GW01375440

THE BEST-EVER
Collection

THE AUSTRALIAN
Women's Weekly

THE BEST-EVER
Collection

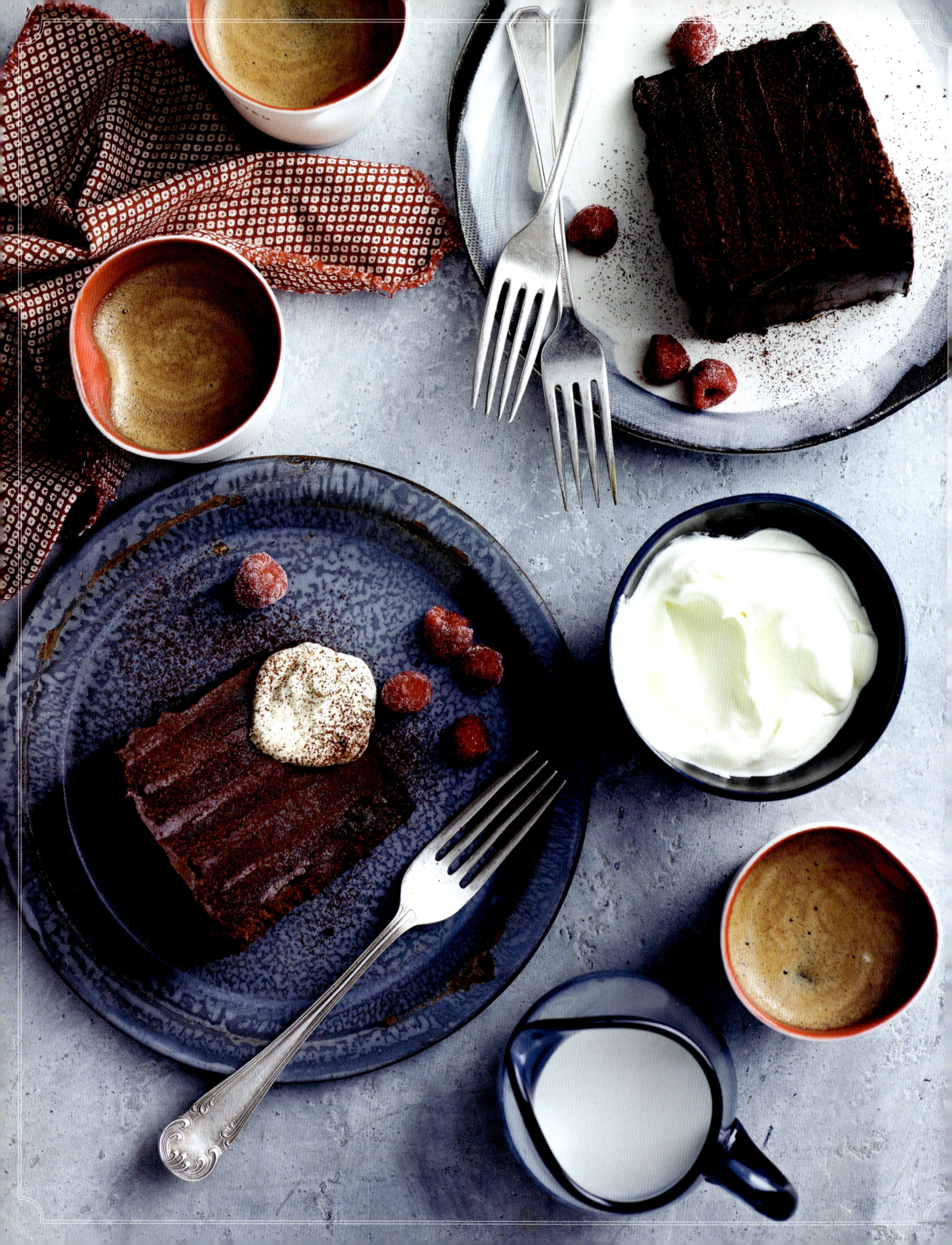

CONTENTS

THE BEST-EVER COLLECTION 6

CHAPTER 1 Soups & Salads 8

CHAPTER 2 Pasta & Rice 42

CHAPTER 3 Barbecues & Picnics 78

CHAPTER 4 Pies & Tarts 110

CHAPTER 5 Casseroles & Curries 138

CHAPTER 6 Roasts & Bakes 176

CHAPTER 7 Puddings & Desserts 206

CHAPTER 8 Cakes & Cupcakes 254

CHAPTER 9 Biscuits & Slices 300

CHAPTER 10 Breads & Scones 326

GLOSSARY 340
CONVERSION CHART 345
INDEX 346

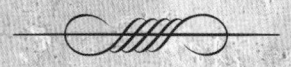

THE BEST-EVER
Collection

This year The Australian Women's Weekly celebrates its 80th birthday – the Test Kitchen isn't quite as old as the magazine but it does date back to the 1950s. However, even before the Test Kitchen came along, The Weekly had always published recipes and various household tips and hints, along with ideas to make a home a more comfortable place to be. The magazine has always been inspirational and aspirational, but within reach – it's led the way for Australians, particularly women. The Weekly has informed and kept its readers on trend in news, fashion, lifestyle and food since it started in 1933.

Choosing a collection of the best-ever recipes for this beautiful book was quite a tall order, so we started by breaking the book into user-friendly chapters. From there it was quite an easy matter to recall frequently requested recipes. Our readers call, write, email and reach us online and then there are our friends' and relatives' requests to consider – they're always asking for recipes and cooking advice.

Our recipes develop as a result of eating out, seeing, reading, chatting or hearing about an idea – we're always on the lookout for a new trend in food or a twist to an old recipe to experiment with in the Test Kitchen. The team who make the Weekly's cookbooks, starting from the most basic idea for a recipe, through to the time the book goes on sale – live, dream and breathe food. Enjoying and sharing food and recipes is what we do – it's our favourite thing. Throughout this book we've selected recipes that we know you'll love, there are some of the classic recipes you'd expect to find in a collection like this, peppered with old favourites that we've modernised to make them acceptable to the way we eat today. Cuisines from all over the world are well-represented in this book. As Australians, we've always been happy to try food from various cultures and, we're lucky to live in a society where the opportunity to try different food is available to us. More Australians travel the world than ever before, they bring home recipes and ideas and want to replicate dishes they've tried – our guess is you'll probably find recipes in this collection for the food you've eaten overseas. Along with each recipe come tips, hints, serving suggestions and often just a little fact about a dish or ingredient that might be of added interest to you.

From soups and salads, to roasts and bakes, puddings and cakes – this book has it all. It really is a superb collection of recipes from the famous Australian Women's Weekly Test Kitchen.

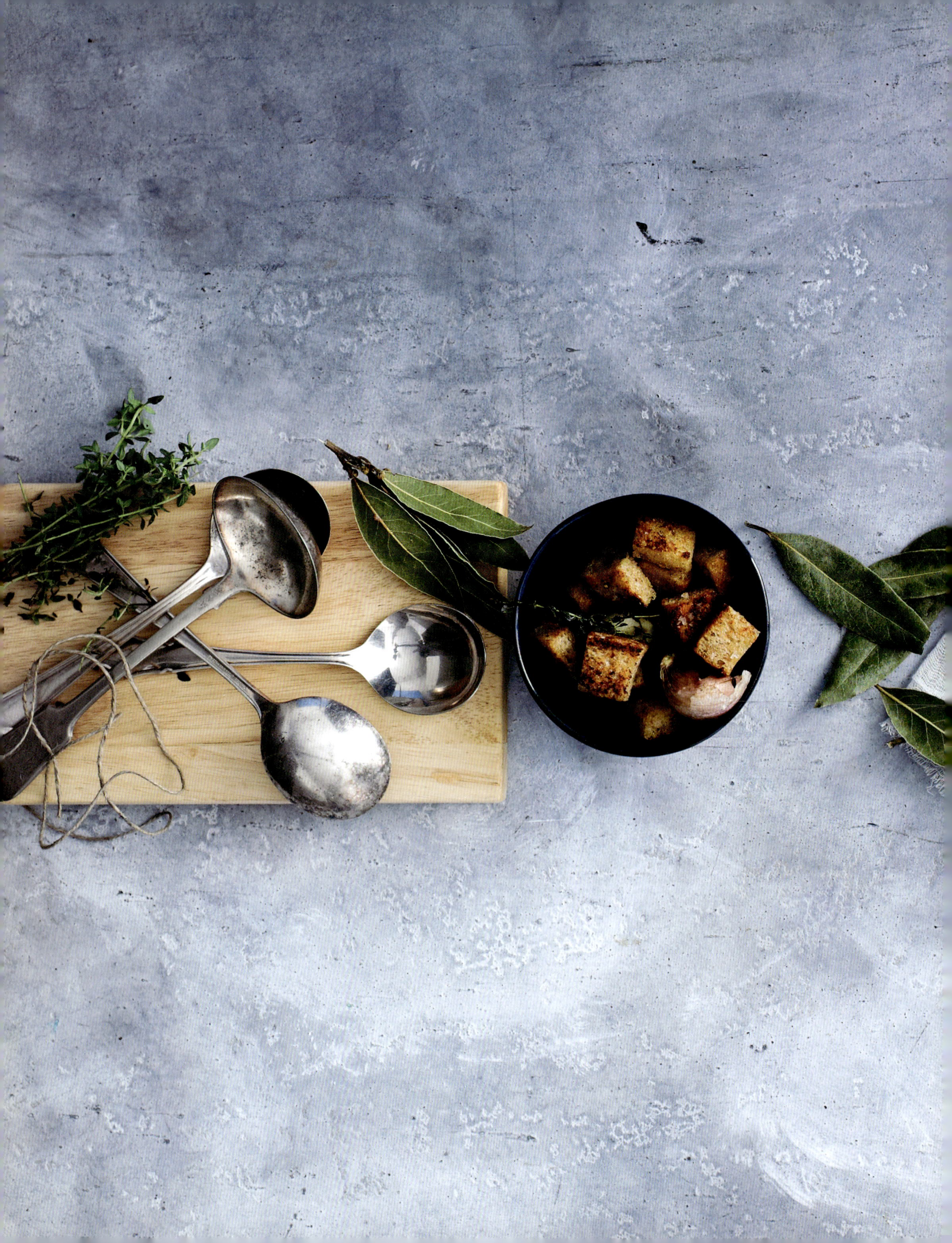

CHAPTER 1
SOUPS & SALADS

CHICKEN, LEMON GRASS
and Rice Soup

PREP + COOK TIME 45 MINUTES SERVES 4

⅔ cup (130g) jasmine rice
1⅓ cups (330ml) water
1 litre (4 cups) chicken stock
2 x 10cm (4-inch) sticks fresh lemon grass (40g), chopped finely
3 shallots (75g), chopped coarsely
1 clove garlic, bruised
1 teaspoon caster (superfine) sugar
2 kaffir lime leaves, torn
400g (12½ ounces) skinless chicken breast fillets
2 tablespoons olive oil
4 cloves garlic, sliced finely, extra
2 tablespoons fish sauce
1 tablespoon lime juice
100g (3 ounces) snow peas, sliced finely lengthways
1 baby buk choy (100g), quartered
1 long red chilli, sliced finely
2 kaffir lime leaves, shredded finely, extra
¼ cup loosely packed fresh coriander (cilantro) leaves

1. Rinse rice under cold running water until water runs clear; drain. Combine rice and the water in a small saucepan; season with salt. Bring to the boil, stirring occasionally. Cover with a tight-fitting lid, reduce heat to low; cook 12 minutes or until water is absorbed. Remove from heat; stand, covered, 10 minutes.
2. Place stock, lemon grass, shallots, bruised garlic, sugar and torn lime leaves in a medium saucepan; bring to the boil. Reduce heat to low; simmer 2 minutes. Add chicken; cook 15 minutes or until cooked through. Remove chicken. Strain broth through a muslin-lined sieve into a large bowl; reserve cooking liquid, discard solids. When cool enough to handle, finely shred chicken.
3. Meanwhile, cook oil and extra garlic in a small frying pan over medium heat, swirling the pan occasionally, for 2 minutes or until light golden. Strain garlic oil through a fine sieve over a small bowl; reserve oil. Drain garlic on paper towel.
4. Return reserved cooking liquid to same medium saucepan with sauce and juice; season to taste. Bring to the boil over medium heat. Stir in shredded chicken, rice, snow peas, buk choy, chilli and extra lime leaves.
5. Ladle soup into bowls; top with coriander, fried garlic and drizzled with a little reserved garlic oil. Serve immediately.

TIPS Save any leftover garlic oil to drizzle over scrambled eggs or to use in a salad dressing. Any remaining kaffir lime leaves can be frozen for another use.
The soup will thicken on standing because of the rice. To prepare this soup ahead, follow the recipe up to the end of step 3; continue with the recipe just before you're ready to serve.

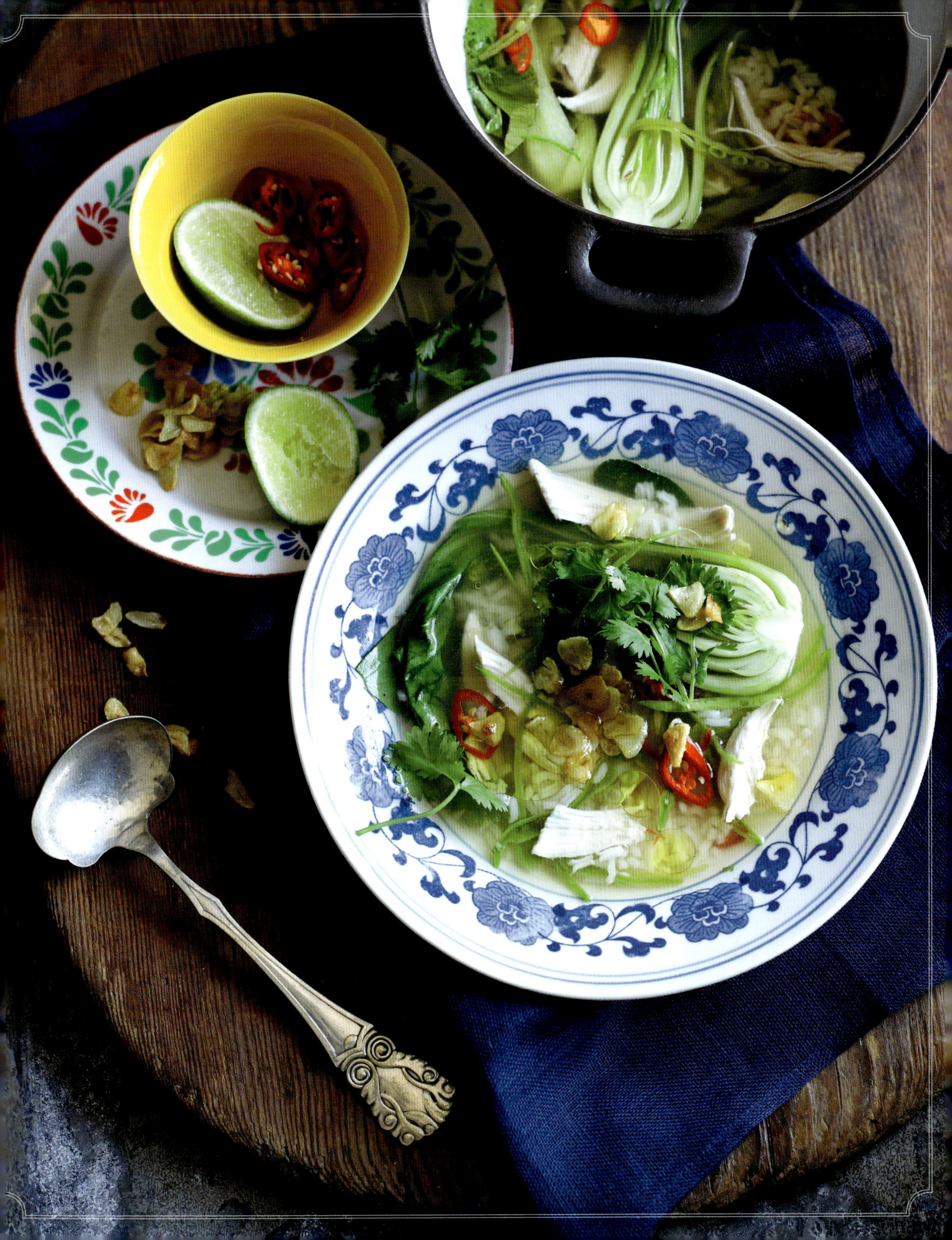

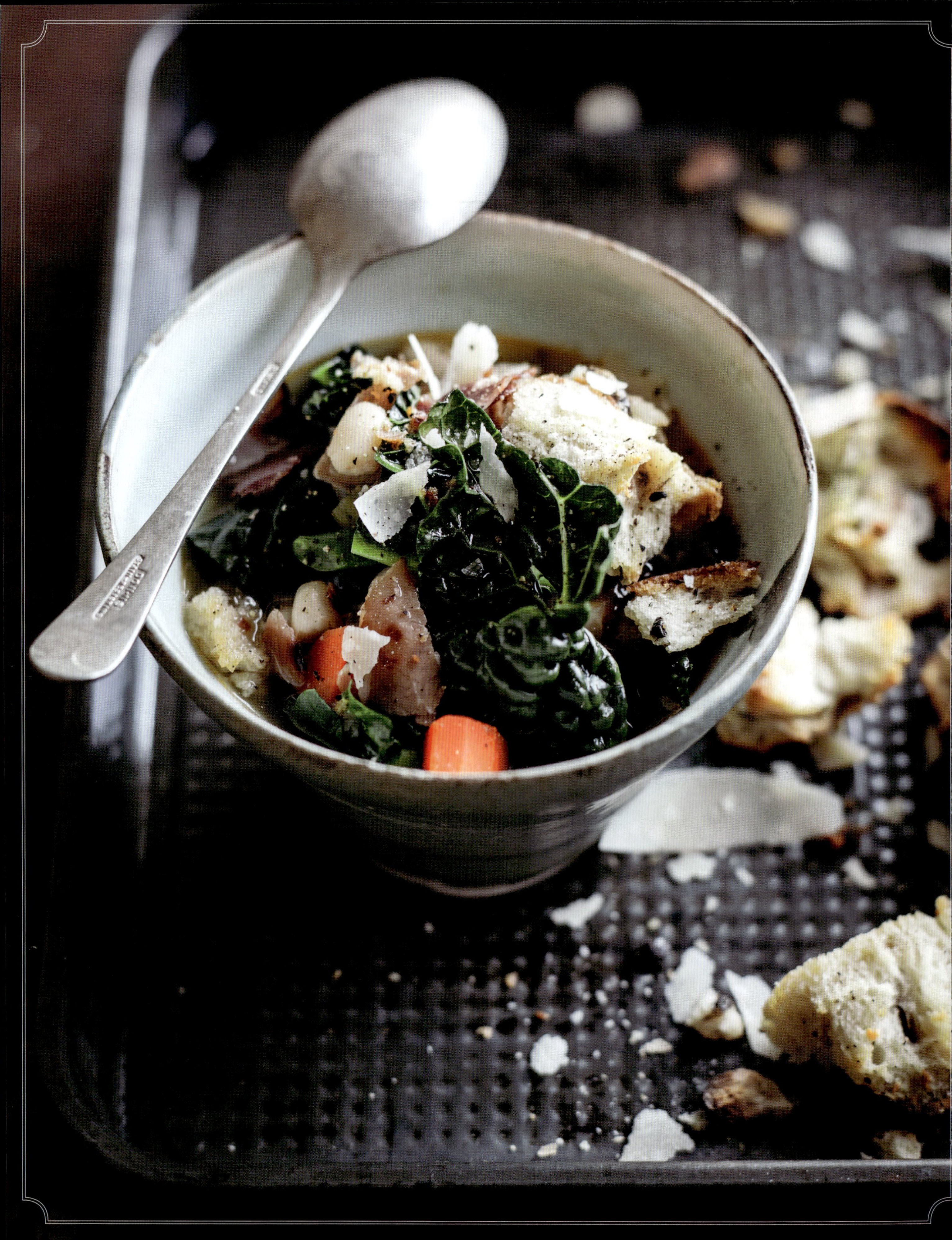

RIBOLLITA

PREP + COOK TIME *45 MINUTES* **SERVES 4**

Ribollita is a Tuscan soup that uses any suitable vegetables available. It is traditionally thickened with stale bread. Instead, we have made chunky garlic breadcrumbs to add some crunch and left the soup more broth-like.

100g (3 ounces) sliced prosciutto
⅓ cup (80ml) olive oil
1 small brown onion (80g), chopped coarsely
1 trimmed celery stick (100g), chopped coarsely
1 medium carrot (120g), chopped coarsely
2 medium tomatoes (300g), chopped coarsely
3 cloves garlic, crushed
1 cinnamon stick
1 sprig fresh rosemary
1 litre (4 cups) water or chicken stock
300g (9½ ounces) loaf olive bread
200g (6½ ounces) cavolo nero
125g (4 ounces) green beans, trimmed, chopped coarsely
400g (12½ ounces) canned cannellini beans, drained, rinsed
¾ cup (60g) shaved parmesan

1. Preheat oven to 200°C/400°F.
2. Coarsely chop half the prosciutto. Heat 1 tablespoon of the oil in a large saucepan; cook onion, celery, carrot and chopped prosciutto, stirring, until vegetables are soft. Add tomato and half the garlic; cook, stirring, until soft. Add cinnamon, rosemary and the water; bring to the boil. Reduce heat; simmer, uncovered, 10 minutes. Discard cinnamon and rosemary.
3. Meanwhile, tear bread into chunks; toss with remaining garlic and remaining oil on an oven tray. Season. Place remaining prosciutto on a wire rack over an oven tray. Bake bread for 10 minutes or until golden and crunchy; bake prosciutto for 5 minutes or until crisp. Break prosciutto into pieces.
4. Remove stalks from cavolo nero; chop leaves coarsely. Add green beans to soup; simmer, uncovered, 5 minutes. Add cavolo nero and cannellini beans; simmer, uncovered, a further 5 minutes or until tender.
5. Serve soup topped with bread, prosciutto pieces and parmesan.

TIP Cavolo nero is also known as tuscan kale or black cabbage.

Soups & Salads

GREEN PEA SOUP
with Mint Pistou

PREP + COOK TIME *30 MINUTES (+ COOLING)* **SERVES** *4*

Pistou, the Provençal equivalent of Italian pesto, generally contains no pine nuts and is based on basil. Our version with mint truly gives it a summery zing.

1 tablespoon olive oil
1 small leek (200g), sliced thinly
1 clove garlic, crushed
2 large potatoes (600g), chopped coarsely
3 cups (360g) frozen peas
3 cups (750ml) water
2 cups (500ml) vegetable stock

MINT PISTOU
2 cups loosely packed fresh mint leaves
¼ cup (20g) finely grated parmesan
1 tablespoon lemon juice
1 clove garlic, quartered
¼ cup (60ml) olive oil

1. Heat oil in a large saucepan over medium heat; cook leek and garlic, stirring, 5 minutes or until leek softens. Add potato, peas, the water and stock; bring to the boil. Reduce heat to low-medium; simmer, covered, 10 minutes or until potato is tender. Cool 15 minutes.
2. Meanwhile, make mint pistou.
3. Blend or process soup, in batches, until smooth. Return soup to same cleaned pan; stir over medium heat until hot.
4. Serve bowls of soup topped with pistou.

MINT PISTOU
Blend or process ingredients until smooth.

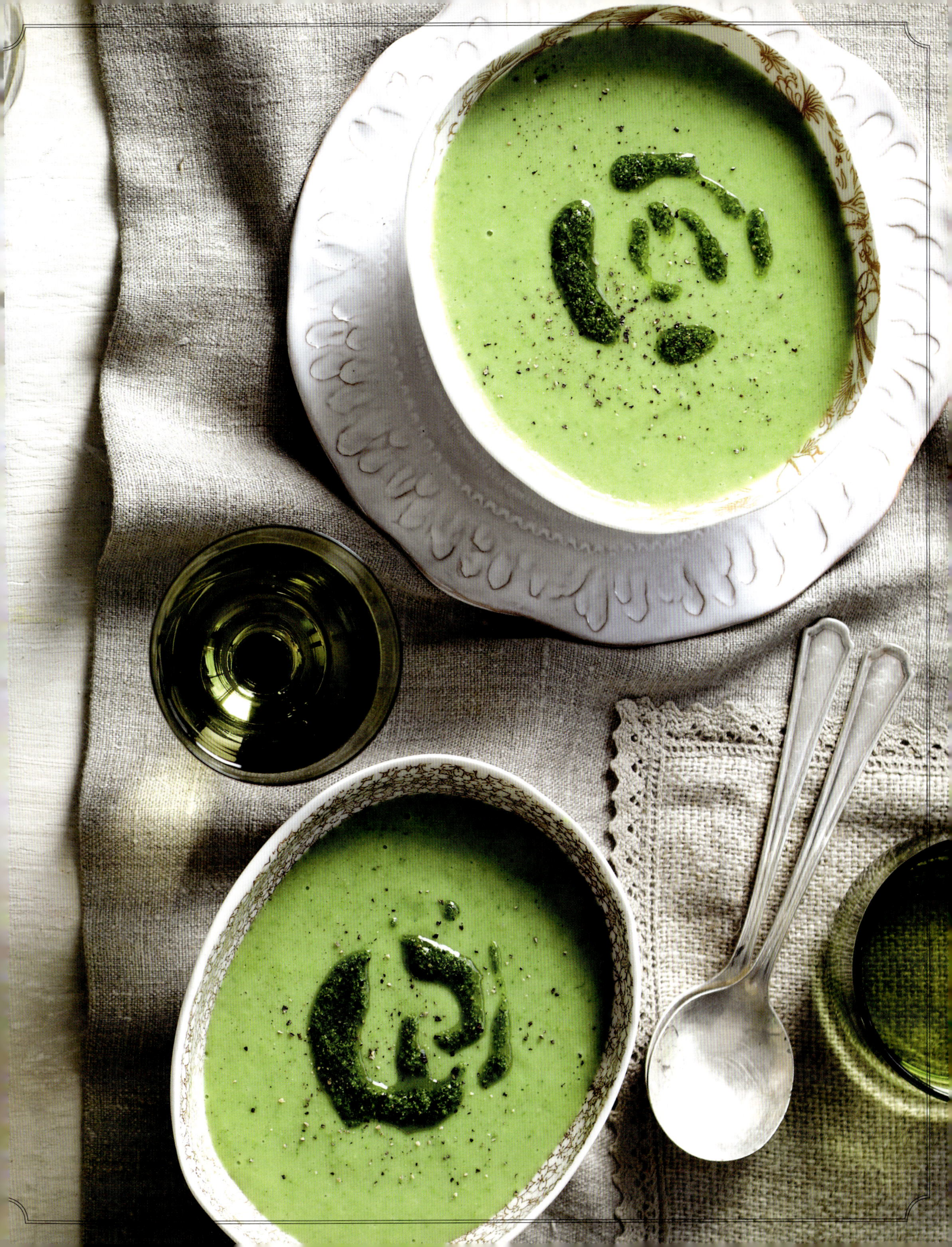

ROAST PUMPKIN SOUP
with Cheese Croûtes

PREP + COOK TIME *1 HOUR* **SERVES 4**

Very few years have passed without The Weekly featuring a pumpkin soup. Our recipes from the 60s were simple, but also (in retrospect), dare we say it, even a little bland. In more recent times, we've added twists, such as roasting the pumpkin, which amplifies the flavour, and dabbled with Asian versions.

1kg (2 pounds) grey pumpkin, peeled, chopped
3 cloves garlic, peeled
1 medium brown onion (150g), chopped
1 tablespoon extra virgin olive oil
3 cups (750ml) salt-reduced chicken stock
⅔ cup (160ml) pouring cream
1 tablespoon finely chopped fresh thyme

CHEESE CROÛTES
¼ cup (60ml) extra virgin olive oil
1 tablespoon wholegrain mustard
2 teaspoons finely chopped fresh thyme
1 small french stick (150g), sliced thinly
⅓ cup (25g) finely grated parmesan

1. Preheat oven to 200°C/400°F.
2. Combine pumpkin, garlic and onion in a large roasting pan; drizzle with oil. Roast 30 minutes or until soft. (Keep oven on.)
3. Blend or process roasted vegetables with stock, in batches, until smooth. Pour mixture into a large saucepan; stir over medium heat until hot. Stir in cream and half the thyme; season to taste.
4. Meanwhile, make cheese croûtes.
5. Serve bowls of soup with croûtes, topped with remaining thyme.

CHEESE CROÛTES
Combine oil, mustard and thyme in a small bowl; brush mixture on bread slices. Place slices on an oven tray; bake 5 minutes. Sprinkle with parmesan; bake 3 minutes or until crisp.

TIP Try adding a squeeze of lemon or lime juice at the very end of cooking, it is much like adding salt – it will balance the sweetness of the pumpkin.

ASIAN VARIATION Omit the thyme and croûtes. In step 2, toss the pumpkin with 2 tablespoons thai red curry paste before roasting; use coconut cream instead of the pouring cream.

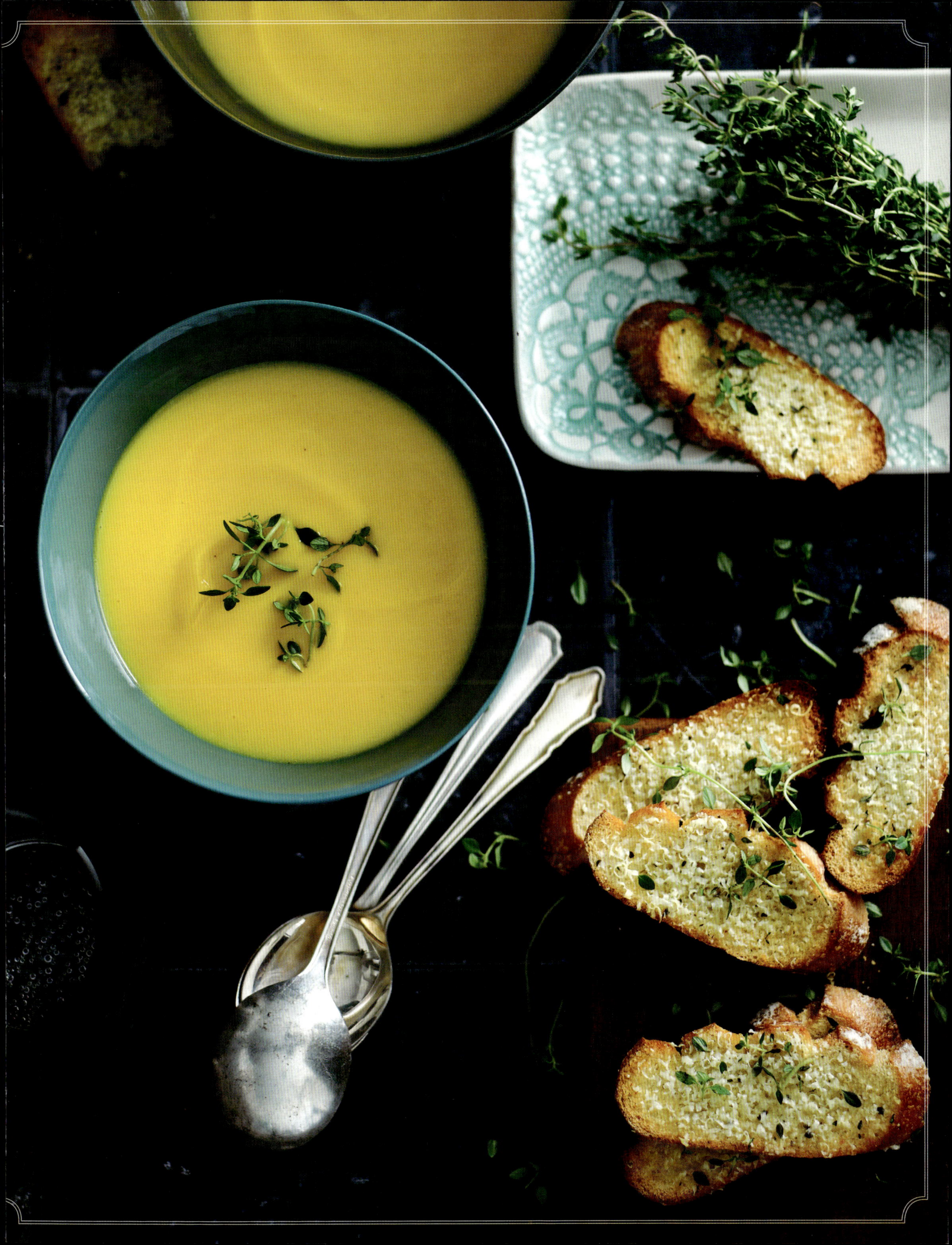

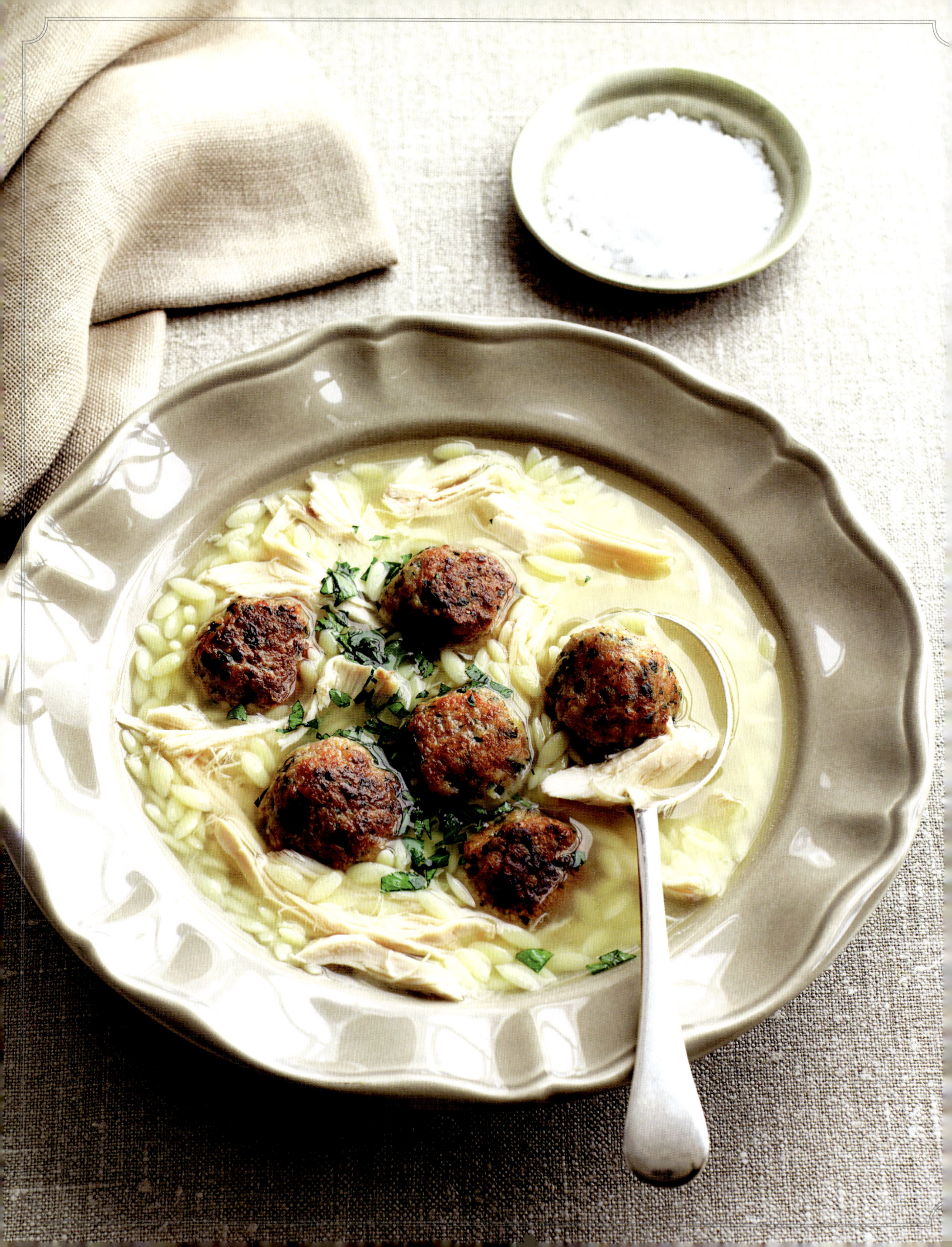

CHICKEN AND RISONI SOUP
with Herbed Meatballs

PREP + COOK TIME 3 HOURS 15 MINUTES (+ REFRIGERATION) **SERVES** 4

This really is the best tasting chicken pasta soup, because you poach the chicken, at the same time creating a comforting golden broth of lusciousness for tender little chicken meatballs and pasta. Start this recipe a day ahead.

1.6kg (3-pound) whole chicken, rinsed
1 medium brown onion (150g), halved
2 trimmed celery sticks (200g), halved
1 large tomato (220g), halved
2 stalks fresh flat-leaf parsley
5 black peppercorns
2.5 litres (10 cups) water
300g (9½ ounces) minced (ground) chicken
½ cup (50g) packaged breadcrumbs
2 tablespoons finely chopped fresh flat-leaf parsley
2 tablespoons finely grated parmesan
1 egg, beaten lightly
1 tablespoon olive oil
¾ cup (165g) risoni pasta
2 tablespoons lemon juice
⅓ cup finely chopped fresh flat-leaf parsley, extra

1. Place whole chicken in a large saucepan with onion, celery, tomato, parsley stalks, peppercorns and the water; bring to the boil. Reduce heat; simmer, covered, 2 hours.
2. Remove chicken from pan. Strain broth through a muslin-lined sieve or colander into a large heatproof bowl; discard solids. Allow broth to cool, cover; refrigerate overnight. When chicken is cool enough to handle, shred meat coarsely, discarding skin and bones. Cover; refrigerate overnight.
3. Combine minced chicken, breadcrumbs, chopped parsley, parmesan and egg in a large bowl. Roll rounded teaspoons of mixture into balls.
4. Heat oil in a medium saucepan over medium heat; cook meatballs, in batches, for 5 minutes or until browned all over. Drain on paper towel.
5. Using a ladle, skim then discard fat from the surface of the broth. Transfer broth to a large saucepan; bring to the boil. Reduce heat to medium; simmer, uncovered, 20 minutes. Add pasta and meatballs; simmer, uncovered, 10 minutes or until pasta is just tender and meatballs are cooked through.
6. Add 2 cups of the shredded chicken (keep remaining chicken for another use) to soup with juice; stir until hot. Serve soup topped with extra chopped parsley.

TIP Risoni is a small, rice-shaped pasta, similar to orzo; you'll find it in the pasta section of major supermarkets. You can use any other small pasta you like or even broken spaghetti.

FRENCH ONION *Soup*

PREP + COOK TIME 1 HOUR 10 MINUTES SERVES 6

This recipe first appeared in the July 1976 issue of The Australian Women's Weekly magazine, and is still as popular now as it was then – a true sign of a classic.

80g (2½ ounces) butter
4 large onions (800g), sliced thinly
1 clove garlic, crushed
1 tablespoon plain (all-purpose) flour
1 litre (4 cups) beef stock
3 cups (750ml) water
⅓ cup (80ml) cider
1 tablespoon sherry
1 small french stick (150g)
125g (4 ounces) butter, extra
1 clove garlic, crushed, extra
250g (8 ounces) gruyère, grated finely
60g (2 ounces) finely grated parmesan
1 tablespoon finely shredded fresh flat-leaf parsely

1. Melt butter in a large heavy-based saucepan over medium heat; cook onion, stirring occasionally, 30 minutes or until caramelised. Add garlic; stir 1 minute or until fragrant.
2. Stir flour into onion mixture; cook, stirring, 1 minute or until mixture thickens.
3. Add stock, the water and cider; stir until combined. Bring to the boil. Reduce heat; simmer, covered, for 45 minutes, stirring occasionally. Stir in sherry; simmer a further 5 minutes.
4. Preheat grill (broiler) to medium-high.
5. Meanwhile, cut bread into 12 x 1cm (½-inch) slices. Melt extra butter in a small saucepan over low heat. Add extra garlic, stir 1 minute or until fragrant. Brush butter mixture on both sides of bread slices; place on a large oven tray. Place under grill until golden on one side only.
6. Ladle hot soup into six 12cm (4¾-inch) ovenproof soup bowls. Place bread, toasted-side down, on to soup. Sprinkle combined gruyère and parmesan on bread, top with thyme; season. Place bowls on an oven tray; place under grill for 2 minutes or until cheeses melt and are golden. Serve immediately.

TIP Using a heavy-based saucepan will make it easier to cook the onions to a deep golden brown; an important step to get the best flavour.

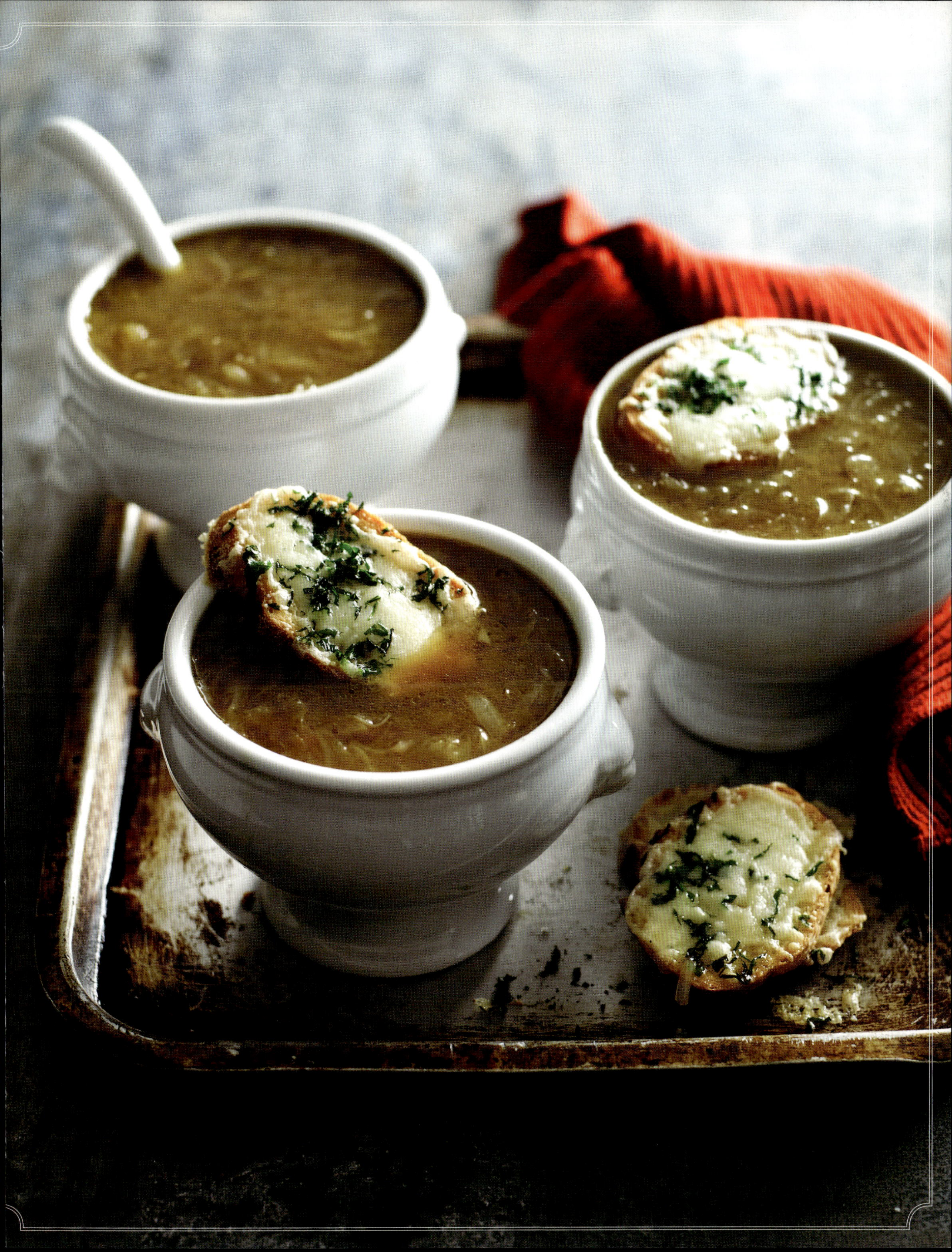

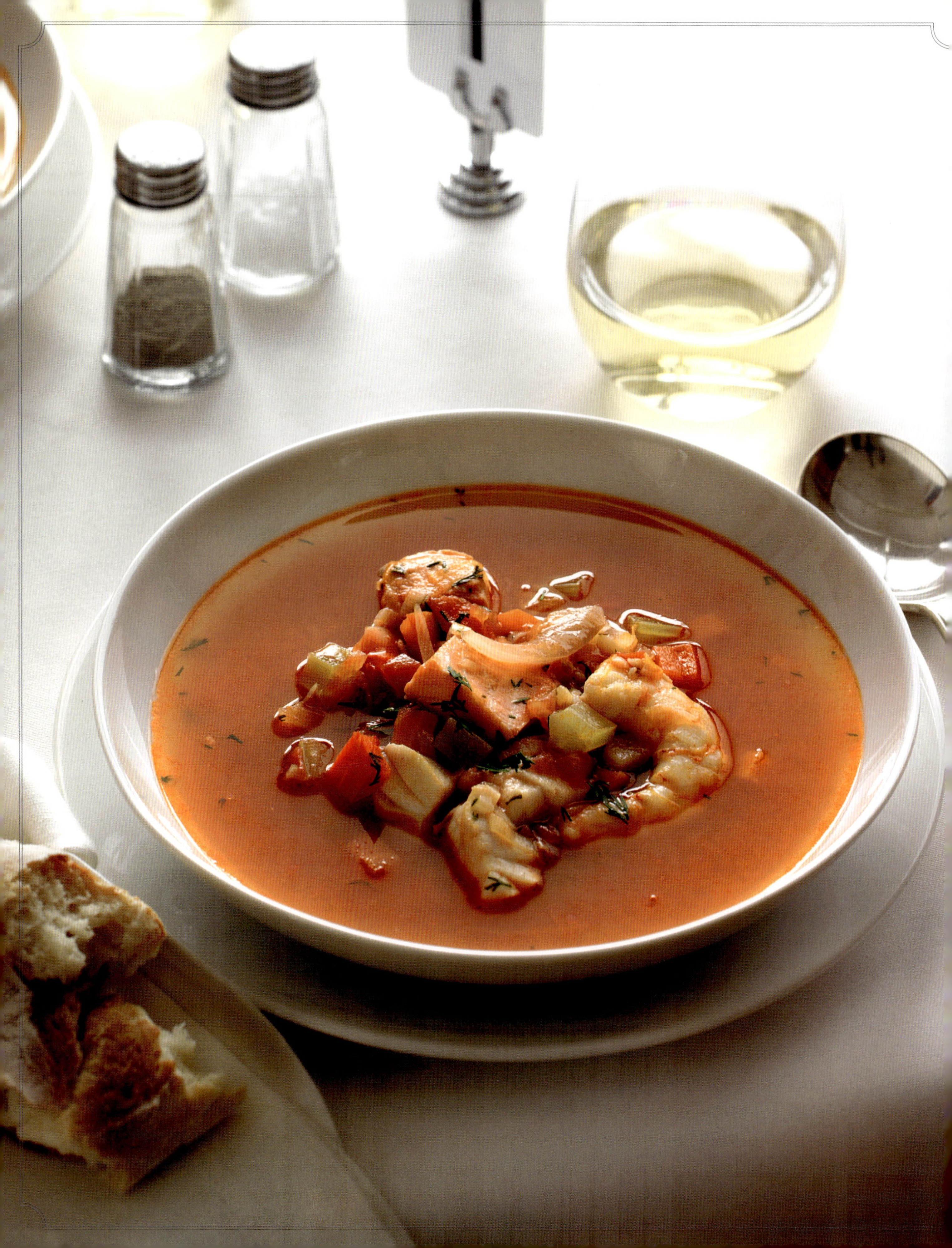

MEDITERRANEAN
Fish Soup

PREP + COOK TIME 1 HOUR   SERVES 4

This robust tomato and vegetable-based fish soup, with hints of orange and a kick of chilli, is influenced by the bold flavours of Provençal fish soups, such as bouillabaisse and Italian fishermen soups.

1 tablespoon olive oil
2 cloves garlic, crushed
1 small red onion (100g), halved, sliced thinly
1 trimmed celery stick (100g), chopped coarsely
1 small carrot (70g), coarsely chopped
1 small leek (200g), halved, sliced thinly
1 small red capsicum (bell pepper) (150g), chopped coarsely
½ teaspoon finely grated orange rind
¼ teaspoon dried chilli flakes
2 tablespoons tomato paste
3 cups (750ml) fish stock
2 cups (500ml) water
¼ cup (60ml) dry white wine
2 large roma (egg) tomatoes (180g), chopped coarsely
200g (6½ ounces) uncooked small king prawns (shrimp)
200g (6½ ounces) skinless blue-eye trevalla fillet, chopped coarsely
200g (6½ ounces) skinless ocean trout fillet, chopped coarsely
¼ teaspoon finely chopped fresh thyme
1 tablespoon finely chopped fresh dill

1. Heat oil in a large saucepan over medium heat; cook garlic, onion, celery, carrot, leek, capsicum, rind and chilli, stirring for 8 minutes or until vegetables soften.
2. Stir in paste, stock, the water, wine and tomato; bring to the boil. Reduce heat to low-medium; simmer, 20 minutes.
3. Meanwhile, shell and devein prawns; chop meat coarsely. Add prawn meat, fish, thyme and half the dill to soup; simmer 3 minutes or until prawn meat and fish are cooked.
4. Serve bowls of soup topped with remaining dill.

TIPS Any firm white-fleshed fish may be substituted for the trevalla.
To ensure even cooking, cut the fish pieces into equal-sized pieces.

Soups & Salads

GREEK LENTIL SPINACH
and Dill Soup

PREP + COOK TIME 1 HOUR SERVES 6

2 tablespoons olive oil
3 medium brown onions (450g), chopped finely
1 trimmed celery stick (100g), chopped finely
1 medium carrot (120g), chopped finely
2 cloves garlic, crushed
1 long red chilli, sliced thinly
2 bay leaves
6 stalks fresh flat-leaf parsley
1½ cups (300g) brown or green lentils
3 litres (12 cups) water
150g (4½ ounces) baby spinach leaves
2 tablespoons red wine vinegar
3 teaspoons sea salt flakes
½ cup lightly packed fresh dill sprigs

1. Heat oil in a large saucepan over medium heat; cook onion, celery and carrot, stirring, 5 minutes or until softened. Add garlic, chilli, bay leaves and parsley stalks; cook, stirring, until fragrant.
2. Add lentils; stir to coat. Add the water; bring to the boil. Reduce heat; simmer, uncovered, 20 minutes or until lentils are tender. Remove bay leaves and parsley stalks.
3. Add spinach, vinegar and salt to soup; stir until spinach wilts. Season with freshly ground black pepper.
4. Serve bowls of soup topped with dill sprigs.

TIP Adding salt during cooking was once thought to make pulses tough – it doesn't. However it does slow down the cooking time, so it's best to season at the very end.

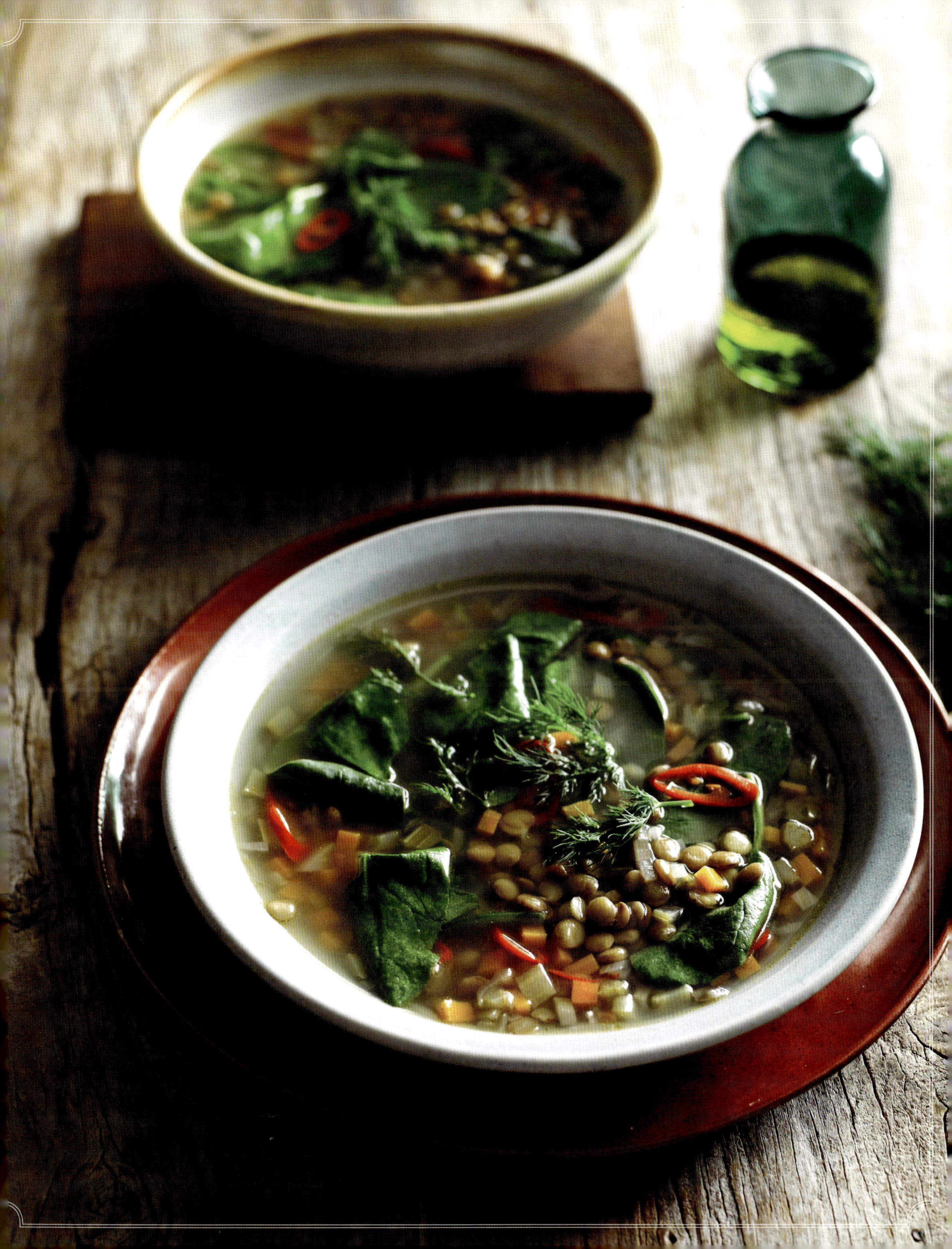

PERFECT POTATO
Salad

PERFECT POTATO *Salad*

PREP + COOK TIME 35 MINUTES SERVES 6

1.5kg (3 pounds) desiree potatoes, cut into wedges
2 tablespoons cider vinegar
½ cup fresh flat-leaf parsley leaves
⅓ cup fresh dill sprigs
⅓ cup fresh mint leaves
4 green onions (scallions), sliced thinly

MAYONNAISE
1 egg yolk
1 tablespoon lemon juice
½ cup (125ml) vegetable oil
1 tablespoon wholegrain mustard

1. Place potatoes in a large saucepan of salted cold water; bring to the boil. Reduce heat; simmer 15 minutes or until potatoes are just tender. Drain well; transfer to a large bowl.
2. Meanwhile, make mayonnaise.
3. Drizzle vinegar over warm potatoes, season to taste; toss gently to combine.
4. Add half the mayonnaise, half the herbs and half the onion; toss gently to combine. Drizzle with remaining mayonnaise; top with remaining herbs and onion.

MAYONNAISE
Whisk egg yolk and juice in a medium bowl until pale and creamy. Gradually add oil, drop by drop then in a steady stream, whisking continuously, until mayonnaise is thick and emulsified. Stir in mustard; season to taste.

TIP You could add some chopped hard-boiled eggs and finely chopped fried bacon, or even flaked smoked trout. Toss through salad just before serving.

PASTA SALAD WITH TOMATO *and Crisp Prosciutto*

PREP + COOK TIME 15 MINUTES SERVES 4

300g (9½ ounces) spiral pasta
6 medium ripe tomatoes (1kg)
¼ cup (50g) small salted capers, rinsed
½ cup coarsely chopped fresh flat-leaf parsley
⅓ cup lightly packed fresh basil leaves
½ cup (125ml) extra virgin olive oil
8 thin slices prosciutto (120g)

1. Cook pasta in a large saucepan of boiling salted water until just tender. Drain. Place pasta in a large serving bowl.
2. Halve tomatoes; squeeze juice and seeds over pasta. Coarsely chop tomato flesh, then add to bowl with capers, herbs and oil; toss gently to combine. Season to taste.
3. Cook prosciutto, in batches, in a large oiled frying pan over medium heat, for 1½ minutes each side or until golden and crisp.
4. Just before serving, crumble prosciutto over salad.

TIPS Store tomatoes at room temperature, rather than in the fridge, which will alter the texture and spoil the flavour. To accelerate ripening, place in a paper bag with a ripe banana.
You can prepare this salad in advance; store the pasta and tomato mixture separately until ready to serve, as the tomatoes will soften the pasta.

(PHOTOGRAPH PAGE 28)

PASTA SALAD WITH TOMATO
and Crisp Prosciutto
(RECIPE PAGE 27)

AVOCADO, BACON
and Cabbage Salad

(RECIPE PAGE 30)

AVOCADO, BACON
and Cabbage Salad

PREP + COOK TIME *15 MINUTES* **SERVES 8**

¼ medium savoy cabbage (400g)
4 rindless bacon slices (260g)
1 bunch chives (15g), cut into 3cm (1¼-inch) lengths
2 large avocados (640g), sliced

GARLIC MUSTARD VINAIGRETTE
½ cup (125ml) extra virgin olive oil
2 tablespoons red wine vinegar
2 teaspoons wholegrain mustard
2 cloves garlic, crushed

1. Using a mandoline or sharp knife, finely shred cabbage.
2. Cook bacon in a small frying pan over medium heat, 2 minutes each side or until crisp; drain on absorbent paper. Chop or break up coarsely.
3. Make garlic mustard vinaigrette.
4. Just before serving, combine cabbage, chives and half the garlic mustard vinaigrette in a large bowl.
5. Place cabbage mixture on a platter, toss gently; top with avocado and bacon. Drizzle with vinaigrette.

GARLIC MUSTARD VINAIGRETTE
Place ingredients in a screw-top jar, season; shake well.

TIPS Savoy cabbage is similar to white cabbage (which may be substituted), except for its crinkled leaves and milder flavour.
This recipe can be prepared several hours ahead. Slice avocado and assemble close to serving.

(PHOTOGRAPH PAGE 29)

COUSCOUS SALAD

PREP + COOK TIME *15 MINUTES* **SERVES 4**

1 cup (200g) couscous
¼ teaspoon salt
1 cup (250ml) boiling water
½ cup coarsely chopped fresh coriander (cilantro)
½ cup coarsely chopped fresh flat-leaf parsley
2 green onions (scallions), sliced thinly
1 medium red capsicum (bell pepper) (200g), trimmed, cut into long strips
1 tablespoon finely chopped preserved lemon rind, cut into strips
2 tablespoons lemon juice
1 teaspoon honey
¼ cup (60ml) extra virgin olive oil
1 teaspoon grated lemon rind

1. Place couscous and salt in a heatproof bowl; cover with the boiling water, mix with a fork. Cover; stand 10 minutes.
2. Fluff couscous with a fork. Stir in herbs, onion and capsicum.
3. Place preserved lemon, juice, honey and oil in a jug or bowl; stir until well combined.
4. Pour dressing over couscous, season to taste, then toss gently. Top with lemon rind.

TIPS Preserved lemons is available from delicastessens and gourmet food stores.
You can add some finely chopped mango pickle, available from the Indian section of supermarkets. Add shelled cooked prawns for an indulgent main-course salad.

SERVING SUGGESTION Serve with barbecued chicken or lamb.

COUSCOUS
SALAD

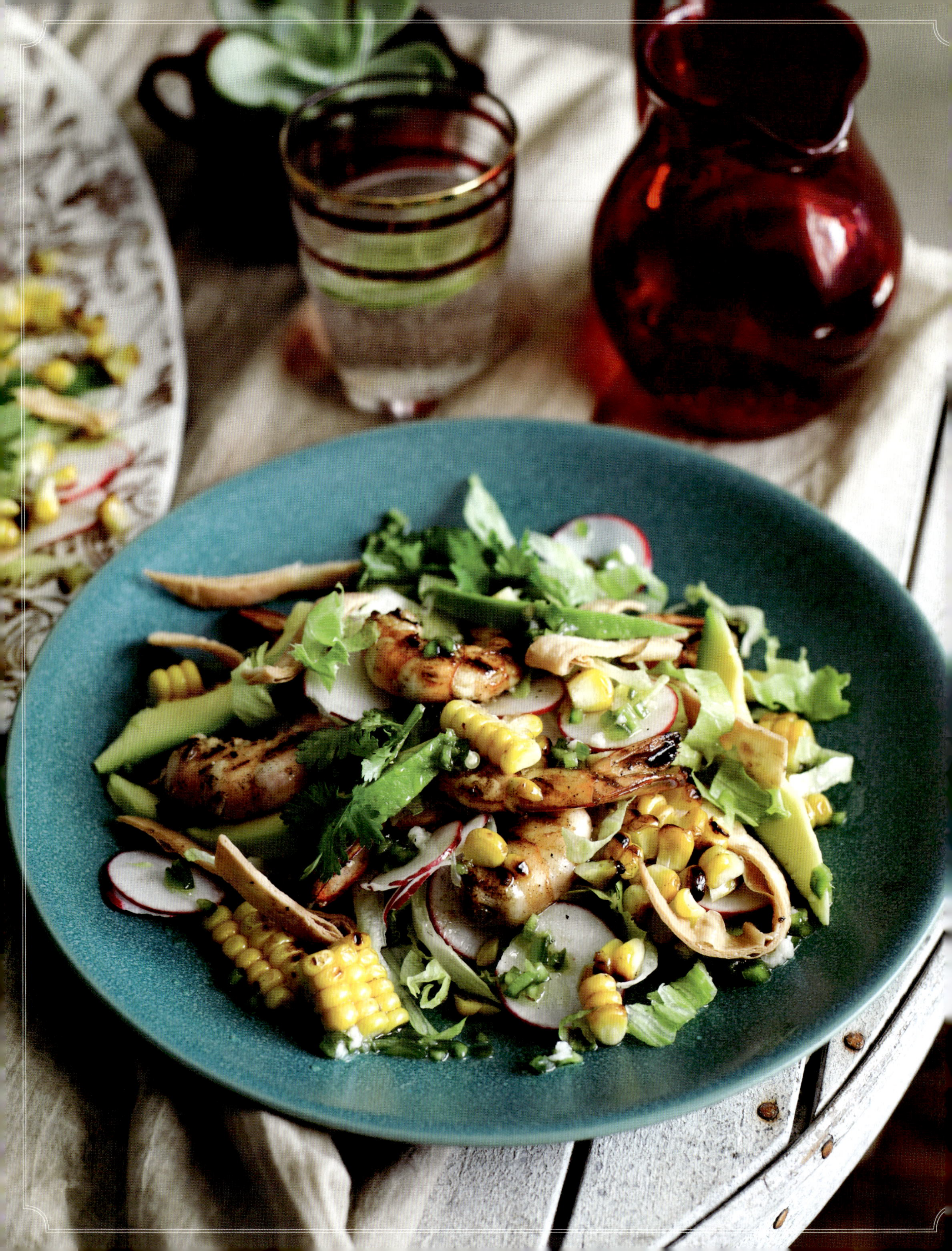

CHAR-GRILLED PRAWN
and Corn Salad

PREP + COOK TIME 40 MINUTES SERVES 4

20 uncooked medium king prawns (shrimp) (1kg)
2 cloves garlic, crushed
2 tablespoons lime juice
½ teaspoon ground cumin
1 teaspoon caster (superfine) sugar
1 tablespoon olive oil
2 trimmed corn cobs (500g)
20g (¾ ounce) butter, softened
2 tablespoons olive oil, extra
3 x 15cm (6-inch) corn tortillas, cut into thin strips
1 medium avocado (250g)
½ medium iceberg lettuce (120g), shredded finely
6 small radishes (100g), trimmed, sliced very thinly
1 cup loosely packed fresh coriander (cilantro) leaves

DRESSING
2 tablespoons lime juice
¼ cup (60ml) olive oil
1 green chilli, seeded, chopped finely
1 clove garlic, crushed
1 teaspoon caster (superfine) sugar

1 Peel and devain prawns, leaving tails intact. Combine prawns, garlic, juice, cumin, sugar and oil in a large bowl. Cover; refrigerate 10 minutes.
2 Meanwhile, make dressing.
3 Brush corn with butter; season. Cook corn on a heated oiled char-grill pan (or barbecue), turning, 10 minutes or until browned lightly and just tender. Using a sharp knife, cut corn kernels from cobs. Transfer to a small bowl; cover to keep warm.
4 Meanwhile, heat extra oil in a medium frying pan over medium heat; fry tortilla strips, in two batches, stirring, 2 minutes or until golden. Remove with a slotted spoon; drain on paper towel. Season with salt to taste.
5 Season prawn mixture; cook on heated char-grill pan for 3 minutes, turning halfway, or until just cooked through.
6 Halve avocado; scoop flesh into a large bowl. Add lettuce, radish and three-quarters of the coriander; toss gently to combine. Arrange lettuce mixture on a platter; layer with prawns and corn, then drizzle with dressing.
7 Serve salad topped with tortilla strips and remaining coriander.

DRESSING
Place ingredients in a screw-top jar; shake well. Season to taste.

TIPS To save time, you can buy shelled prawns from the fishmonger.
The tortilla strips can be prepared a day ahead; cool and store in an airtight container.

CHICKEN CAESAR SALAD

PREP + COOK TIME *35 MINUTES* SERVES *4*

1 teaspoon sea salt
2 chicken breasts (400g)
⅔ cup (200g) aïoli
2 anchovy fillets, chopped finely
2 teaspoons dijon mustard
⅓ cup (80ml) extra virgin olive oil
4 rindless bacon slices (260g), chopped coarsely
12 thin slices crusty italian bread (140g)
2 cos (romaine) lettuce, leaves separated
1 cup (80g) shaved parmesan

1. Half-fill a medium frying pan with water, add salt; bring to the boil. Add chicken, reduce heat to low; cook, covered, in barely simmering water 10 minutes or until chicken is just cooked through, turning halfway. Remove chicken from pan; cover, stand 5 minutes before slicing thinly.
2. Combine aïoli, anchovy and mustard in a small bowl. (If necessary, add 1 tablespoon of hot water to thin the dressing to a drizzling consistency.)
3. Heat oil in a large non-stick frying pan over medium heat; cook bacon 2 minutes each side or until browned. Drain on paper towel. Add bread to pan; cook, in two batches, 2 minutes on each side or until golden.
4. Layer lettuce (tearing any large leaves into smaller pieces) in a large bowl or on a platter with bacon, bread, chicken and parmesan. Drizzle with dressing.

TIPS Aïoli is garlic mayonnaise, and is available from delicatessens and supermarkets (sometimes in the refrigerated section of the fruit and veg department). Substitute with regular mayonnaise and 1 clove crushed garlic.
You can use 1 teaspoon of worcestershire sauce instead of the anchovy fillets.
This salad is a great way to use up leftover roast chicken. Shred the chicken and add to the salad instead of the poached chicken breasts.

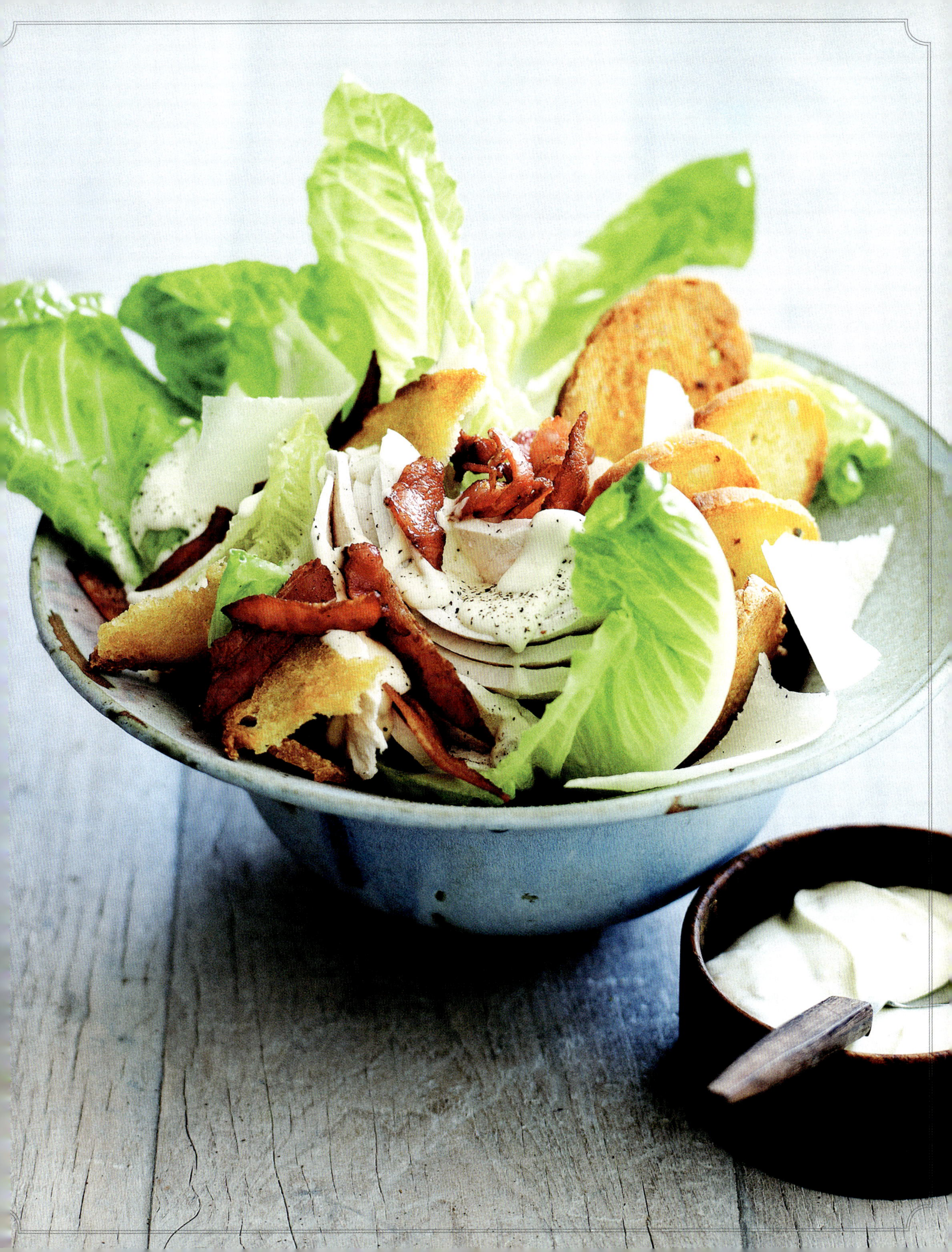

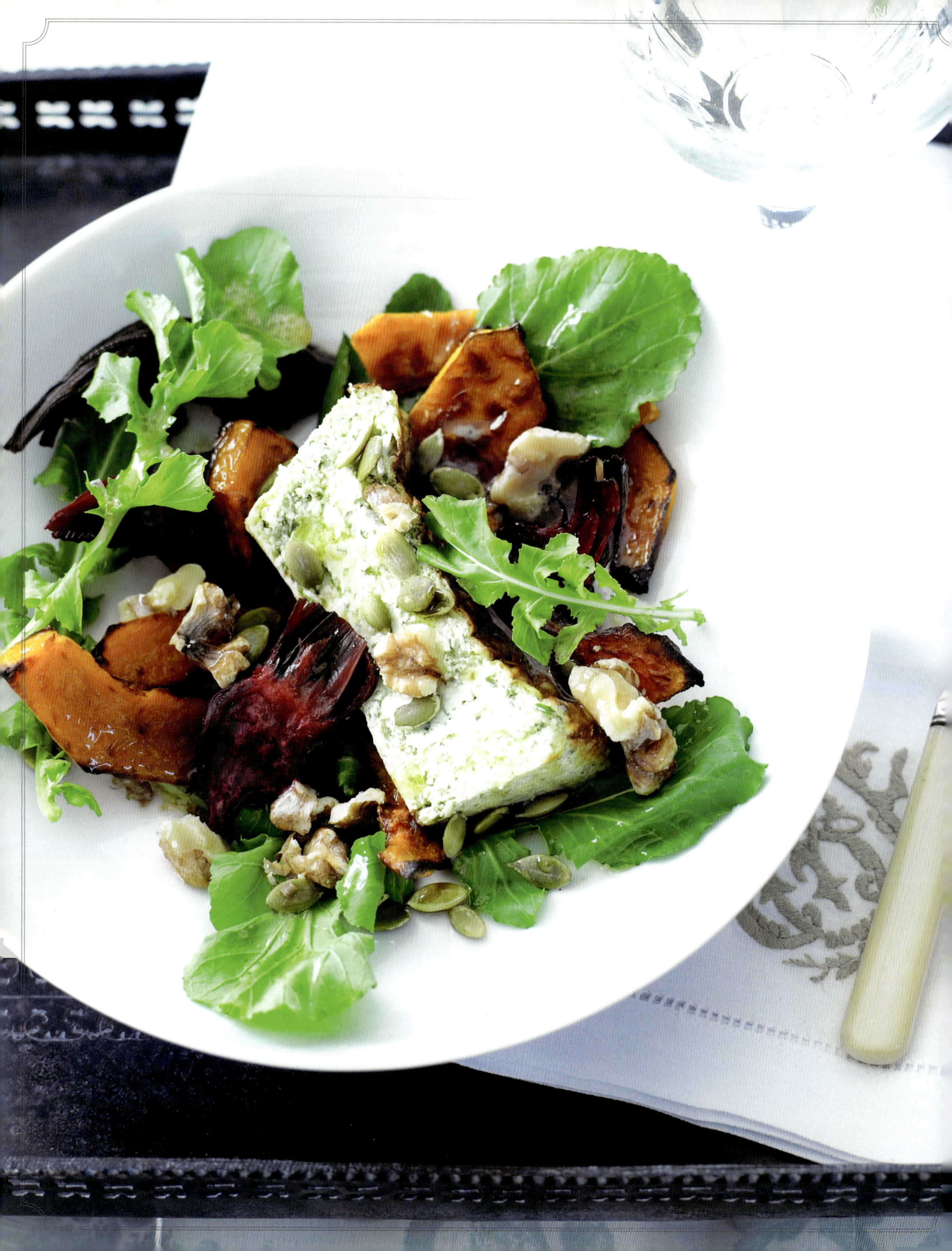

ROAST VEGETABLE SALAD
with Herbed Ricotta

PREP + COOK TIME *1 HOUR 10 MINUTES* **SERVES** *4*

500g (1 pound) baby beetroots (beets), leaves trimmed
500g (1 pound) pumpkin, peeled, sliced thinly
1 tablespoon olive oil
200g (6½ ounces) rocket (arugula)
⅓ cup (35g) coarsely chopped roasted walnuts
1 tablespoon roasted pepitas

HERBED RICOTTA
1 cup loosely packed fresh basil leaves
½ cup loosely packed fresh mint leaves
½ cup loosely packed fresh flat-leaf parsley leaves
⅓ cup (80ml) pouring cream
500g (1 pound) fresh ricotta
2 eggs, beaten lightly
1¼ cups (100g) finely grated parmesan

RED WINE VINEGAR DRESSING
2 tablespoons red wine vinegar
2 tablespoons olive oil
1 teaspoon dijon mustard

1. Preheat oven to 200°C/180°C. Oil a 8cm x 22.5cm (3¼-inch x 9-inch) loaf pan (base measurement); line base and sides with baking paper.
2. Place beetroot on an oven tray; bake 45 minutes or until just tender. Wearing gloves, rub off stalks and skin from beetroot while still warm. Cool. Halve or quarter larger beetroot, if necessary.
3. Make herbed ricotta.
4. Place pumpkin on an oven tray; drizzle with oil. Bake 25 minutes or until just tender.
5. Make red wine vinegar dressing.
6. Arrange beetroot, pumpkin and rocket on serving plates; top with sliced herbed ricotta, walnuts and pepitas. Just before serving, drizzle with dressing.

HERBED RICOTTA
Process herbs until finely chopped. Add cream and half the ricotta; process until smooth. Add egg, parmesan and remaining ricotta; process until just combined. Season. Spoon mixture into loaf pan. Bake for 30 minutes or until browned lightly. Cool in pan for 15 minutes.

RED WINE VINEGAR DRESSING
Place ingredients in a screw-top jar; shake well. Season to taste.

SPICY CHICKEN SALAD

PREP + COOK TIME *45 MINUTES* **SERVES** *4*

This light and aromatic chicken salad, known as larb in Laos and Thailand, is eaten wrapped in lettuce leaves for a textural contrast.

2 tablespoons long-grain white rice
1 tablespoon peanut oil
10cm (4-inch) stick lemon grass (20g), chopped finely
2 red bird's-eye chillies, seeded, chopped finely
2 cloves garlic, crushed
1 tablespoon finely chopped galangal
750g (1½ pounds) minced (ground) chicken
1 small red onion (100g), sliced thinly
1 lebanese cucumber (130g), seeded, sliced thinly
100g (3 ounces) bean sprouts
½ cup loosely packed fresh thai basil leaves
1 cup loosely packed fresh coriander (cilantro) leaves
4 large iceberg lettuce leaves

DRESSING
⅓ cup (80ml) lime juice
2 tablespoons fish sauce
2 tablespoons kecap manis
2 tablespoons peanut oil
2 teaspoons grated palm sugar
½ teaspoon sambal oelek

1 Heat a dry wok over medium heat; stir-fry rice for 1 minute or until browned lightly. Blend or process (or crush using a mortar and pestle) rice until it resembles fine breadcrumbs.
2 Make dressing.
3 Heat oil in wok over medium heat; stir-fry lemon grass, chilli, garlic and galangal until fragrant. Remove from wok. Stir-fry chicken, in batches, until changed in colour and just cooked through.
4 Return chicken and lemon grass mixture to wok with one-third of the dressing; stir-fry 5 minutes or until mixture thickens slightly.
5 Place chicken mixture in a large bowl with onion, cucumber, sprouts, herbs and remaining dressing; toss gently to combine. Place lettuce leaves on serving plates; spoon larb into leaves, sprinkle with ground rice.

DRESSING
Place ingredients in a screw-top jar; shake well.

TIPS Sambal oelek is a hot chilli paste, available from major supermarkets and Asian food stores. You can use ½ small seeded, finely chopped red chilli or ¼ teaspoon dried chilli flakes instead. Kecap manis is a thick sweet Indonesian soy sauce, substitute regular soy sauce mixed with either 1 tablespoon palm, white or brown sugar. Sambal oelek and kecap manis are available from major supermarkets and Asian food stores.

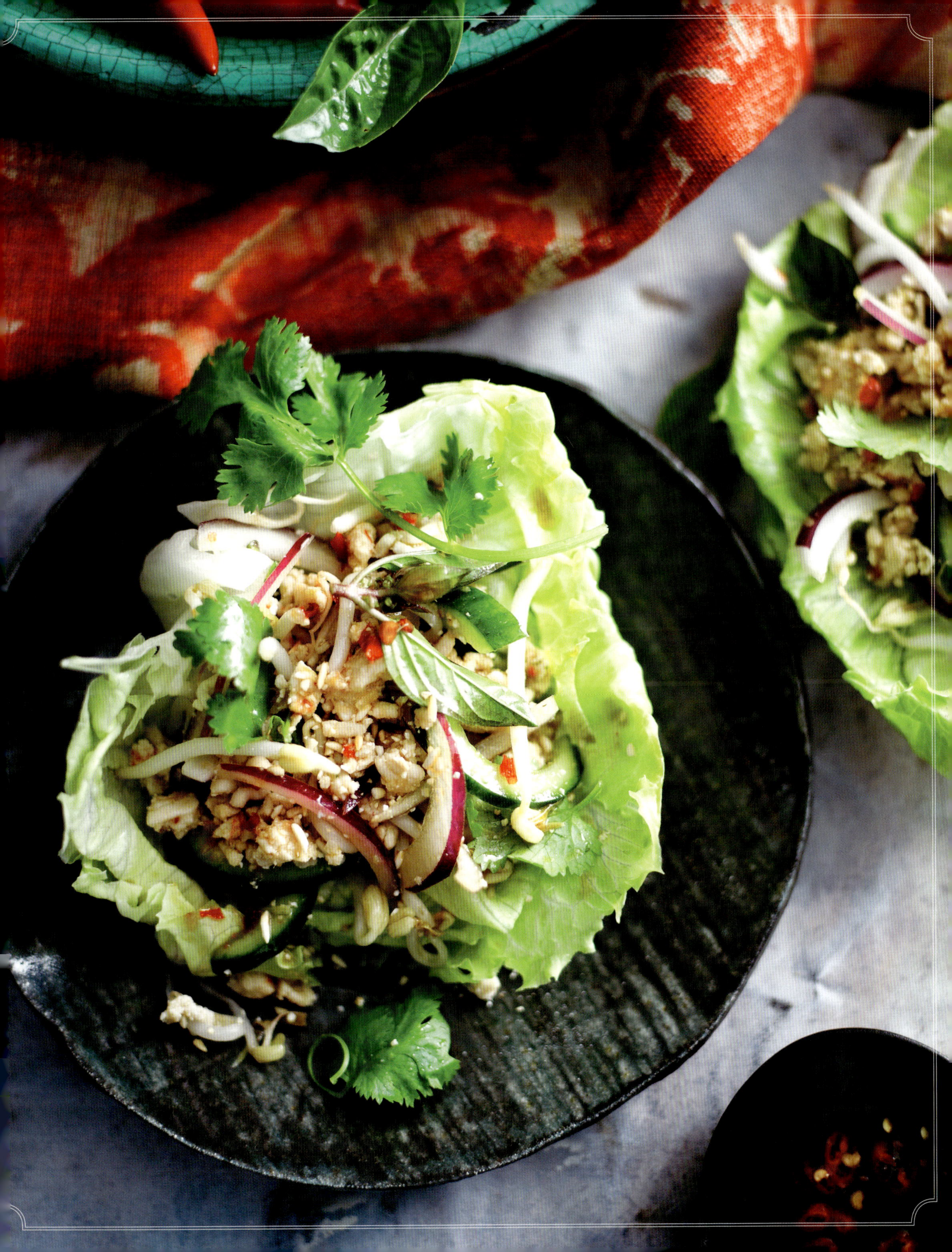

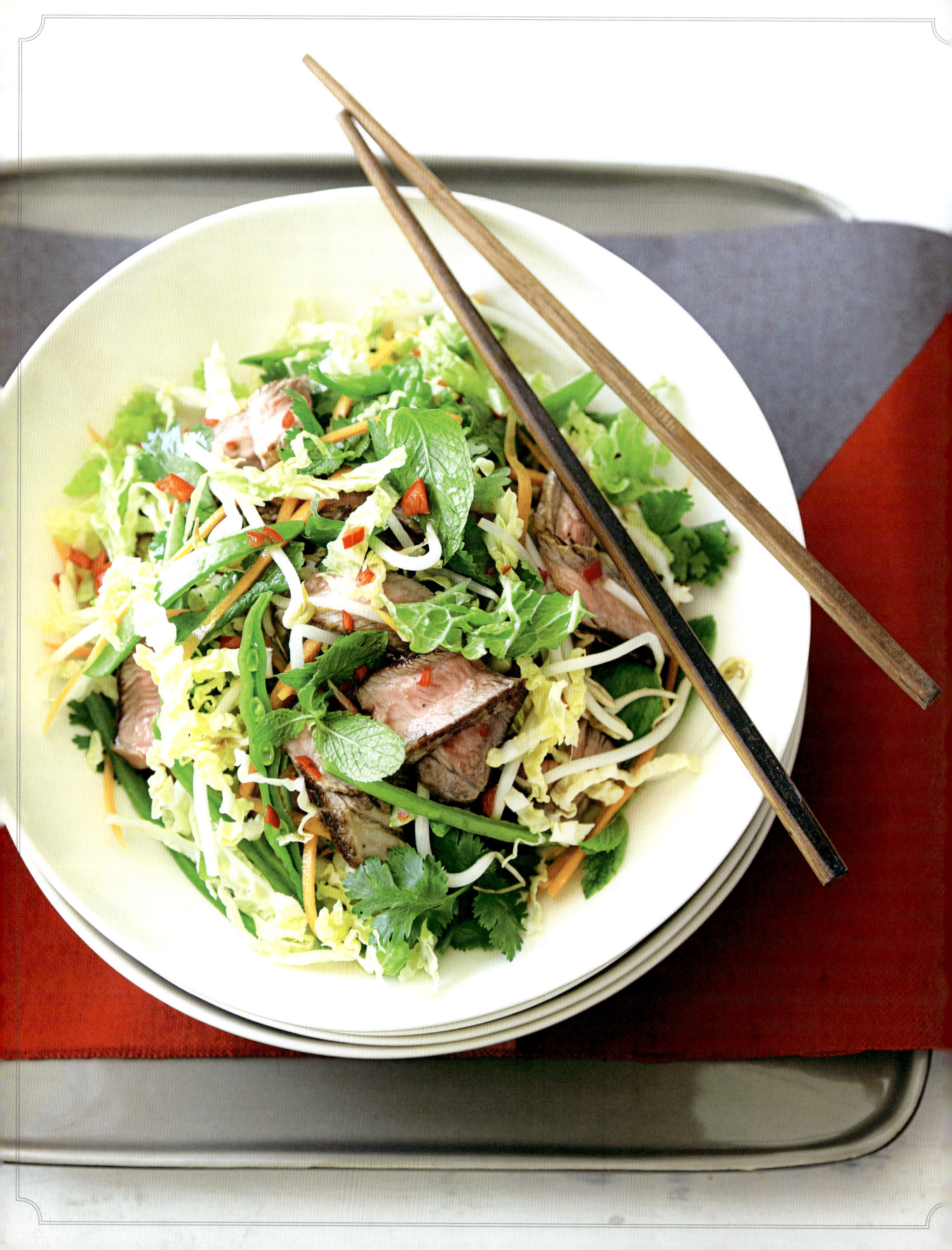

BEEF AND CRUNCHY
Wombok Salad

PREP + COOK TIME 25 MINUTES SERVES 4

500g (1 pound) beef sirloin steaks
½ medium wombok (napa cabbage) (800g), trimmed, shredded finely
1 medium carrot (120g), grated coarsely
150g (4½ ounces) snow peas, sliced thinly lengthways
2 cups (160g) bean sprouts
½ cup loosely packed fresh mint leaves
½ cup loosely packed fresh coriander (cilantro) leaves

DRESSING
½ cup (125ml) lime juice
2 tablespoons fish sauce
¼ cup (65g) grated palm sugar or brown sugar
2 red bird's-eye chillies, seeded, chopped finely

1 Preheat an oiled grill plate (or grill or barbecue) to medium-high. Cook beef 2 minutes each side, depending on the thickenss, for medium-rare or until cooked as desired. Transfer to a plate, cover with foil; stand 5 minutes. Slice thinly.
2 Make dressing.
3 Place wombok, carrot, snow peas, sprouts and herbs in a large bowl with beef and dressing; toss gently to combine.

DRESSING
Place ingredients in a screw-top jar; shake well.

TIP The shape and thickness of a steak will create differences in cooking time, so use the following guide. For perfect medium rare, cook steaks until moisture is just visible on the surface; turn over and repeat cooking on the other side. To check: press with the back of a pair of tongs; the steak should feel soft when pressed.

CHAPTER 2
PASTA & RICE

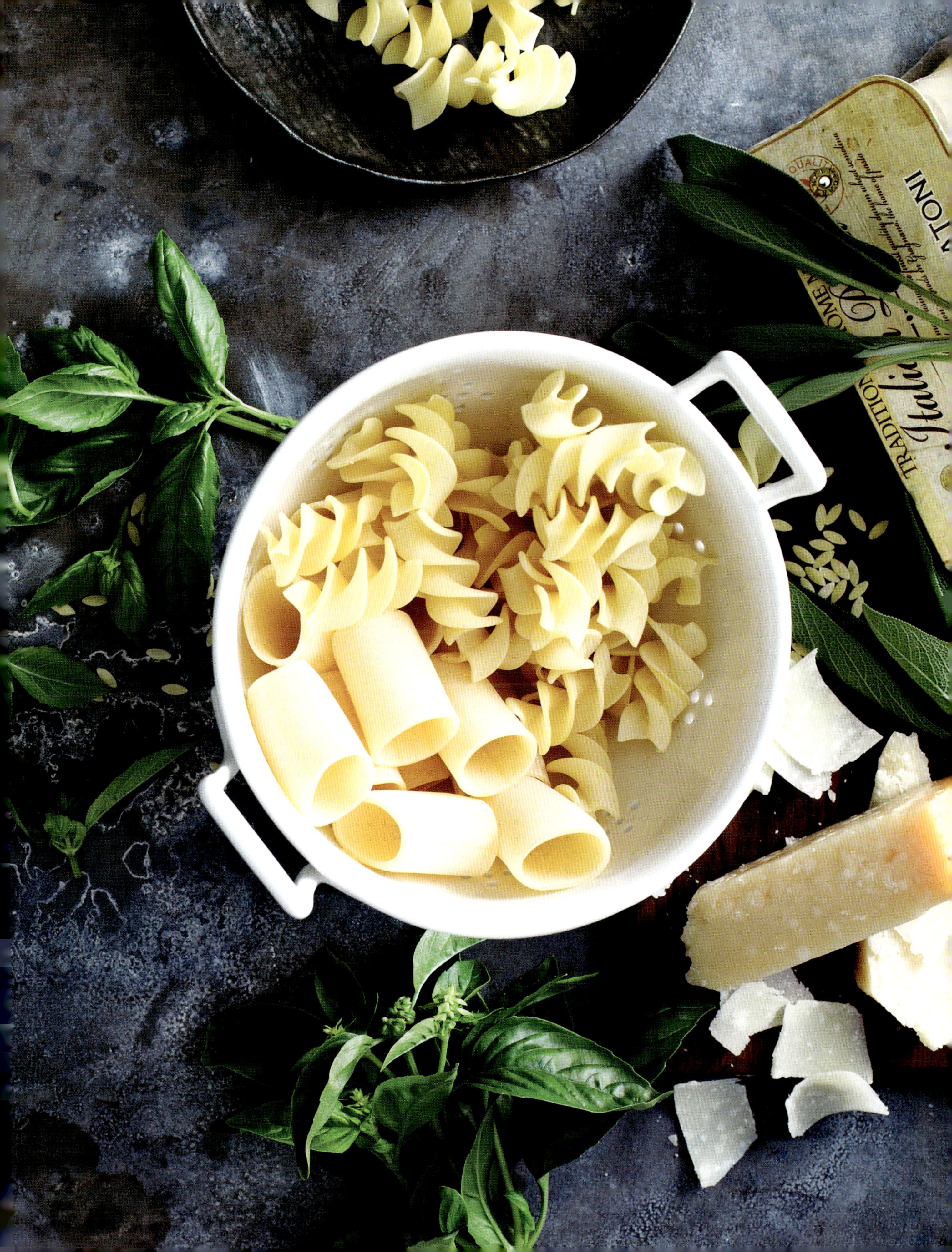

LASAGNE

PREP + COOK TIME *2 HOURS* **SERVES** *6*

1 tablespoon olive oil
1 medium onion (150g), chopped
2 cloves garlic, crushed
1kg (2 pounds) minced (ground) pork and veal
575g (1¼ pounds) bottled tomato pasta sauce
800g (1½ pounds) canned diced tomatoes
2 tablespoons chopped fresh oregano
2 tablespoons chopped fresh basil
2 tablespoons chopped fresh flat-leaf parsley
80g (2½ ounces) butter
½ cup (75g) plain (all-purpose) flour
3 cups (750ml) milk
1¼ cups (250g) fresh ricotta
½ cup (40g) grated parmesan
375g (12 ounces) instant lasagne sheets
1½ cups (125g) grated cheddar

1. Heat oil in a large saucepan over medium heat; cook onion and garlic, stirring 5 minutes or until soft. Add minced pork and veal; cook, stirring until browned. Stir in pasta sauce and tomatoes; simmer, uncovered, 40 minutes, stirring occasionally, until mixture is thickened. Stir in herbs.
2. Melt butter in a medium saucepan over low-medium heat, add flour; cook, stirring until bubbling. Gradually stir in milk; stir until sauce boils and thickens. Remove from heat, whisk in ricotta and parmesan.
3. Preheat oven to 180°C/350°F.
4. Oil a 3-litre (12-cup) ovenproof dish. Cover base with one-third of the lasagne sheets; top with half the mince mixture and ⅓ cup of the ricotta mixture. Repeat layers. Top with remaining lasagne sheets and ricotta mixture; sprinkle with cheddar.
5. Bake lasagne, covered with greased foil, 30 minutes. Remove foil; bake a further 25 minutes or until hot. Stand 10 minutes before cutting.

TIP The secret to our delicious lasagne is the pork and veal mince in the meat sauce, which gives it a balanced and rich flavour. While ricotta in our white sauce gives it an extra creaminess and lusciousness without much guilt.

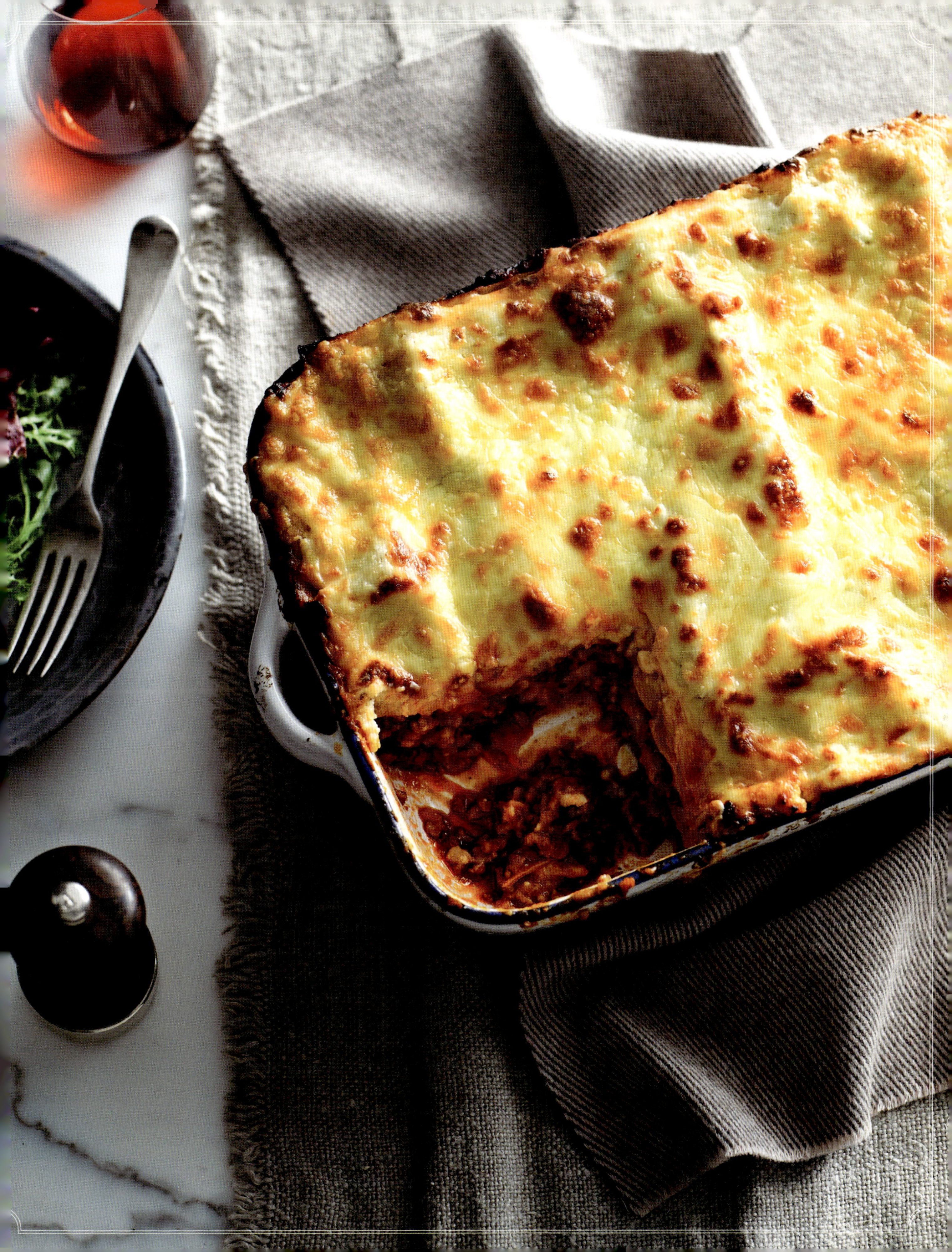

EGGPLANT AND
Pesto Baked Pasta

EGGPLANT AND
Pesto Baked Pasta

PREP + COOK TIME *1 HOUR 30 MINUTES* **SERVES** *6*

500g (1 pound) small pasta
2 large zucchini (300g), grated coarsely
¾ cup (200g) pesto
2 large eggplants (1kg), sliced thinly lengthways
¾ cup (180ml) olive oil
2 cups (200g) grated mozzarella
¼ cup (20g) grated parmesan
500g (1 pound) cherry tomatoes, halved

1. Cook pasta in a large saucepan of boiling salted water until just tender; drain. Return to pan with zucchini and pesto; toss to combine.
2. Meanwhile, brush both sides of eggplant with oil. Cook eggplant, in batches, in a large non-stick frying pan over medium heat until browned on both sides. Drain on paper towel.
3. Preheat oven to 180°C/350°F.
4. Spoon pasta mixture into a shallow 4-litre (16-cup) ovenproof dish; top with eggplant, slightly overlapping the slices. Scatter with combined cheeses; top with tomatoes, cut-side up.
5. Bake 45 minutes or until heated through and cheese is lightly browned; cover with foil if it starts to overbrown.

TIPS You can use any small pasta you like, such as spirals, macaroni or mini penne.
The eggplant can also be cooked under the grill (broiler) or on a barbecue.

SERVING SUGGESTION Serve with a green leaf salad.

SPICY PRAWN
Linguine

PREP + COOK TIME *20 MINUTES* **SERVES** *4*

400g (12½ ounces) dried linguine
⅓ cup (80ml) extra virgin olive oil
500g (1 pound) uncooked prawns (shrimp), peeled, deveined, with tails intact
3 cloves garlic, crushed
2 long red chillies, chopped finely
2 tablespoons coarsely chopped fresh flat-leaf parsley

1. Cook pasta in a large saucepan of salted boiling water until tender. Drain, reserving ⅓ cup of cooking water. Return to pan.
2. Meanwhile, heat half the oil in a large non-stick frying pan over high heat; cook prawns 2 minutes or until browned lightly. Add garlic and chilli; cook, stirring, until prawns are just cooked.
3. Add prawns with any pan juices to pasta with parsley, reserved cooking water and remaining oil; toss gently to combine.

TIP For perfectly cooked pasta, bring at least 5 litres (20 cups) water to the boil. Although it may sound like a lot, add at least 1 tablespoon salt – but don't worry, most of it will be drained away. Next add pasta and give it a good stir to separate the strands. Cook until 'al dente', meaning firm to the tooth; pasta should have a little resistance when you bite into a piece.

(PHOTOGRAPH PAGE 48)

SPICY PRAWN
Linguine
(RECIPE PAGE 47)

FARFALLE WITH ZUCCHINI LEMON
Garlic Sauce
(RECIPE PAGE 50)

FARFALLE WITH ZUCCHINI LEMON
Garlic Sauce

PREP + COOK TIME *25 MINUTES* **SERVES 4**

375g (12 ounces) farfalle pasta
3 medium green zucchini (280g)
3 medium yellow zucchini (280g)
30g (1 ounce) butter
1 tablespoon olive oil
2 cloves garlic, crushed
⅓ cup (80ml) vegetable stock
½ cup (125ml) pouring cream
2 teaspoons finely grated lemon rind
75g (2½ ounces) baby spinach leaves
⅓ cup coarsely chopped fresh chives
¼ cup (20g) shaved parmesan

1. Cook pasta in a large saucepan of boiling salted water until just tender; drain. Return to pan.
2. Meanwhile, cut zucchini in half lengthways; slice thinly on the diagonal.
3. Heat butter and oil in a large, non-stick frying pan over high heat; cook zucchini and garlic, stirring, 8 minutes or until zucchini is just tender. Add stock; bring to the boil. Reduce heat; stir in cream, rind, spinach and chives until hot.
4. Add pasta to zucchini mixture, season; toss to combine. Serve topped with parmesan.

TIP You can use yellow squash instead of the yellow zucchini, if you like.

SERVING SUGGESTION Serve with a multi-coloured tomato salad tossed in a balsamic dressing.

(PHOTOGRAPH PAGE 49)

TAGLIATELLE WITH CREAMY MUSHROOM
and Bacon Sauce

PREP + COOK TIME *25 MINUTES* **SERVES 4**

20g (¾ ounce) butter
4 rindless bacon slices (260g), chopped
300g (9½ ounces) button mushrooms, sliced
100g (3 ounces) shiitake mushrooms, sliced
2 cloves garlic, crushed
1½ cups (375ml) chicken stock
1½ cups (375ml) pouring cream
375g (12 ounces) tagliatelle pasta
½ cup (40g) grated parmesan
2 tablespoons fresh lemon thyme leaves

1. Melt butter in a large frying pan over medium heat; cook bacon and mushrooms, stirring, 5 minutes or until browned lightly. Add garlic; cook, stirring, until fragrant.
2. Stir in stock; simmer 8 minutes or until reduced by half. Add cream; bring to the boil. Reduce heat; simmer 5 minutes or until thickened slightly.
3. Meanwhile, cook pasta in a saucepan of boiling salted water until just tender; drain.
4. Add pasta to sauce, toss to coat. Serve immediately topped with parmesan and thyme.

TIPS Discard the stems from the shiitake mushrooms before slicing as they are too tough to eat. If you like, replace the shiitakes with the same quantity of either button or swiss brown mushrooms. You could also add a handful of frozen (or cooked fresh) peas at the same time as the cream.

TAGLIATELLE WITH CREAMY MUSHROOM
and Bacon Sauce

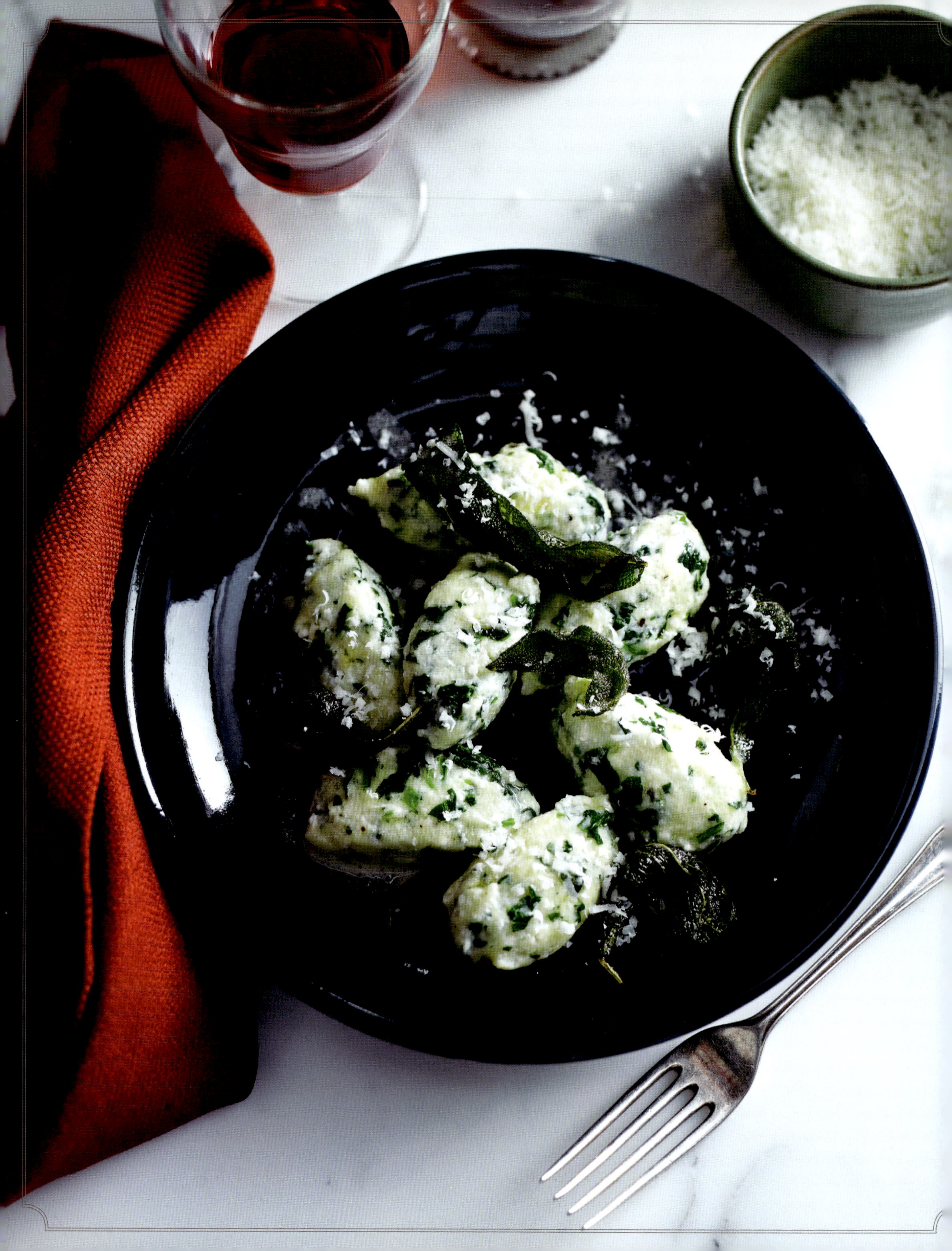

SPINACH AND RICOTTA GNOCCHI
with Sage Butter

PREP + COOK TIME *35 MINUTES* **SERVES** *4*

200g (6½ ounces) baby spinach leaves
500g (1 pound) firm fresh ricotta
1 cup (80g) finely grated parmesan
½ cup (75g) plain (all-purpose) flour
2 eggs, beaten lightly
1 tablespoon extra virgin olive oil
80g (2½ ounces) butter, chopped
16 sage leaves
¼ cup (20g) shaved parmesan

1. Briefly cook spinach in a large saucepan of boiling salted water; drain. Refresh in iced water; drain. Squeeze spinach firmly to remove excess liquid; chop finely.
2. Place spinach in a large bowl with ricotta, grated parmesan, flour, egg and oil; season, then mix well.
3. Preheat oven to 150°C/300°F.
4. Meanwhile, bring a large saucepan of salted water to the boil. Shape level tablespoons of spinach mixture into ovals. Drop gnocchi, in batches, into boiling water; cook 1-2 minutes or until gnocchi float to the surface. Using a slotted spoon, remove immediately; drain well. Transfer to a tray; cover, keep warm in oven.
5. Cook butter in a large frying pan over medium heat until browned lightly. Add sage; remove from heat.
6. Divide gnocchi among bowls, drizzle with sage butter. Serve topped with shaved parmesan.

TIPS Blanching the spinach in step 1 prevents the spinach from overcooking.
Make sure you use firm fresh ricotta otherwise the gnocchi may not hold together. It is available from the deli section of supermarkets.
Gnocchi can be prepared several hours ahead. Store, covered, in the fridge. Cook just before serving.

PASTA SHELLS
with Italian Sausages

PREP + COOK TIME *35 MINUTES* **SERVES 4**

750g (1½ pounds) Italian-style sausages
1 tablespoon extra virgin olive oil
4 cloves garlic, chopped finely
1.2kg (2½ pounds) canned crushed tomatoes
2 tablespoons pouring cream
2 cups loosely packed fresh basil leaves
500g (1 pound) conchiglioni (large pasta shells)
⅓ cup (40g) finely grated parmesan

1. Make a slit lengthways down the sausages; remove sausage meat, discard skins. Coarsely crumble sausage meat.
2. Heat a large frying pan over high heat; cook sausage meat, stirring, 8 minutes or until browned. Remove with a slotted spoon; drain on paper towel. Discard fat in pan.
3. Heat oil in same pan over low-medium heat; cook garlic, stirring, 3 minutes without browning. Increase heat, add tomatoes and sausage meat; simmer 10 minutes or until sauce is thick. Season to taste. Stir in cream and half the basil.
4. Meanwhile, cook pasta in a large saucepan of boiling salted water until just tender. Drain, reserving ½ cup cooking water.
5. Add pasta to sauce mixture; stir to combine. Remove from heat, stir in parmesan. If mixture feels dry, add some of the pasta cooking water.
6. Serve pasta topped with remaining basil.

TIP Conchiglie is a shell-shaped pasta, available in several sizes. Conchiglioni is the large version, which works well with chunky sauces and when stuffed or baked. If you can't find it, use a short pasta such as rigatoni or penne instead.

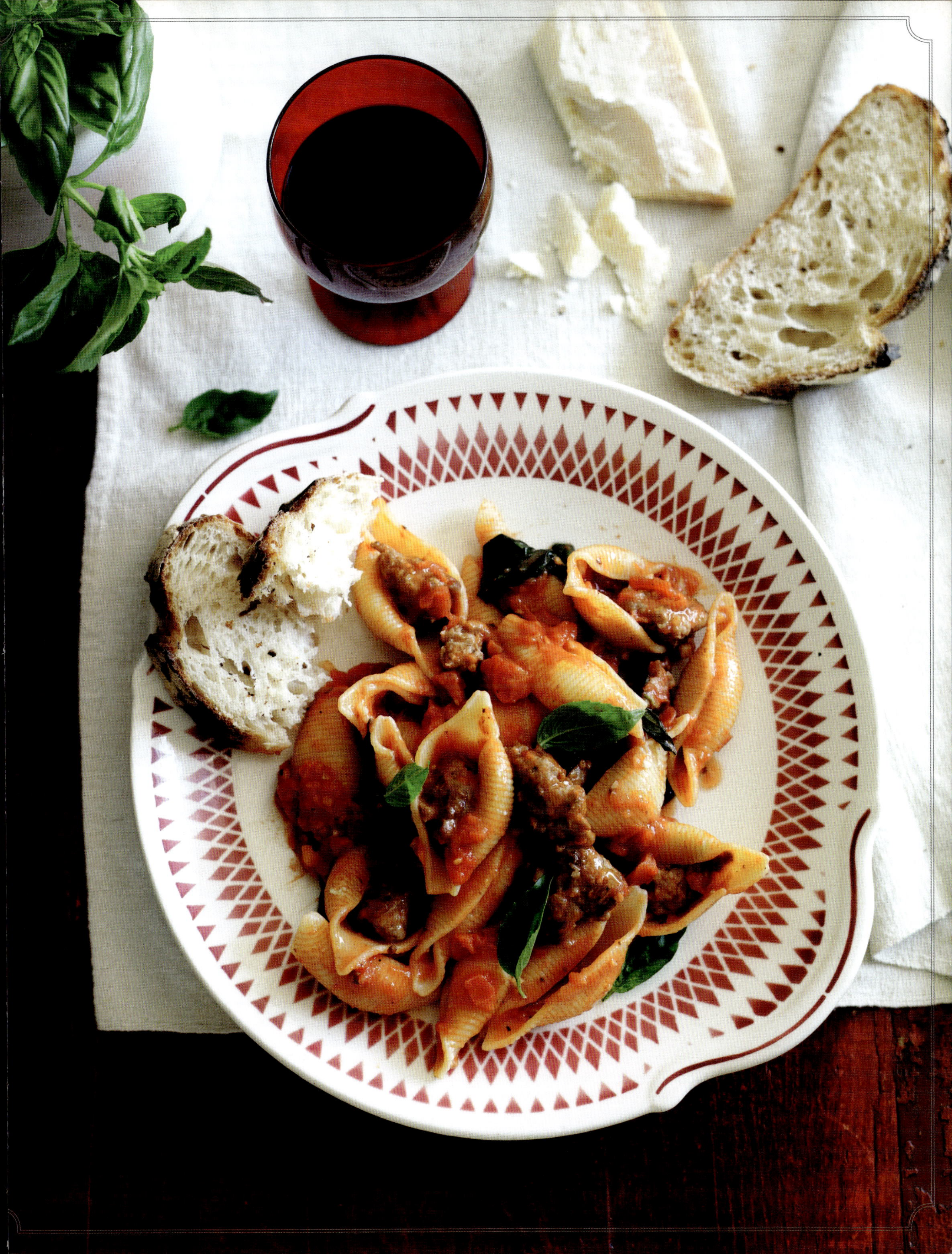

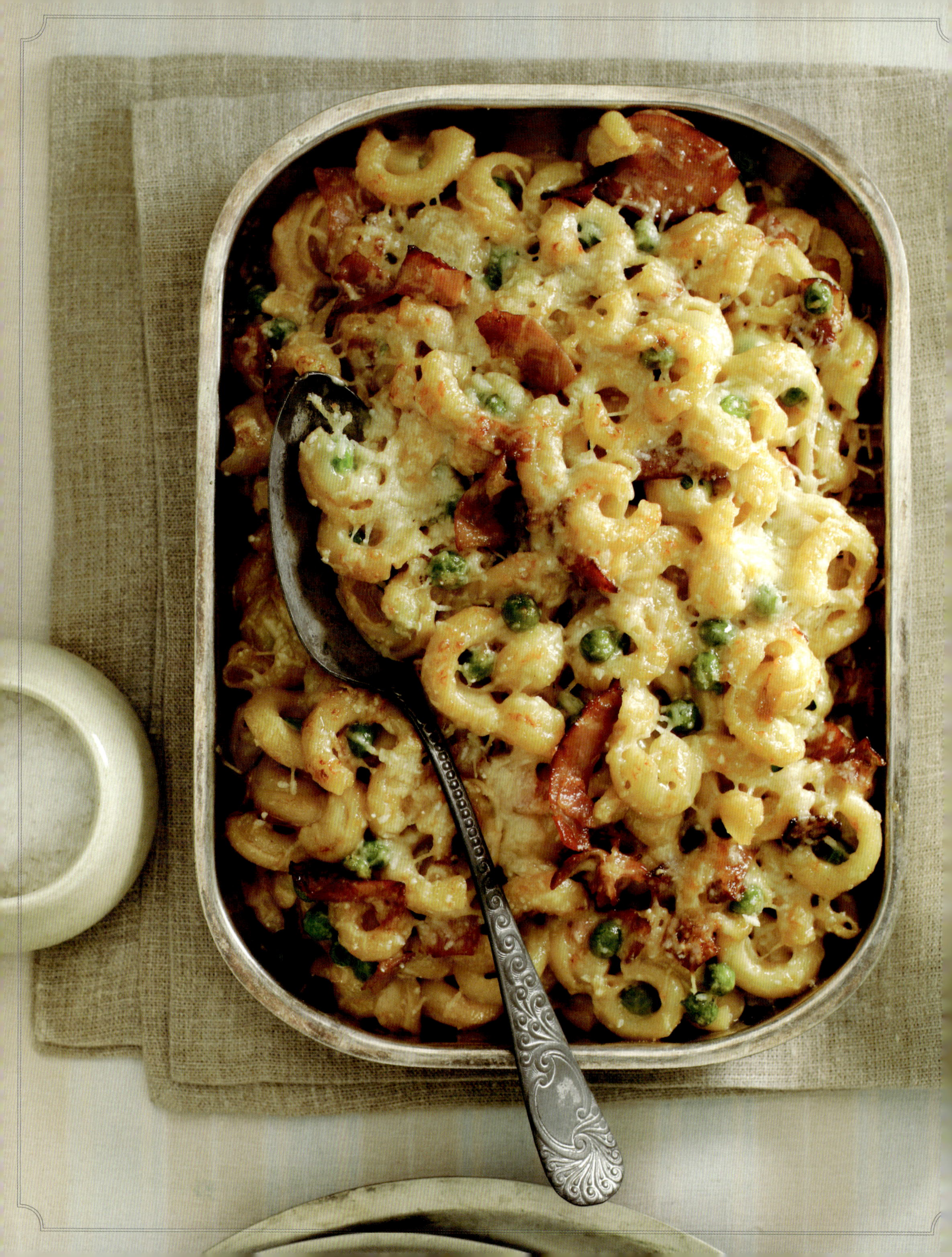

PROSCIUTTO AND PEA
Pasta Gratin

PREP + COOK TIME 30 MINUTES SERVES 4

375g (12 ounces) curly pasta
1 teaspoon cornflour (cornstarch)
300ml (½ pint) pouring cream
20g (¾ ounce) butter
8 slices prosciutto (120g), chopped coarsely
¾ cup (90g) frozen peas, thawed
1 cup (80g) finely grated parmesan

1. Cook pasta in a large saucepan of boiling, salted water until just tender; drain. Return to pan.
2. Blend cornflour and a little of the cream until smooth; stir in remaining cream.
3. Melt butter in a large frying pan over medium heat; cook prosciutto, stirring, 3 minutes or until browned lightly. Add cream mixture, peas and half the parmesan, stirring, until sauce boils and thickens slightly. Pour sauce over hot pasta; toss to combine. Season to taste.
4. Preheat grill (broiler) to high.
5. Spoon pasta mixture into an oiled 2-litre (8-cup) ovenproof dish; sprinkle with remaining parmesan. Place under hot grill for 8 minutes or until top has browned lightly.

TIPS You can use any variety of short pasta you like in this recipe.
For extra vegie content, add 300g (9½ ounces) cooked broccoli or cauliflower florets in step 3, at the same time as the peas.

SPAGHETTI AND MEATBALLS

PREP + COOK TIME *35 MINUTES* SERVES 4

500g (1 pound) minced (ground) pork or beef
¾ cup (50g) stale breadcrumbs
½ small red onion (50g), chopped finely
2 tablespoons coarsely chopped fresh flat-leaf parsley
1 clove garlic, crushed
2 tablespoons milk
2 tablespoons tomato paste
2 tablespoons olive oil
800g (1½ pounds) canned crushed tomatoes
1 teaspoon caster (superfine) sugar
400g (12½ ounces) spaghetti
⅓ cup (25g) finely grated pecorino romano or parmesan

1. Combine minced pork, breadcrumbs, onion, parsley, garlic, milk and half the paste in a large bowl. Roll level tablespoonfuls of mixture into balls.
2. Heat oil in a large non-stick frying pan over high heat; cook meatballs, in batches, 8 minutes or until browned all over.
3. Place tomatoes and remaining paste in same pan; bring to the boil over high heat. Reduce heat; simmer 10 minutes or until thickened slightly. Stir in sugar.
4. Add meatballs to sauce; reduce heat to low and simmer, stirring occasionally, 5 minutes or until meatballs are cooked through.
5. Meanwhile, cook spaghetti in a large saucepan of salted boiling water until just tender; drain.
6. Divide spaghetti among serving bowls, top with meatballs and sauce; sprinkle with pecorino and, if you like, some extra chopped parsley.

TIP The best way to thoroughly mix the meatball mixture is with your hands. Dampen your hands with a little water before rolling the mixture into balls – this will prevent the mixture from sticking.

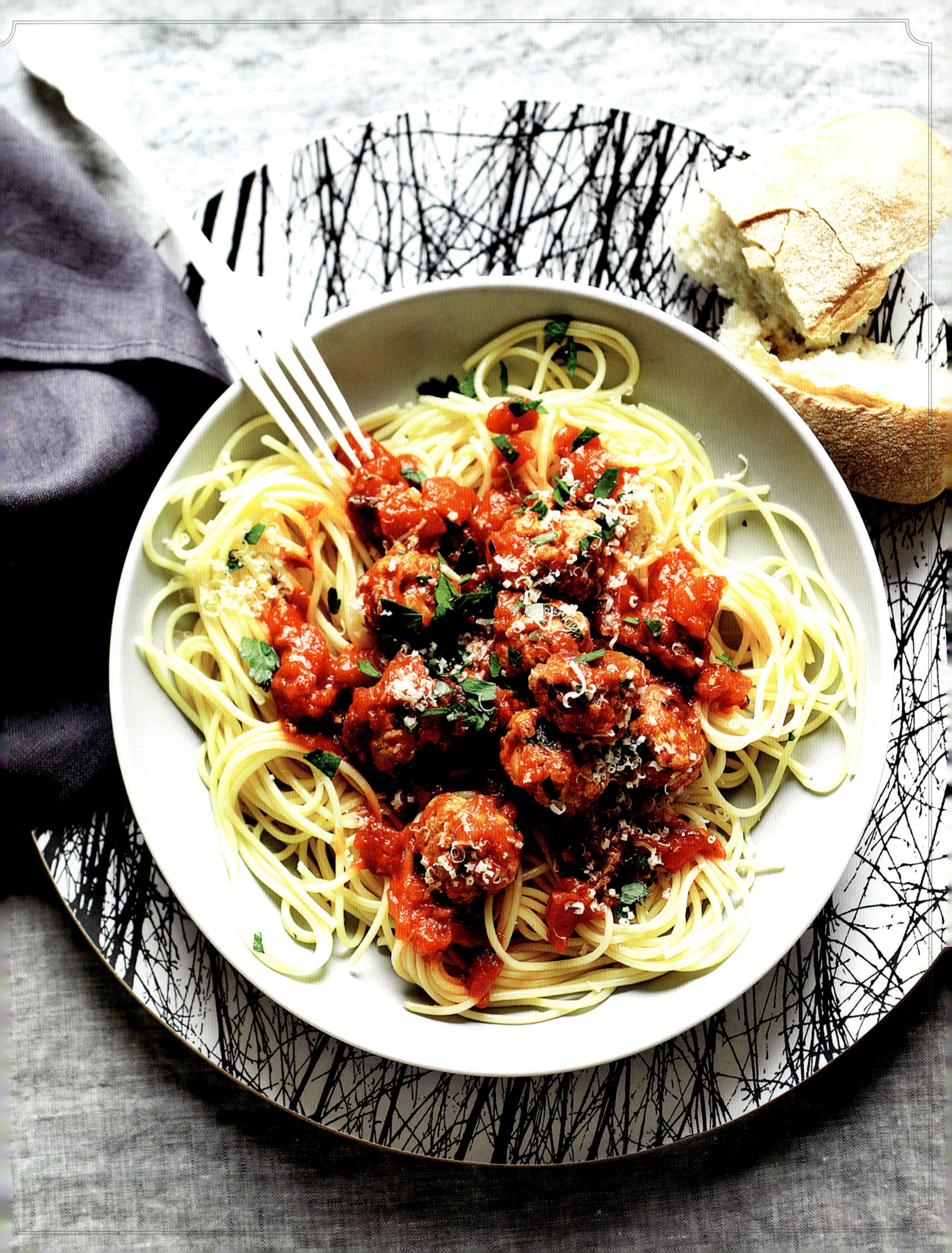

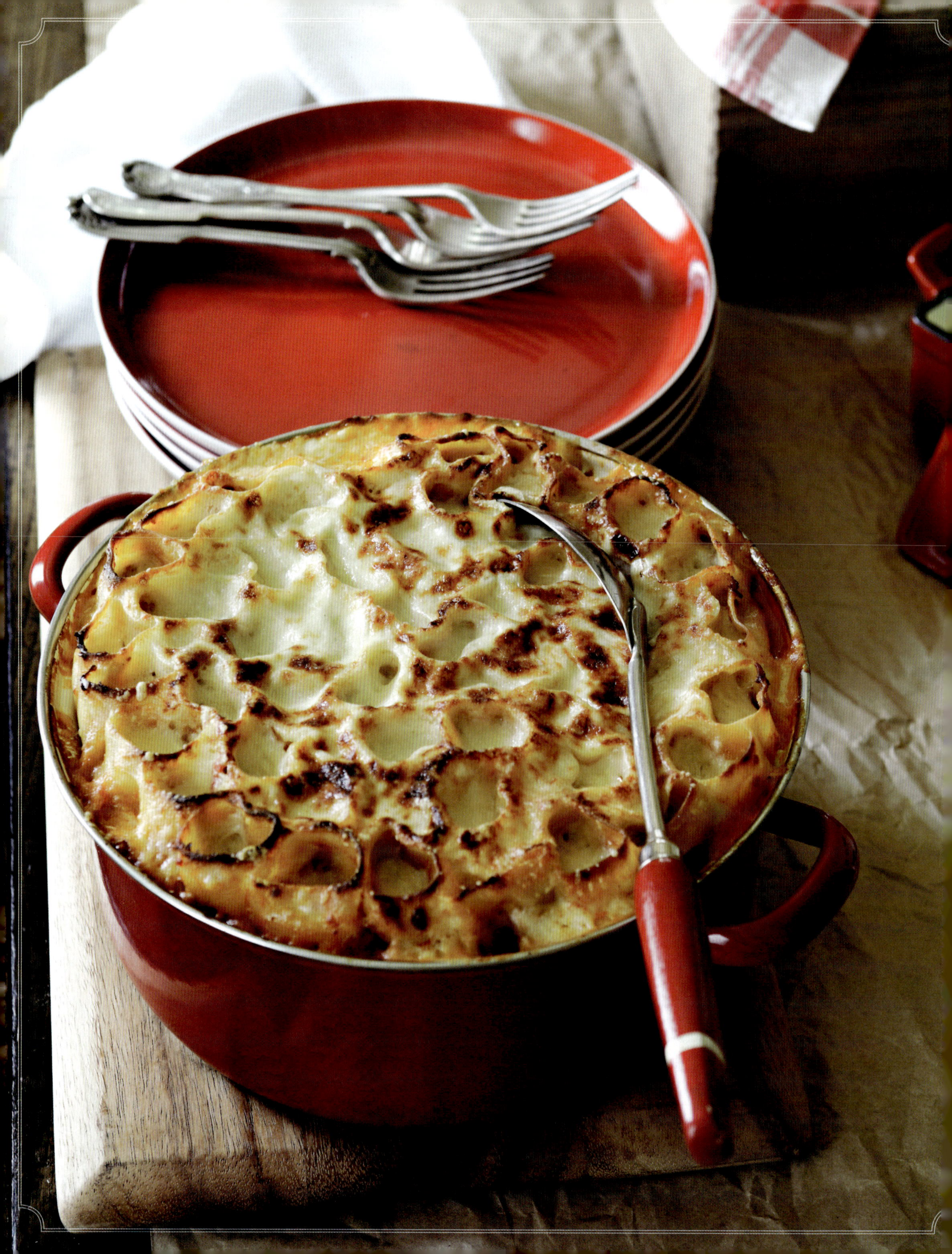

CANNELLONI STRAIGHT-UP

PREP + COOK TIME *2 HOURS 30 MINUTES* SERVES 8

3 x 250g (8-ounce) packets cannelloni tubes
⅔ cup (70g) grated mozzarella
2 tablespoons grated parmesan

FILLING
¼ cup (60ml) olive oil
2 large brown onions (400g), chopped finely
4 cloves garlic, crushed
2 medium carrots (240g), chopped finely
2 trimmed celery sticks (200g), chopped
1.5kg (3 pounds) minced (ground) beef
800g (1½ pounds) canned diced tomatoes
¾ cup (210g) tomato paste
1 litre (4 cups) water
2 teaspoons dried oregano
1 cup chopped fresh flat-leaf parsley

CHEESE SAUCE
60g (2 ounces) butter
⅓ cup (50g) plain (all-purpose) flour
3 cups (750ml) milk
1 cup (80g) grated parmesan

1. Make filling.
2. Make cheese sauce.
3. Preheat oven to 180°C/350°F.
4. Spoon a quarter of the filling over the base of a 26cm (10½-inch) round, 11.5cm (4¾-inch) deep ovenproof dish (make sure the dish is taller than the length of the cannelloni tubes). Stand tubes upright in filling, pressing gently into mixture, allowing a little room between them to expand. Spoon remaining filling into tubes; gently tap dish on bench to settle mixture.
5. Pour sauce over cannelloni, sprinkle with cheeses.
6. Bake 40 minutes or until cannelloni is tender and cheese is golden.

FILLING
Heat oil in a large saucepan over medium heat; cook onion, garlic, carrot and celery stirring, 8 minutes or until soft. Remove from pan. Add beef; cook, stirring, over high heat, until browned, breaking up any lumps. Return vegetables to pan with tomatoes, paste, water and oregano; bring to the boil. Reduce heat; simmer, partially covered, 1 hour or until thickened slightly, stirring occasionally. Remove from heat, stir in parsley; season to taste.

CHEESE SAUCE
Melt butter in a medium saucepan over medium heat, add flour; stir 1 minute or until mixture is grainy. Gradually stir in milk; cook, stirring, until sauce boils and thickens. Remove from heat; stir in parmesan. Season to taste.

PUMPKIN RAVIOLI
with Sage Butter

PREP + COOK TIME 1 HOUR 30 MINUTES SERVES 12

1 quantity pasta dough (recipe page 64)
250g (8 ounces) butter, chopped
4 cloves garlic, sliced thinly
1 bunch sage, leaves picked
¼ cup (20g) shaved parmesan

PUMPKIN AND RICOTTA FILLING
1kg (2 pound) butternut pumpkin, peeled, chopped coarsely
100g (3 ounces) fresh ricotta
⅔ cup (50g) grated parmesan
⅔ cup (50g) fresh breadcrumbs
½ teaspoon grated nutmeg

1. Make pumpkin and ricotta filling.
2. Roll pasta dough to the thinnest setting on a pasta machine to form pasta sheets (see page 64). Immediately prepare ravioli or the pasta will dry out. Roll two sheets at a time; keep remaining dough wrapped in plastic wrap. Place pasta sheet on a semolina-dusted surface. Place rounded teaspoons of filling 5cm (2-inches) apart in two rows, 2cm (¾-inch) from the edges. Brush around filling with a little water. Place another freshly rolled pasta sheet on top.
3. Press around each mound of filling to remove any air. Using a knife or cutter, cut into squares or rounds. Place ravioli on a tray dusted with a little semolina. Repeat with remaining pasta sheets, filling and water.
4. Cook ravioli, in batches, in a large saucepan of boiling salted water 3 minutes or until cooked through; remove from pan with a slotted spoon.
5. While the last batch of ravioli is cooking, melt butter in a frying pan over medium heat, add garlic and sage leaves; cook until butter just begins to colour.
6. Serve ravioli drizzled with sage butter; top with shaved parmesan.

PUMPKIN AND RICOTTA FILLING
Preheat oven to 200°C/400°F. Place pumpkin on an oiled oven tray, season; roast 30 minutes or until tender. Cool. Process pumpkin until smooth; add remaining ingredients, process until smooth.

TIP Making ravioli is time-consuming to prepare and this recipe makes a large batch. You can either halve the recipe or freeze half for another meal. Open-freeze uncooked ravioli on trays in a single layer until solid, then pack into airtight containers. Cook ravioli from frozen.

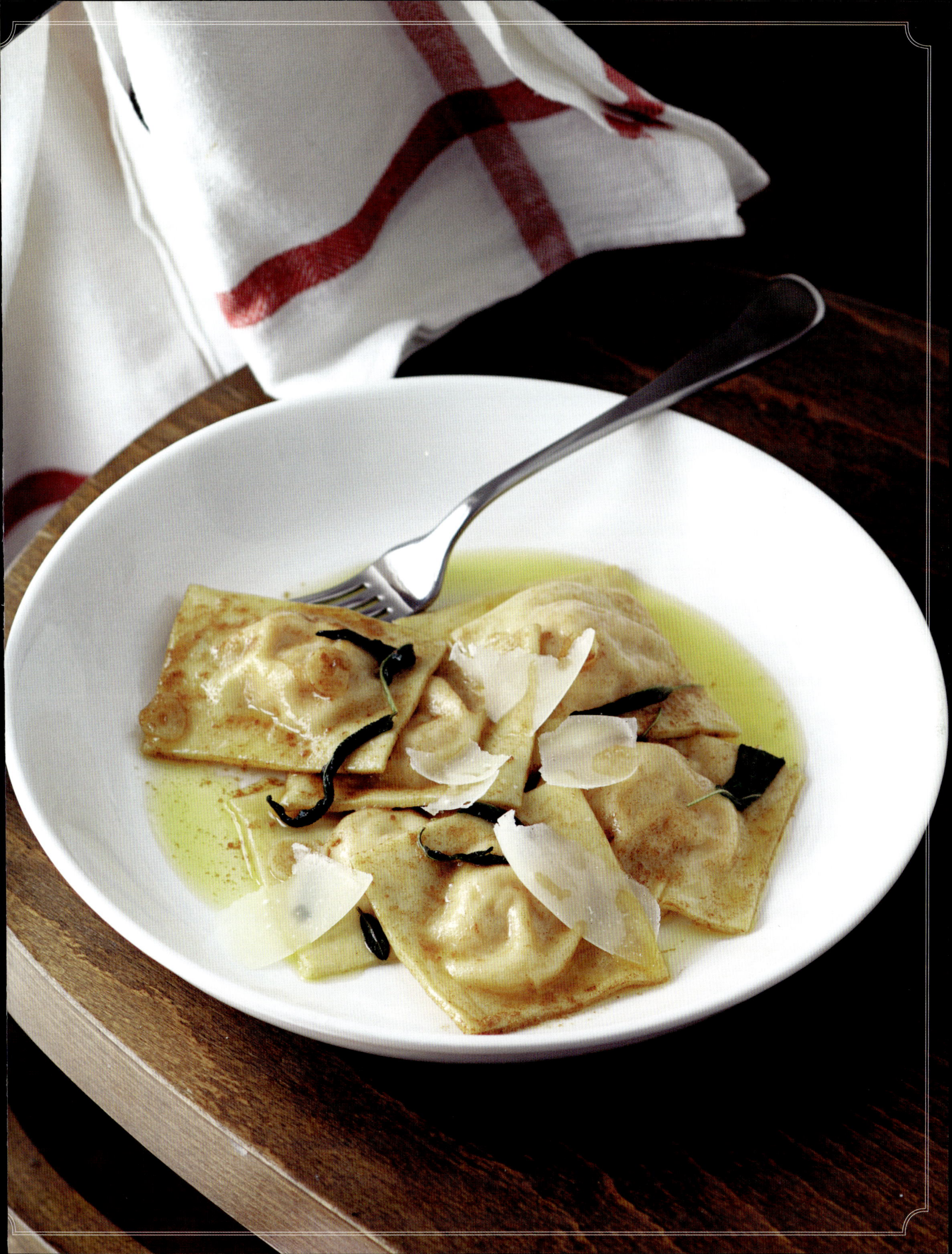

PASTA DOUGH

PREP TIME *30 MINUTES* **SERVES** *6*

4 cups (600g) 00 flour or bakers' flour (see tip)
6 eggs, at room temperature
1 teaspoon fine salt
tablespoon olive oil (see tip)
tablespoons water (see tip)
fine semolina or extra flour, for dusting

1. Pulse flour, eggs, salt and olive oil in a food processor until ingredients are well combined. Add water if needed – the dough should be firm.
2. Place dough on a work surface; knead into a ball. Knead dough for 5 minutes or until smooth. Wrap in plastic wrap; refrigerate 30 minutes.
3. Divide dough into quarters; wrap three pieces in plastic. Shape one piece of dough into a rectangle narrower than the rollers of the pasta machine.
4. Sprinkle dough and rollers of pasta machine with a little extra flour to prevent sticking. Roll one piece of dough through the pasta machine on its thickest setting. Fold short sides of dough into the centre, turn it 90 degrees and roll through the machine about six times until it is the width of the rollers. Repeat rolling several times, without folding or turning, adjusting the setting each time so the dough becomes thinner with each roll. Roll to second thinnest or thinnest setting, depending on thickness required. (The thinnest setting is used for lasagne sheets, ravioli and pappardelle.) Sprinkle pasta sheets with a little semolina or flour. Repeat with remaining dough. Pasta can be cooked immediately.
5. For machine-cut pastas such as tagliatelle and linguine, insert the attachment into the machine. Cut rolled pasta sheets to desired lengths. Dust with flour. Roll sheets through the machine. Dust the cut pasta with semolina or flour; place, in a single layer, on a tray. If you're not cooking it straight away, dry it out to help prevent it sticking and clumping. Drape the cut pasta, in a single layer, over an opened cupboard door or on a clean clothes drying rack.
6. To cook, add pasta to a large saucepan of boiling, salted water until just tender, this can take up to 2 minutes, depending on the shape and thickness. Fresh pasta cooks quickly so watch it carefully. Drain pasta; return to pan, add sauce, toss gently.

TIP 00 flour is imported from Italy and available from some delicatessens and major supermarkets. If you use 00 flour you will only need 1 tablespoon of olive oil and no water. If you use bread flour, you will need 2 tablespoons each of oil and water.

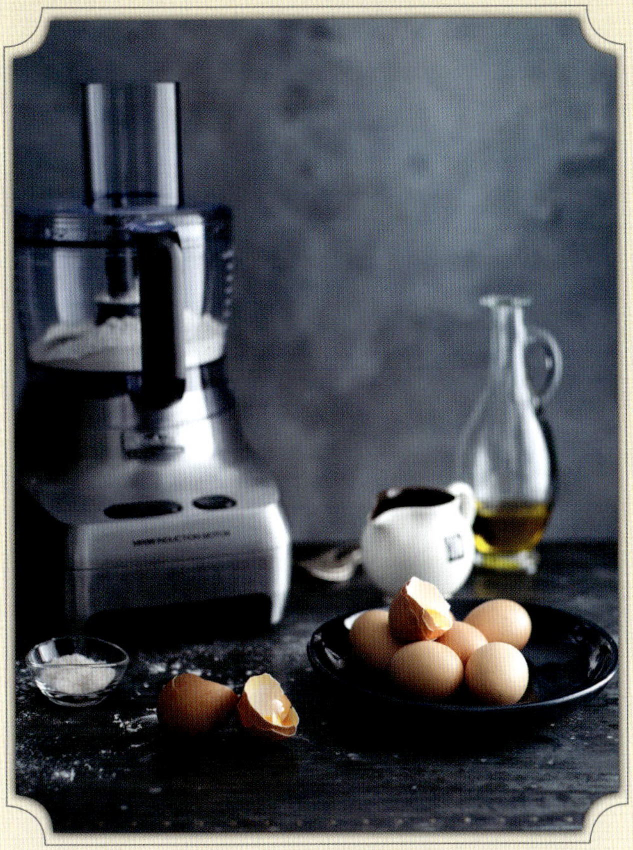
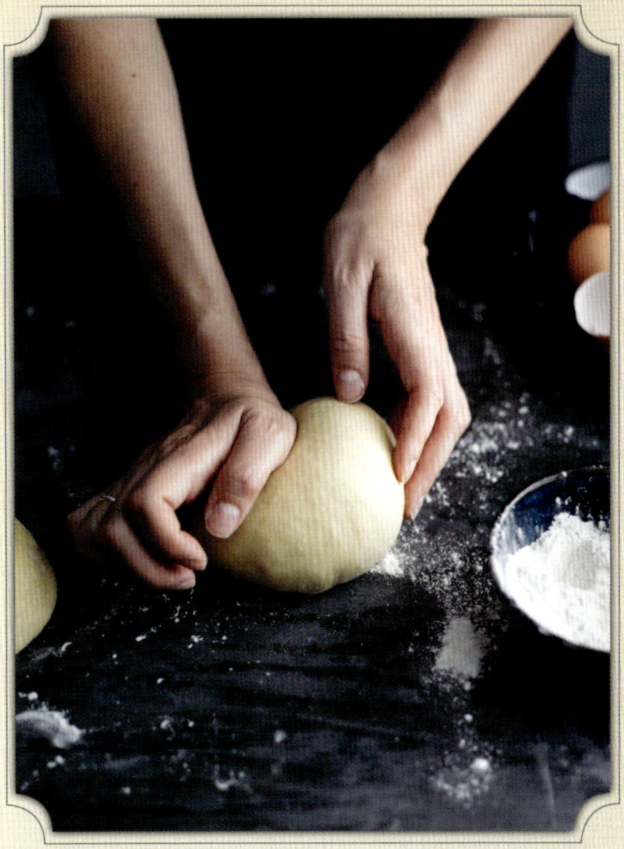
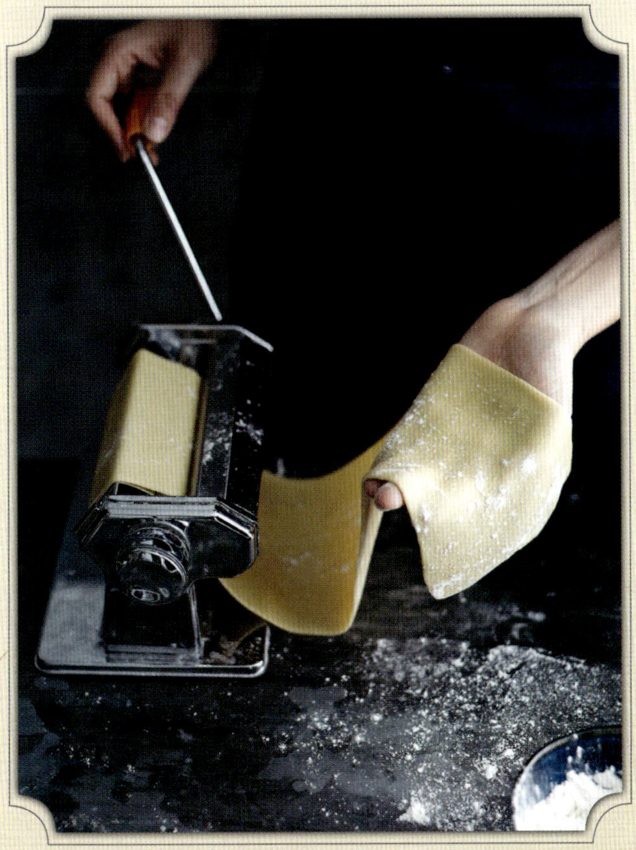
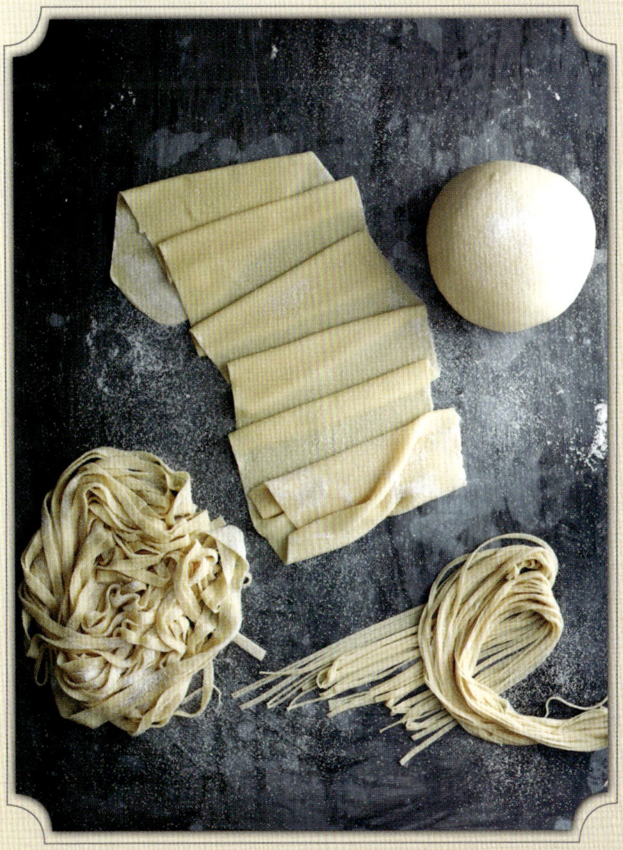

LAMB BIRYANI

PREP + COOK TIME *3 HOURS (+ REFRIGERATION)* **SERVES** *8*

Biryani are some of the most elaborate of Indian rice dishes synonymous with the Moghul emperors. Meat, rice and spices are layered in this fragrant one-pot dish. Start the recipe a day ahead.

1.5kg (3 pounds) boneless lamb shoulder, cut into 2cm (¾-inch) cubes
5cm (2-inch) piece fresh ginger (25g), grated finely
3 cloves garlic, crushed
2 fresh red bird's-eye chillies, chopped finely
1 cup (280g) Greek-style yoghurt
2 tablespoons coarsely chopped fresh coriander (cilantro)
3 teaspoons garam masala
¼ teaspoon ground turmeric
½ teaspoon ground chilli powder
1 teaspoon sea salt
80g (2½ ounces) ghee (clarified butter) or butter
1 cup (140g) flaked almonds
⅓ cup (55g) sultanas
3 large brown onions (600g), sliced thickly
1 cup (250ml) water
500g (1 pound) basmati rice, rinsed
large pinch saffron threads
2 tablespoons hot milk
½ cup fresh coriander (cilantro) leaves, extra

1 Combine lamb, ginger, garlic, chilli, yoghurt, coriander, spices and salt in a medium bowl. Cover; refrigerate overnight.
2 Heat half the ghee in a large, heavy-based saucepan over medium heat; fry almonds and sultanas until browned lightly. Remove from pan with a slotted spoon.
3 Heat remaining ghee in same pan over medium heat; cook onion, covered, 5 minutes or until soft. Remove lid; cook another 5 minutes or until onion is browned lightly. Remove half the onion from pan.
4 Add lamb mixture to pan; cook, stirring, until lamb is browned lightly. Add the water; bring to the boil. Reduce heat; simmer, covered, over low heat, stirring occasionally, 1 hour. Remove lid; simmer, uncovered, a further 30 minutes or until lamb is tender. Season to taste.
5 Meanwhile, cook rice in a saucepan of boiling, salted water 5 minutes or until half-cooked; drain.
6 Combine saffron and milk in a small bowl; stand 15 minutes.
7 Preheat oven to 180°C/350°F.
8 Spread half the lamb mixture in an oiled 3.5-litre (14-cup) ovenproof dish; top with half the rice, then remaining lamb and rice. Drizzle saffron milk mixture over rice; cover tightly with oiled foil and lid. Bake 40 minutes or until rice is tender.
9 Serve biryani topped with reheated reserved onion, almond mixture and extra coriander.

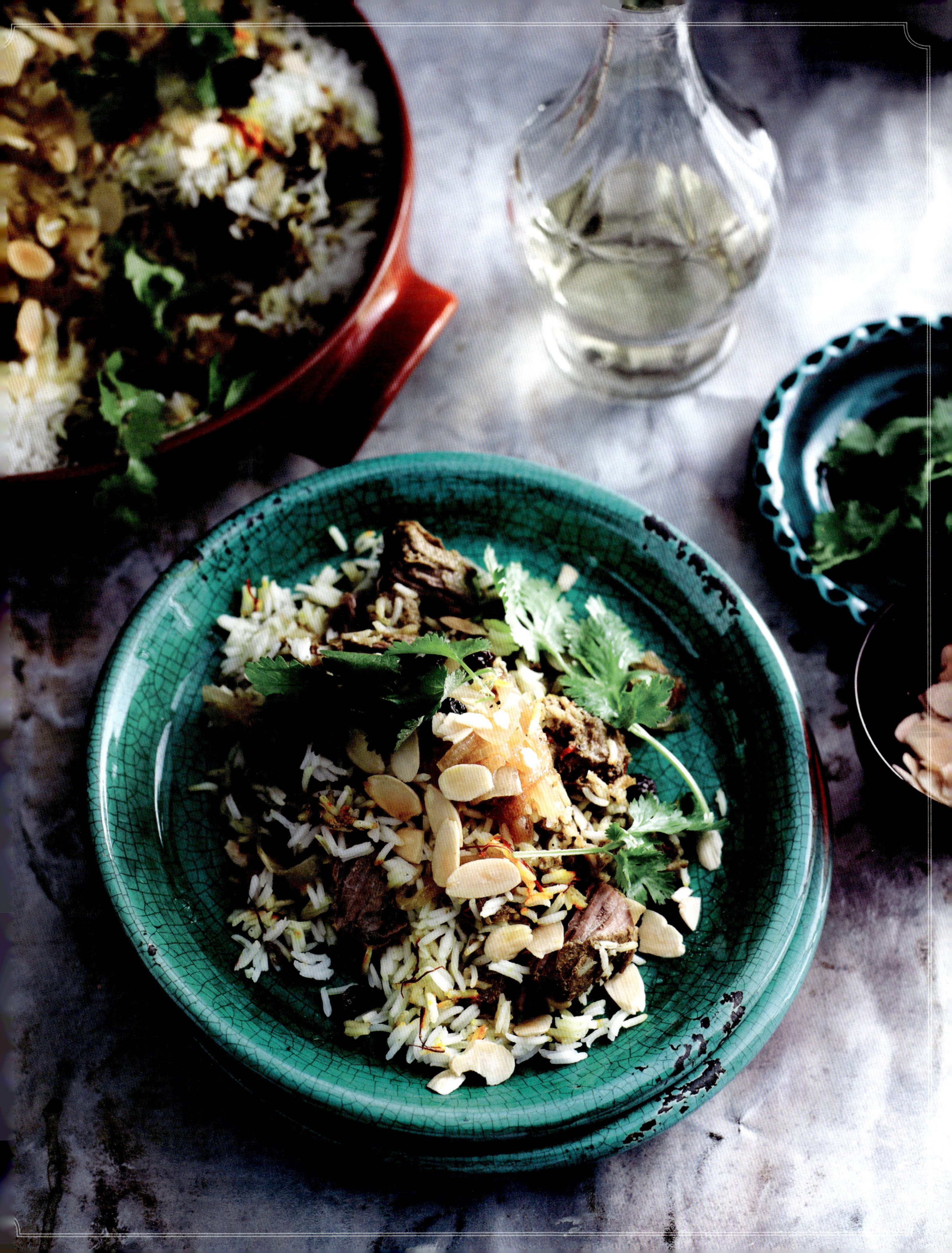

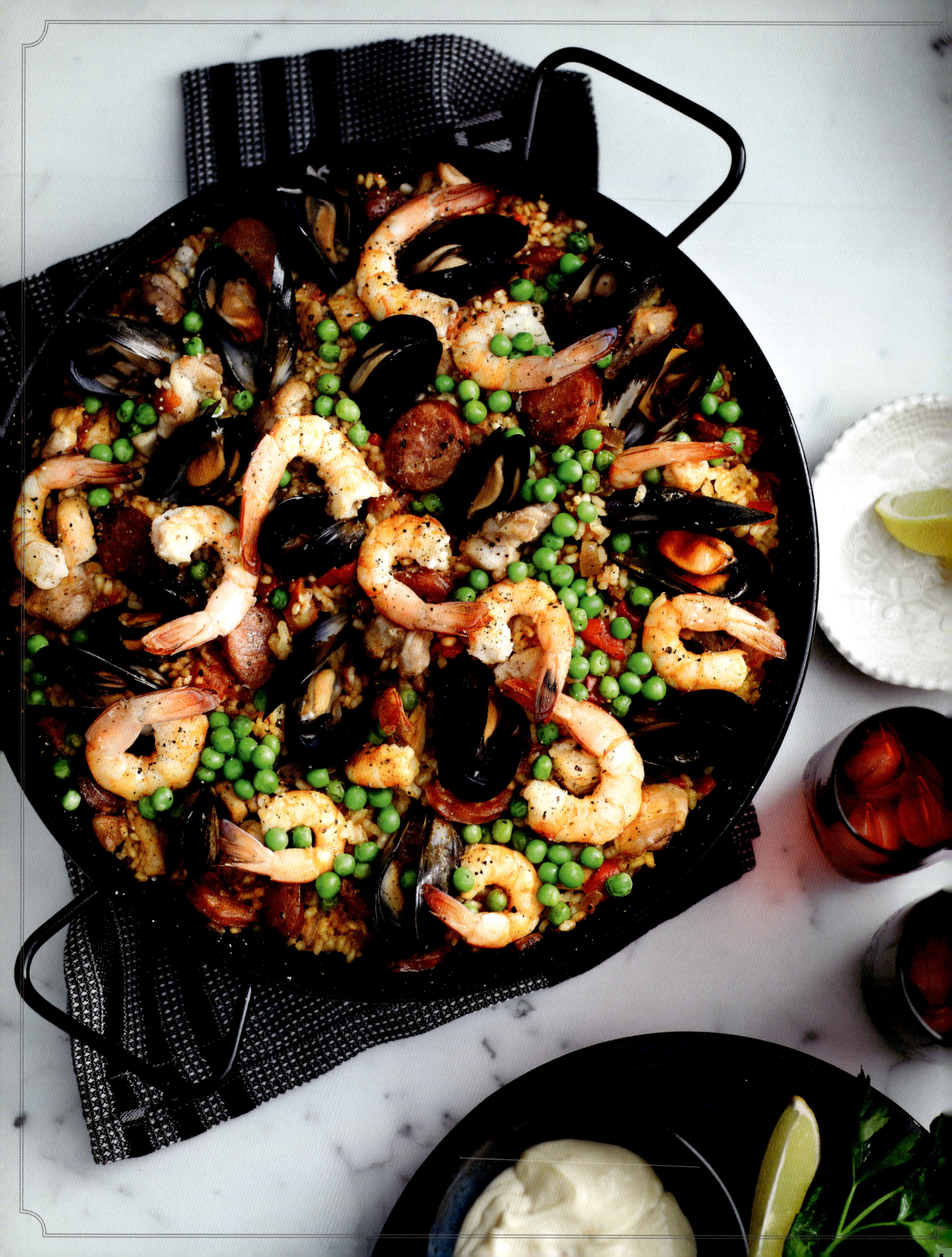

SEAFOOD PAELLA
with Alioli

PREP + COOK TIME *1 HOUR* **SERVES** *4*

Alioli, similar to the French aïoli, is the traditional accompaniment to paella.

large pinch saffron threads
¼ cup (60ml) boiling water
1 tablespoon olive oil
500g (1 pound) chicken thigh fillets, chopped coarsely
200g (6½ ounces) cured chorizo sausage, sliced thinly
1 large red onion (300g), chopped finely
1 large red capsicum (bell pepper) (300g), chopped finely
2 cloves garlic, crushed
1 teaspoon smoked paprika
400g (12½ ounces) canned diced tomatoes
1½ cups (300g) calasparra rice (or medium-grain rice)
3 cups (750ml) chicken stock
½ cup (60g) frozen peas
500g (1 pound) uncooked medium king prawns (shrimp), shelled, deveined, with tails intact
500g (1 pound) black mussels, cleaned
2 tablespoons torn fresh flat-leaf parsley

ALIOLI
2 egg yolks
4 cloves garlic, quartered
1 teaspoon sea salt
¾ cup (180ml) olive oil
1 tablespoon lemon juice
1 tablespoon boiling water

1. Make alioli.
2. Place saffron and the water in a small bowl; stand 15 minutes.
3. Heat oil in a 30cm (12-inch) paella pan or frying pan over medium heat; cook chicken 5 minutes or until browned all over. Remove from pan.
4. Cook chorizo in same pan, 2 minutes each side or until browned; drain on paper towel.
5. Cook onion, capsicum, garlic and paprika in same pan, stirring, 5 minutes or until soft. Stir in tomatoes. Add rice; stir to coat in mixture. Return chicken and chorizo to pan with stock and saffron mixture; stir only until combined. Don't stir again. Bring to the boil; simmer, uncovered, 15 minutes or until rice is almost tender.
6. Sprinkle peas over rice; place prawns and mussels evenly over surface of paella. Cover pan with foil; simmer 10 minutes or until prawns are just cooked through and mussels have opened (rotate the pan during cooking so heat distributes evenly.)
7. Serve paella with parsley and alioli.

ALIOLI
Process egg yolks, garlic and salt until smooth. With the motor operating, gradually add oil, drop by drop at first, then in a steady stream until mixture is thick and emulsified. Stir in juice and water. Cover surface with plastic wrap.

NASI GORENG

PREP + COOK TIME *40 MINUTES* SERVES *4*

Nasi goreng is the delicious Indonesian version of fried rice, traditionally made from the previous night's leftover rice and eaten for breakfast.

2 tablespoons peanut oil
250g (8 ounces) pork fillet, sliced thinly
1 medium brown onion (150g), sliced thinly
1 medium red capsicum (bell pepper) (200g), sliced thinly
3 fresh long red chillies, sliced thinly
2 cloves garlic, crushed
2cm (¾-inch) piece fresh ginger (10g), grated finely
1 teaspoon shrimp paste
250g (8 ounces) uncooked small prawns (shrimp), peeled, deveined
4 cups cold cooked long-grain white rice (see tips)
1 tablespoon kecap manis
6 green onions (scallions), sliced thinly
1 tablespoon peanut oil, extra
4 eggs
2 tablespoons chopped unsalted roasted peanuts

1 Heat half the oil in a wok over high heat; stir-fry pork, in batches, until browned. Remove from wok.
2 Heat remaining oil in wok; stir-fry onion, capsicum, chilli, garlic, ginger and shrimp paste until fragrant and softened. Add prawns; stir-fry 2 minutes or until changed in colour. Add rice; stir-fry 1 minute or until well combined.
3 Return pork to wok with kecap manis and two-thirds of the green onion; stir-fry to coat rice in sauce.
4 Meanwhile, heat extra oil in a large frying pan over medium heat; cook eggs, sunny-side up, 2 minutes or until whites are set.
5 Serve rice mixture topped with an egg; sprinkle with peanuts and remaining green onion.

TIPS You will need to cook 1½ cups (300g) long-grain white rice for this recipe. When cooked, spread it out in a thin layer on a tray; refrigerate, uncovered, for several hours or overnight.
You can use chicken, prawns or tofu instead of the pork, if you like.

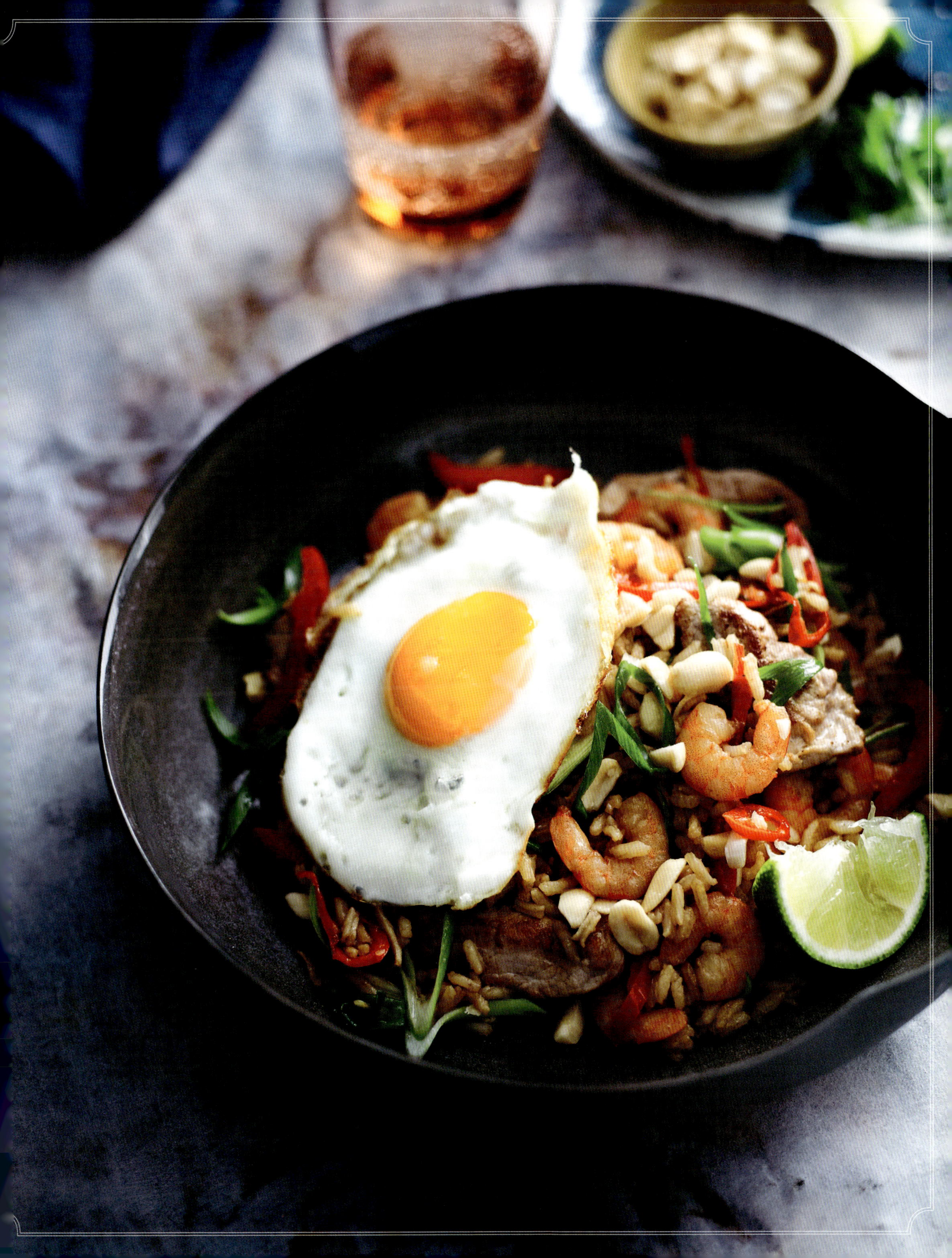

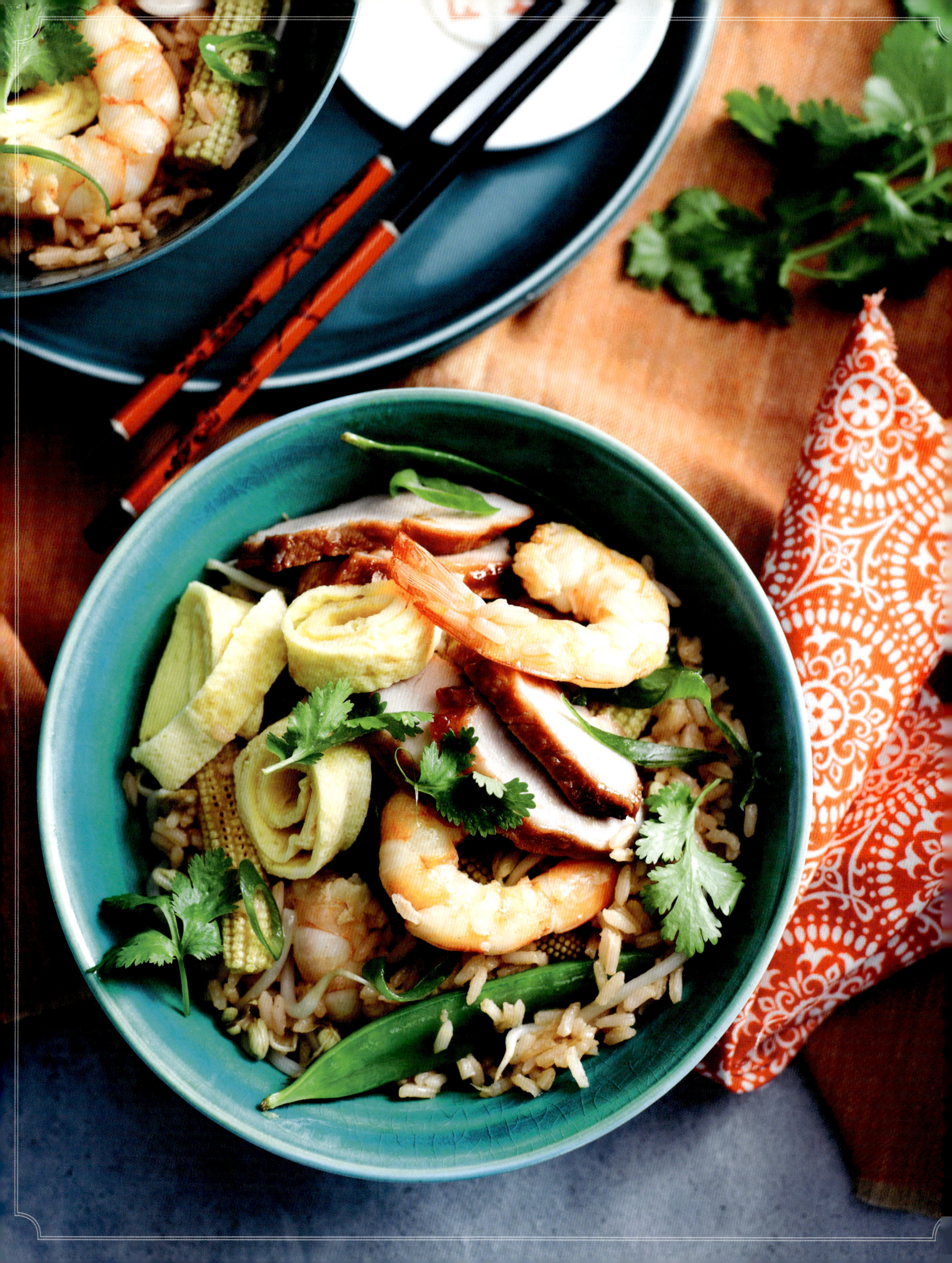

CHAR SIU PORK
Fried Rice

PREP + COOK TIME *40 MINUTES (+ REFRIGERATION)* **SERVES 4**

2 tablespoons char siu sauce
1 tablespoon hoisin sauce
500g (1 pound) pork fillet
1 tablespoon peanut oil
2 eggs, beaten lightly
2 tablespoons sesame oil
8 uncooked medium prawns (shrimp) (200g), peeled, deveined, with tails intact
3 cloves garlic, crushed
4cm (1½-inch) piece fresh ginger (20g), grated finely
115g (3½ ounces) baby corn, halved lengthways
150g (4½ ounces) snow peas, trimmed
3 green onions (scallions), sliced thinly
1 cup fresh coriander (cilantro) leaves
4 cups cold cooked long-grain white rice (see tip)
1 cup bean sprouts, trimmed
2 tablespoons soy sauce

1 Combine sauces in a medium bowl with pork. Cover; refrigerate 2 hours or overnight.
2 Preheat oven to 220°C/400°F. Line an oven tray with baking paper.
3 Drain pork mixture; reserve marinade. Place pork on tray; roast 20 minutes or until just cooked through, brushing occasionally with reserved marinade. Transfer pork to a plate, cover; rest 5 minutes, then slice thinly.
4 Heat a large wok or frying pan over medium heat, add peanut oil, then egg; swirl to cover base of wok, cook until just set. Remove from pan. Roll omelette tightly, slice thinly.
5 Heat wok, add sesame oil, prawns, garlic and ginger; stir-fry 2 minutes or until prawns just change colour. Remove from wok. Add corn, snow peas and green onion; stir-fry 2 minutes or until just tender. Add half the omelette and half the coriander, then rice, bean sprouts, sauce and prawn mixture; stir-fry until hot.
6 Serve rice mixture in bowls, topped with pork, remaining omelette and remaining coriander.

TIP You will need to cook 1½ cups (300g) long-grain white rice for this recipe. When cooked, spread it out in a thin layer on a tray; refrigerate, uncovered, for several hours or overnight.

CREAMY Pumpkin Risotto

PREP + COOK TIME *50 MINUTES* **SERVES 4**

The secret to a great risotto lies with the type of risotto rice you use; you want one that will absorb a lot of liquid while maintaining some texture. Italian arborio is better than locally grown, however even better is carnaroli – it is available from some supermarkets and delicatessens.

1kg (2 pound) butternut pumpkin, cut into 2cm (¾-inch) pieces
¼ cup (60ml) extra virgin olive oil
¼ teaspoon dried chilli flakes
1.5 litres (6 cups) chicken or vegetable stock
50g (1½ ounces) butter
2 medium onions (300g), chopped finely
2 cloves garlic, chopped finely
2 cups (400g) arborio rice
½ cup (125ml) dry white wine
¼ cup fresh sage leaves
¼ cup (60g) mascarpone cheese
½ cup (40g) grated parmesan
2 tablespoons toasted pine nuts

1. Preheat oven to 200°C/400°F.
2. Combine pumpkin and 2 tablespoons of the oil on a large baking-paper-lined oven tray; season with salt. Roast 25 minutes or until tender and browned lightly. Sprinkle with chilli. Reserve one third of the pumpkin; cover to keep warm. Divide remaining pumpkin in half; mash one half in a small bowl.
3. Meanwhile, bring stock to a gentle simmer in a medium saucepan.
4. Melt butter in a large heavy-based saucepan over medium heat; cook onion, stirring, 5 minutes or until soft. Add garlic and rice, stir to coat well; cook, stirring, 1 minute. Add wine; simmer until liquid has evaporated.
5. Add ½ cup of the hot stock to rice mixture; cook, stirring until liquid is absorbed. Continue adding stock, ½ cup at a time, stirring after each addition, until half the stock has been added. Stir in both mashed and unmashed pumpkin, then continue adding stock, ½ cup at a time, stirring after each addition, until all liquid has been absorbed (this will take about 20 minutes).
6. Heat remaining oil in a small frying pan over high heat; fry sage leaves for 20 seconds or until crisp. Remove with a slotted spoon; drain on paper towel.
7. Remove risotto from heat; stir in mascarpone and parmesan. Season to taste. Serve topped with reserved pumpkin, pine nuts and sage. If you like, sprinkle with some extra grated parmesan.

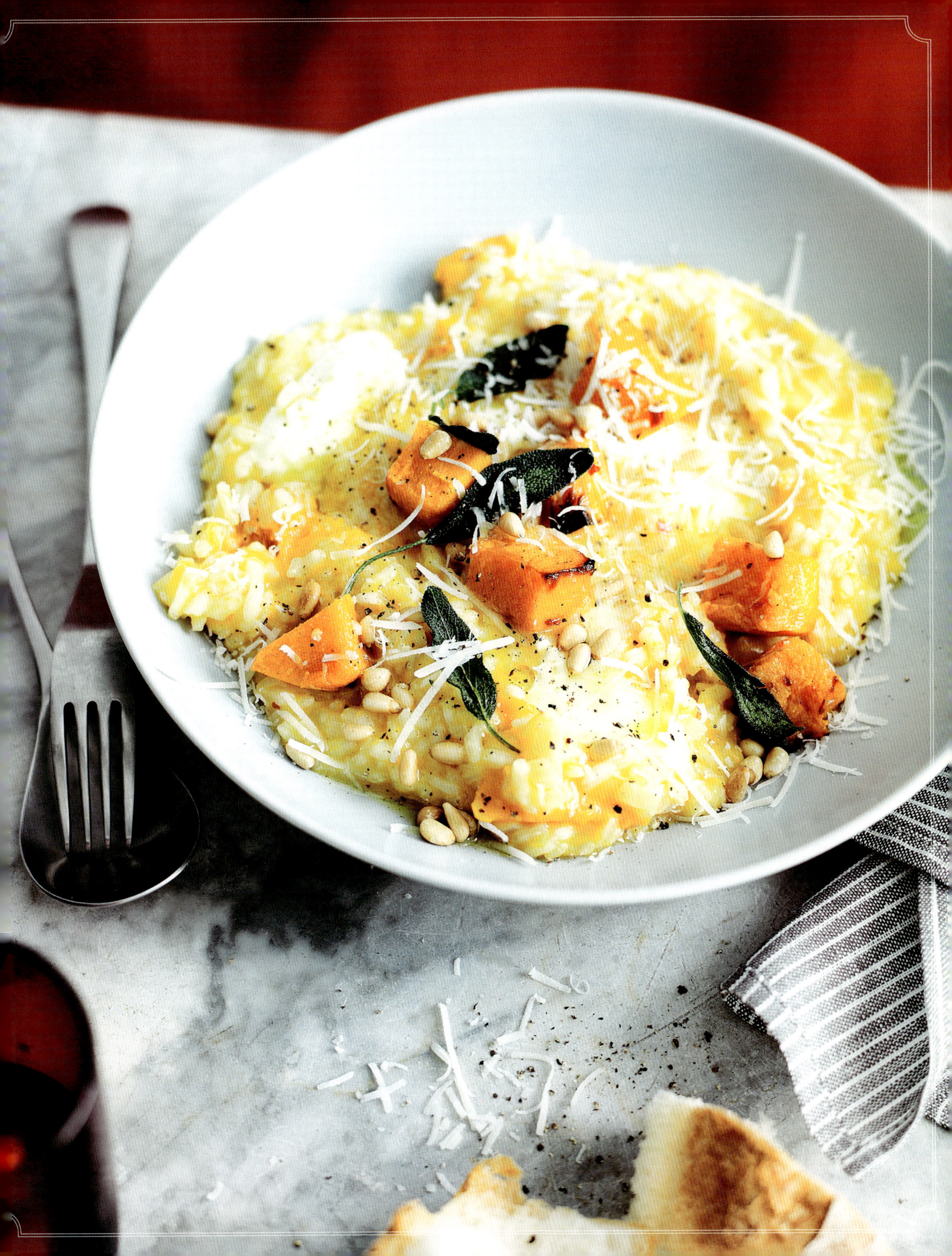

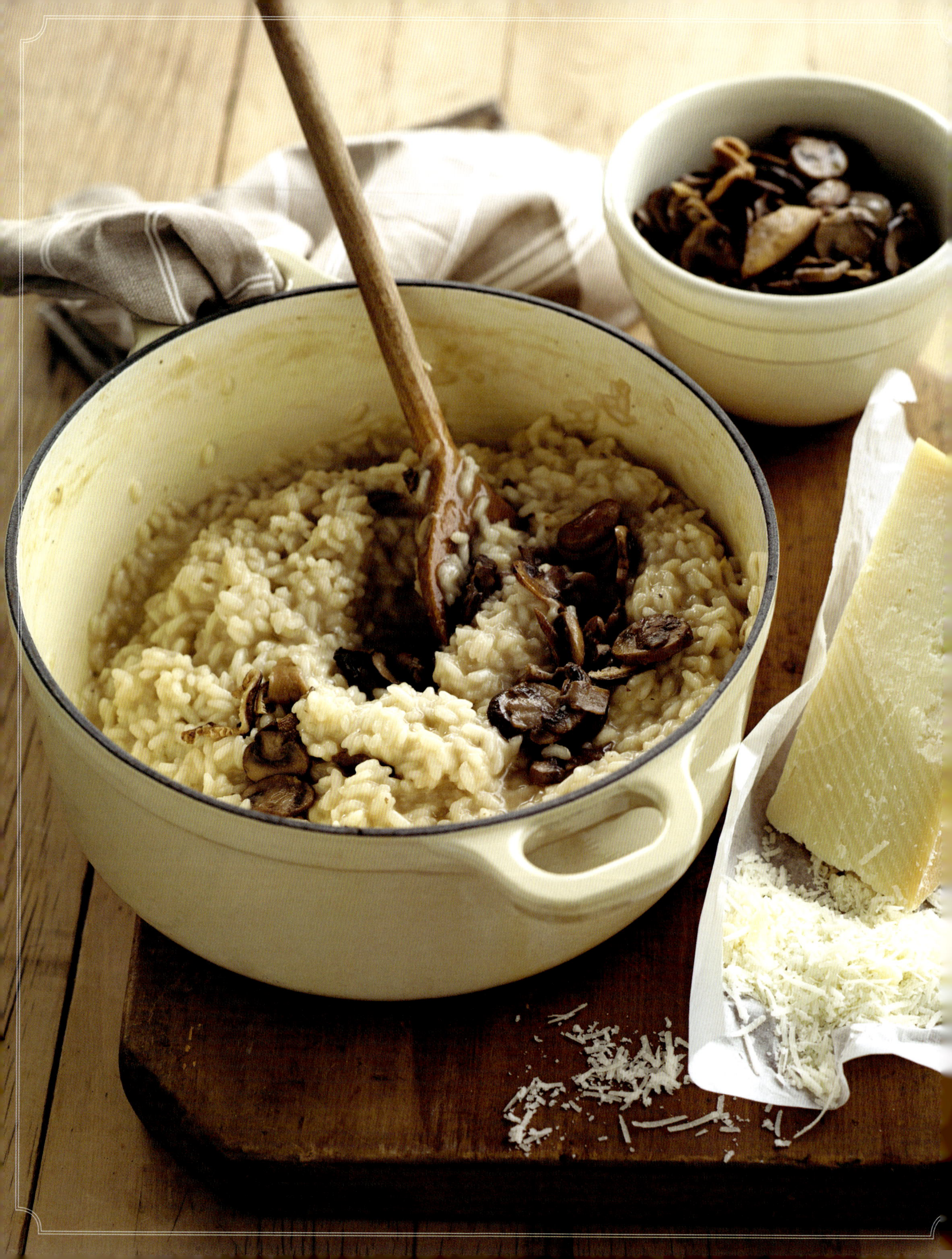

REALLY GOOD
Mushroom Risotto

PREP + COOK TIME *1 HOUR* SERVES *4*

10g (½ ounce) dried porcini mushrooms
½ cup (125ml) warm water
1.5 litres (6 cups) chicken or vegetable stock
100g (3 ounces) butter
100g (3 ounces) swiss brown mushrooms, sliced
200g (6½ ounces) button mushrooms, sliced
100g (3 ounces) flat mushrooms, sliced
2 cloves garlic, crushed
1 large onion (200g), chopped finely
2 cups (400g) arborio rice
⅓ cup (80ml) dry white wine
½ cup (40g) grated parmesan

1. Place porcini mushrooms and the water in a small bowl; stand 15 minutes. Drain into a small jug; reserve soaking liquid.
2. Meanwhile, bring stock to a gentle simmer in a medium saucepan.
3. Heat 30g (1 ounce) of the butter in a large, heavy-based saucepan over medium heat; cook swiss brown, button and flat mushrooms for 5 minutes or until softened and browned lightly. Add garlic; cook, stirring, until fragrant. Remove from pan.
4. Stir porcini and the reserved liquid into stock.
5. Melt 50g (1½ ounces) of the butter in same heavy-based pan; cook onion, stirring, for 5 minutes or until soft. Add rice, stir to coat well; cook, stirring, 1 minute. Add wine; simmer, until all liquid has evaporated.
6. Add ½ cup of the hot stock mixture to rice mixture; cook, stirring until liquid is absorbed. Continue adding stock mixture, ½ cup at a time, stirring after each addition, until all liquid has been absorbed (this will take about 20 minutes).
7. Stir in cooked mushrooms, parmesan and remaining butter; season to taste. Stir until hot.
8. Serve risotto topped with freshly ground black pepper and a little extra parmesan, if you like.

TIP In Italy, porcini mushrooms are available fresh and dried, but fresh ones are rarely seen anywhere else. The dried version, available from delicatessens and some supermarkets and greengrocers, is far more pungent and gives the risotto a delicious earthy taste.

CHAPTER 3
BARBECUES
& PICNICS

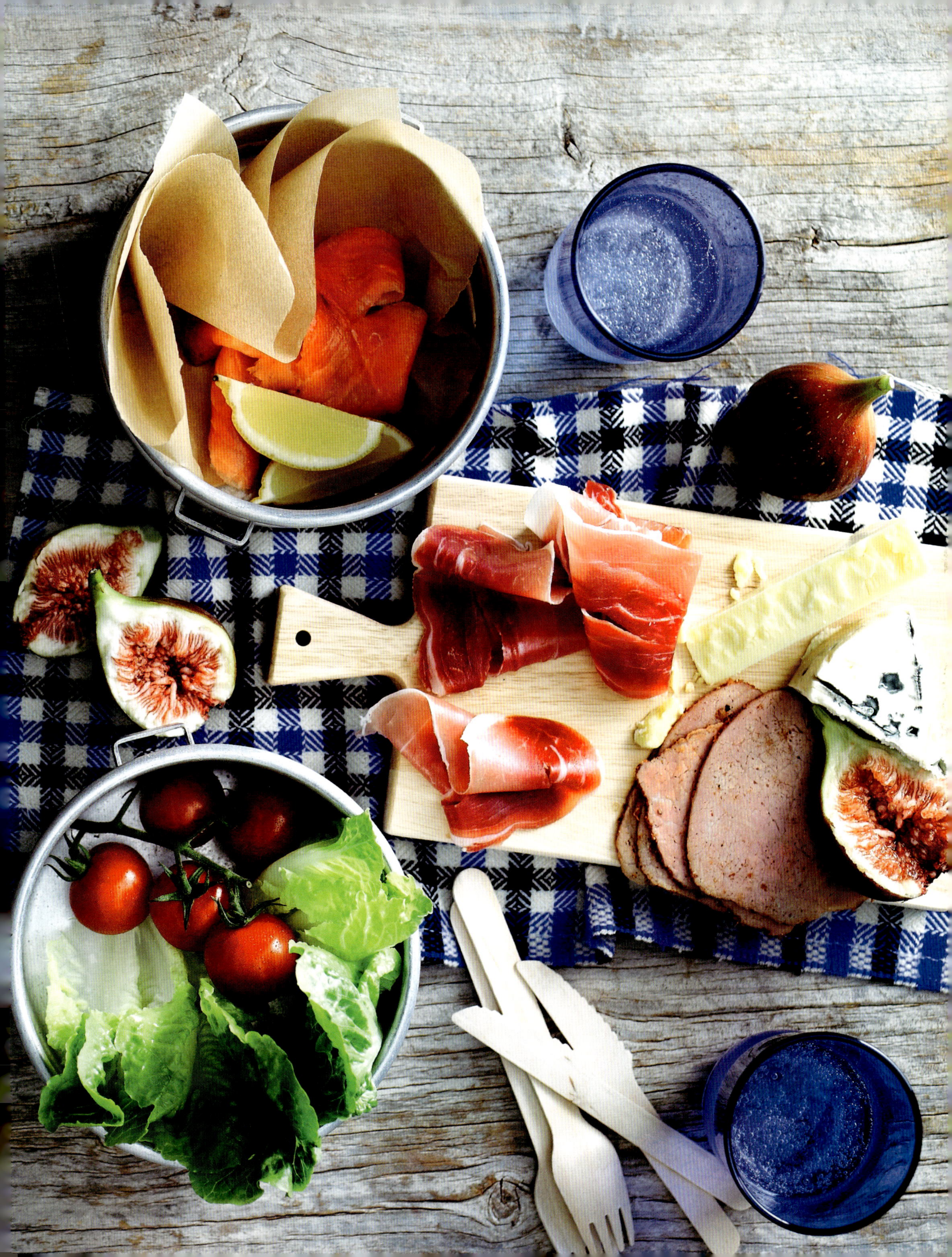

CHICKEN BURGER
with Avocado and Bacon

PREP + COOK TIME 40 MINUTES MAKES 4

¾ cup (50g) fresh breadcrumbs
1 tablespoon milk
500g (1 pound) minced (ground) chicken
4 green onions (scallions), sliced thinly
2 tablespoons fresh flat-leaf parsley, chopped finely
2 anchovy fillets, chopped finely
¼ cup (75g) whole-egg mayonnaise
1 clove garlic, crushed
1 teaspoon wholegrain mustard
1½ teaspoons lemon juice
4 centre-cut rindless bacon slices (260g), each cut into thirds
2 teaspoons olive oil
4 wholegrain rolls (260g), split
4 baby cos (romaine) lettuce leaves (40g)
1 medium avocado (250g), sliced thickly

1. Place breadcrumbs and milk in a medium bowl. Add chicken, green onion, parsley and anchovies. Season. Using your hands, mix until well combined. Using slightly damp hands, shape mixture into four 10cm (4-inch) round patties.
2. Combine mayonnaise, garlic, mustard and juice in a small bowl.
3. Cook bacon in a large non-stick frying pan over medium-high heat 2 minutes each side or until browned and crisp. Drain on paper towel.
4. Heat oil in same cleaned pan over medium until hot; cook patties 5 minutes each side or until just cooked through.
5. Meanwhile, preheat an oiled char-grill pan over high heat; place rolls, cut-side down, for 30 seconds or until marked and toasted.
6. Spread bottom of the rolls with half the mayonnaise mixture; top with lettuce, patties, avocado and bacon. Replace the roll tops and serve immediately with remaining mayonnaise mixture.

TIP You will need two thick slices of bread, crusts removed, to make enough fresh breadcrumbs.

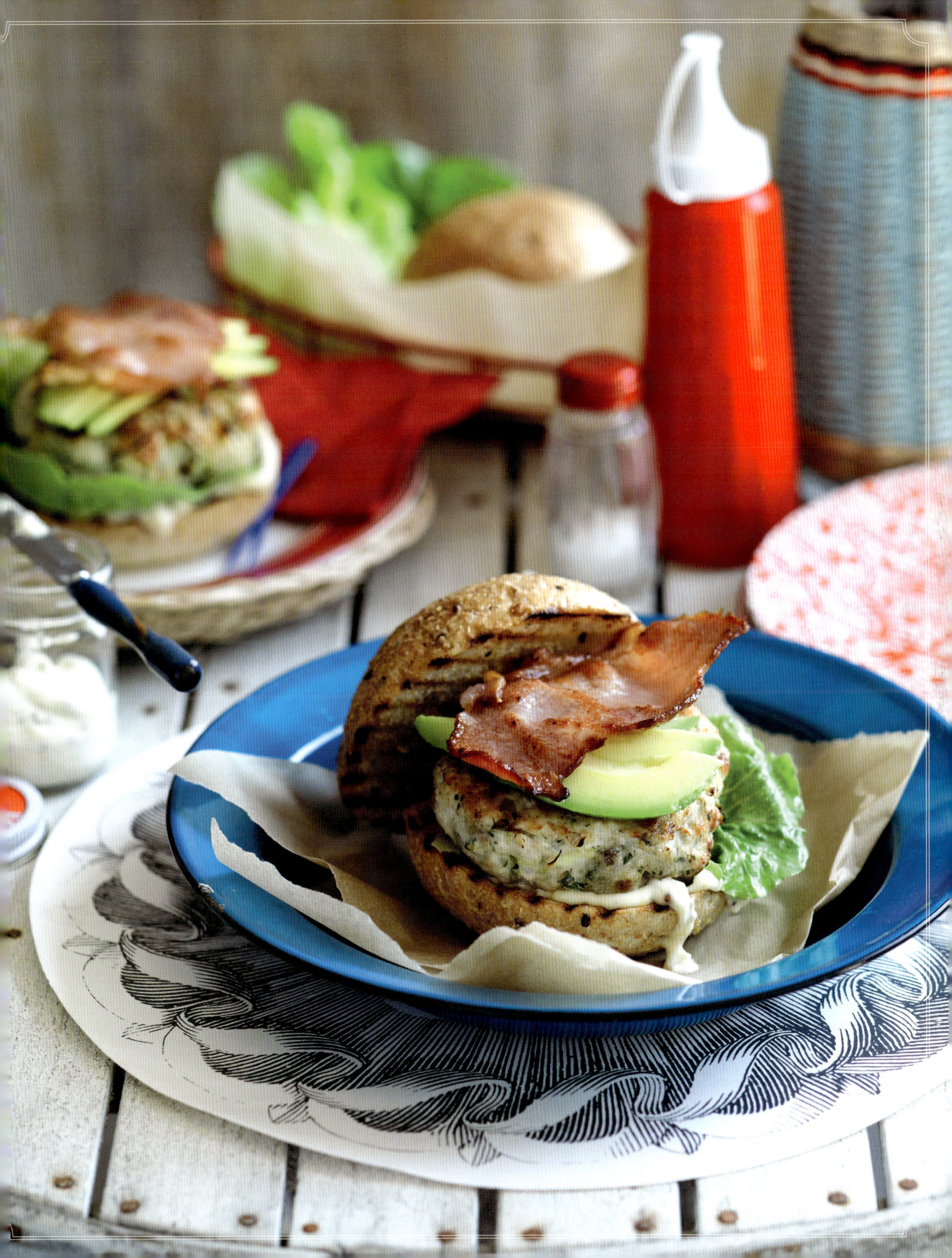

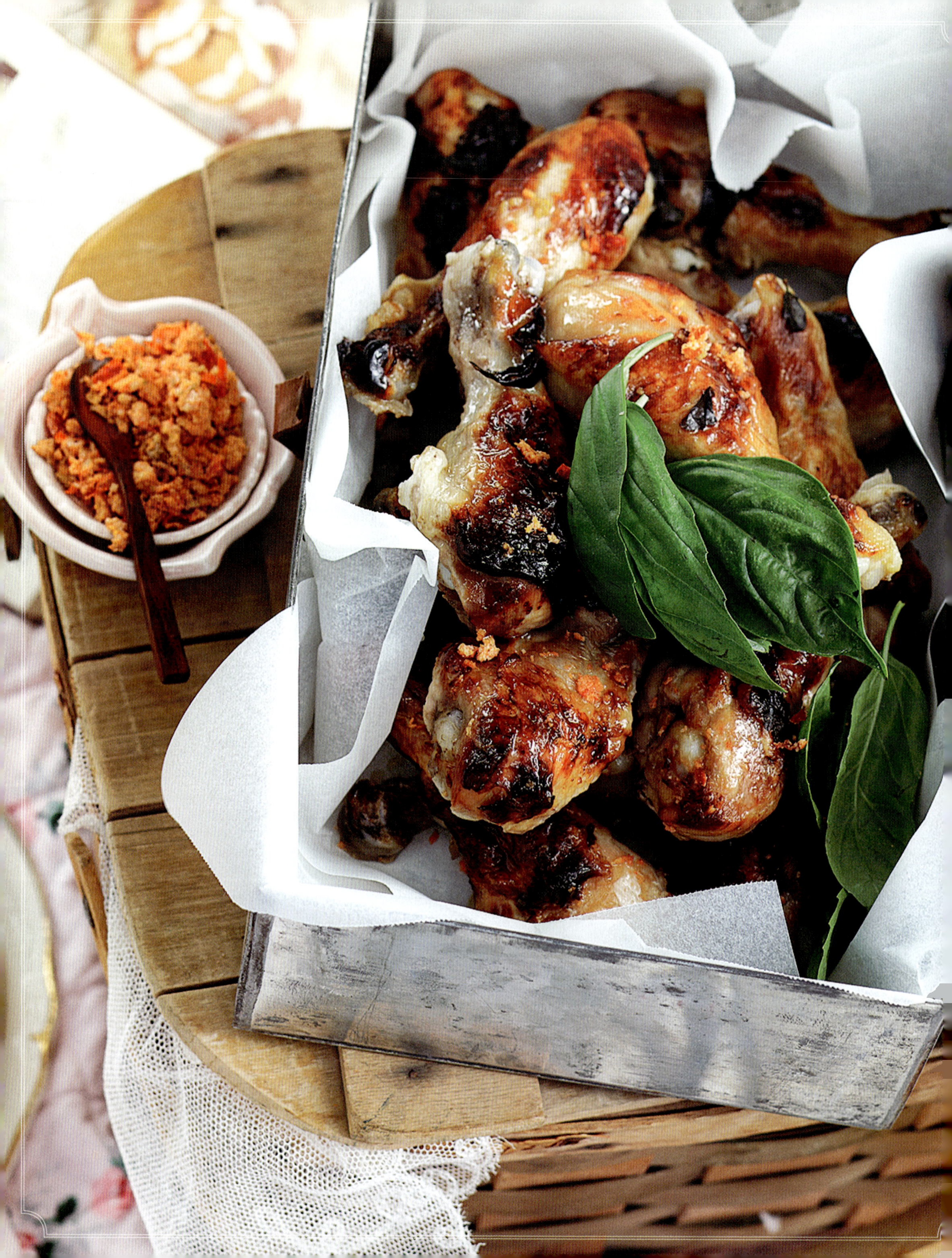

LEMON CHICKEN DRUMSTICKS
with Citrus Chilli Salt

PREP + COOK TIME *1 HOUR 10 MINUTES (+ COOLING)* **SERVES** *6*

½ cup (60g) sea salt flakes
1 long red chilli, seeded, sliced thinly
3 teaspoons finely grated orange rind
2 teaspoons finely grated lemon rind
1 teaspoon finely grated lime rind
⅓ cup (80ml) orange juice
¼ cup (60ml) lemon juice
2 tablespoons lime juice
¼ cup (60ml) extra virgin olive oil
2 tablespoons honey
12 chicken drumsticks (1.8kg)
12 fresh basil leaves

1. Preheat oven to 180°C/350°F.
2. Pound salt, chilli and rinds with a mortar and pestle or process until fine flakes form. Spread salt mixture out on a small oven tray. Bake 5 minutes or until dry; cool. Store in an airtight jar or container.
3. Whisk juices, oil and honey in a large bowl until combined, then add chicken; stir to coat. Transfer chicken and marinade to a large baking dish with basil.
4. Bake chicken 50 minutes, turning occasionally, or until cooked through. Cool.
5. Transfer chicken and pan juices to a storage container. Refrigerate until ready to serve. Serve sprinkled with citrus salt.

TIP Care should be taken to store items in a cooler, especially meats on a picnic. Anything that has been left unrefrigerated for up 2 hours, should be consumed immediately, or after this time discarded.

SERVING SUGGESTION Serve with avocado, bacon and cabbage salad (see page 30).

VEGETABLE PAN BAGNA

PREP + COOK TIME 30 MINUTES (+ COOLING & REFRIGERATION) SERVES 6

Start this recipe a day ahead.

2 medium red capsicums (bell pepper) (400g)
1 medium yellow capsicum (bell pepper) (200g)
¼ cup (60ml) extra virgin olive oil
1 teaspoon balsamic vinegar
2 tablespoons chopped fresh flat-leaf parsley
1½ tablespoons capers, chopped
1 medium zucchini (120g), sliced thinly
50cm (20-inch) long sourdough baguette (300g)
1 clove garlic, bruised
4 soft-boiled eggs, halved
10 marinated artichoke hearts (125g), sliced
10 large fresh basil leaves

1. Preheat oven to 200°C/400°F.
2. Place capsicums on an oven tray; roast 20 minutes or until skins begin to blister and blacken. Transfer to a bowl; cover with plastic wrap. Cool. Remove skin and seeds from capsicums; thinly slice.
3. Combine oil, vinegar, parsley and capers in a medium bowl. Add zucchini and capsicum, season; toss to combine.
4. Split baguette in half lengthways, without cutting all the way through; open out flat. Scoop out soft bread, leaving a 1cm (½-inch) shell; rub garlic over the inside of the baguette.
5. Fill the base of the baguette with eggs; top with artichoke, capsicum mixture and basil. Fold the top of the baguette over to enclose.
6. Wrap baguette in plastic wrap; place on a tray. Top with another tray; weight down with several cans of food. Refrigerate overnight. Cut into thick slices to serve.

TIPS The success of this recipe depends on the quality of the bread and its ability to absorb the flavoured oil. Pan bagna can also be made in a round loaf. Simply cut off the top of a small cob loaf and scoop out the bread.
For a heartier version, add well-drained canned tuna, prosciutto or smoked salmon.

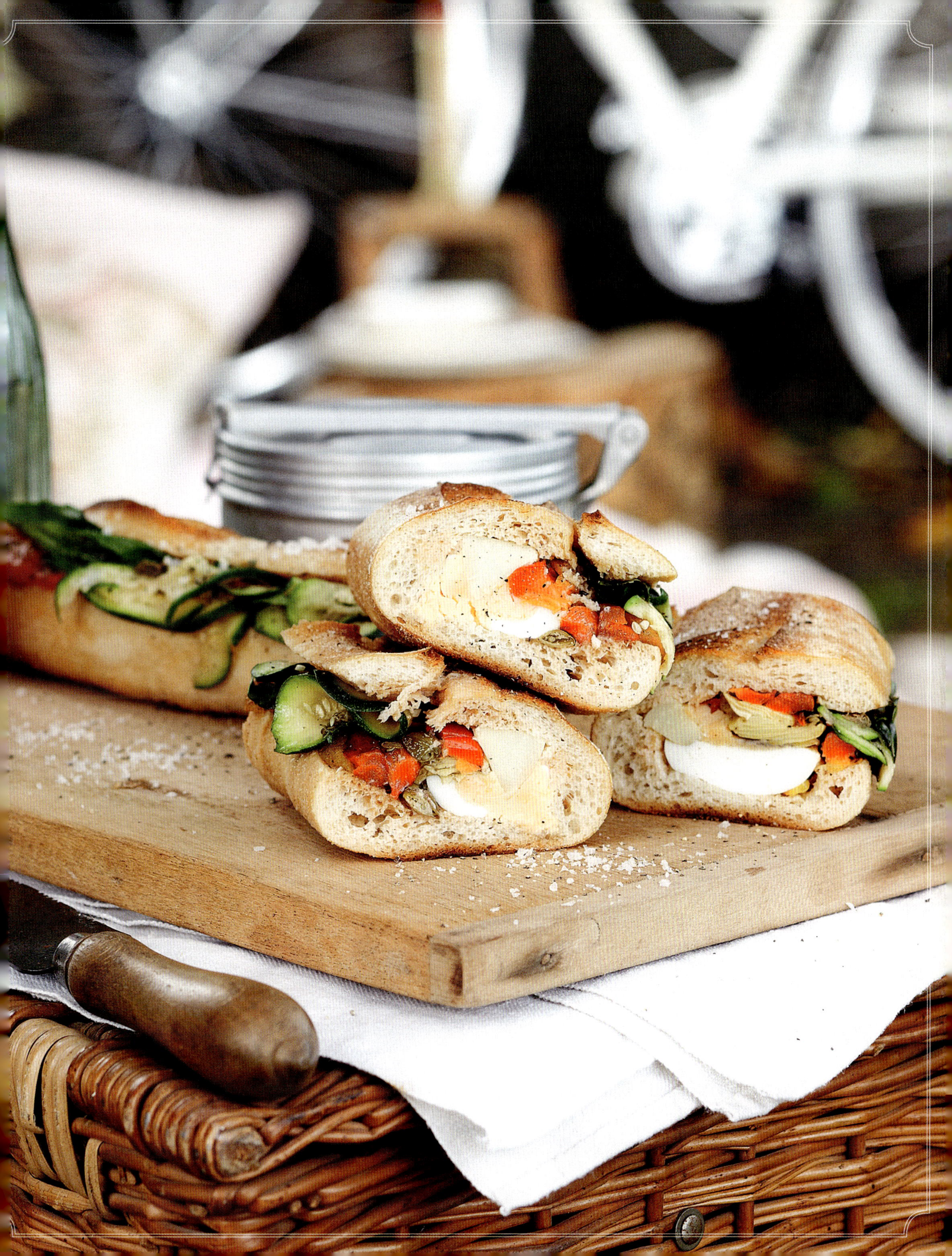

MEXICAN FIESTA

MEXICAN PORK CUTLETS
with Avocado Salsa
(RECIPE PAGE 89)

CHAR-GRILLED PRAWN
and Corn Salad
(RECIPE PAGE 33)

FROZEN MANGO
Macadamia Crunch
(RECIPE PAGE 236)

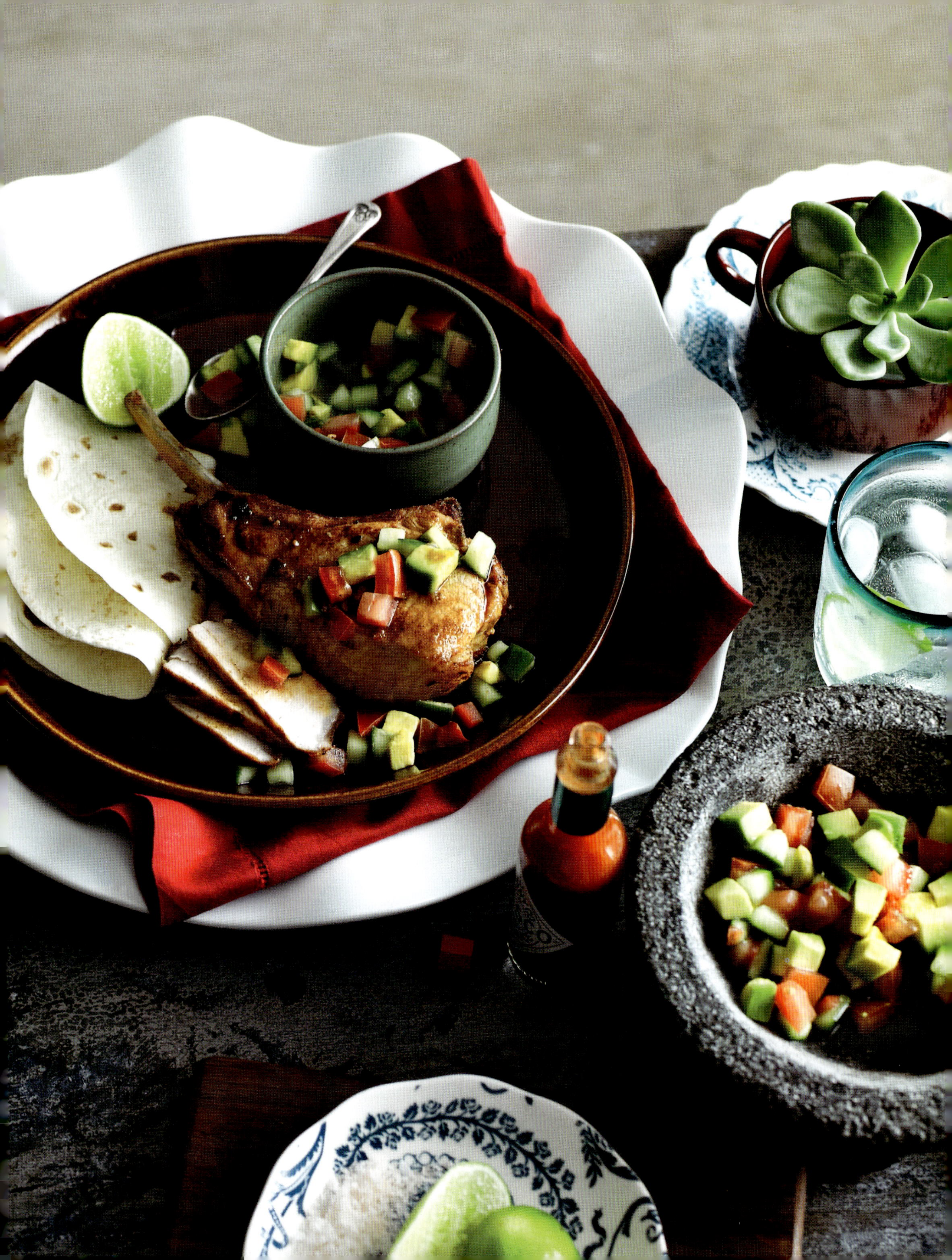

MEXICAN PORK CUTLETS
with Avocado Salsa

MEXICAN PORK CUTLETS
with Avocado Salsa

PREP + COOK TIME 20 MINUTES SERVES 4

2 tablespoons taco seasoning mix
⅓ cup (80ml) olive oil
4 x 230g (7-ounce) pork cutlets
3 small tomatoes (270g), seeded, chopped finely
1 small avocado (200g), chopped finely
1 lebanese cucumber (130g), seeded, chopped finely
1 tablespoon lemon juice
240g (8 ounces) tortillas

1. Combine seasoning and 2 tablespoons of the oil in a large bowl with pork.
2. Preheat a barbecue grill or flatplate to medium-high.
3. Brush pork with 1 tablespoon of the oil; cook on barbecue 4 minutes each side or until browned and just cooked through. Transfer to a plate; rest 5 minutes.
4. Meanwhile, place tomato, avocado, cucumber, juice and remaining oil in a medium bowl, season; toss gently to combine.
5. Warm tortillas according to packet instructions.
6. Serve pork with avocado salsa and tortillas.

CHICKEN STICKS
with Harissa Mayonnaise

PREP + COOK TIME 25 MINUTES SERVES 6

2 tablespoons dukkah
1½ teaspoons sweet paprika
2 tablespoons olive oil
6 chicken thigh fillets (600g), halved lengthways

HARISSA MAYONNAISE
½ cup (150g) whole-egg mayonnaise
2 teaspoons harissa
2 teaspoons lemon juice

1. Combine dukkah, paprika and oil in a medium bowl with chicken; season. Thread onto skewers.
2. Heat an oiled grill plate or barbecue to medium high. Cook skewers 8 minutes or until browned all over and cooked through.
3. Make harissa mayonnaise.
4. Serve chicken skewers with harissa mayonnaise.

HARISSA MAYONNAISE
Combine ingredients in a small bowl.

TIPS Dukkah is an Egyptian mix of coarsely ground spices and nuts, eaten as a dip with olive oil and bread. Typically, it includes cumin, coriander and sesame seeds with variants on the nuts used. We have used one with pistachios.
Harissa is a fiery chilli-based North African condiment. It is available from delicatessens and Middle Eastern food stores. Substitute 1 seeded finely chopped red bird's-eye chilli and a pinch each of ground cumin and coriander.

SERVING SUGGESTION Serve with rocket (arugula) leaves.

(PHOTOGRAPH PAGE 90)

CHICKEN STICKS
with Harissa Mayonnaise

(RECIPE PAGE 89)

PORK RIBS WITH STICKY
Barbecue Sauce

(RECIPE PAGE 92)

PORK RIBS WITH STICKY
Barbecue Sauce

PREP + COOK TIME 45 MINUTES SERVES 4

1.75kg (3½ pounds) american-style pork spare ribs
1 cup (250ml) tomato sauce (ketchup)
½ cup (110g) firmly packed brown sugar
2 cloves garlic, crushed
2 tablespoons worcestershire sauce
1 tablespoon cider vinegar
2 teaspoons smoked paprika

1. Bring a large saucepan of water to the boil. Reduce heat to medium, add ribs; simmer, covered, 40 minutes or until tender. Drain.
2. Combine remaining ingredients in a large bowl with the ribs.
3. Preheat an oiled barbecue (or grill or grill pan).
4. Cook ribs on barbecue for 15 minutes, turning and basting with remaining marinade every 5 minutes.
5. Cut ribs into serving-sized portions.

SERVING SUGGESTION Serve with barbecued corn.

(PHOTOGRAPH PAGE 91)

BAKED RICOTTA
with Olives

PREP + COOK TIME 50 MINUTES (+ COOLING) SERVES 6

600g (1¼ pounds) fresh ricotta
1 teaspoon thyme leaves
¼ cup (40g) pitted kalamata olives, chopped coarsely
⅓ cup (25g) coarsely grated parmesan
1 egg
125g (4 ounces) cherry truss tomatoes

1. Preheat oven to 180°C/350°F. Oil a 20cm (8-inch) springform tin; place on an oven tray.
2. Combine ricotta, thyme, olives, parmesan and egg in a large bowl; season. Spoon mixture into tin.
3. Bake ricotta 35 minutes or until firm and lightly golden. Cool.
4. Serve ricotta on a platter topped with tomatoes.

SERVING SUGGESTION Serve drizzled with a little olive oil and with crispbread or a baguette.

BAKED RICOTTA
with Olives

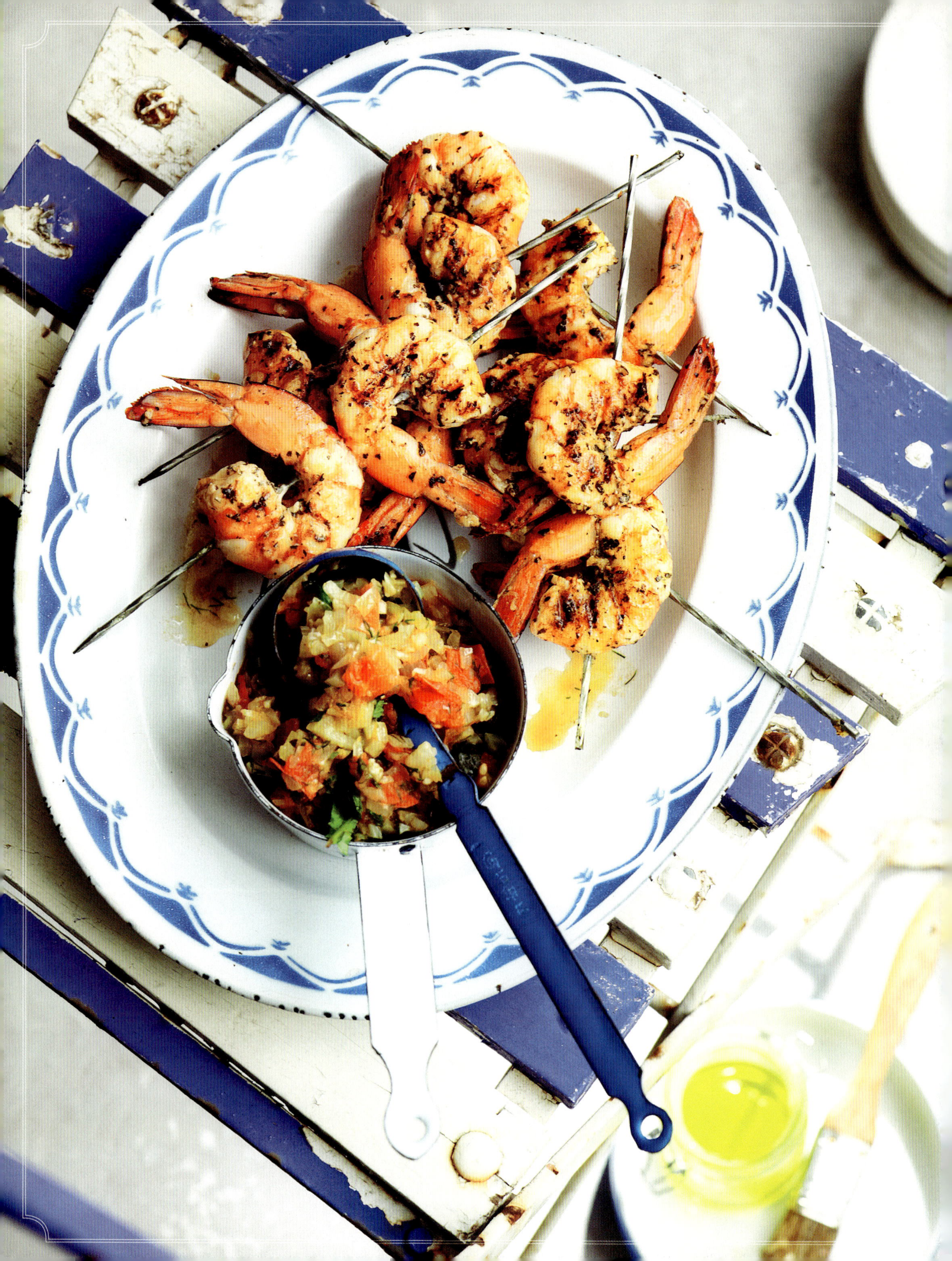

PRAWN SOUVLAKIA
with Tomato and Fennel Sauce

PREP + COOK TIME *35 MINUTES (+ REFRIGERATION)* **SERVES 8**

---

16 uncooked large prawns (shrimp) (1kg)
2 tablespoons olive oil
3 cloves garlic, crushed
2 teaspoons dried mint
1 teaspoon finely grated lemon rind
2 tablespoons lemon juice

TOMATO AND FENNEL SAUCE
2 baby fennel bulbs (260g), chopped finely
1 tablespoon olive oil
1 medium brown onion (150g), chopped finely
2 cloves garlic, chopped finely
3 medium ripe tomatoes (450g), chopped coarsely
¼ cup (60ml) ouzo, pernod or dry white wine
1 cup coarsely chopped fresh mint

1. Shell and devein prawns, leaving tails intact. Place prawns in a large bowl with remaining ingredients; toss to combine. Cover; refrigerate 1 hour.
2. Meanwhile, make tomato and fennel sauce.
3. Preheat a grill plate (or grill or barbecue or grill pan) to medium.
4. Thread prawns onto eight metal skewers; reserve marinade. Cook prawn skewers on heated oiled grill plate brushing with the reserved marinade 1 minute each side or until just cooked through.
5. Serve prawns with tomato and fennel sauce.

TOMATO AND FENNEL SAUCE
Trim then chop fennel fronds finely; set aside. Heat oil in a medium saucepan over medium heat; cook onion, garlic and fennel 5 minutes or until softened. Add tomato and ouzo; cook until heated through. Just before serving, stir in fronds and mint; season to taste.

TIP If you don't have metal skewers, use bamboo skewers – soak them in water while the prawns are in the fridge in step 1.

GRILLED PORTUGUESE
Chicken and Rice

PREP + COOK TIME 35 MINUTES SERVES 4

⅓ cup (80ml) lemon juice
1 tablespoon olive oil
1 tablespoon sweet paprika
2 teaspoons dried oregano leaves
1 teaspoon sea salt flakes
2 red bird's-eye chillies, seeded, chopped finely
1 clove garlic, crushed
8 x 110g (3½-ounce) chicken thigh fillets
⅓ cup (110g) tomato chutney

RICE
1 tablespoon olive oil
4 green onions (scallions), chopped finely
1 clove garlic, crushed
1 medium red capsicum (bell pepper) (200g), chopped finely
125g (4 ounces) canned corn kernels, drained, rinsed
2 x 250g (8-ounce) packets cooked long-grain white rice (see tip)
⅓ cup (40g) pitted green olives, chopped coarsely
¼ cup chopped fresh coriander (cilantro)

1 Combine juice, oil, paprika, oregano, salt, chilli, garlic and chicken in a large bowl.
2 Preheat an oiled grill plate (or grill or barbecue) to medium.
3 Cook chicken on grill plate, covered loosely with foil, 6 minutes each side or until browned and cooked through.
4 Meanwhile, make rice.
5 Serve chicken with rice and chutney.

RICE
Heat oil in a large frying pan; cook onion, garlic, capsicum and corn, stirring, until vegetables have softened. Add rice; cook, stirring, 5 minutes, to separate rice grains and heat through. Stir in olives and coriander; season to taste.

TIPS For a more intense flavour, marinate the chicken overnight.
You can substitute 1 cup uncooked long-grain rice, cooked in boiling water 15 minutes, then drained.

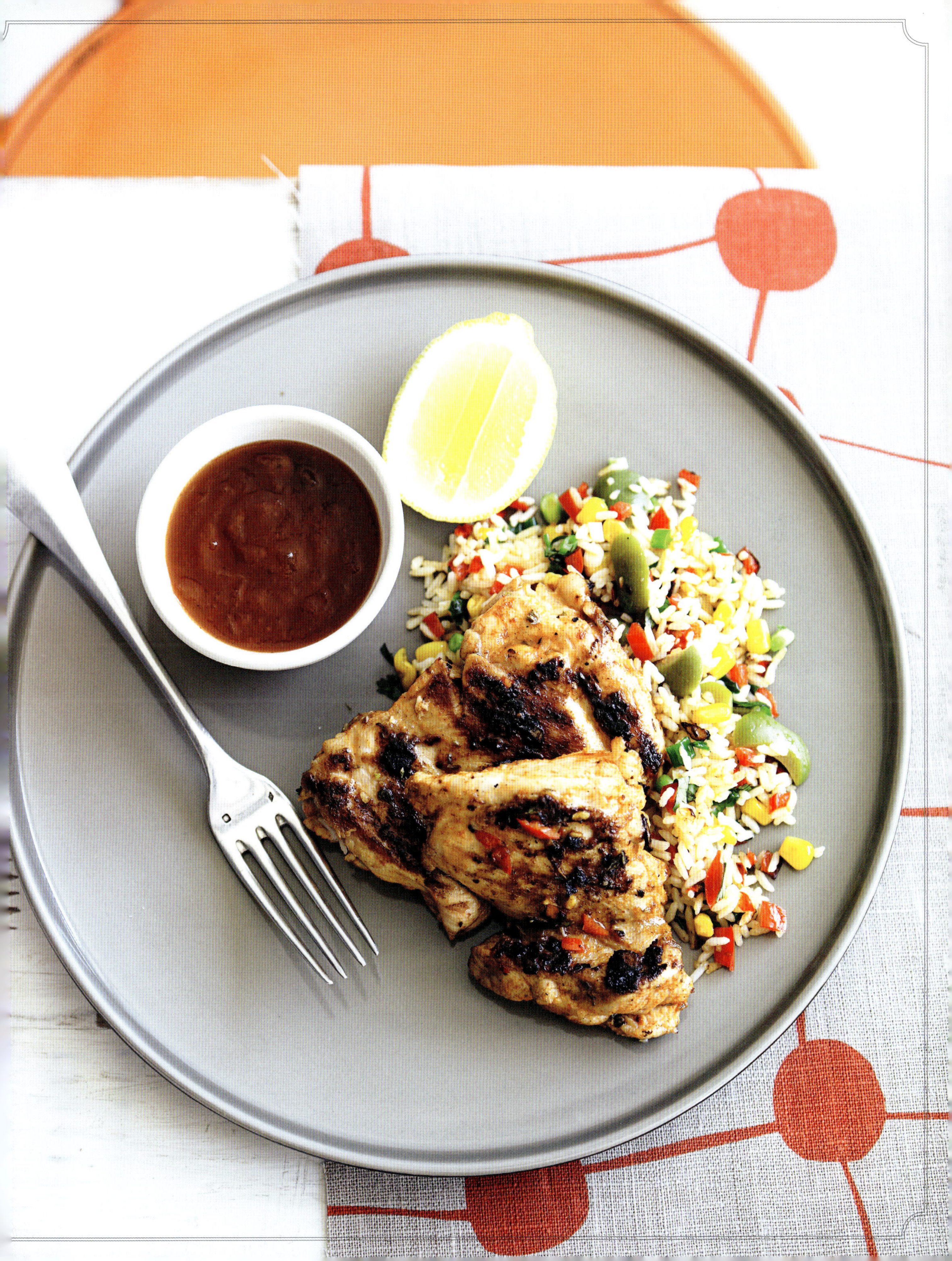

SUMMER PICNIC

BARBECUED SALMON
with Capsicum and Olive Salsa

(RECIPE PAGE 100)

PERFECT POTATO
Salad

(RECIPE PAGE 27)

COUSCOUS
Salad

(RECIPE PAGE 30)

PASSIONFRUIT
Meringue Cake

(RECIPE PAGE 280)

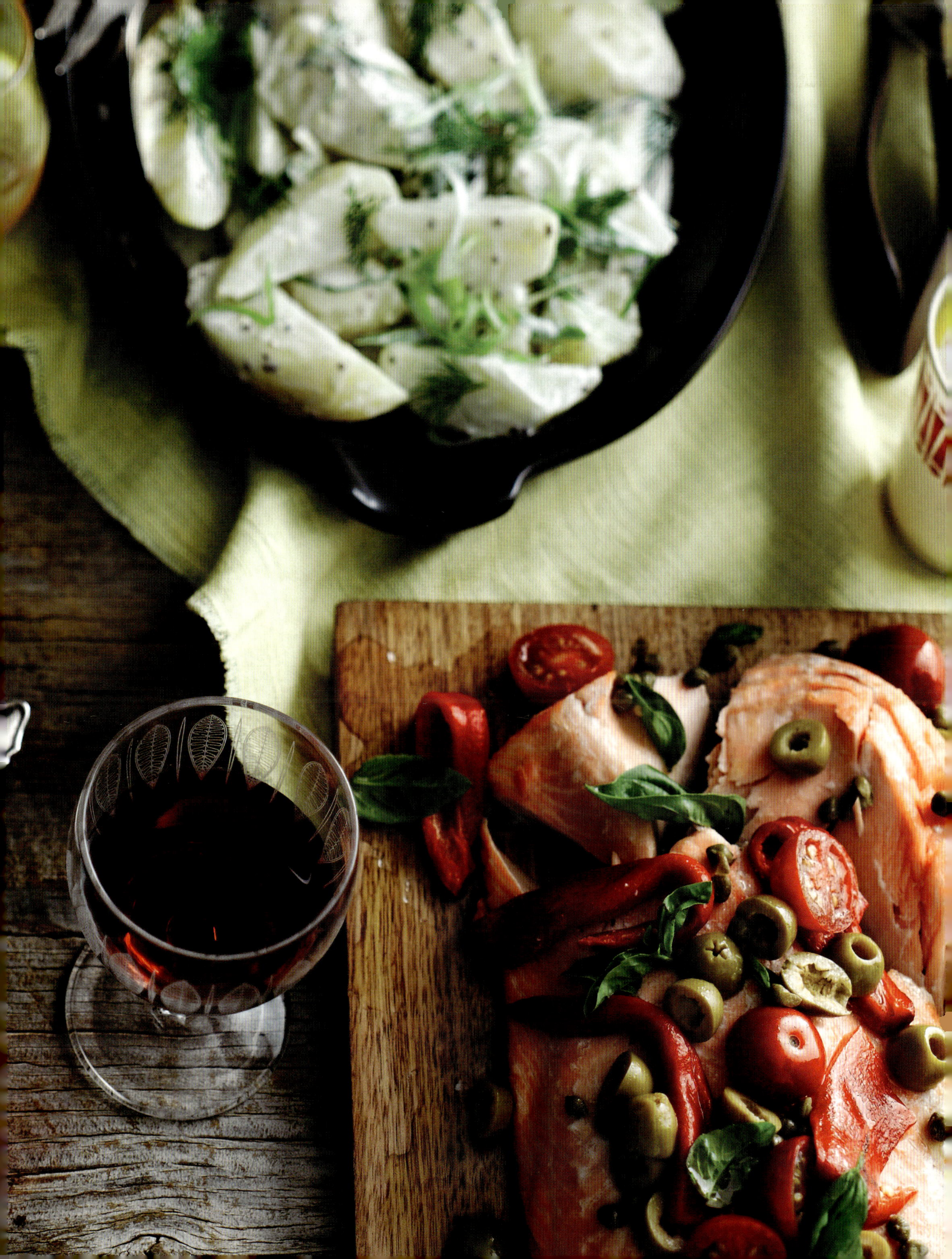

BARBECUED SALMON
with Capsicum and Olive Salsa

PREP + COOK TIME *40 MINUTES* **SERVES 8**

---

1 large red capsicum (bell pepper) (350g), seeded, quartered
125g (4 ounces) cherry tomatoes, halved (or quartered if large)
2 tablespoons baby capers
¼ cup (60g) pitted green olives, quartered
¼ cup (60ml) extra virgin olive oil
cooking-oil spray or olive oil
1.5kg (3-pound) side of salmon (fillet)
2 teaspoons sea salt
½ cup loosely packed fresh baby basil leaves

1. Preheat grill (broiler) to high and a barbecue (or grill plate) to medium.
2. Place capsicum under grill, skin-side-up, 10 minutes or until skin blisters and blackens. Place capsicum in a small bowl, cover; stand 5 minutes. Peel skin from capsicum; cut flesh into thick strips, then into 1.5cm (¾-inch) pieces.
3. Place capsicum pieces in a medium bowl with tomatoes, capers, olives and oil, then season; toss to gently combine.
4. Place a double layer of foil about 1 metre (3 feet) long on a work surface; spray with cooking-oil or brush lightly with olive oil. Place a 45cm (18-inch) sheet of baking paper in centre of foil.
5. Pat salmon dry with paper towel. Remove any fine bones in centre of fillet with tweezers. Rub salt over skin. Place salmon, skin-side-down, on baking-paper-lined foil. Wrap to enclose salmon.
6. Cook wrapped salmon, skin-side-down, on heated barbecue 10 minutes, for medium-rare or until cooked as desired.
7. Just before serving, add basil leaves to capsicum and olive salsa. Serve salmon topped with salsa.

TIPS You will need extra-wide foil for this recipe. The fish can be prepared and wrapped up to 1 hour ahead. The salsa can be made 2 hours ahead; add the basil just before serving.

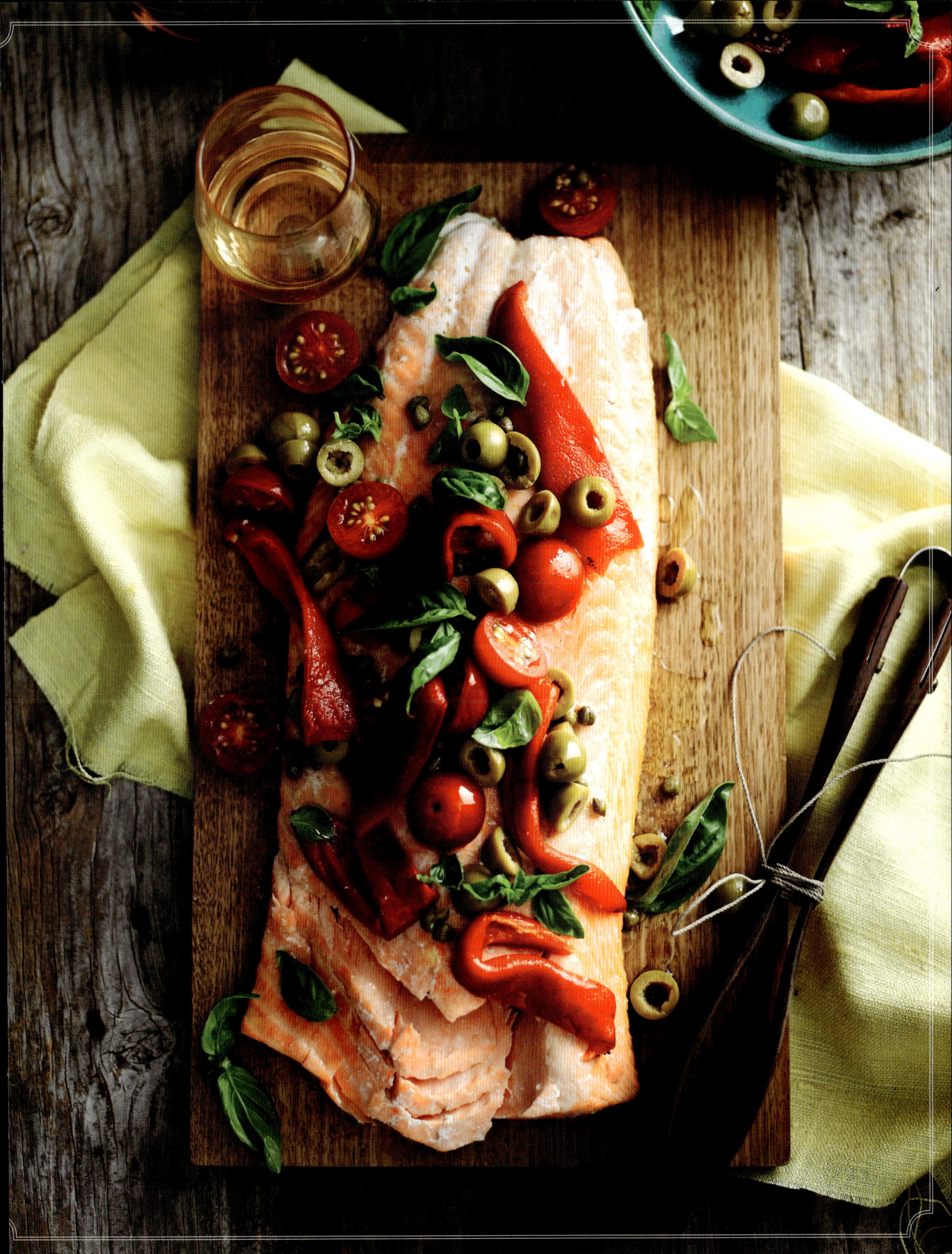

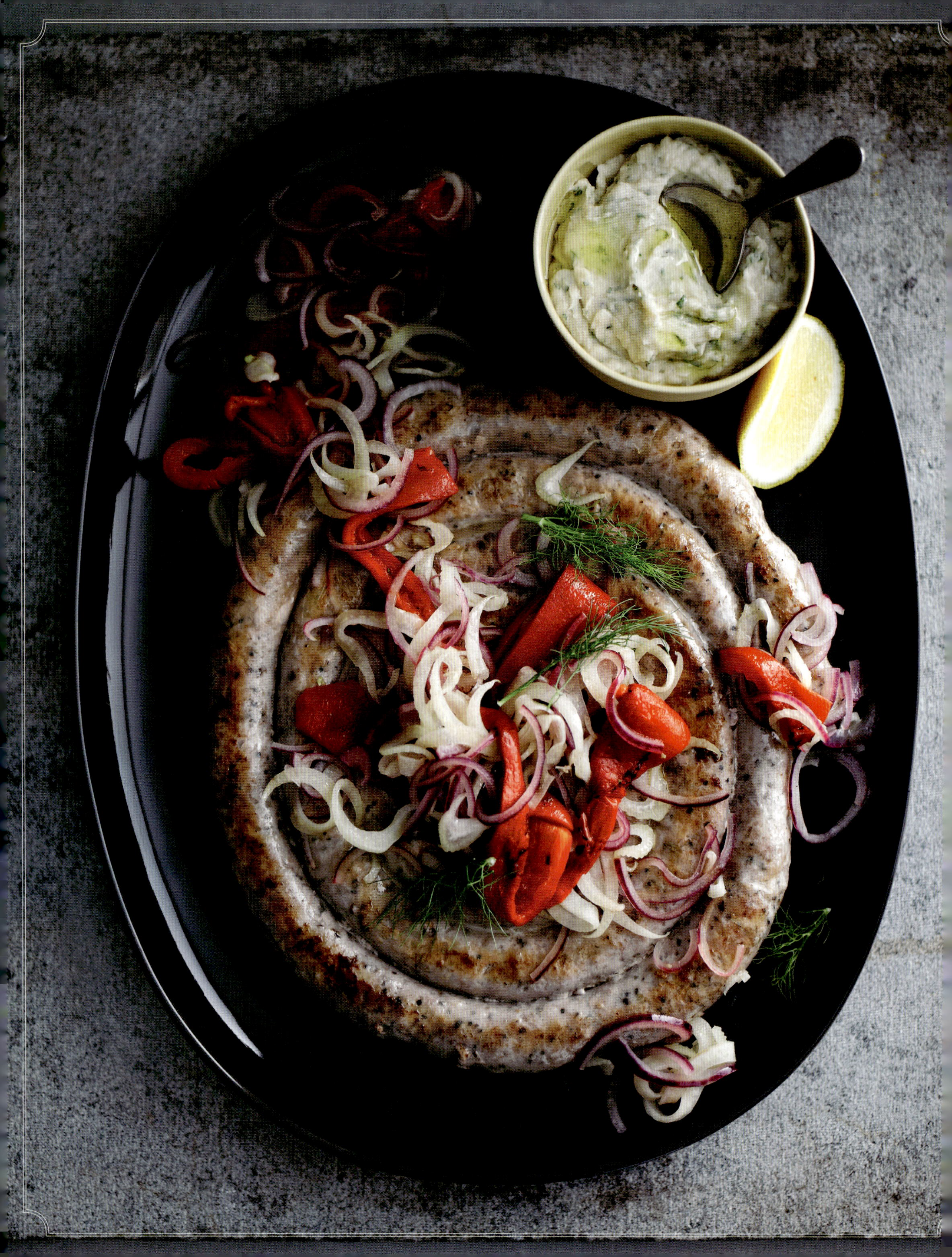

SAUSAGE SPIRAL WITH GRILLED CAPSICUM
and Whipped White Beans

PREP + COOK TIME 45 MINTUES SERVES 4

2 medium red capsicums (bell peppers) (400g)
1kg (2 pounds) Italian-style pork and fennel sausage (see tips)
2 tablespoons extra virgin olive oil
2 tablespoons red wine vinegar
1 tablespoon brown sugar
1 baby fennel bulb (130g), trimmed, sliced thinly
1 large red onion (300g), sliced thinly

WHIPPED WHITE BEANS

400g (12½ ounces) canned cannellini beans, drained, rinsed
100g (3 ounces) fresh ricotta
2 teaspoons dijon mustard
1 clove garlic, crushed
2 tablespoons olive oil
2 tablespoons lemon juice
¼ cup finely chopped fresh flat-leaf parsley

1. Make whipped white beans.
2. Preheat a barbecue grill and flatplate to medium-high heat.
3. Cook capsicums on heated flatplate, turning occasionally, for 15 minutes or until skin blisters and blackens; cool. Peel away skin, remove seeds; cut flesh into strips.
4. Coil sausage length into one large spiral; push two metal skewers, at right angles, through the centre of the spiral to secure. Cook sausage spiral on heated barbecue for 10 minutes each side or until cooked through.
5. Meanwhile, combine oil, vinegar and sugar in a medium bowl. Add capsicum, fennel and onion, then season; toss to combine. Cook capsicum mixture on heated barbecue flatplate, stirring mixture occasionally, for 10 minutes or until soft.
6. Serve sausage spiral topped with capsicum mixture, accompanied with whipped beans.

WHIPPED WHITE BEANS

Process ingredients until smooth; season to taste. Spoon into a bowl; set aside.

TIPS Ask the butcher for a 2-metre (6½-foot) length of unlinked sausages. Alternatively, you can unlink a length of sausages and use short lengths together to form the spiral.
If your barbecue doesn't include a flatplate, cook the capsicum mixture in a heavy-based frying pan on the barbecue.

MARINATED LAMB
Skewers

PREP + COOK TIME 40 MINUTES SERVES 4

---

2 tablespoons extra virgin olive oil
2 teaspoons grated lemon rind
1 teaspoon dried oregano
1 clove garlic, crushed
800g (1½ pounds) lamb backstraps, cut into 3cm (1¼-inch) pieces
250g (8 ounces) baba ghanoush
2 tablespoons chopped fresh flat-leaf parsley
2 teaspoons lemon juice
8 pitta breads
1 medium lemon (140g), cut into wedges

GREEK SALAD
2 large tomatoes (440g), chopped coarsely
1 lebanese cucumber (130g), halved lengthways, sliced diagonally
½ small red onion (50g), sliced thinly
½ cup (60g) pitted black olives
125g (4 ounces) fetta, cut into cubes
1 tablespoon extra virgin olive oil
¼ teaspoon dried oregano

1 Combine oil, rind, oregano and garlic in a small bowl; season, mix well. Thread lamb onto eight skewers. Rub lemon mixture all over lamb; set aside.
2 Make greek salad.
3 Preheat an oiled grill plate (or grill or barbecue) to medium.
4 Combine baba ghanoush, parsley and juice in a small bowl; season to taste.
5 Cook lamb skewers on heated grilled plate, turning on all sides, 8 minutes or until browned and still slightly pink in the centre. Rest meat 5 minutes.
6 Place pitta on heated oiled grill plate until charred and heated through.
7 Serve skewers with greek salad, baba ghanoush mixture, pitta bread and lemon wedges.

GREEK SALAD
Place ingredients in a medium bowl, season to taste; toss gently to combine.

TIP If you're using bamboo skewers, soak them in water for at least 30 minutes before using to prevent scorching during cooking.

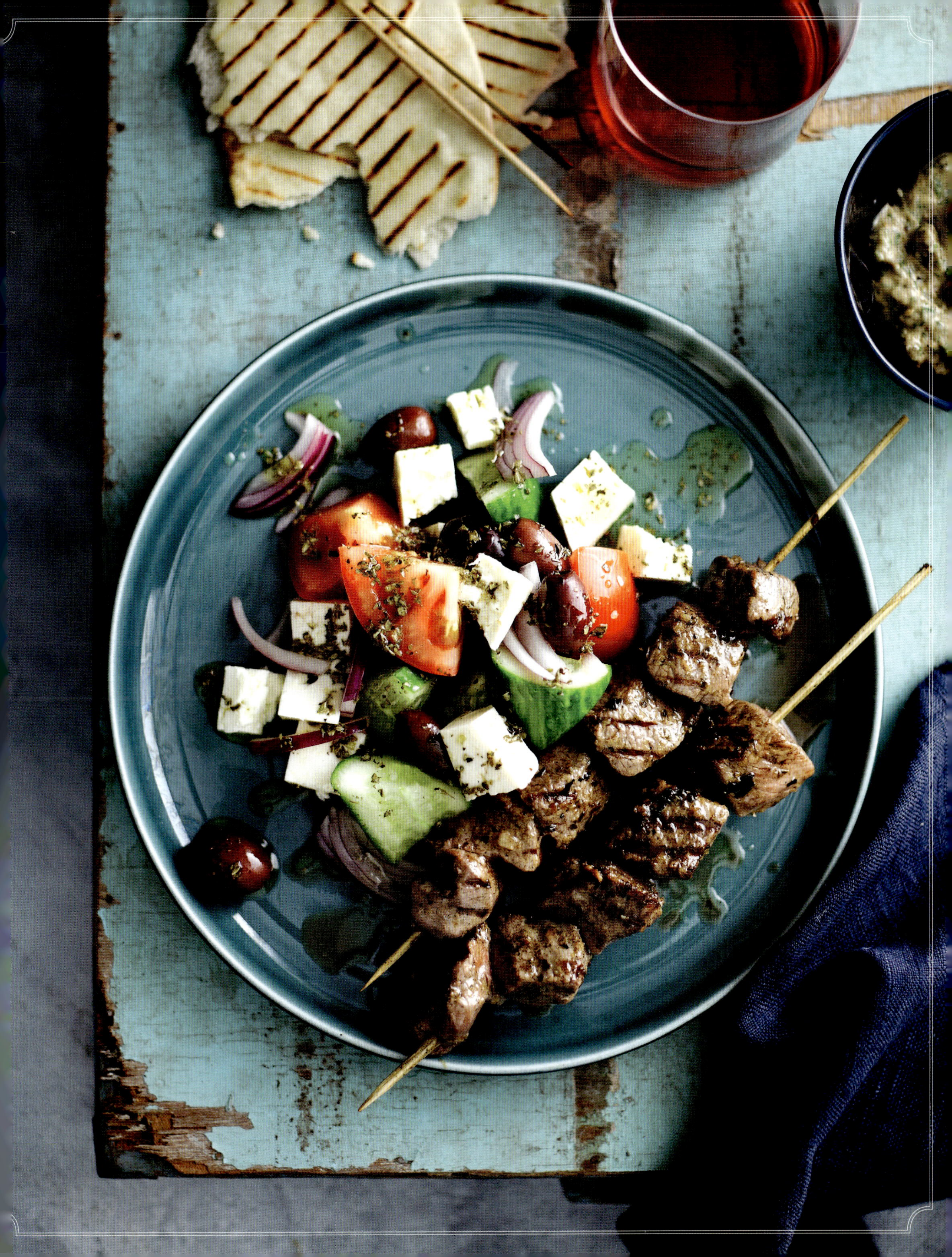

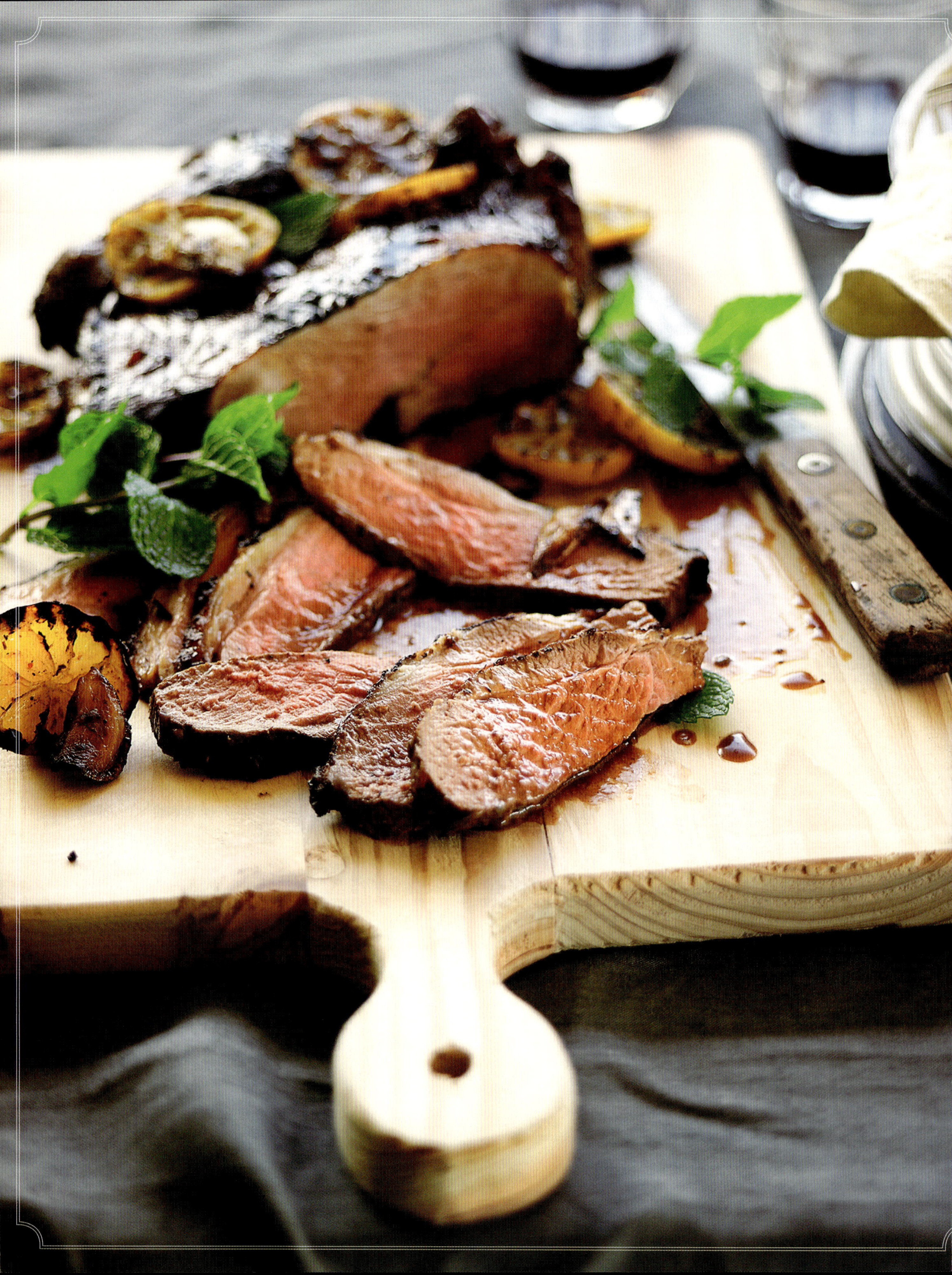

BUTTERFLIED LAMB
with Lemon and Herbs

PREP + COOK TIME *40 MINUTES (+ REFRIGERATION)* **SERVES 10**

1.6kg (3¼-pound) butterflied leg of lamb

LEMON MARINADE

¼ cup (60ml) extra virgin olive oil
6 cloves garlic, bruised
2 tablespoons coarsely chopped fresh mint
1 tablespoon rigani
1 tablespoon fig jam
1 medium lemon (140g), sliced into thin rounds

1. Make lemon marinade.
2. Add lamb to marinade; rub all over lamb, season. Cover; refrigerate at least 3 hours or overnight, turning occasionally.
3. Preheat a barbecue to medium heat.
4. Remove lemon and garlic from lamb; reserve. Place lamb, fat-side down, on barbecue. Cover with foil or a large upturned metal baking dish (or if using a covered barbecue, close the lid); cook 15 minutes or until browned underneath. Turn lamb; cook, covered, a further 20 minutes for medium, or until cooked as desired. A few minutes before lamb is cooked, add reserved lemon and garlic to barbecue; cook until browned on both sides. Transfer lamb, lemon and garlic to a warm platter; cover, rest 15 minutes. before slicing lamb.
5. Serve lamb with lemon and garlic, and some extra fresh mint leaves, if you like.

LEMON MARINADE

Combine ingredients in a large shallow dish.

TIPS Rigani is a dried Greek oregano, often sold in dried bunches, which the leaves crumble off easily. It is available from delicatessens or greengrocers. If it's hard to find, use dried oregano leaves instead. You can also roast the lamb in a 220ºC/425ºF oven for 35 minutes.

ZUCCHINI AND FETTA
Fritters

PREP + COOK TIME 30 MINUTES SERVES 4

3 large zucchini (450g)
200g (6½ ounces) fetta, crumbled finely
5 green onions (scallions), sliced thinly
2 eggs, beaten lightly
1 tablespoon chopped fresh oregano
2 tablespoons chopped fresh mint
⅓ cup (50g) plain (all-purpose) flour
2 tablespoons olive oil
4 medium roma (egg) tomatoes (300g), chopped coarsely
½ cup (75g) pitted kalamata olives, halved
270g (8½ ounces) bottled char-grilled capsicum (bell pepper), drained, cut into thin strips
1½ tablespoons red wine vinegar
1 tablespoon extra virgin olive oil

1. Preheat oven to 160°C/325°F. Line an oven tray with baking paper.
2. Coarsely grate zucchini; squeeze firmly to remove excess liquid with paper towel. Place zucchini in a large bowl with fetta, green onion, egg, herbs and flour, season; stir to combine.
3. Heat 2 tablespoons of the oil in a large non-stick frying pan over medium heat; cook level tablespoons of zucchini mixture, in batches, for 2½ minutes each side or until browned and cooked through. Drain on paper towel. Place fritters on oven tray; keep warm in oven between batches.
4. Place tomato, olives, capsicum, vinegar and extra virgin olive oil in a medium bowl; toss gently to combine. Season to taste.
5. Serve fritters with tomato salad.

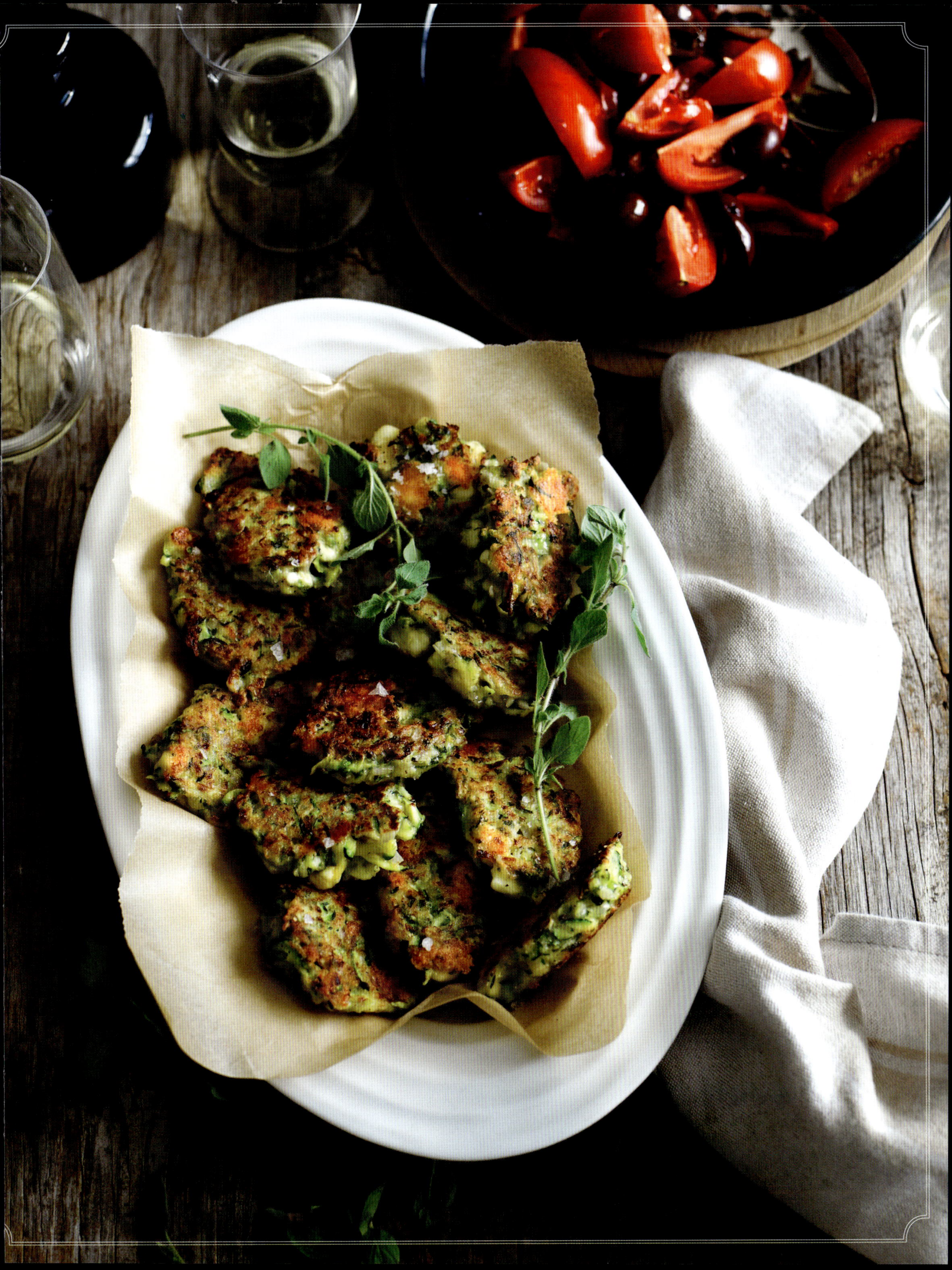

CHAPTER 4
PIES & TARTS

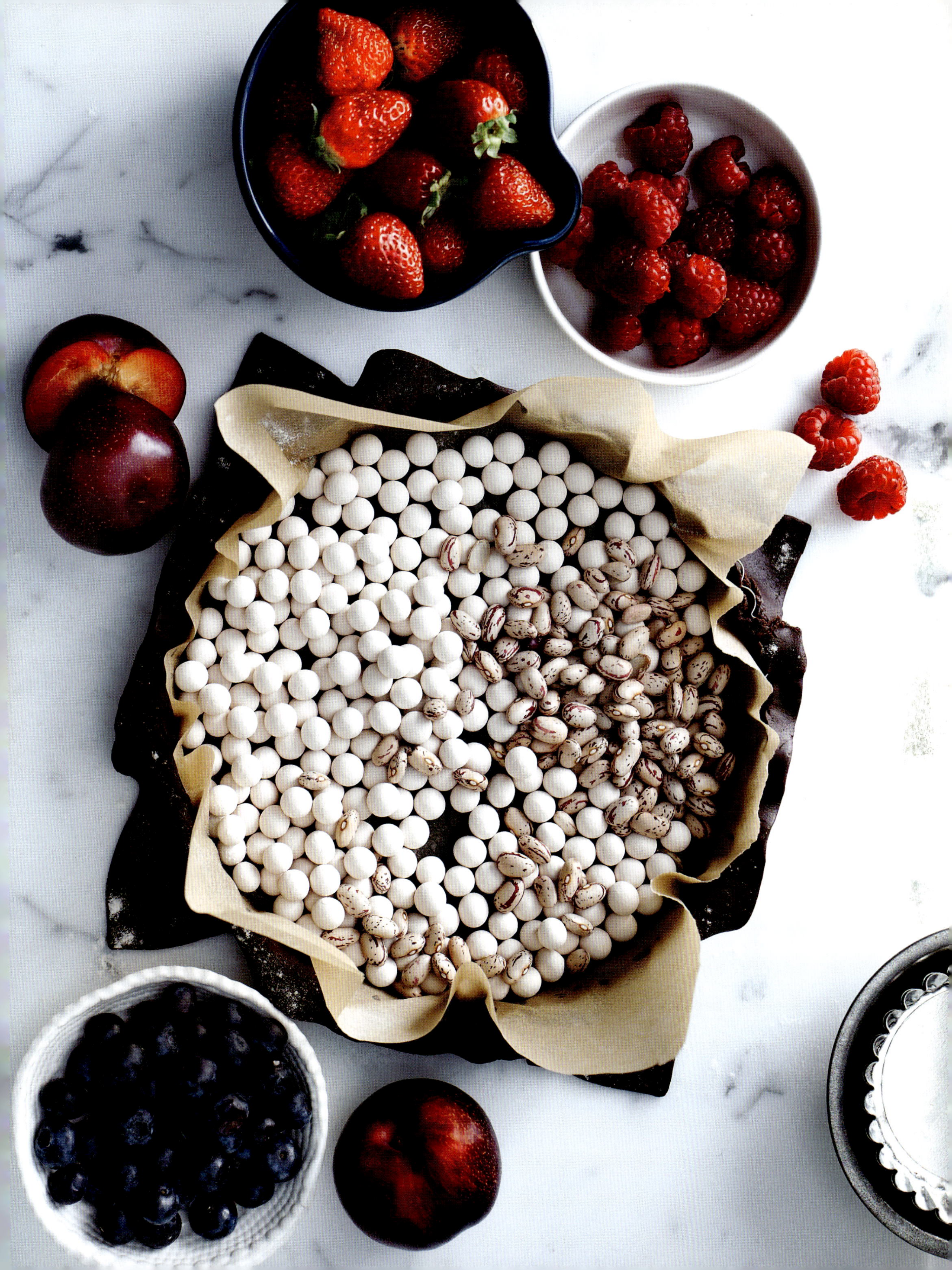

BEEF AND MUSHROOM
Family Pie

PREP + COOK TIME *50 MINUTES (+ COOLING)* **SERVES 4**

---

1 tablespoon olive oil
2 medium brown onions (300g), chopped finely
500g (1 pound) minced (ground) beef
200g (6½ ounces) button mushrooms, sliced finely
2 tablespoons tomato paste
1 tablespoon worcestershire sauce
⅓ cup (65g) powdered gravy mix
1 cup (250ml) water
1 sheet shortcrust quiche pastry
1 egg, beaten lightly
1 sheet butter puff pastry

1. Heat oil in a large frying pan over medium heat; cook onions, stirring, for 5 minutes or until soft. Add beef; cook, stirring with a wooden spoon to break up lumps, until changed in colour. Stir in mushrooms. Add paste, sauce, gravy mix and water; bring to the boil. Reduce heat; simmer 10 minutes or until mixture is thick. Cool.
2. Preheat oven to 220°C/425°F.
3. Oil a 22cm (9-inch) pie dish. Line base and side of dish with shortcrust pastry; trim to fit. Spoon in beef mixture. Brush rim of pastry with a little egg; top with puff pastry, pressing edges to seal. Trim excess pastry; brush top of pie with a little more egg. Place pie on an oven tray.
4. Bake pie, on lower oven shelf, for 40 minutes or until pastry is browned and crisp. Stand 10 minutes before serving.

SERVING SUGGESTION Serve with green vegetables.

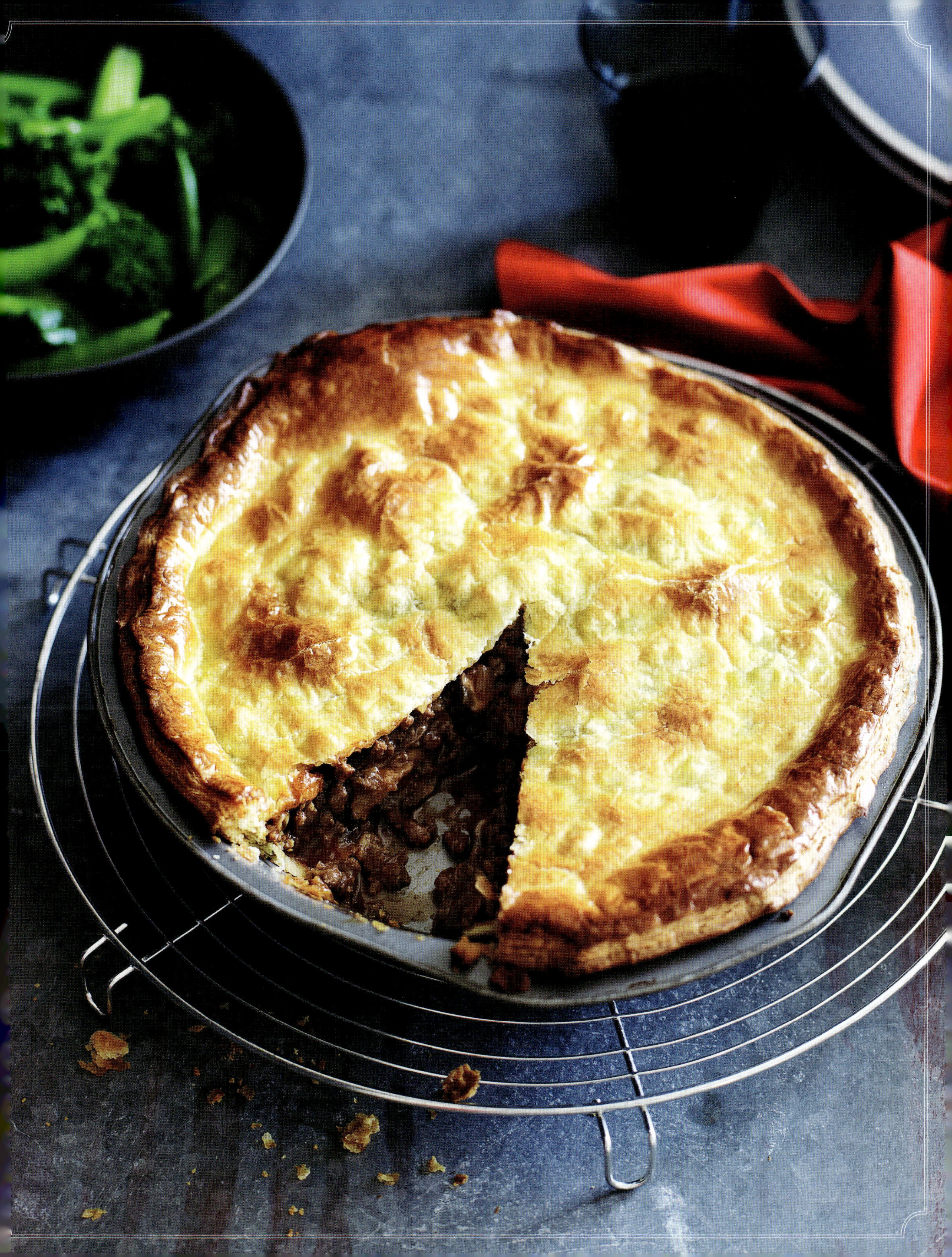

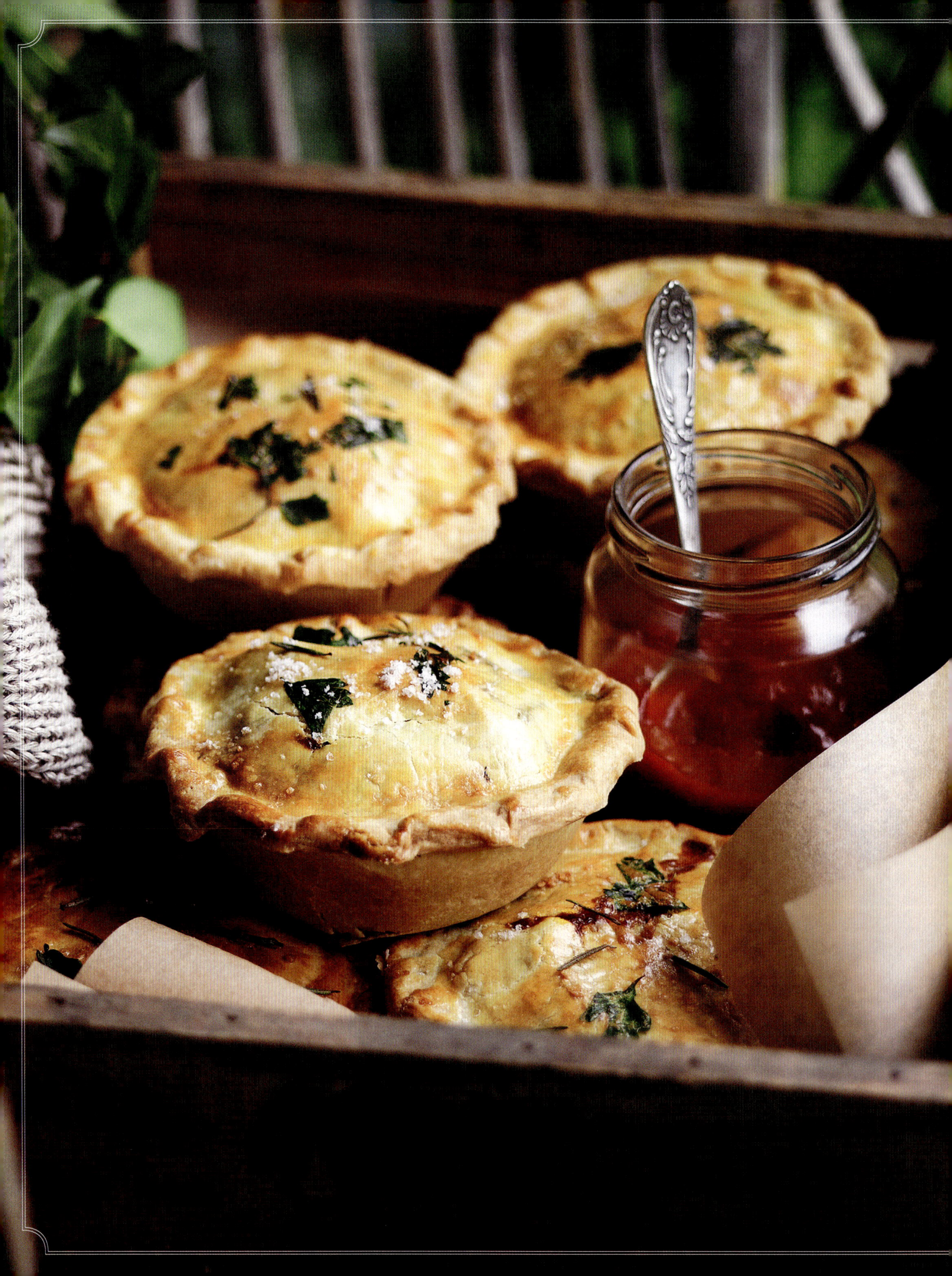

LAMB AND ROSEMARY PIES

PREP + COOK TIME 2 HOURS 25 MINUTES MAKES 6

2 tablespoons olive oil
650g (1¼ pounds) lamb shoulder, cut into 2cm (¾-inch) pieces
2 medium brown onions (300g), chopped coarsely
2 cloves garlic, crushed
1 tablespoon tomato paste
½ cup (125ml) dry red wine
1 tablespoon fresh rosemary leaves
2 cups (500ml) beef stock
3 small parsnips (360g), chopped coarsely
fresh rosemary and flat-leaf parsley leaves
1 egg, beaten lightly

RICH SHORTCRUST PASTRY
3 cups (450g) plain (all-purpose) flour
250g (8 ounces) cold butter, chopped
2 egg yolks
¼ cup (60ml) cold water

1. Heat half the oil in a large frying pan over medium-high; cook lamb, turning occasionally, 5 minutes or until browned. Remove from pan.
2. Heat remaining oil in same pan; cook onion and garlic, stirring, for 5 minutes or until onion is soft.
3. Add tomato paste; cook, stirring, 1 minute. Stir in wine, then rosemary, stock and lamb; bring to the boil. Reduce heat; simmer, covered, for 1 hour. Stir in parsnip; cook a further 45 minutes or until lamb is tender and mixture is thickened. Season to taste.
4. Meanwhile, make pastry.
5. Preheat oven to 200°C/400°F. Grease six pie tins (7.5cm/3-inch base measure, 11cm/4½-inch top).
6. Divide pastry in half; divide one half into six portions. Roll portions on a floured surface until large enough to line tins. Ease rounds into pie tins, trim edge. Place tins on an oven tray, refrigerate while rolling remaining pastry.
7. Divide remaining pastry into six portions. Using your fingers, shape each portion into a small round, press a few rosemary and parsley leaves on top. Gently roll over dough, pressing herbs in and rolling the dough until large enough to cover tops of tins.
8. Spoon lamb mixture into pastry cases; top each with herbed pastry, pressing edges together firmly to seal; trim pastry. Brush pies with egg.
9. Bake pies, on low oven shelf, 40 minutes or until browned. Stand pies for 10 minutes before removing from tins.

RICH SHORTCRUST PASTRY
Process flour and butter until crumbly; add egg yolks and the water, pulse until mixture just comes together. Knead on a floured surface until smooth. Form into a disc, enclose in plastic wrap; refrigerate 30 minutes.

SERVING SUGGESTION Serve with a green leaf salad.

FISH PIE WITH
Potato and Celeriac Mash

PREP + COOK TIME *1 HOUR 10 MINUTES* **SERVES** *6*

1 medium celeriac (celery root) (750g), peeled, chopped coarsely
4 medium desiree potatoes (800g), peeled, chopped coarsely
25g (¾ ounce) butter
¼ cup (60ml) milk, warmed
90g (3 ounces) butter, extra
3 small leeks (600g), sliced thickly
¼ cup (35g) plain (all-purpose) flour
1½ cups (375ml) milk
1kg (2 pounds) boneless white fish fillets, chopped coarsely
2 teaspoons lemon juice
¼ cup coarsely chopped fresh chives

1. Boil or steam celeriac and potato until soft; drain. Mash celeriac and potato with butter and warmed milk until smooth. Season to taste.
2. Meanwhile, melt 60g (2 ounces) of the extra butter in a large saucepan over medium heat; cook leek, covered, until soft. Add flour; cook, stirring, for 2 minutes. Gradually stir in milk; bring to the boil, stirring continuously.
3. Add fish to pan; cook, covered, 3 minutes. Gently stir in juice and chives without breaking up the fish.
4. Preheat oven to 220°C/425°F.
5. Spoon fish mixture into a 2.5-litre (10-cup) ovenproof dish. Melt remaining butter. Top fish mixture with potato and celeriac mash; brush top liberally with melted butter. Place dish on an oven tray.
6. Bake pie 25 minutes or until mash is golden.

TIPS You can substitute celeriac with more potato, if you prefer. You may need a little more milk to make a light, fluffy mash.
We used ocean perch fillets for this recipe.

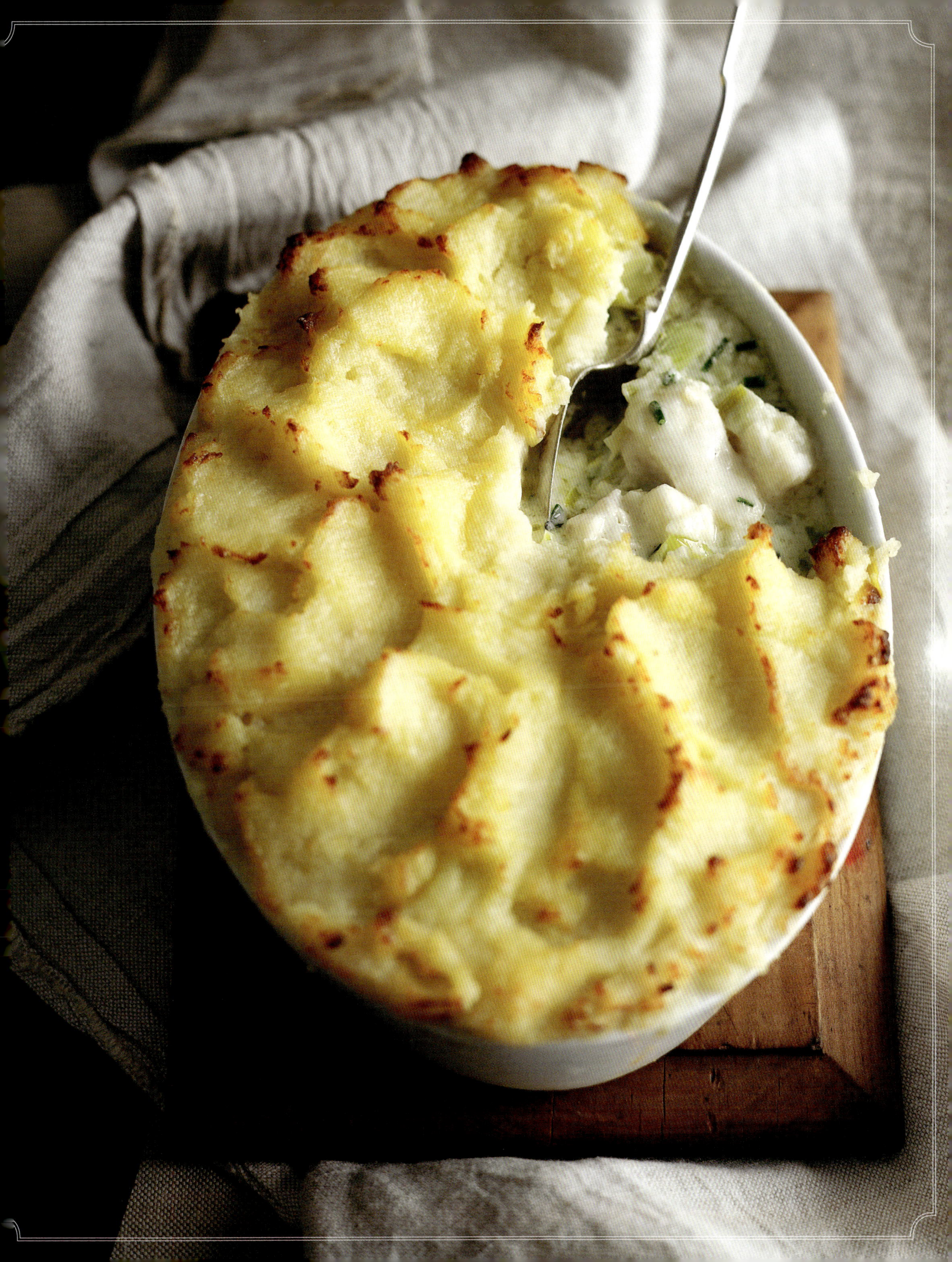

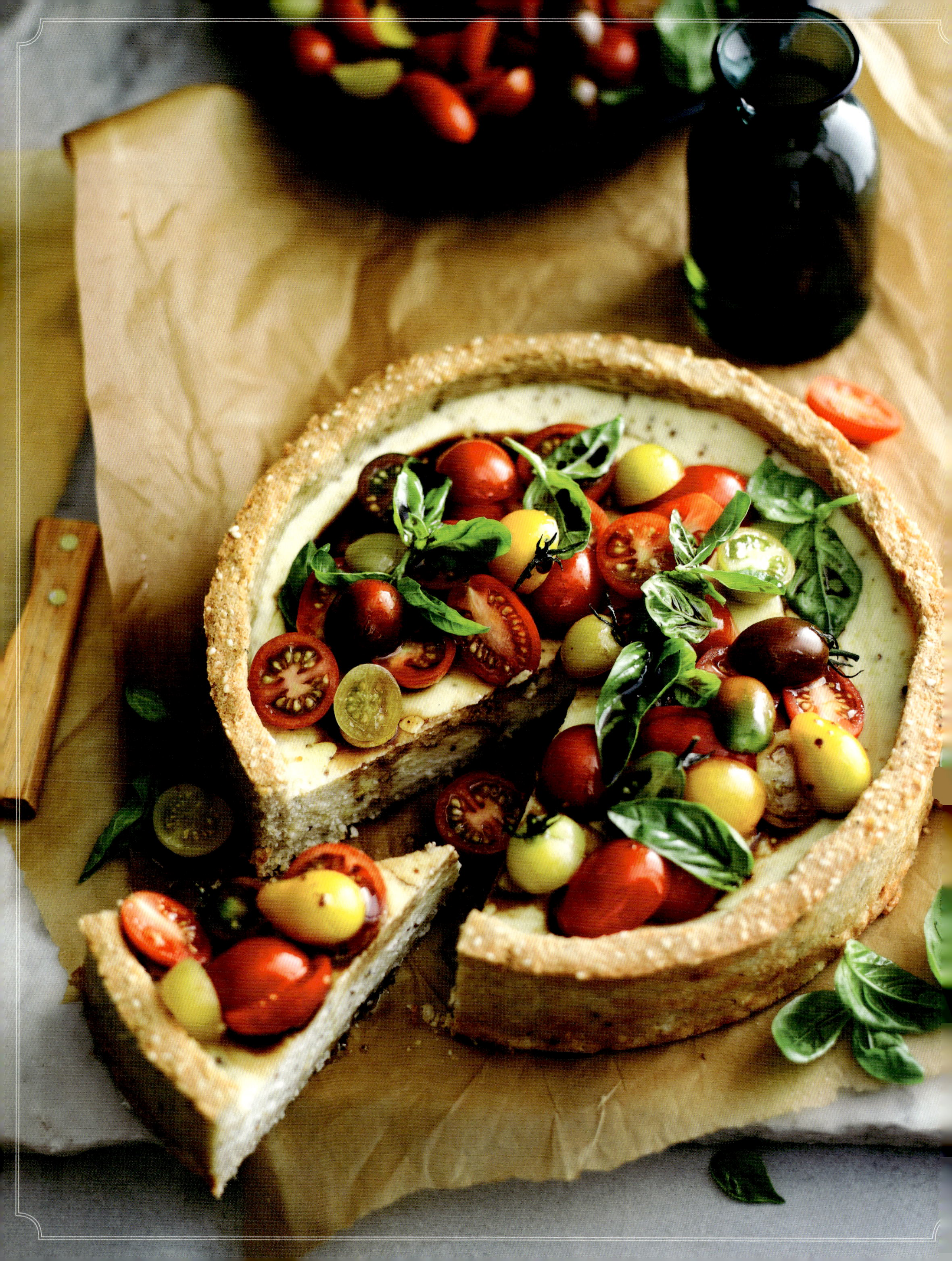

TOMATO AND GOAT'S CHEESE TART
with Rice and Seed Crust

PREP + COOK TIME 1 HOUR (+ COOLING) SERVES 8

Nutty brown rice and sesame seeds replace flour to form a delicious crust for this tangy cheese and heirloom tomato tart. Perfect for coeliacs.

500g (1 pound) packaged ready-steamed brown basmati rice
⅓ cup (50g) sesame seeds
1½ cups (120g) finely grated parmesan
3 eggs
1 teaspoon sea salt flakes
500g (1 pound) fresh ricotta
150g (4½ ounces) soft goat's cheese
¼ cup (60ml) milk
1 tablespoon wholegrain mustard
1 clove garlic, chopped finely
400g (12½ ounces) mixed baby heirloom tomatoes, halved
2 tablespoons small fresh basil leaves
1 tablespoon extra virgin olive oil
2 teaspoons balsamic vinegar

1. Preheat oven to 200°C/400°F. Grease a 24cm (9½-inch) springform pan.
2. Process rice, seeds and half the parmesan until rice is finely chopped. Add 1 egg and half the salt; process until mixture forms a coarse dough.
3. Using damp hands, press rice dough over base and up the side of the pan, stopping 5mm (¼ inch) from the top.
4. Bake crust 25 minutes or until golden and dry to the touch.
5. Meanwhile, process ricotta, goat's cheese, milk, mustard and garlic with remaining parmesan, eggs and salt until smooth.
6. Pour cheese mixture into warm rice crust. Reduce oven to 180°C/350°F; bake tart 30 minutes or until a skewer inserted into the centre comes out clean. Cool 1 hour.
7. Just before serving, arrange tomatoes and basil over top of tart; drizzle with oil and vinegar. Season with freshly ground black pepper.

TIPS Ready-steamed brown basmati rice is available in packets from the rice section of supermarkets. Use fresh ricotta, sold in wheels from delis and the deli section of supermarkets for the best taste and texture.
If heirloom tomatoes are not available, use baby grape or cherry truss tomatoes.

GOAT'S CHEESE
and Leek Tart

PREP + COOK TIME *45 MINUTES (+ REFRIGERATION)* **SERVES** *8*

375g (12-ounce) block butter puff pastry
1 tablespoon olive oil
20g (¾ ounce) butter
1 large leek (500g), white part only, sliced thinly
2 teaspoons chopped fresh thyme leaves
140g (4½ ounces) soft goat's cheese, crumbled
3 eggs
1 cup (250ml) pouring cream
60g (2 ounces) curly endive (frisée) lettuce

LEMON AND MUSTARD DRESSING
¼ cup (60ml) olive oil
2 tablespoons lemon juice
1 tablespoon white wine vinegar
1 tablespoon dijon mustard

1. Oil a 24cm (9½-inch) round, loose-based tart pan. Roll out pastry on a floured surface until large enough to line pan. Lift pastry into pan, gently ease into base and side (do not stretch pastry or it will shrink during cooking). Prick base with a fork; place pan on an oven tray. Refrigerate 20 minutes.
2. Preheat oven to 220°C/425°F.
3. Line pastry case with baking paper; fill with dried beans or rice. Bake 15 minutes. Carefully remove paper and beans; bake a further 1 minute or until browned. Cool. Reduce oven to 180°C/350°F.
4. Meanwhile, heat oil and butter in a medium frying pan over medium heat; cook leek and thyme, stirring, 10 minutes or until very soft. Spread leek mixture into pastry case; top with goat's cheese.
5. Whisk eggs and cream in a small bowl; season. Pour over leek filling.
6. Bake tart 25 minutes or until set. Cool in pan for 5 minutes before lifting out.
7. Combine endive and dressing in a medium bowl.
8. Serve warm tart with endive.

LEMON AND MUSTARD DRESSING
Place ingredients in a screw-top jar; shake well.

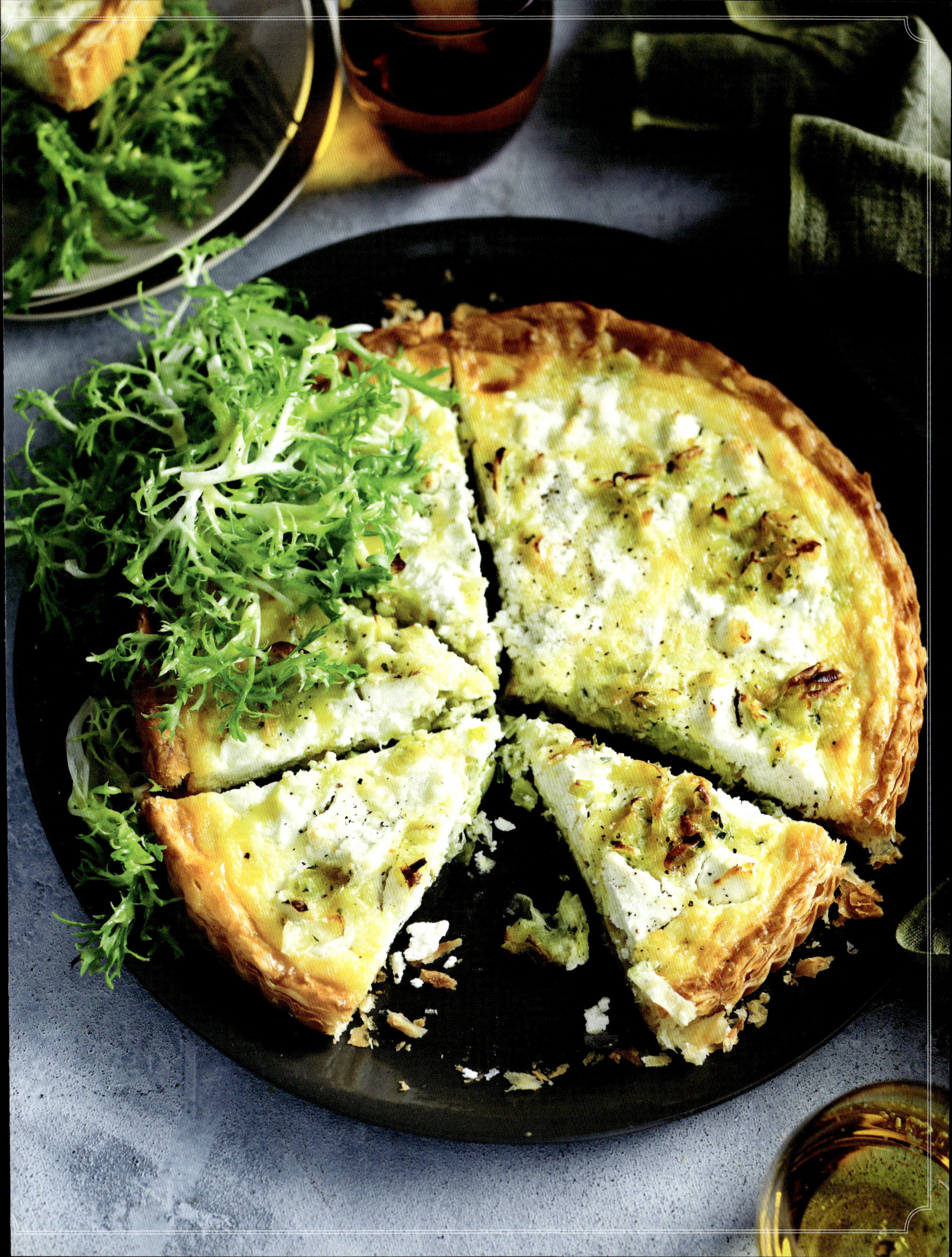

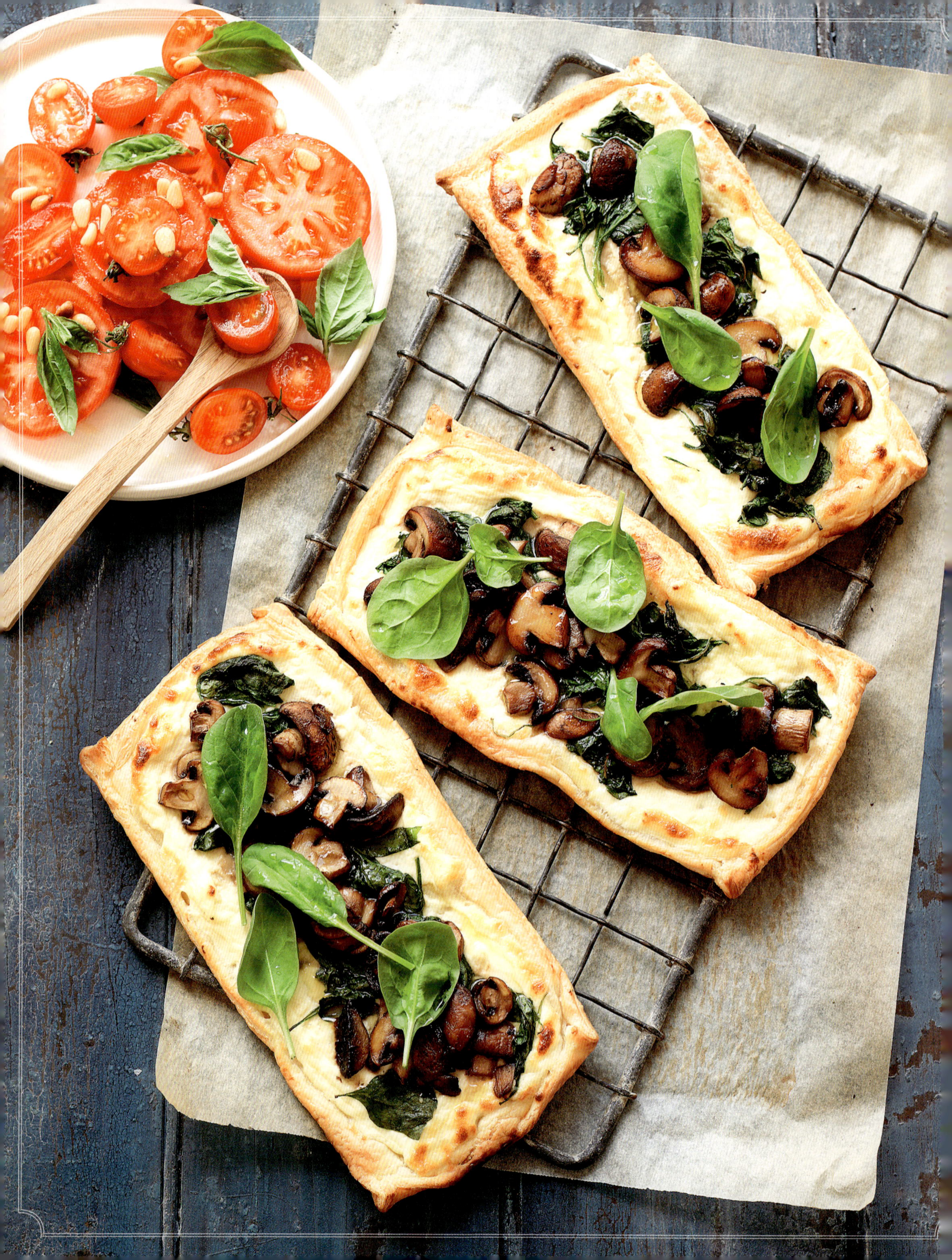

MUSHROOM AND SPINACH TARTS
with Tomato Salad

PREP + COOK TIME *40 MINUTES* SERVES 4

150g (4½ ounces) baby spinach leaves
20g (¾ ounce) butter
300g (9½ ounces) button mushrooms, sliced thinly
1 egg, beaten lightly
250g (8 ounces) fresh ricotta
2 tablespoons finely shredded fresh basil
2 sheets butter puff pastry, halved

TOMATO SALAD
2 tablespoons pine nuts, toasted
250g (8 ounces) grape tomatoes, halved
2 small vine-ripened tomatoes (180g), sliced thickly
1 tablespoon olive oil
1 tablespoon lemon juice
½ cup loosely packed fresh basil leaves

1. Preheat oven to 220°C/425°F. Line two large oven trays with baking paper. Reserve 1 cup of loosely packed spinach leaves.
2. Heat butter in a large frying pan over high heat; cook mushrooms 5 minutes or until browned and tender. Add remaining spinach; cook, stirring, until beginning to wilt. Drain mixture on paper towel.
3. Combine egg, ricotta and shredded basil in a medium bowl. Season.
4. Place pastry rectangles on trays. Spread ricotta evenly over pastry, leaving a 1.5cm (¾-inch) border; fold in borders. Top with mushroom mixture.
5. Bake tarts 20 minutes or until pastry is browned.
6. Make tomato salad.
7. Serve tarts topped with reserved spinach leaves and tomato salad.

TOMATO SALAD
Combine ingredients in a large bowl. Season.

FREE-FORM SPINACH,
Herb and Ricotta Pies

PREP + COOK TIME 35 MINUTES **SERVES** 4

1 tablespoon olive oil
1 medium brown onion (150g), chopped
1 clove garlic, crushed
2 sheets puff pastry
250g (8 ounces) frozen spinach, thawed, drained
1½ cups (300g) fresh ricotta
¼ cup coarsely chopped fresh flat-leaf parsley
¼ cup coarsely chopped fresh dill
2 tablespoons coarsely chopped fresh mint
2 teaspoons finely grated lemon rind

1. Preheat oven to 240°C/475°F.
2. Heat oil in a small frying pan over medium heat; cook onion and garlic 5 minutes or until soft. Transfer to a large bowl.
3. Meanwhile, heat two oven trays in the oven. Place pastry on two sheets of baking paper.
4. Using your hands, squeeze out excess liquid from spinach. Add spinach, ricotta, herbs and rind to onion mixture; mix well. Season well.
5. Spread spinach mixture on pastry sheets into a 20cm (8-inch) round. Fold edges of pastry roughly over filling. Carefully transfer pies to hot trays.
6. Bake pies 20 minutes or until pastry is golden. Cut in half to serve.

TIP For best results, use a pizza tray with holes in the base – this will make it possible to cook the pastry evenly.

SERVING SUGGESTION Serve with a Greek-style salad.

CHICKEN AND
Mushroom Party Pies

PREP + COOK TIME 55 MINUTES **MAKES** 24

1 tablespoon olive oil
1 small brown onion (80g), chopped finely
1 clove garlic, crushed
400g (12½ ounces) minced (ground) chicken
100g (3 ounces) button mushrooms, chopped finely
2 teaspoons plain (all-purpose) flour
¾ cup (180ml) pouring cream
2 tablespoons finely chopped fresh chives
3 sheets shortcrust pastry
1 egg, beaten lightly
2 sheets puff pastry
2 teaspoons sesame seeds

1. Heat oil in a medium frying pan over medium heat; cook onion and garlic, stirring, 5 minutes or until onion softens. Add chicken and mushrooms; cook, stirring, until chicken changes colour. Add flour; cook, stirring, 1 minute. Gradually stir in cream; cook, stirring, until mixture boils and thickens. Stir in chives; cool.
2. Preheat oven to 200°C/400°F. Oil two 12-hole (2-tablespoon/40ml) deep flat-based patty pans.
3. Cut 24 x 7cm (2¾ inch) rounds from shortcrust pastry; press into pan holes. Brush edges with a little of the egg. Spoon chicken mixture into pastry cases.
4. Cut 24 x 6cm (2½-inch) rounds from puff pastry; top pies with puff pastry lids. Press edges firmly to seal; brush tops with remaining egg, sprinkle with sesame seeds. Cut a small slit in top of each pie.
5. Bake pies 20 minutes or until browned lightly. Stand in pan 5 minutes before serving.

FREE-FORM SPINACH,
Herb and Ricotta Pies

CHICKEN AND
Mushroom Party Pies

APPLE CROSTATA

PREP + COOK TIME *1 HOUR 20 MINUTES (+ REFRIGERATION)* **SERVES** *8*

A crostata is a type of rustic Italian free-form tart, the beauty of which is, that it requires no special pan for baking.

4 medium green apples (600g)
1 cup (220g) caster (superfine) sugar
2 teaspoons finely grated lemon rind
1 tablespoon lemon juice
3 cups (750ml) water
2 cups (300g) plain (all-purpose) flour
125g (8 ounces) cold unsalted butter, chopped
¼ cup (55g) caster (superfine) sugar, extra
⅓ cup (80ml) iced water, approximately
2 tablespoons milk

1. Preheat oven to 180°C/350°F.
2. Peel and core apples; cut into eighths. Place apples in a medium saucepan with sugar, rind, juice and the water; bring to the boil. Reduce heat; simmer over a low heat 10 minutes or until apple is tender. Remove apple with a slotted spoon into a medium bowl. Simmer syrup 15 minutes or until reduced to 200ml. Remove from heat.
3. Meanwhile, process flour, butter and 1 tablespoon of the extra sugar until crumbly. Add enough iced water to process until the ingredients come together. Press dough into a ball. Wrap in plastic wrap; refrigerate 30 minutes.
4. Roll dough out between two large sheets of baking paper into a 35cm (14-inch) round. Remove top layer of paper; carefully lift dough onto a large oven tray.
5. Pile apples into the centre of the dough, leaving a 7cm (2¾-inch) border. Fold pastry edge up and around apple, pleating it as you go. Brush pastry edges with milk, then sprinkle with remaining sugar.
6. Bake tart for 40 minutes or until pastry is golden. Spoon some syrup over the tart before serving.

TIP If you would like to give the pie some colour, add a handful of frozen raspberries or blueberries to the apples before placing on the pastry.

SERVING SUGGESTION Serve with cream or custard.

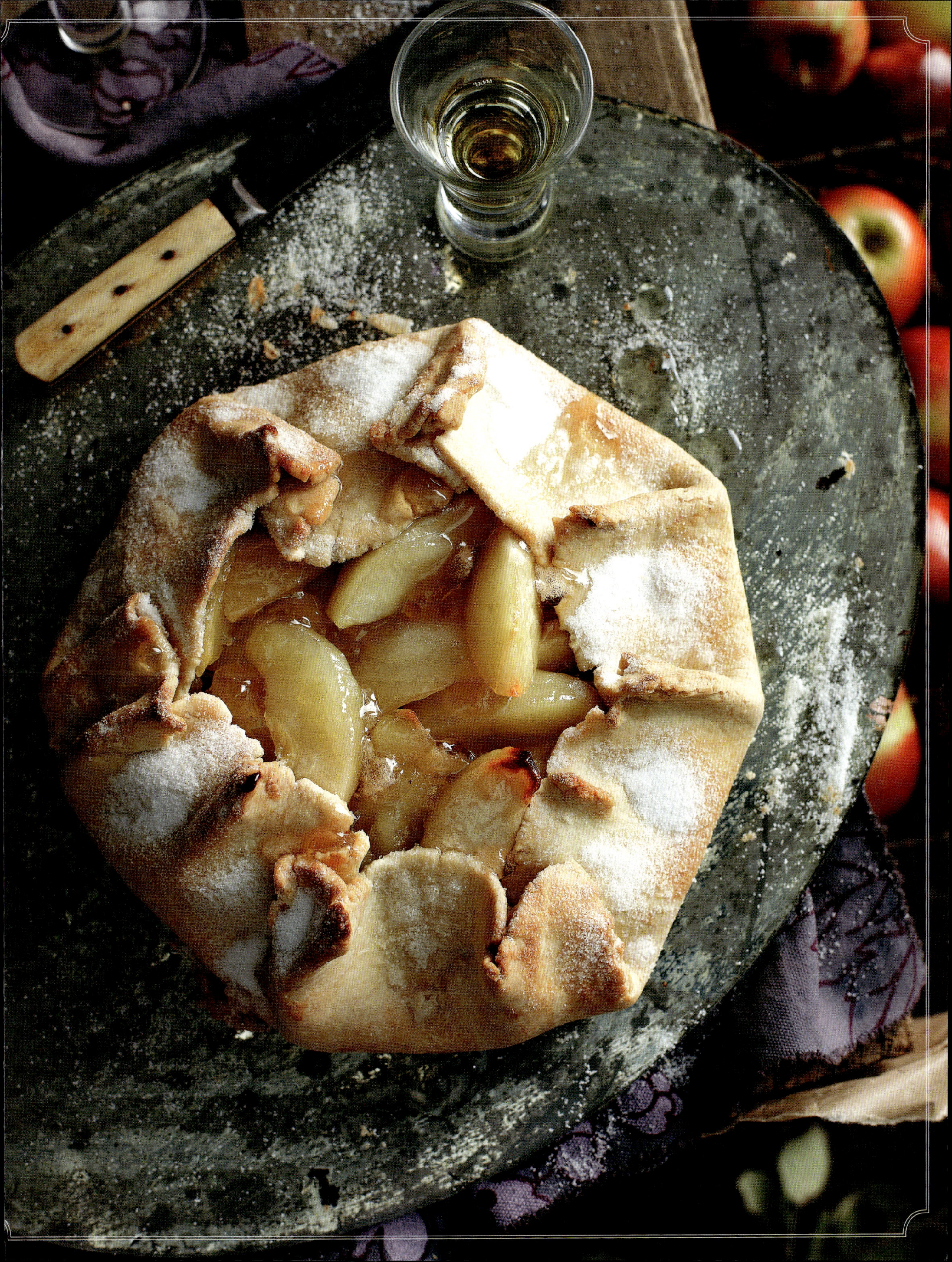

RICH CHOCOLATE
and Coconut Tart

RICH CHOCOLATE
and Coconut Tart

PREP + COOK TIME *30 MINUTES (+ REFRIGERATION)* **SERVES** *12*

1 cup (90g) desiccated coconut
1 egg white, beaten lightly
¼ cup (55g) caster (superfine) sugar
300ml (½ pint) thickened (heavy) cream
300g (9½ ounces) dark (semi-sweet) chocolate, chopped finely
4 egg yolks
2 teaspoons coffee-flavoured liqueur
2 tablespoons cocoa powder

1. Preheat oven to 140°C/250°F. Grease a 20cm (8-inch) non-stick springform pan.
2. Combine coconut, egg white and sugar. Press mixture evenly over base and 4cm (1½-inches) up the side of pan. Bake, on the lowest shelf, for 40 minutes or until golden. Cool.
3. Heat cream in a small saucepan until almost boiling. Add chocolate; stir until smooth. Cool slightly.
4. Whisk egg yolks and liqueur into chocolate mixture; strain. Pour chocolate mixture into coconut shell.
5. Refrigerate tart 6 hours or until set. Serve dusted with cocoa.

TIPS The crust of this tart is delicate. To help with removal from the pan, ensure that the pan base is smooth and clip it in upside down; this will eliminate any lip, providing a flat surface that a spatula can easily slide under.
You can use Kahlua or Tia Maria for the coffee-flavoured liqueur.
This tart can be made a day ahead.

SERVING SUGGESTION Serve with fresh strawberries and thick (double) cream.

PEACH AND
Nectarine Tart

PREP + COOK TIME *55 MINUTES* **SERVES** *8*

60g (2 ounces) butter, softened
⅓ cup (75g) caster (superfine) sugar
1 egg
½ teaspoon orange blossom water
¾ cup (75g) ground almonds
2 tablespoons plain (all-purpose) flour
2 x 375g (12-ounce) blocks puff pastry
4 large peaches (880g)
1 nectarine (170g)
150g (4½ ounces) raspberries
¼ cup (35g) coarsely chopped pistachios
¼ cup (90g) honey

1. Beat butter and sugar in a small bowl with an electric mixer until creamy. Beat in egg and orange blossom water until combined. Stir in ground almonds and flour.
2. Preheat oven to 220°C/425°F.
3. Roll out each block of pastry on a floured sheet of baking paper into a 16cm x 34cm (6½-inch x 13½-inch) rectangle. Lift each pastry rectangle onto an oven tray. Spread almond mixture thinly over pastry, leaving a 1cm (½-inch) border.
4. Cut peaches and nectarine in half; remove stones. Cut halves into thin wedges. Arrange fruit wedges, overlapping slightly, on almond mixture.
5. Bake tart for 30 minutes or until browned and pastry is cooked underneath. Serve tarts topped with raspberries and pistachios; drizzle with honey.

SERVING SUGGESTION Serve warm or cool with thick (double) cream or ice-cream.

(PHOTOGRAPH PAGE 130)

PEACH AND
Nectarine Tart

(RECIPE PAGE 129)

PEAR TARTE TATIN

(RECIPE PAGE 132)

PEAR TARTE TATIN

PREP + COOK TIME 2 HOURS SERVES 8

6 medium firm pears (1.4kg)
80g (2½ ounces) unsalted butter, chopped
¾ cup (165g) firmly packed brown sugar
2 tablespoons lemon juice
375g (12-ounce) block frozen puff pastry, thawed

1. Peel, quarter and core pears.
2. Melt butter in a 19cm (7¾-inch) heavy-based ovenproof frying pan, large enough to hold almost all of the pears in a single layer. Add pears; sprinkle with sugar and juice. Simmer, uncovered, over a very low heat, 1 hour 20 minutes, turning as pears caramelise. Pears should be soft and well caramelised (if the heat is too high, use a simmer mat or occasionally cover the pan if necessary to prevent excess evaporation or burning). As pears become softer, gently push them into a single layer; remove from heat.
3. Preheat oven to 200°C/350°F.
4. Roll pastry out on a floured surface until slightly larger than the frying pan; cut pastry into a 27cm (10¾-inch) round, using a bowl or plate as a guide. Place pastry over pears. Tuck edge of the pastry around pears.
5. Bake tart 15 minutes or until well browned. Stand 5 minutes before turning out onto a platter with a lip to collect juices.

TIPS We used beurre bosc pears for this recipe as they hold their shape well when baked.
You need a frying pan with a heatproof handle. If the handle of your pan is not heatproof, wrap it in two layers of foil. The 19cm (7¾-inch) pan we used has a top measurement of 26cm (10½ inches).

SERVING SUGGESTION Serve with ice-cream or cream.

(PHOTOGRAPH PAGE 131)

QUICK AND EASY
Plum Tart

PREP + COOK TIME 30 MINUTES SERVES 6

This tart is a breeze to whip up in next to no time for a mid-week dessert or easy entertaining. Swap the plums for peaches, nectarines or apricots if you prefer, or use a combination.

1 sheet butter puff pastry
4 medium plums (330g), stones removed, sliced
⅓ cup (55g) icing (confectioners') sugar

1. Preheat oven to 180°C/350°F. Line an oven tray with baking paper.
2. Place pastry on tray; fold edges in by 1cm (½-inch) to form a border.
3. Arrange plum slices, slightly overlapping, on pastry. Dust with 2 tablespoons of the sifted icing sugar.
4. Bake tart 20 minutes or until pastry is puffed and lightly brown. Serve tart dusted with remaining sifted icing sugar.

SERVING SUGGESTION Serve with vanilla or chocolate ice-cream, or whipped cream.

QUICK AND EASY
Plum Tart

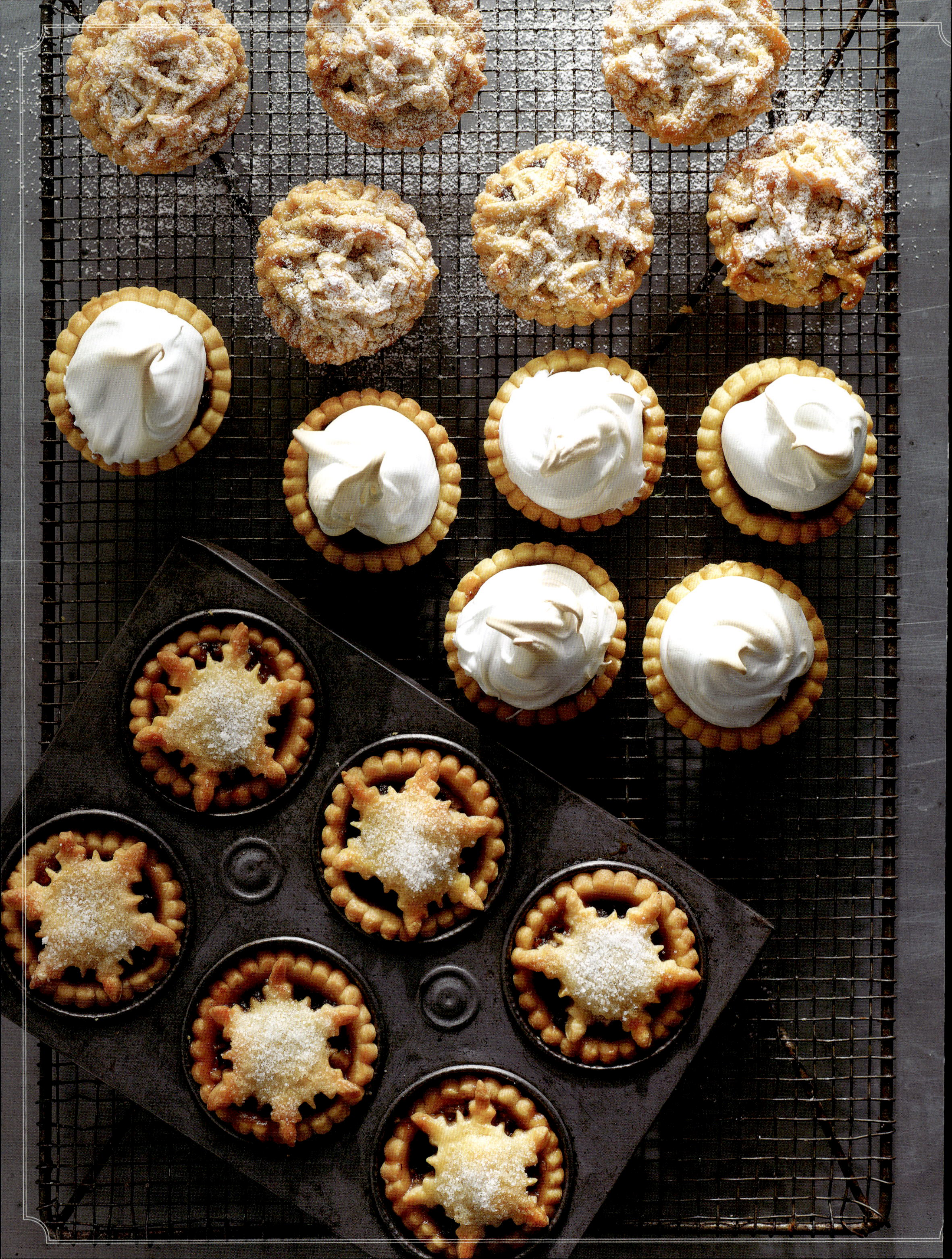

MINCE PIES

PREP + COOK TIME *1 HOUR (+ REFRIGERATION & COOLING)* **MAKES** *24*

475g (13½ ounces) bottled fruit mince
½ cup (125g) finely chopped glacé peaches
⅓ cup (45g) finely chopped roasted slivered almonds
¼ cup (30g) ground almonds
1 tablespoon brandy
2 egg whites, beaten lightly
½ cup (110g) caster (superfine) sugar
2 teaspoons icing (confectioners') sugar

PASTRY
1½ cups (225g) plain (all-purpose) flour
2 tablespoons custard powder
¼ cup (55g) caster (superfine) sugar
125g (4 ounces) cold butter, chopped
1 egg yolk
2 tablespoons cold water

1. Combine fruit mince, glacé peaches, slivered and ground almonds, and brandy in a medium bowl.
2. Make pastry.
3. Preheat oven to 200°C/400°F. Grease two 12-hole (2-tablespoon/40ml) patty pans.
4. Roll two-thirds of the pastry between sheets of baking paper until 3mm (⅛-inch) thick. Cut 24 x 7.5cm (3-inch) rounds from pastry, re-rolling scraps as necessary. Press pastry rounds into pan holes; reserve pastry scraps. Spoon fruit mince mixture into pastry cases.
5. Roll remaining third of pastry between sheets of baking paper until 3mm (⅛-inch) thick. Cut out eight snowflakes or stars using cutters; place on eight pies.
6. Knead all pastry scraps into a ball; freeze until firm. Coarsely grate frozen pastry; sprinkle on eight pies. Brush a little egg white on pastry tops, sprinkle with 1 tablespoon of the caster sugar. Cover remaining eight pies with greased foil.
7. Bake all pies for 20 minutes or until pastry is browned lightly. Transfer the 16 pastry-topped pies to a wire rack.
8. Beat remaining egg white in a small bowl with an electric mixer until soft peaks form. Gradually add remaining caster sugar, beating until sugar dissolves. Spoon meringue onto remaining eight pies; bake for 5 minutes or until browned lightly. Cool.
9. Dust struesel-topped pies with sifted icing sugar.

PASTRY
Process flour, custard powder, sugar and butter until combined. Add egg yolk and enough water to make ingredients cling together. Knead dough on floured surface until smooth; wrap in plastic wrap. Refrigerate 30 minutes.

DIVINE CHOCOLATE
and Raspberry Tarts

PREP + COOK TIME 1 HOUR MAKES 6

125g (4 ounces) unsalted butter
½ cup (50g) dutch cocoa
⅓ cup (110g) raspberry jam
⅔ cup (150g) caster (superfine) sugar
2 eggs, beaten lightly
⅔ cup (100g) plain (all-purpose) flour
¼ teaspoon bicarbonate of soda (baking soda)
125g (4 ounces) cream cheese, softened
1 egg yolk
½ cup (75g) frozen raspberries

1. Preheat oven to 160°C/325°F. Grease six 10cm (4-inch) round, loose-based tart pans; place on an oven tray.
2. Melt butter in a medium saucepan, add sifted cocoa; whisk over low heat until mixture boils. Remove from heat; whisk in jam and ½ cup of the sugar. Stir in egg, then sifted flour and soda. Spoon mixture into pans.
3. Beat cream cheese, remaining sugar and egg yolk in a small bowl with an electric mixer until smooth; stir in raspberries.
4. Drop spoonfuls of cheese mixture on chocolate mixture; pull a knife backwards and forwards several times for a marbled effect.
5. Bake tarts for 30 minutes. Serve warm or at room temperature.

SERVING SUGGESTION Serve with thick (double) cream and fresh raspberries.

MACADAMIA FILLO TARTS
with Caramelised Pineapple

PREP + COOK TIME 1 HOUR SERVES 6

½ cup (70g) unsalted macadamias
⅓ cup (75g) firmly packed brown sugar
¼ teaspoon ground cardamom
6 sheets fillo pastry
60g (2 ounces) butter, melted
1 small pineapple (900g)
2 tablespoons caster (superfine) sugar

1. Preheat oven to 180°C/350°F. Line two large oven trays with baking paper.
2. Process macadamias until finely ground. Combine macadamias, brown sugar and cardamom in a small bowl.
3. Place a sheet of pastry on a clean work surface. Brush with a little of the butter; sprinkle with a thin layer of the nut mixture. Repeat layering with remaining pastry, butter and nut mixture. Press down lightly.
4. Cut six 12cm (4¾-inch) rounds from layered pastry; discard scraps. Carefully transfer layered pastry rounds to one tray; cover with a sheet of baking paper, then top with second tray.
5. Peel and quarter pineapple; remove core. Thinly slice pineapple. Place pineapple slices, in a single layer, on top tray.
6. Bake trays on top of each other for 20 minutes. Remove top tray, then the baking paper from pastry rounds. Place pineapple on pastry rounds; sprinkle with caster sugar. Bake for a further 10 minutes or until pastry is golden.

SERVING SUGGESTION Serve with vanilla or butterscotch ice-cream.

DIVINE CHOCOLATE
and Raspberry Tarts

MACADAMIA FILLO TARTS
with Caramelised Pineapple

CHAPTER 5
CASSEROLES & CURRIES

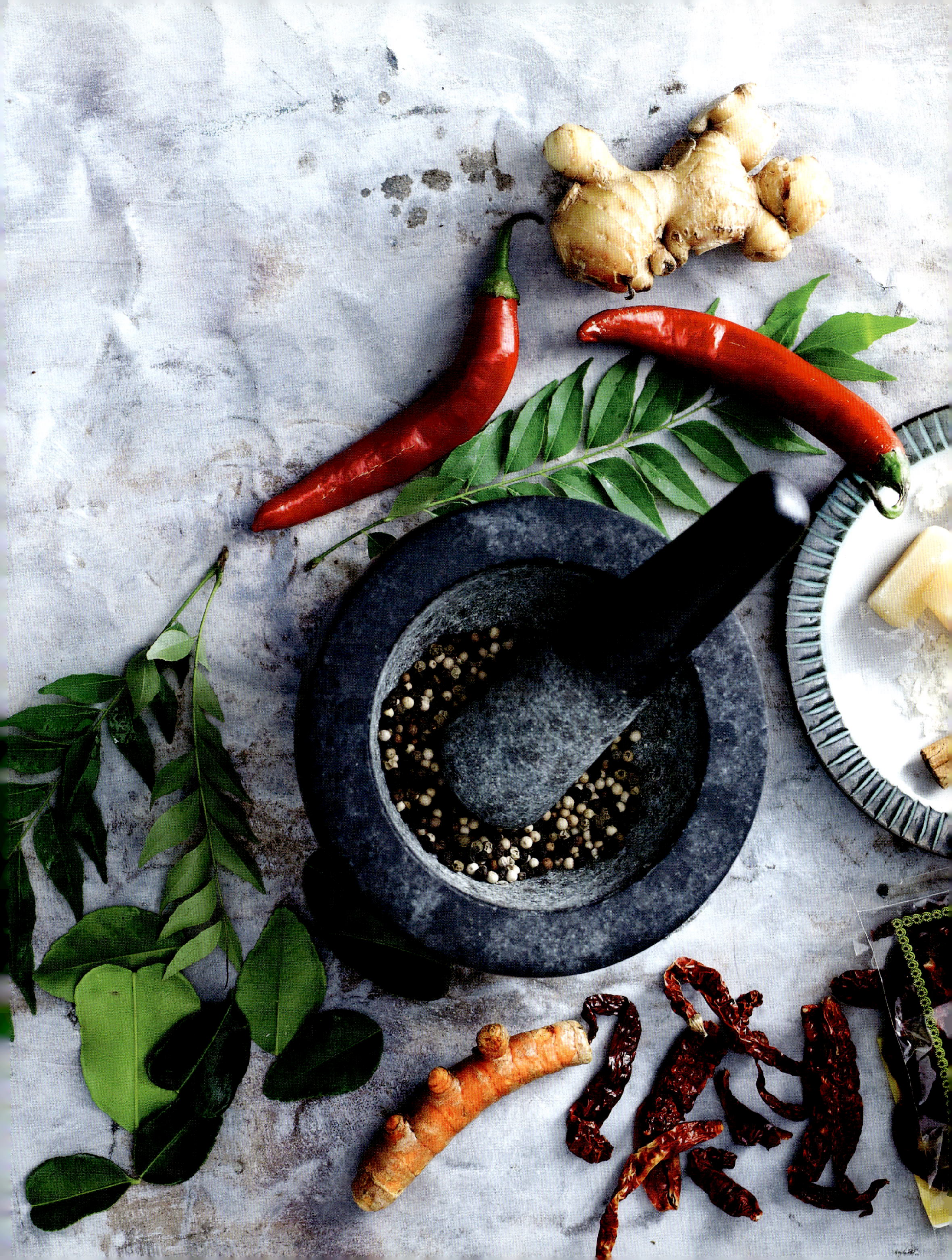

PANANG BEEF CURRY

PREP + COOK TIME 1 HOUR SERVES 4

500g (1 pound) beef rump steak
1 tablespoon kecap manis
1 clove garlic, crushed
2 tablespoons peanut oil
2 tablespoons fish sauce
2 tablespoons grated palm sugar
8 kaffir lime leaves, torn
400ml (12½ ounces) canned coconut milk
100g (3 ounces) snake beans, cut into 8cm (3¼-inch) lengths
125g (4 ounces) baby corn
¼ cup coarsely chopped coriander (cilantro)
1 long red chilli, seeded, sliced thinly

CURRY PASTE
5 long red chillies, chopped
1 teaspoon table salt
2 teaspoons chopped coriander (cilantro) root
3cm piece ginger (15g), sliced
10cm (4-inch) stick lemon grass (20g), sliced
2 red shallots (50g), chopped
2 cloves garlic, chopped
¼ cup (60ml) water
½ cup (75g) roasted peanuts

1. Combine beef, kecap manis, garlic and half the oil in a medium bowl, turning the beef to coat. Cover; refrigerate for 1 hour.
2. Make curry paste.
3. Heat remaining oil in a wok or large frying pan; stir-fry ½ cup of the paste until fragrant. Add fish sauce, sugar and kaffir lime leaves; stir-fry 1 minute. Add coconut milk; bring to the boil. Reduce heat; simmer 10 minutes or until thickened.
4. Meanwhile, preheat an oiled grill pan (or barbecue or grill) over medium heat.
5. Cook beef on a heated grill pan for 3 minutes each side for medium rare. Transfer to a plate, cover; rest for 5 minutes. Slice beef thickly.
6. Stir beans and corn into wok; simmer 5 minutes or until just tender. Serve curry topped with beef, coriander and chilli.

CURRY PASTE
Blend or process all the ingredients, except for peanuts, until smooth. Add peanuts; blend until combined.

TIPS Although the curry paste recipe makes 1 cup, you only need ½ cup for the curry recipe. Freeze the remaining paste for up to 3 months.
The beef can be marinated and curry paste made up to 3 days ahead.

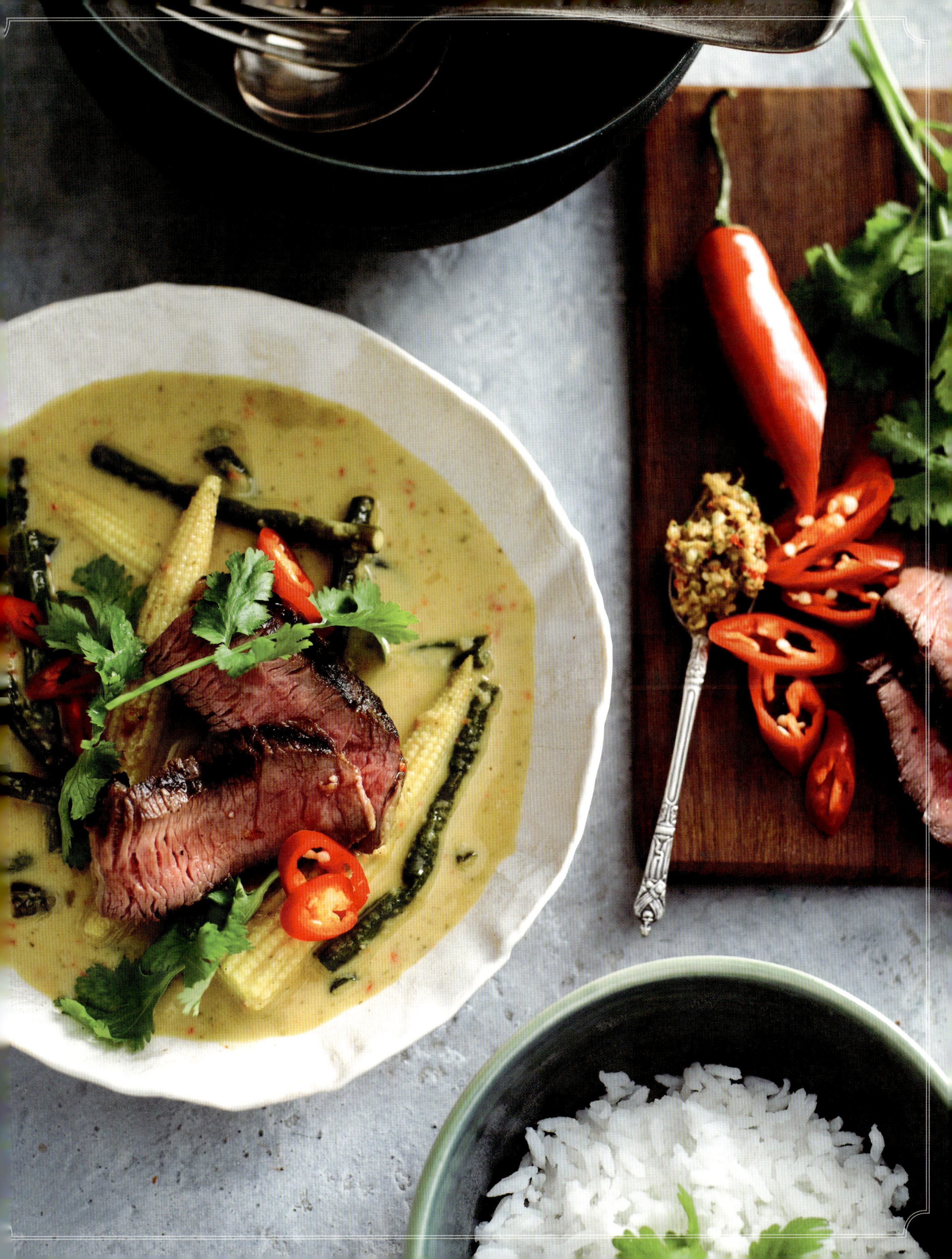

CREAMY COCONUT
Pork Curry

PREP + COOK TIME *30 MINUTES* **SERVES** *4*

1 tablespoon peanut oil
600g (1¼ pounds) pork fillet, cut into 2cm (¾-inch) pieces
1 large brown onion (300g), sliced thinly
¼ cup (75g) thai red curry paste
1 large red capsicum (bell pepper) (350g), sliced thinly
150g (4½ ounces) snake or green beans, cut into lengths
400g (12½ ounces) canned chopped tomatoes
1⅔ cups (400ml) coconut milk
⅓ cup fresh coriander (cilantro) leaves

1. Heat half the oil in a large non-stick frying pan over high heat; cook pork, in batches, for 5 minutes or until browned and just cooked through. Remove from pan.
2. Heat remaining oil in same pan over medium heat; cook onion, stirring, for 5 mintues or until soft. Add curry paste; cook, stirring, until fragrant. Add capsicum, beans and tomatoes, bring to the boil; cook for 5 minutes or until beans are just tender and mixture has thickened slightly.
3. Return pork and any juices to the pan with coconut milk; stir until heated through. Stir in half the coriander leaves.
4. Serve curry topped with remaining coriander leaves.

SERVING SUGGESTION Serve with steamed jasmine rice.

SPICY DHAL

PREP + COOK TIME *50 MINUTES* **SERVES** *10*

1½ tablespoons vegetable oil or ghee
1 large brown onion (200g), chopped finely
4 cloves garlic, crushed
1½ teaspoons ground cumin
1½ teaspoons garam masala
½ teaspoon ground turmeric
pinch chilli powder
1½ cups (300g) yellow split peas, rinsed
1.125 litres (4½ cups) water
2 large brown onions (400g), extra sliced thinly
¼ cup coarsely chopped fresh coriander (cilantro)

1. Heat half the oil in a medium saucepan over medium heat; cook onion and garlic, stirring, for 5 minutes or until onion softens. Add spices; cook, stirring, until fragrant.
2. Add split peas and the water; bring to the boil. Reduce heat; simmer for 40 minutes or until split peas are tender. Season with salt.
3. Heat remaining oil in a medium heavy-based frying pan over medium heat; cook extra onions, stirring occasionally, for 15 minutes or until browned.
4. Serve dhal topped with onion and coriander.

TIP For a more fragrant dhal, add 6 fresh curry leaves with the split peas. Any leftover curry leaves can be frozen, then used directly from the freezer as you need them.

CREAMY COCONUT
Pork Curry

SPICY DHAL

ASIAN BANQUET

THAI GREEN
Prawn Curry

(RECIPE PAGE 146)

SPICY CHICKEN
Salad

(RECIPE PAGE 38)

MACADAMIA FILLO TARTS
with Caramelised Pineapple

(RECIPE PAGE 136)

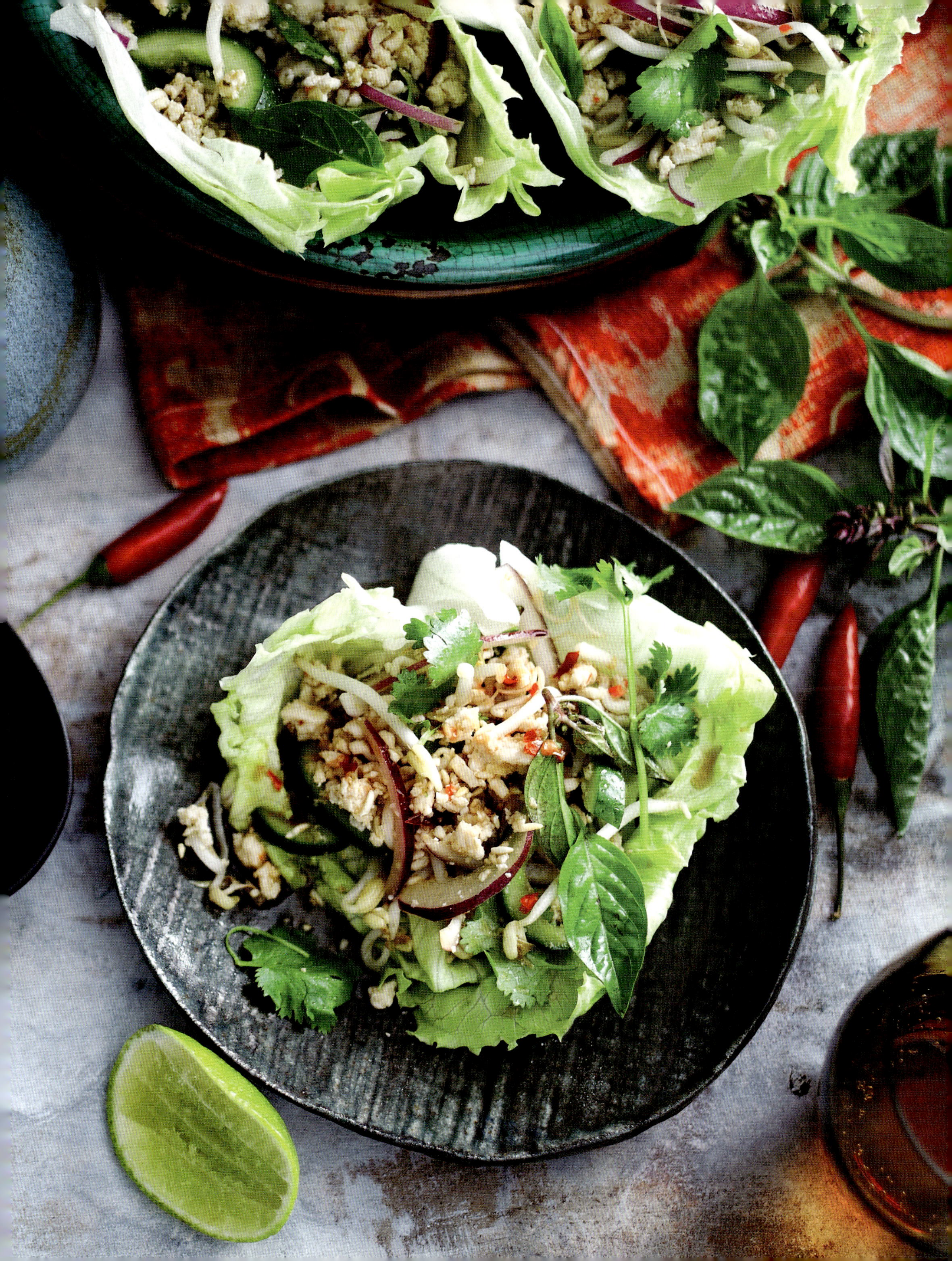

THAI GREEN PRAWN CURRY

PREP + COOK TIME *25 MINUTES* **SERVES** *4*

24 uncooked medium prawns (shrimp) (1kg)
1 tablespoon vegetable oil
¼ cup (75g) thai green curry paste
4 kaffir lime leaves
10cm (4-inch) stick lemon grass (20g), cut into three pieces
2 cups (500ml) coconut milk
¾ cup (180ml) water
1½ tablespoons fish sauce
150g (4½ ounces) snake beans, cut into 4cm (1½-inch) pieces
⅓ cup (50g) fresh or frozen peas
2 teaspoons grated palm sugar or brown sugar
½ cup fresh thai basil leaves
2 limes, cut into wedges

1. Shell and devein prawns, leaving tails intact. Butterfly prawns by cutting along the centre back of prawns, without cutting all the way through.
2. Heat oil in a large frying pan over medium heat; cook curry paste, lime leaves and lemon grass, stirring for 3 minutes or until fragrant. Add coconut milk, the water, sauce, beans and peas; simmer, stirring, for 3 minutes or until beans and peas are almost tender.
3. Add prawns; cook for 1 minute or until prawns are just cooked through. Stir in sugar. Season to taste with extra fish sauce or sugar, if needed.
4. Serve curry with basil and lime wedges.

TIP You can use green beans if snake beans are not available and coriander if you can't find thai basil.

SERVING SUGGESTION Serve with steamed jasmine rice.

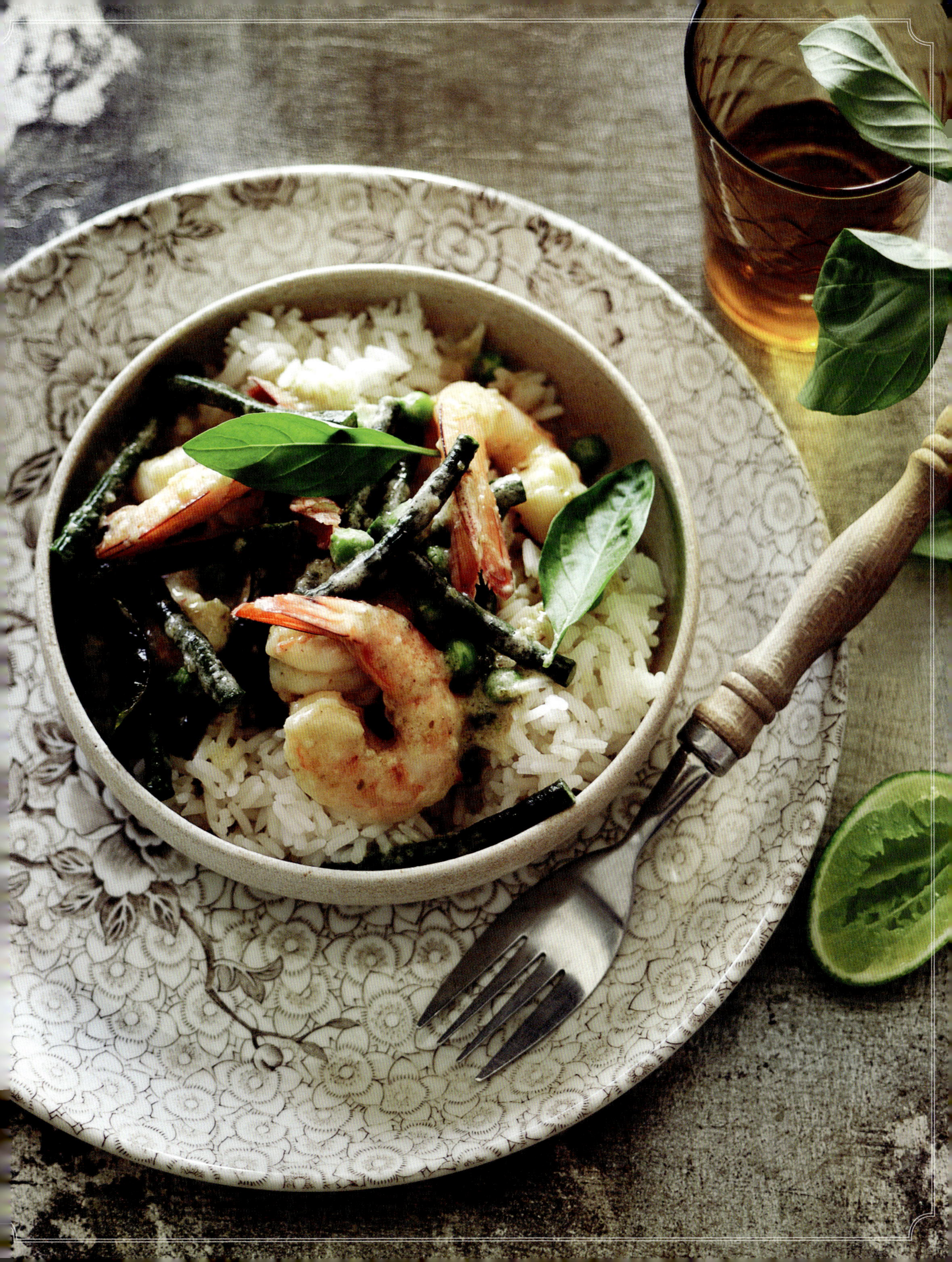

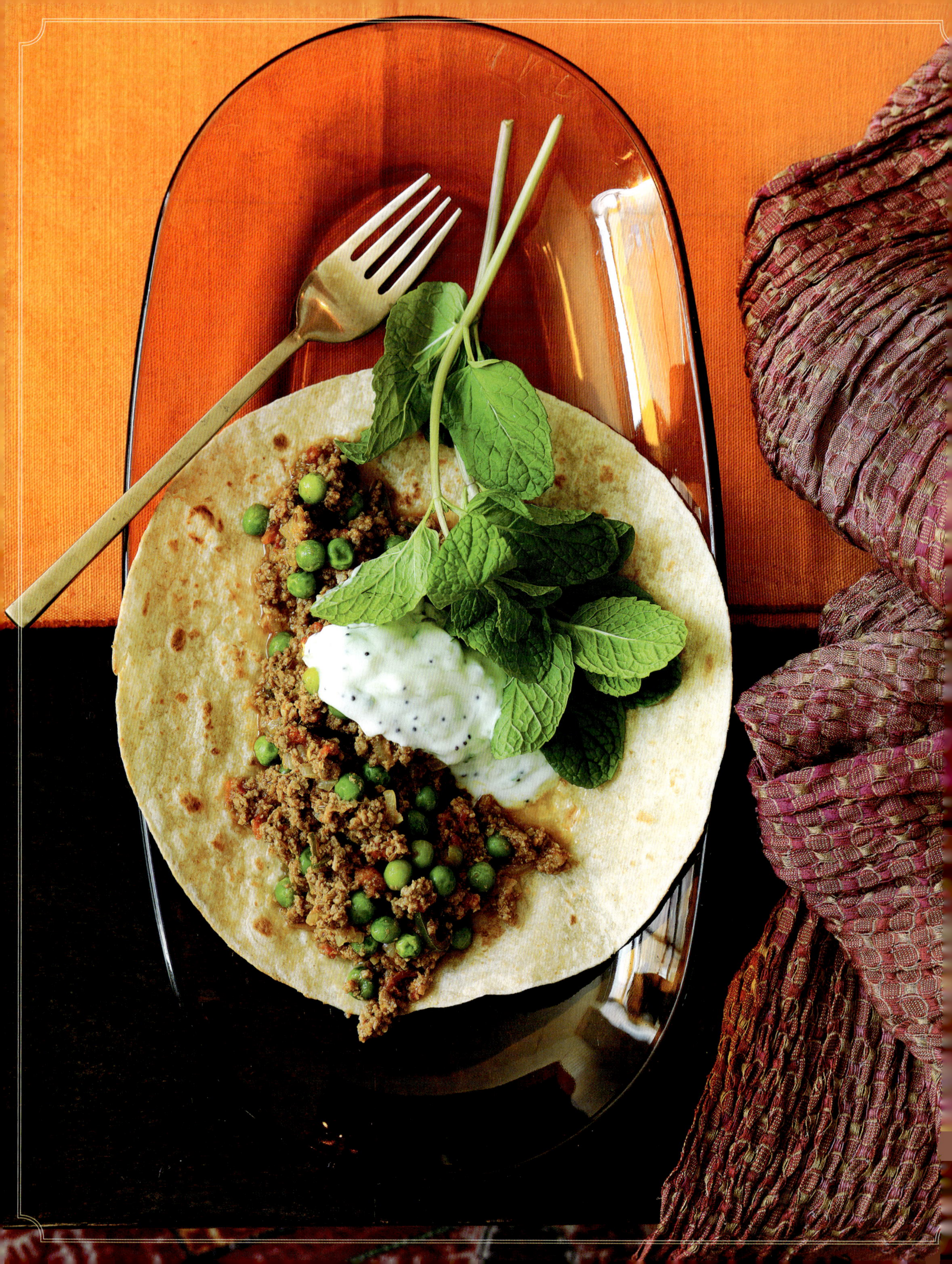

LAMB KEEMA

PREP + COOK TIME *1 HOUR* **SERVES** *10*

2 tablespoons vegetable oil or ghee
2 medium brown onions (300g), chopped finely
10cm (4-inch) piece fresh ginger (50g), grated finely
4 cloves garlic, crushed
4-6 long green chillies, chopped finely
1 tablespoon cumin seeds
1 tablespoon ground coriander
1 teaspoon ground turmeric
1 tablespoon garam masala
1.5kg (3 pounds) minced (ground) lamb
800g (1½ pounds) canned chopped tomatoes
2 cups (240g) frozen peas
2 tablespoons lemon juice
⅔ cup (200g) yoghurt
10 indian flat breads (chapatti, naan or paratha)
¼ cup fresh mint sprigs

1 Heat oil in a large heavy-based saucepan over medium heat; cook onion, ginger, garlic and two-thirds of the chilli, stirring, for 5 minutes or until onion softens. Add spices; cook, stirring, until fragrant. Add lamb; cook, stirring, breaking up the lumps with a spoon until browned.
2 Add tomatoes; cook, stirring, occasionally, for 20 minutes or until mince mixture has thickened. Season with salt.
3 Stir in remaining chilli and peas; cook for 3 minutes or until peas are tender. Stir in juice and yoghurt.
4 Serve keema with flat breads and mint sprigs.

SERVING SUGGESTION Serve with a cucumber raita: combine 1 seeded, coarsely grated lebanese cucumber with 1 cup (280g) Greek-style yoghurt, 1 teaspoon ground cumin and 2 tablespoons finely chopped mint in a small bowl.

Casseroles & Curries

SLOW-COOKER BUTTER CHICKEN

PREP + COOK TIME *4 HOURS 30 MINUTES (+ REFRIGERATION)* **SERVES 6**

12 chicken thigh cutlets (2.4kg), skin removed
2 tablespoons lemon juice
1 teaspoon chilli powder
¾ cup (200g) Greek-style yoghurt
5cm (2-inch) piece fresh ginger (25g), grated
2 teaspoons garam masala
45g (1½ ounces) butter
1 tablespoon vegetable oil
1 medium brown onion (150g), chopped finely
4 cloves garlic, crushed
1 teaspoon ground coriander
1 teaspoon ground cumin
1 teaspoon sweet paprika
2 tablespoons tomato paste
410g (13 ounces) canned tomato purée
⅔ cup (160ml) chicken stock
2 tablespoons honey
1 cinnamon stick
⅓ cup (80ml) pouring cream
⅓ cup (80g) fresh ricotta
½ cup loosely packed fresh coriander (cilantro) leaves

1. Combine chicken, juice and chilli powder in a large bowl. Cover; refrigerate 30 minutes.
2. Stir yoghurt, ginger and half the garam masala into chicken mixture.
3. Heat butter and oil in a large frying pan over medium heat; cook chicken, in batches, for 5 minutes or until browned all over. Transfer mixture to a 4.5-litre (18-cup) slow cooker.
4. Cook onion and garlic in same frying pan until onion softens. Add remaining garam masala and ground spices; cook, stirring, until fragrant. Remove from heat; stir in tomato paste, purée, stock, honey and cinnamon. Transfer mixture to slow cooker. Cook, covered, on low, for 4 hours.
5. Stir in cream; season to taste. Serve topped with ricotta and coriander leaves.

TIP If you don't have a slow cooker, after browning the chicken, simmer in a heavy-based saucepan on the stove top for 1½ hours or until tender.

SERVING SUGGESTION Serve with steamed basmati rice and warm naan bread.

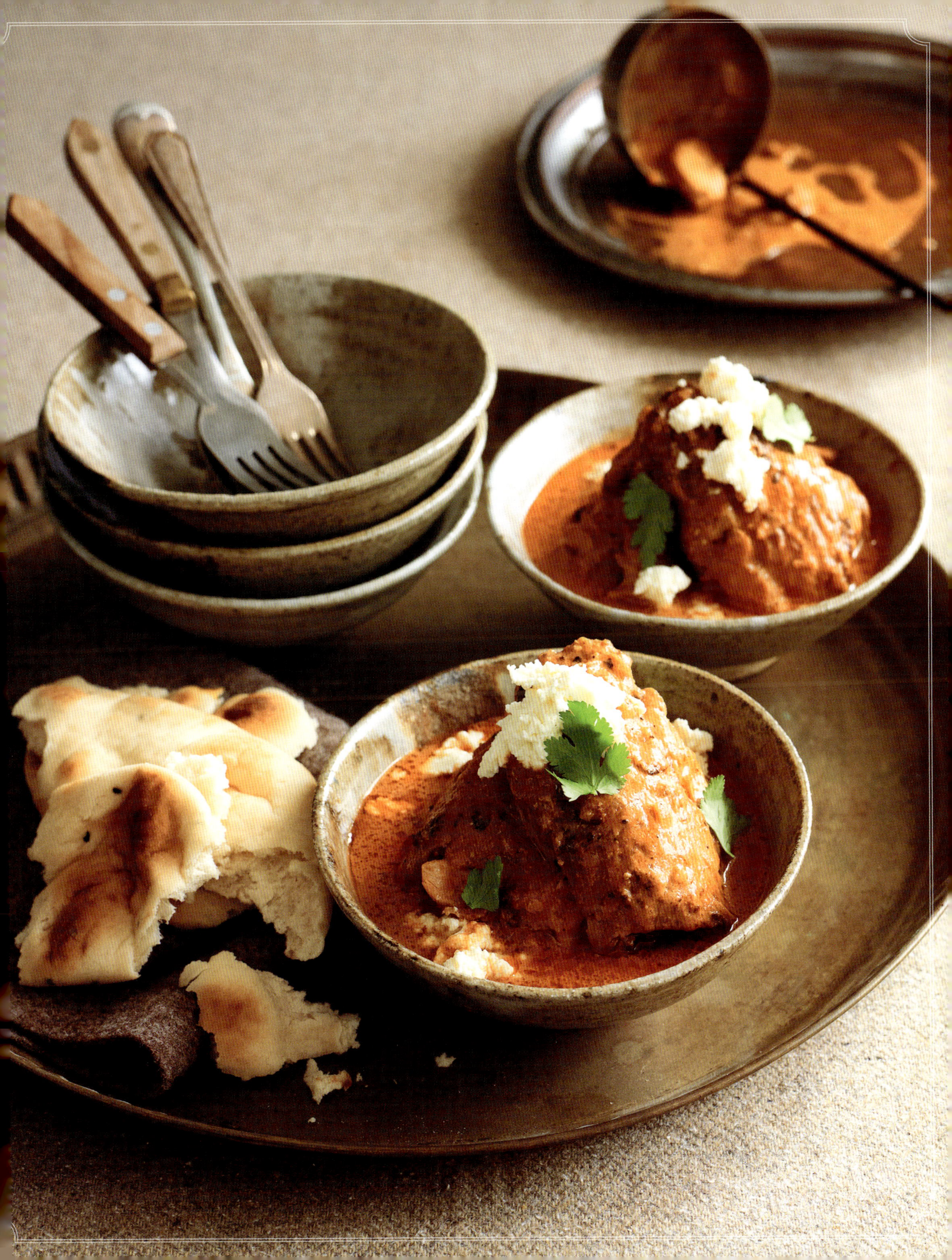

NEPALESE PORK
Mince Curry

NEPALESE PORK
Mince Curry

PREP + COOK TIME *35 MINUTES* **SERVES 4**

This dry, fragrant Nepalese curry, traditionally served with steamed rice and lime wedges, is one of this remote Himalayan country's most popular meat dishes.

2 tablespoons peanut oil
2 tablespoons yellow mustard seeds
2 teaspoons ground cumin
1 teaspoon ground turmeric
2 teaspoons garam masala
3 cloves garlic, crushed
4cm (1½-inch) piece fresh ginger (20g), grated
2 medium brown onions (300g), chopped finely
800g (1½ pounds) minced (ground) pork
1 cup (250ml) chicken stock
¼ cup coarsely chopped fresh coriander (cilantro)
1 lebanese cucumber (130g), sliced

1 Heat oil in a large frying pan over medium heat; cook seeds, stirring, for 2 minutes or until seeds pop. Add cumin, turmeric and garam masala; cook, stirring, for 2 minutes or until fragrant.
2 Add garlic, ginger and onion; cook, stirring, for 5 minutes or until onion softens.
3 Add mince; cook, stirring, breaking up with a spoon, until cooked through. Add stock; simmer 15 minutes for flavours to develop. Season to taste.
4 Remove from heat, stir in coriander. Serve with cucumber slices.

CAULIFLOWER
and Green Pea Curry

PREP + COOK TIME *50 MINUTES* **SERVES 4**

This is a fabulous simple curry for a vegetarian or serve it with one of the meat curries as part of an Indian banquet.

2 tablespoons ghee or oil
1 medium brown onion (150g), chopped finely
2 cloves garlic, crushed
2cm (¾-inch) piece fresh ginger (10g), grated
¼ cup (75g) hot curry paste
¾ cup (180ml) pouring cream
600g (1¼ pounds) cauliflower florets
2 large tomatoes (440g), chopped coarsely
1 cup (120g) frozen peas
1 cup (280g) yoghurt
3 hard-boiled eggs, sliced thinly
¼ cup finely chopped fresh coriander (cilantro)

1 Heat ghee or oil in a large saucepan over medium heat; cook onion, garlic and ginger, stirring, 5 minutes or until onion softens. Add paste; cook, stirring, until mixture is fragrant.
2 Add cream; bring to the boil, then reduce heat. Add cauliflower and tomato; simmer, uncovered, for 5 minutes, stirring occasionally.
3 Add peas and yoghurt; stir over low heat for 5 minutes or until peas and cauliflower are just cooked.
4 Serve curry with egg and coriander.

SERVING SUGGESTION Serve with rice and/or indian flatbreads such as naan, chapatti or paratha.

(PHOTOGRAPH PAGE 154)

CAULIFLOWER
and Green Pea Curry

(RECIPE PAGE 153)

CHICKEN KORMA
(RECIPE PAGE 156)

CHICKEN KORMA

PREP + COOK TIME *1 HOUR 10 MINUTES (+ REFRIGERATION)*
SERVES *10*

The Australian Women's Weekly has been at the forefront of culinary trends introducing readers as far back as the early 1960s, to curries from not just India but, Java, Nepal and Pakistan. Korma is a mild and creamy curry perfect for those who don't like too much spice or heat.

290g (9 ounces) bottled korma curry paste
⅔ cup (200g) yoghurt
4 cloves garlic, crushed
1.75kg (3½ pounds) chicken thigh fillets, sliced thickly
2 tablespoons vegetable oil or ghee
4 medium onions (600g), sliced thinly
3 medium tomatoes (450g), chopped
2 cups (500ml) water
⅓ cup (40g) ground almonds
½ cup coarsely chopped fresh coriander (cilantro)

1 Combine paste, yoghurt and garlic in a large bowl with chicken. Cover; refrigerate 3 hours or overnight.
2 Heat oil in a large heavy-based saucepan over medium heat; cook onion, stirring, for 10 minutes or until soft and browned lightly. Increase heat to high, add chicken mixture; cook, stirring, until chicken is sealed and has changed colour.
3 Add tomatoes and the water; bring to the boil. Reduce heat; simmer, covered, for 20 minutes. Stir in almonds; simmer, uncovered, for another 20 minutes or until sauce has thickened slightly. Season with salt.
4 Serve korma topped with coriander.

SERVING SUGGESTION Serve with naan bread.

(PHOTOGRAPH PAGE 155)

LAMB SHANKS
with Risoni and Tomato

PREP + COOK TIME *2 HOURS 50 MINUTES* **SERVES** *6*

8 french-trimmed lamb shanks (2kg)
½ cup (75g) plain (all-purpose) flour
2 tablespoons olive oil
4 cloves garlic, crushed
½ cup (125ml) white wine
400g (12½ ounces) canned chopped tomatoes
2 tablespoons tomato paste
1 litre (4 cups) chicken stock
1 cup (220g) risoni pasta
3 small zucchini (270g), chopped coarsely
½ cup fresh flat-leaf parsley leaves
1 teaspoon thinly sliced lemon rind

1 Preheat oven to 160°C/325°F.
2 Toss lamb in flour, shake away excess flour. Heat oil in a large casserole over medium heat; cook lamb, in two batches, turning for 5 minutes or until well browned all over.
3 Add garlic to pan; cook, stirring, for 1 minute or until fragrant. Add wine; boil until almost evaporated. Stir in tomatoes, paste and stock; bring to the boil. Cover pan tightly with foil; transfer to the oven, cook for 2 hours.
4 Add risoni and zucchini to dish; cook, covered, for a further 40 minutes or until tender.
5 Serve lamb and risoni topped with parsley and rind.

LAMB SHANKS
with Risoni and Tomato

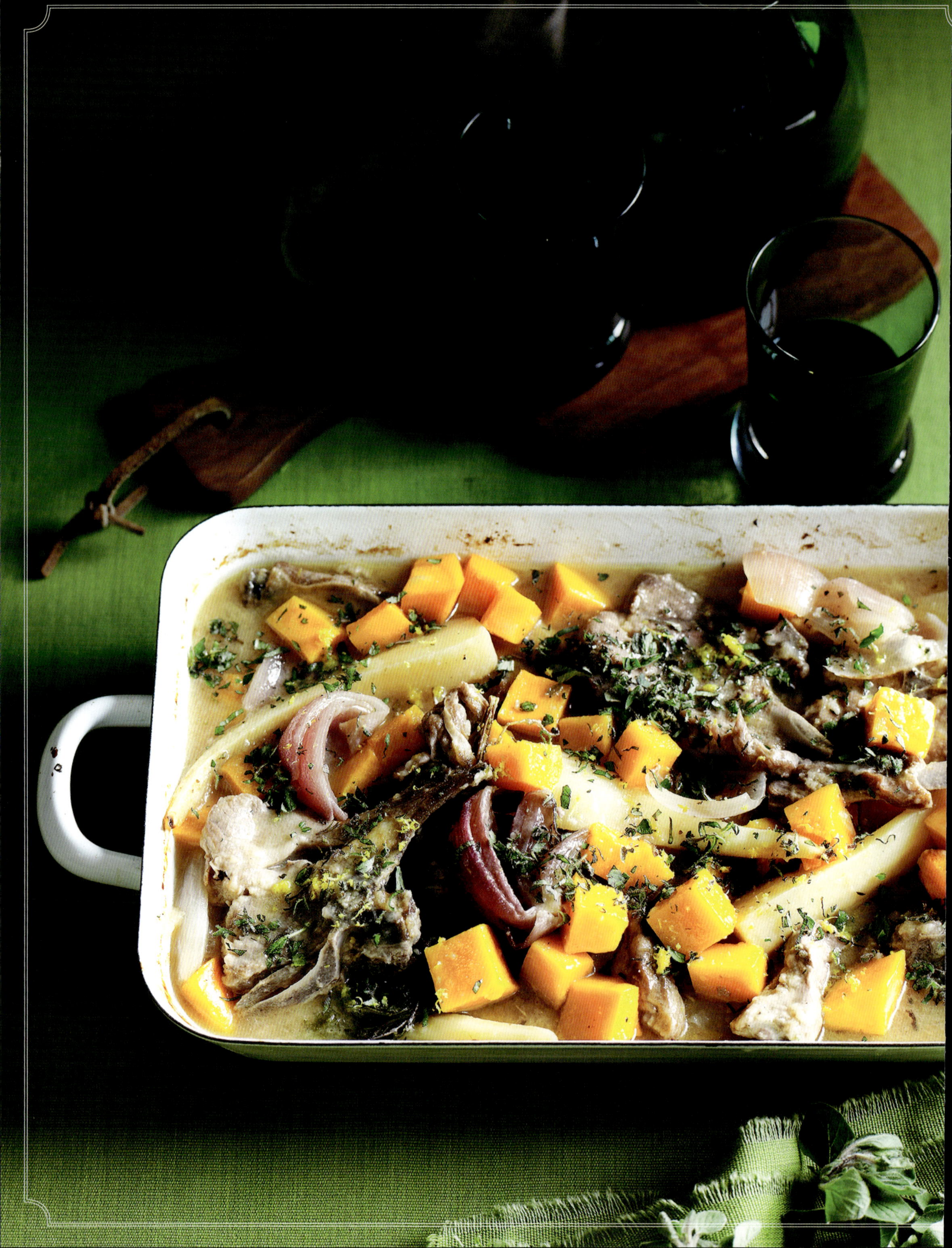

LEMON-SCENTED LAMB CASSEROLE
with Winter Vegetables

PREP + COOK TIME 3 HOURS SERVES 4

1 bay leaf
3 sprigs fresh oregano
3 stalks fresh flat-leaf parsley
1kg (2 pounds) best neck lamb chops
2 tablespoons plain (all-purpose) flour
2 tablespoons olive oil
3 small red onions (300g), quartered
3 cloves garlic, sliced
⅓ cup (80ml) lemon juice
3 cups (750ml) salt-reduced chicken stock
2 medium parsnips (500g), halved, quartered lengthways
800g (1½ pounds) butternut pumpkin, cut into 2cm (¾-inch) cubes
2 teaspoons finely grated lemon rind
1 tablespoon chopped fresh oregano

1. Preheat oven to 160°C/325°F. Make a bouquet garni by tying the bay leaf, oregano sprigs and parsley stalks together with kitchen string.
2. Coat lamb in flour seasoned with some salt and freshly ground black pepper; shake away excess flour.
3. Heat 1 tablespoon of the oil in a large ovenproof dish over medium-high heat; cook lamb, in two batches, for 5 minutes or until browned all over. Remove from pan.
4. Heat remaining oil in same dish over medium heat; cook onion for 5 minutes or until soft. Add garlic; cook, stirring, for 1 minute or until fragrant.
5. Add ¼ cup (60ml) of the juice; bring to the boil. Cook, stirring, until juice is reduced by about half.
6. Return lamb with any juices to dish with bouquet garni; stir in stock and parsnips. Bring to the boil. Cover; cook in oven for 1½ hours or until lamb is very tender. Place pumpkin on top of casserole (don't stir in); cook, covered, a further 10 minutes or until pumpkin is tender.
7. Add remaining juice; top with rind and oregano.

SERVING SUGGESTION Serve with mashed potatoes.

COQ AU VIN

PREP + COOK TIME *1 HOUR 50 MINUTES* **SERVES** *8*

20g (¾ ounce) butter
1 tablespoon extra virgin olive oil
100g (3 ounces) speck, rind removed, cut into 1cm (½-inch) pieces
16 small chicken thigh cutlets (3.2kg), skin on, trimmed
1kg (2 pounds) pickling onions, peeled
2 medium carrots (240g), sliced thickly
2 trimmed celery sticks (200g), sliced thickly
3 cloves garlic, sliced
4 sprigs fresh thyme
4 bay leaves
2 cups (500ml) dry red wine
2 cups (500ml) chicken stock
400g (12½ ounces) button mushrooms
2 tablespoons cornflour (cornstarch)
¼ cup (60ml) water
½ cup fresh flat-leaf parsley leaves

1. Preheat oven to 150°C/300°F.
2. Heat butter and oil in a large casserole or baking dish over medium heat; cook speck, stirring occasionally for 8 minutes or until browned. Remove with a slotted spoon; drain on paper towel.
3. Cook chicken in same dish, in batches, 3 minutes each side or until browned; drain on paper towel. Remove all but 2 teaspoons of fat from the dish.
4. Add onions, carrot, celery, garlic, thyme and bay leaves to same dish; cook, stirring, until vegetables are fragrant. Add wine; bring to the boil. Reduce heat; simmer, uncovered, until reduced by half.
5. Add stock, then speck and chicken; bring to the boil. Cover with a tight-fitting lid; cook in oven for 1 hour. Add mushrooms; cook, covered, for a further 30 minutes or until chicken is tender. Using a slotted spoon, transfer chicken and vegetables to a serving dish; cover to keep warm.
6. Add blended cornflour and the water to sauce; stir until sauce boils and thickens. Season. Pour sauce over chicken and vegetables. Serve topped with parsley.

TIPS You can use 8 thighs and 8 drumsticks instead of the chicken thigh cutlets, if you like.
Cut the button mushrooms into quarters if they are large.

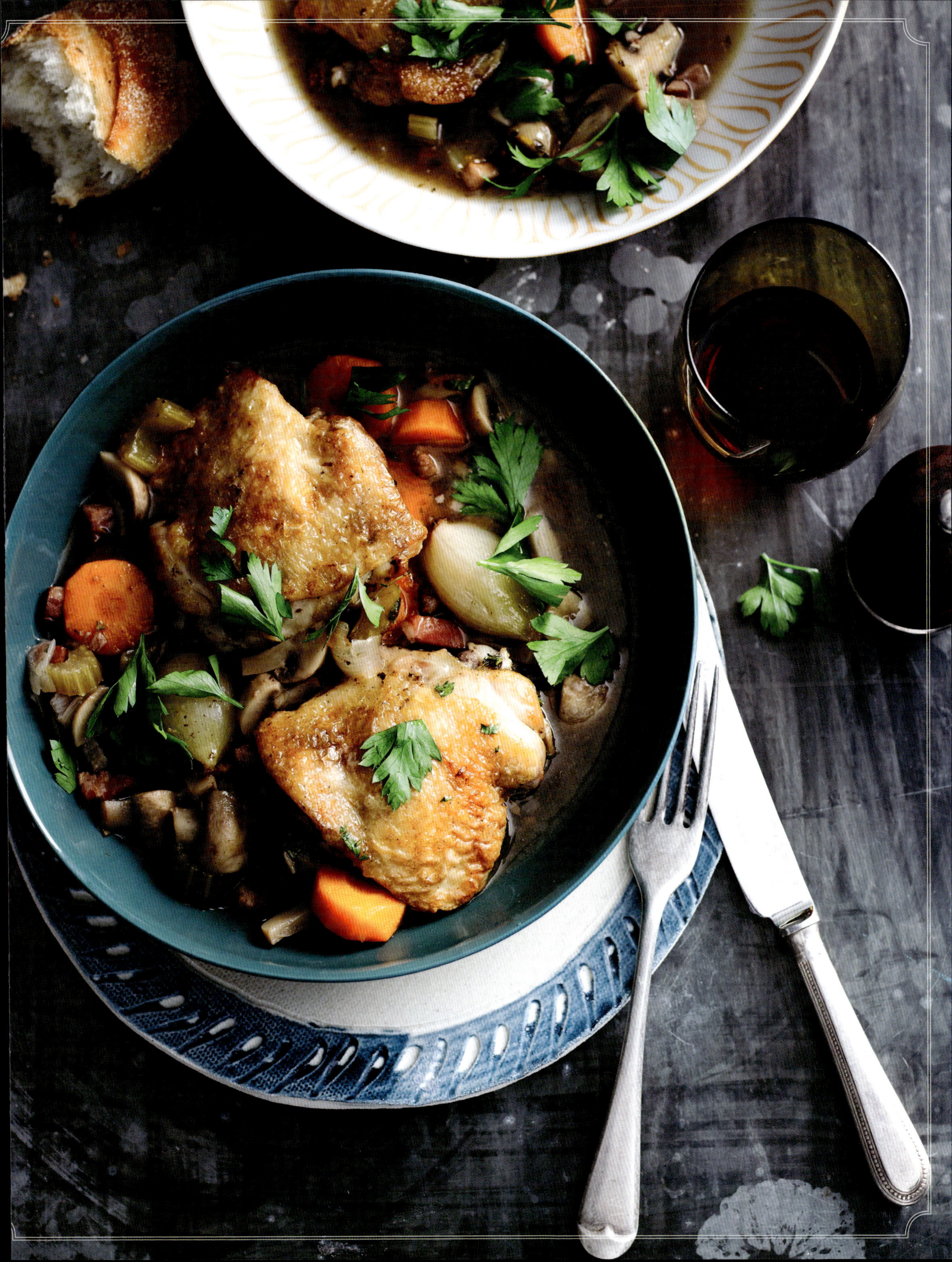

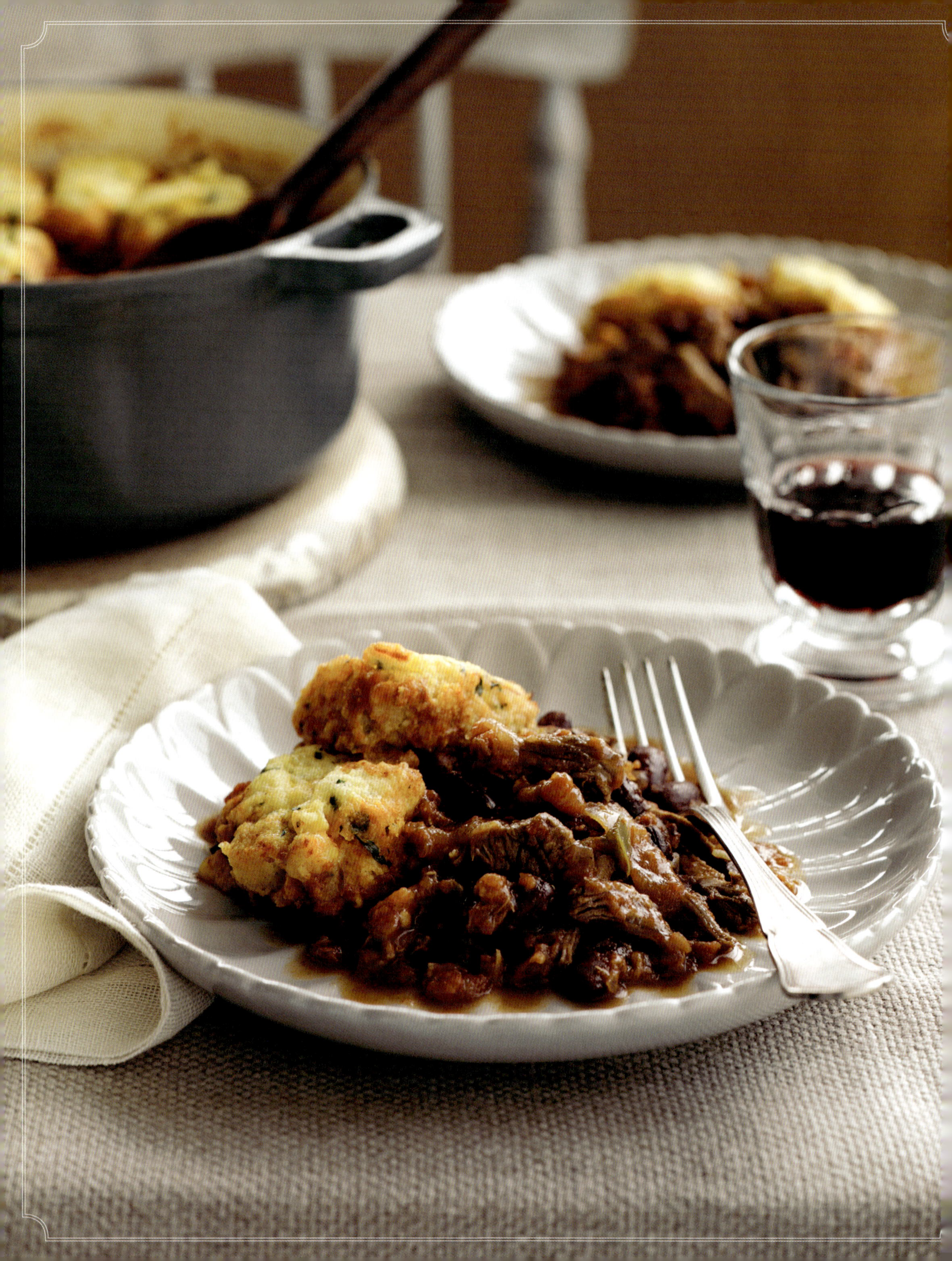

CHILLI CON CARNE
with Corn Dumplings

PREP + COOK TIME 3 HOURS 10 MINUTES SERVES 6

2 tablespoons olive oil
1.5kg (3 pounds) chuck steak, cut into 4cm (1½-inch) cubes
2 medium brown onions (300g), chopped
2 cloves garlic, crushed
1 large green capsicum (bell pepper) (350g), chopped coarsely
2 teaspoons sweet paprika
2 teaspoons ground cumin
2 teaspoons chilli powder
800g (1½ pounds) canned whole peeled tomatoes
2 tablespoons tomato paste
1 cup (250ml) beef stock
400g (12½ ounces) canned red kidney beans, drained, rinsed

CORN DUMPLINGS
½ cup (75g) self-raising flour
½ cup (85g) polenta
50g (1½ ounces) butter, chopped
1 egg, beaten lightly
¼ cup (30g) coarsely grated cheddar
¼ cup chopped fresh coriander (cilantro)
130g (4 ounces) canned corn kernels, drained
1 tablespoon milk, approximately

1. Heat half the oil in a large casserole over high heat; cook steak, in batches, for 5 minutes or until browned all over. Remove from dish.
2. Heat remaining oil in same dish; cook onion, garlic and capsicum, stirring, for 5 minutes or until vegetables soften. Add spices; cook, stirring until fragrant.
3. Return steak to dish with tomatoes, paste and stock; bring to the boil. Reduce heat; simmer, covered, for 2½ hours or until tender.
4. Remove a quarter of the steak; shred coarsely using two forks. Return to pan with kidney beans. Season to taste with salt. If sauce is too liquid, simmer, uncovered, until reduced.
5. Make corn dumplings.
6. Drop level tablespoons of corn dumpling mixture, about 2cm (¾ inch) apart, on top of the steak mixture. Simmer, covered, for 20 minutes or until dumplings are cooked through.

CORN DUMPLINGS
Place flour and polenta in a medium bowl; rub in butter. Stir in egg, cheese, coriander, corn and enough milk to make a soft, sticky dough.

PORTUGUESE
Seafood Stew

PREP + COOK TIME *1 HOUR 15 MINUTES* **SERVES** *8*

8 small cleaned squid (320g)
16 small black mussels (325g)
16 uncooked medium prawns (shrimp) (400g)
4 uncooked small blue swimmer crabs (1kg)
800g (1½ pounds) canned whole tomatoes
2 tablespoons olive oil
2 large brown onions (400g), sliced
3 cloves garlic, crushed
1 large red capsicum (bell pepper) (350g), sliced
150g (4½ ounces) prosciutto, chopped coarsely
½ cup (125ml) dry white wine
1 bay leaf
2 tablespoons tomato paste
2 tablespoons fresh flat-leaf parsley leaves

1. Cut squid into rings. Scrub mussels; remove beards. Shell and devein prawns, leaving tails intact. Cut crabs into quarters, rinse well; remove grey gills.
2. Blend or process tomatoes until smooth.
3. Heat oil in a large saucepan over medium heat; cook onion and garlic, stirring, for 5 minutes or until onion is soft. Add capsicum and prosciutto; cook, stirring, for 5 minutes or until soft.
4. Add wine, bay leaf, paste and pureed tomato; bring to the boil. Reduce heat; simmer, uncovered, until sauce is reduced by half.
5. Add seafood to pan; stir to coat in sauce. Simmer, covered, for 10 minutes or until seafood is just cooked through. Season to taste.
6. Serve stew topped with parsley.

TIPS Use a selection of seafood of your choice for this recipe. Lobster, octopus, clams and any firm white fish would all make suitable substitutes. You can also use red onions instead of the brown we used here.

SERVING SUGGESTION Serve with lemon wedges and crusty bread.

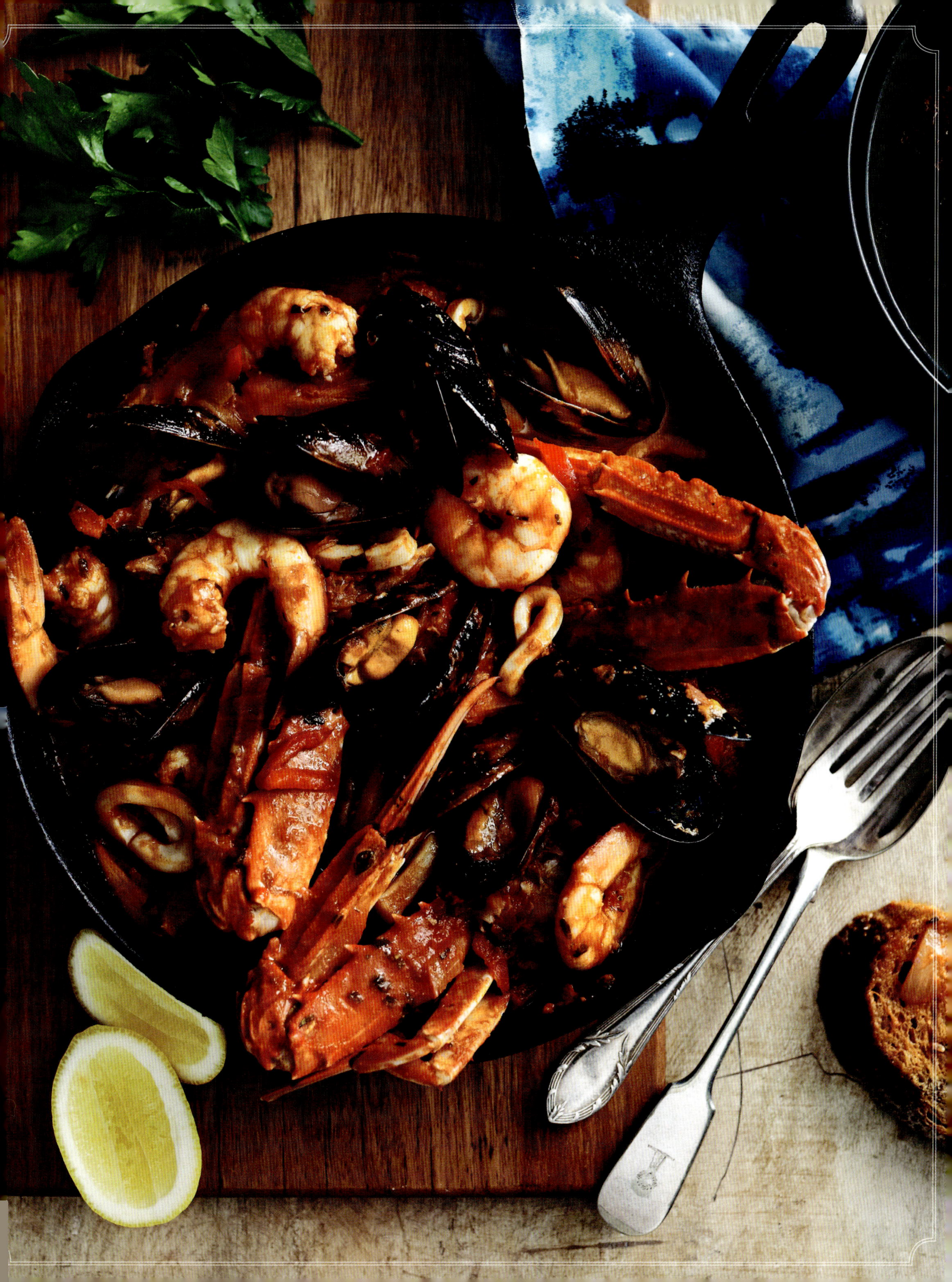

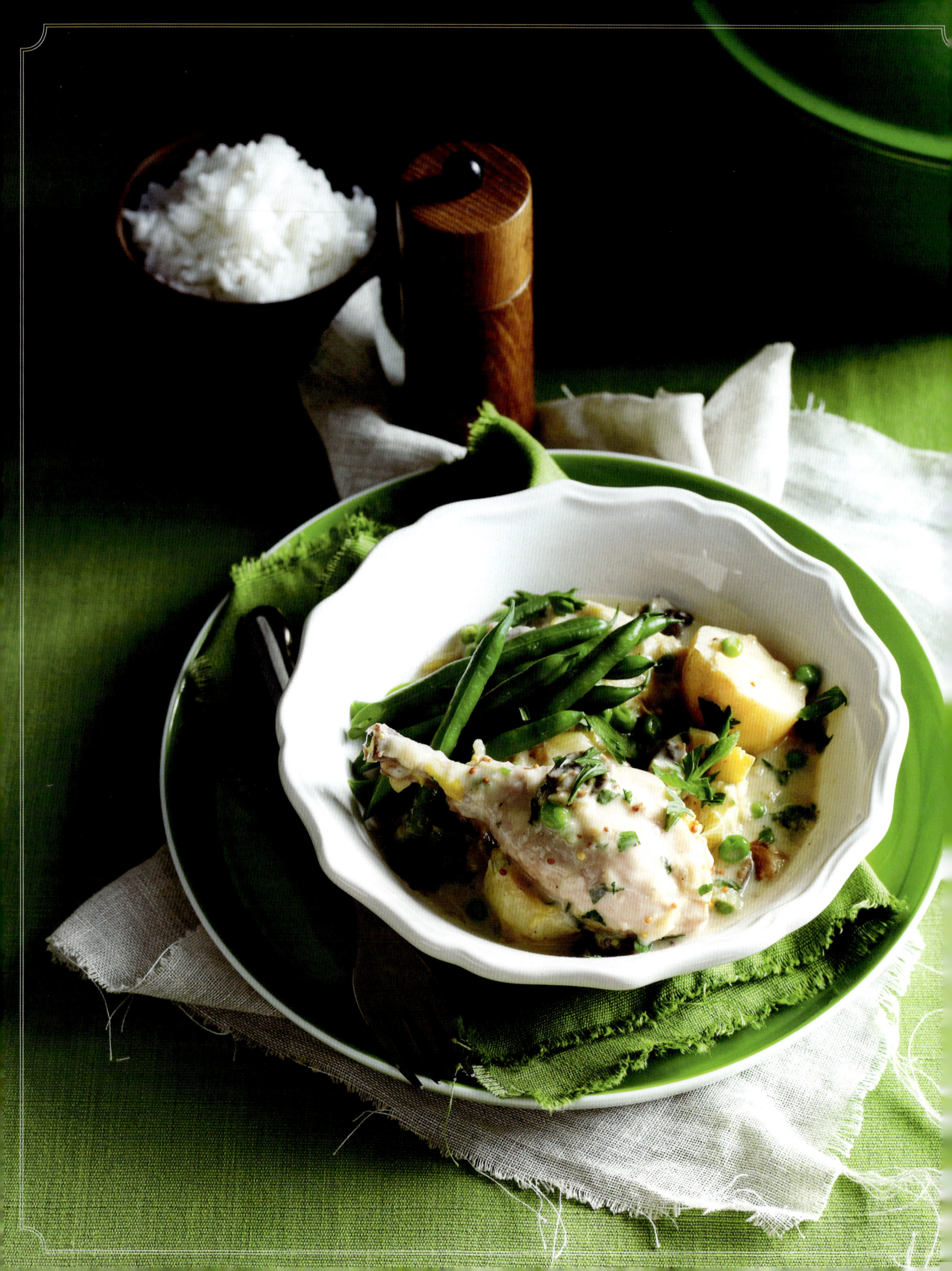

MUSTARD CHICKEN
Casserole

PREP + COOK TIME *1 HOUR 30 MINUTES* **SERVES** *4*

1 bay leaf
3 sprigs fresh thyme
3 stalks fresh flat-leaf parsley
4 trimmed skinless chicken drumsticks (520g)
4 chicken thigh fillets (800g), trimmed, halved
2 tablespoons plain (all-purpose) flour
2 tablespoons olive oil
2 medium leeks (700g), white part only, halved lengthways, sliced
2 cloves garlic, crushed
½ cup (125ml) dry white wine
1 cup (250ml) salt-reduced chicken stock
8 baby new potatoes (320g), halved
120g (4 ounces) button mushrooms, sliced thickly
1 tablespoon wholegrain mustard
¼ cup (60ml) pouring cream
¾ cup (90g) frozen baby peas, thawed
2 tablespoons chopped fresh flat-leaf parsley

1. Preheat oven to 160°C/325°F. Make a bouquet garni by tying the bay leaf, thyme sprigs and parsley stalks together with kitchen string.
2. Coat chicken in flour seasoned with salt and freshly ground black pepper; shake away excess flour.
3. Heat half the oil in a large casserole over medium-high heat; cook chicken, in two batches, 5 minutes or until browned all over. Remove from pan.
4. Heat remaining oil in same dish over medium heat; cook leek, for 2 minutes or until softened slightly. Add garlic; cook, stirring, 1 minute or until fragrant.
5. Add wine; bring to the boil. Cook, stirring until reduced by half.
6. Return chicken and any juices to dish with bouquet garni, stock, potatoes and mushrooms. Bring to the boil. Cover; cook in the oven for 1 hour or until chicken is very tender. Stir in mustard, cream, peas and parsley; stand, covered, for 5 minutes. Remove bouquet garni before serving.

TIP Trimmed skinless chicken drumsticks are sometime called "lovely legs" and are available from specialty chicken shops. If you can't find them, just remove the skin from regular drumsticks.

SERVING SUGGESTION Serve with green vegetables.

FAST FISH TAGINE

PREP + COOK TIME *30 MINUTES* **SERVES 4**

4 blue-eye trevalla fillets (800g), skin on, halved widthways
2 tablespoons chermoulla or moroccan spice mix
2 tablespoons olive oil
1 large brown onion (200g), sliced thinly
3 cloves garlic, crushed
1 medium lemon (140g), sliced thinly
¾ cup (95g) pitted green olives
1 cup (250ml) salt-reduced chicken stock
1 teaspoon caster (superfine) sugar
2 tablespoons coarsely chopped fresh coriander (cilantro)

CORIANDER COUSCOUS
1 cup (200g) couscous
1 cup (250ml) boiling water
½ cup firmly packed fresh coriander (cilantro) leaves

1. Preheat oven to 200°C/400°F.
2. Place fish and chermoulla in a large bowl; toss fish to coat well.
3. Heat half the oil in a large flameproof baking dish over medium heat; cook onion and garlic, stirring, for 5 minutes or until softened. Remove from dish.
4. Heat remaining oil in same dish; cook fish, in batches, for 1 minute each side or until browned all over. Remove from dish.
5. Return onion mixture to dish with lemon slices, olives, stock and sugar; bring to the boil. Transfer dish to oven; bake, uncovered, for 10 minutes or until fish is just cooked through. Remove from oven; sprinkle with chopped coriander.
6. Meanwhile, make coriander couscous.
7. Serve tagine with couscous.

CORIANDER COUSCOUS
Combine couscous and the water in a medium heatproof bowl. Cover; stand 5 minutes or until the liquid is absorbed, fluffing with a fork occasionally. Stir in coriander.

TIP If your baking dish isn't flameproof, cook the onion, garlic and fish in a large non-stick frying pan as per the recipe. Transfer the mixture to the baking dish with lemon, olives, stock and sugar before placing it in the oven.

SERVING SUGGESTION Serve with steamed zucchini.

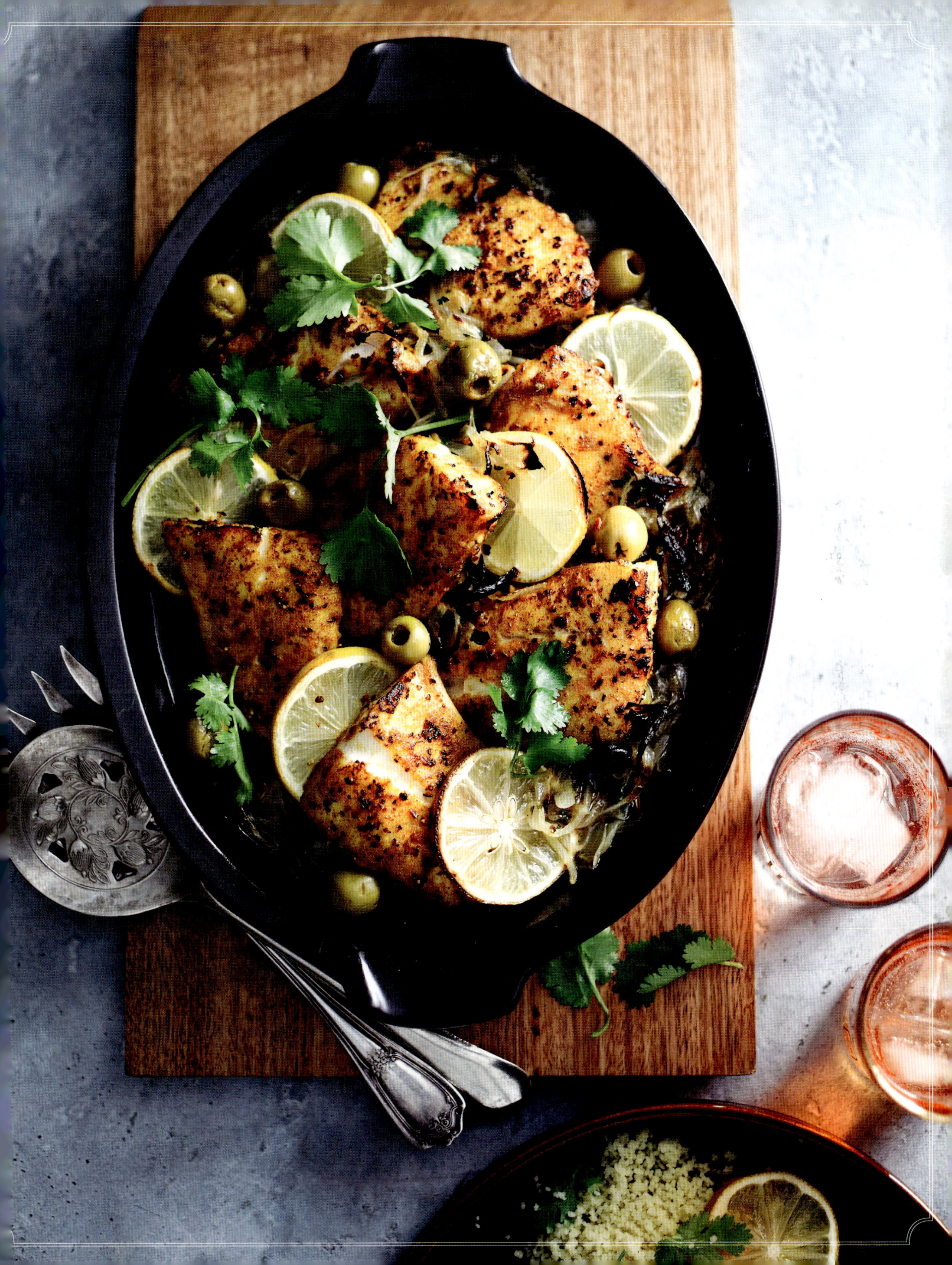

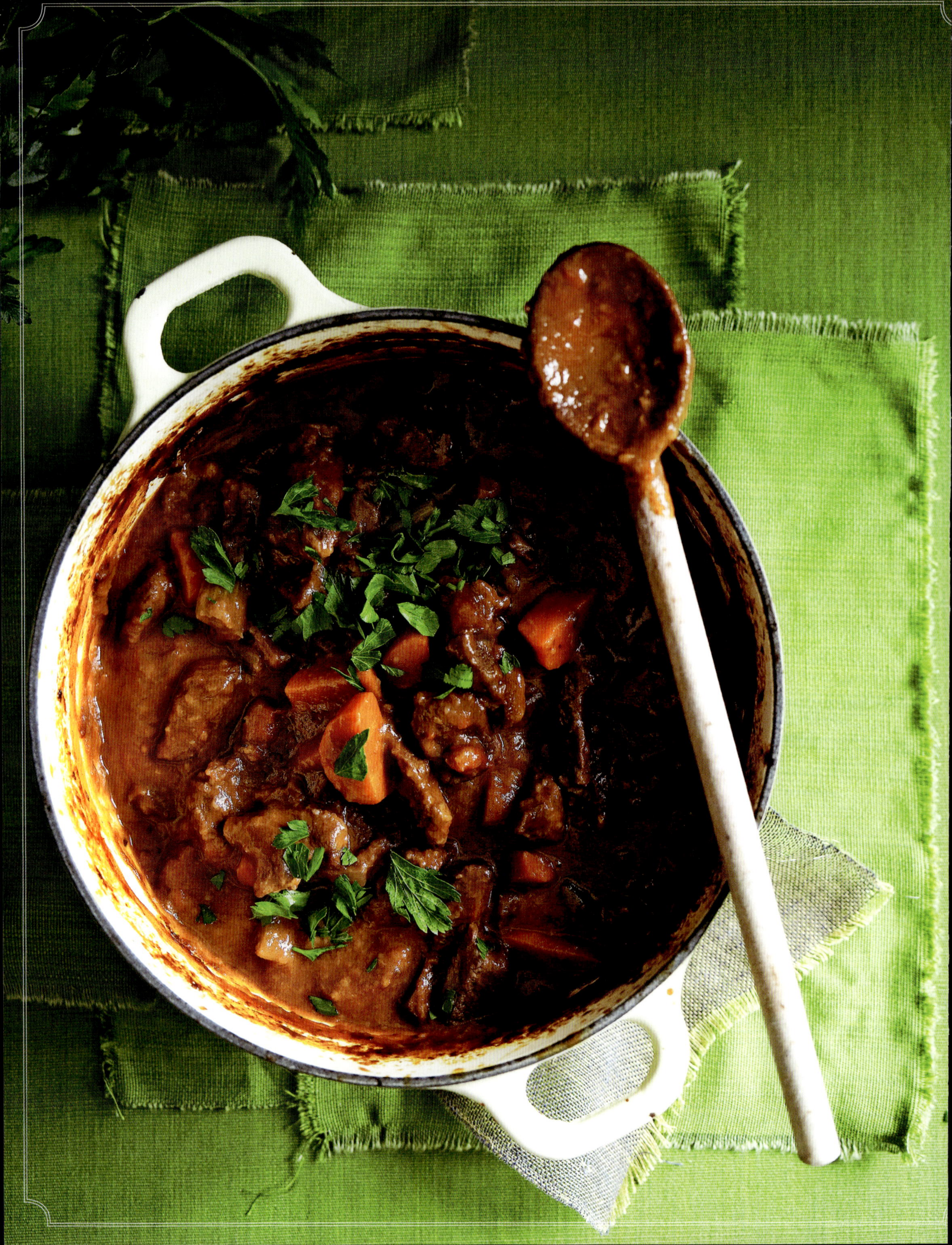

TRADITIONAL BEEF
Casserole

PREP + COOK TIME *2 HOURS 45 MINUTES* **SERVES 4**

Casseroles are the great backbone of winter cooking, asking little of the cook with their simple ingredients and cheaper cuts of meat, except perhaps a little patience as ingredients meld creating a great depth of flavour.

2 bay leaves
3 sprigs fresh thyme
3 stalks fresh flat-leaf parsley
1kg (2 pounds) chuck steak, trimmed, cut into 3cm (1¼-inch) cubes
2 tablespoons plain (all-purpose) flour
2 tablespoons olive oil
1 medium brown onion (150g), chopped
2 medium carrots (240g), halved, sliced thickly
2 trimmed celery sticks (200g), sliced thickly
2 garlic cloves, crushed
1 cup (250ml) dry red wine
1 cup (250ml) salt-reduced beef stock
400g (12½ ounces) canned diced tomatoes
2 tablespoons chopped fresh flat-leaf parsley

1. Preheat oven to 160°C/325°F. Make a bouquet garni by tying the bay leaves, thyme sprigs and parsley stalks together with kitchen string.
2. Coat beef in flour seasoned with salt and freshly ground black pepper; shake away excess flour.
3. Heat half the oil in a large casserole over medium-high heat; cook beef, in two batches, for 5 minutes or until browned on all sides. Remove from dish.
4. Add remaining oil to same dish; cook onion, carrot and celery over medium heat for 2 minutes or until browned lightly. Add garlic; cook, stirring, for 1 minute or until fragrant.
5. Add wine; increase heat to medium-high, bring to the boil. Cook, stirring, until wine is reduced by half.
6. Return beef and any juices to dish with stock, tomatoes and bouquet garni; stir to combine. Bring to the boil. Cover; cook in the oven for 2 hours or until meat is very tender. Remove bouquet garni. Serve casserole sprinkled with parsley.

SERVING SUGGESTION Serve with mashed potatoes.

OSSO BUCO

PREP + COOK TIME *3 HOURS* **SERVES 4**

This popular recipe first appeared in the September 1975 issue of The Australian Women's Weekly magazine. Osso buco are cross sections of the shank, they require long, slow cooking but reward the cook with tender moist meat. While the traditional accompaniment is risotto milanese, soft polenta or mashed potatoes also work really well.

8 pieces veal osso buco (2kg)
½ cup (75g) plain (all-purpose) flour
90g (3 ounces) butter
1 tablespoon olive oil
2 large brown onions (400g), chopped
2 medium carrots (240g), chopped
3 trimmed celery sticks (300g), chopped
2 cloves garlic, crushed
2 tablespoons tomato paste
1 cup (250ml) dry red wine
1½ cups (375ml) beef stock
800g (1½ pounds) canned whole tomatoes
1 teaspoon fresh thyme leaves
1 bay leaf
2.5cm (1-inch) strip lemon rind

GREMOLATA
1 clove garlic, crushed
2 tablespoons thinly sliced lemon rind
¼ cup fresh flat-leaf parsley leaves

1. Preheat oven to 160°C/325°F.
2. Coat veal in flour seasoned with salt and freshly ground black pepper; shake away excess.
3. Heat 60g (2 ounces) of the butter with the oil in a large casserole over medium heat; cook veal, in batches, 3 minutes each side or until browned all over. Remove from pan.
4. Add remaining butter to pan; cook onion, carrot, celery and garlic, stirring for 10 minutes or until vegetables soften.
5. Return veal to pan with tomato paste, stirring for 2 minutes or until meat is coated with vegetables. Add remaining ingredients; bring to the boil. Cover; bake in oven for 1¾ hours or until meat is tender. Season to taste.
6. Meanwhile, make gremolata.
7. Serve osso buco sprinkled with gremolata.

GREMOLATA
Combine ingredients in a small bowl.

TIP Don't overlook the marrow in the bones when you are eating the osso buco; it's considered one of the great delicacies of this dish.

SERVING SUGGESTION Serve with risotto milanese (recipe page 174).

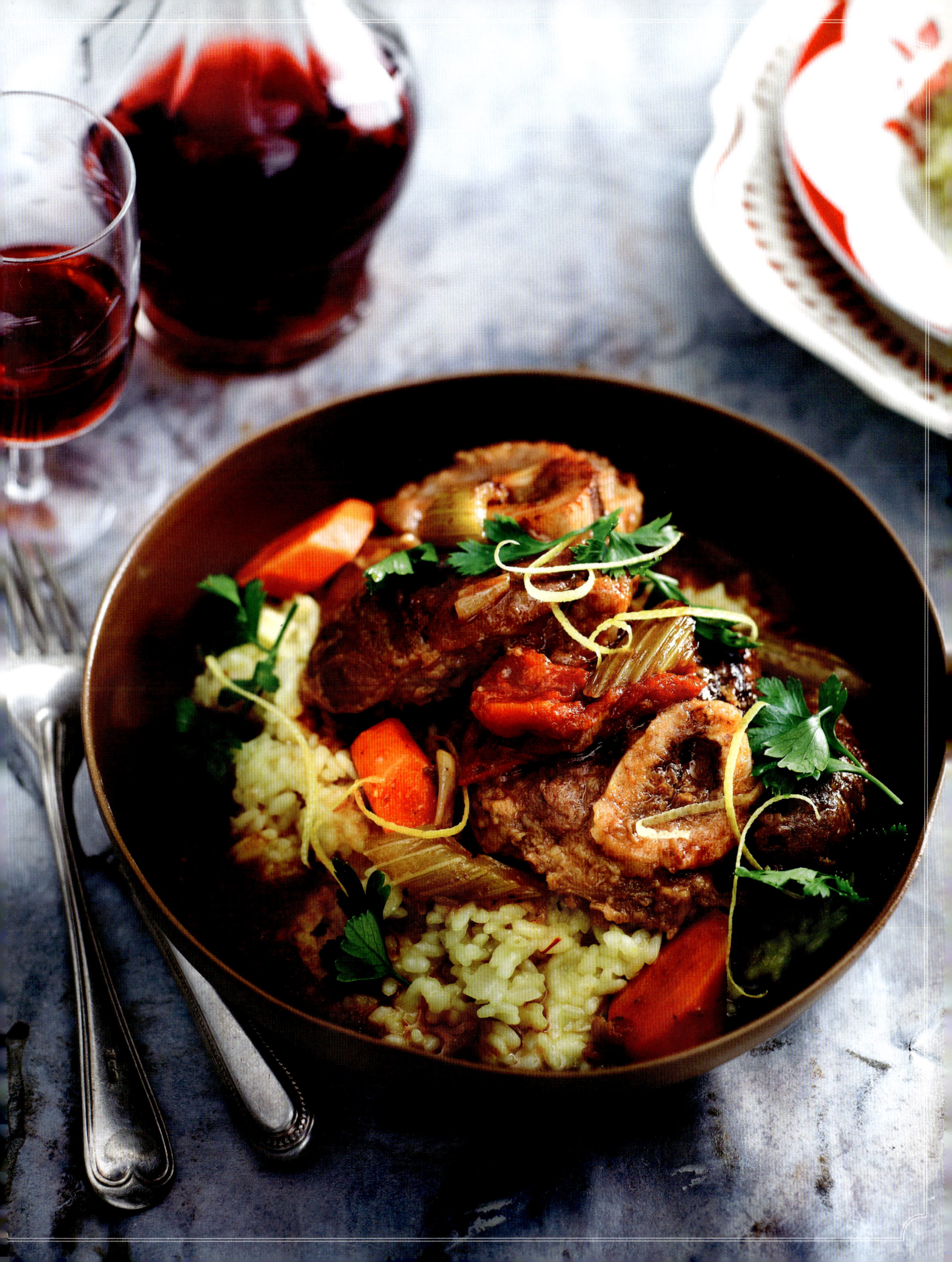

RISOTTO MILANESE

PREP + COOK TIME *45 MINTUES* **SERVES 4**

1 litre (4 cups) chicken stock
¼ teaspoon saffron threads
90g (3 ounces) butter
1 large brown onion (200g), chopped finely
½ cup (125ml) dry white wine
200g (6½ ounces) arborio rice
80g (2½ ounces) finely grated parmesan

1 Bring stock and saffron to the boil in a medium saucepan. Reduce heat to low, cover and keep at a gentle simmer.
2 Heat 60g (2 ounces) of the butter in a large saucepan over medium heat; cook onion, stirring for 5 minutes or until soft. Increase heat to high; add wine, stir for 2 minutes or until reduced by half. Reduce heat to medium; add rice, stir for 2 minutes or until slightly transparent.
3 Add stock, ½ cup at a time, stirring between each addition until liquid has been absorbed and rice is tender. (This will take about 20 minutes.) Stir in parmesan and season to taste. Serve with osso buco (recipe page 172).

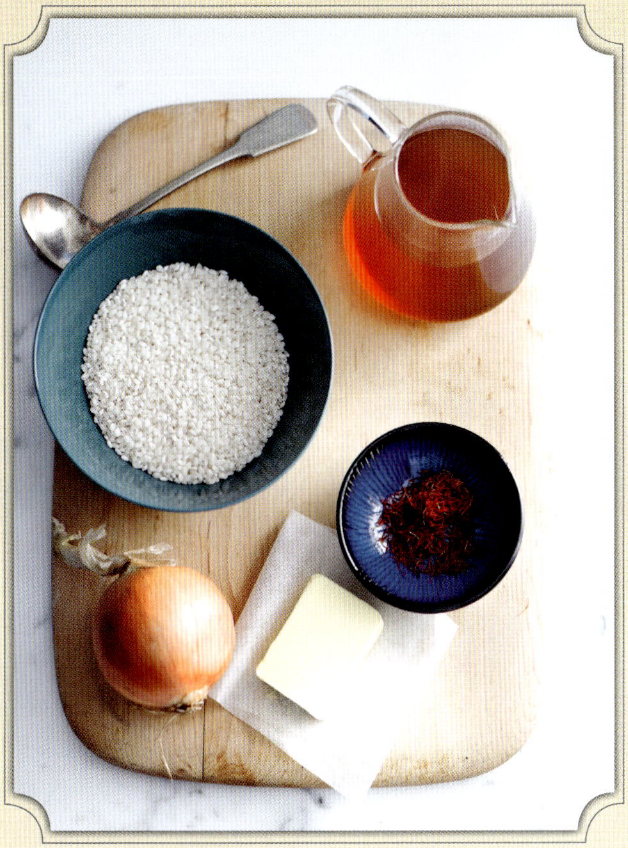
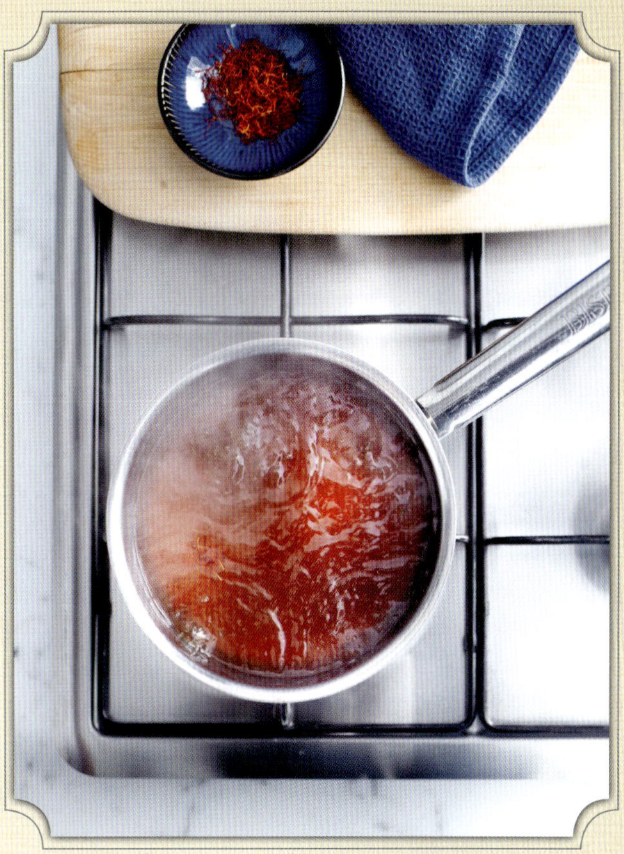
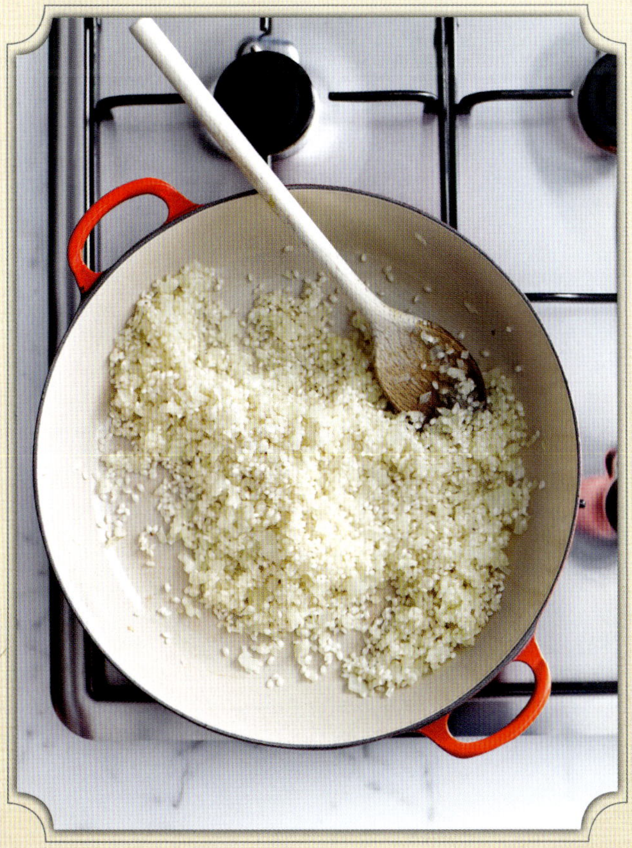
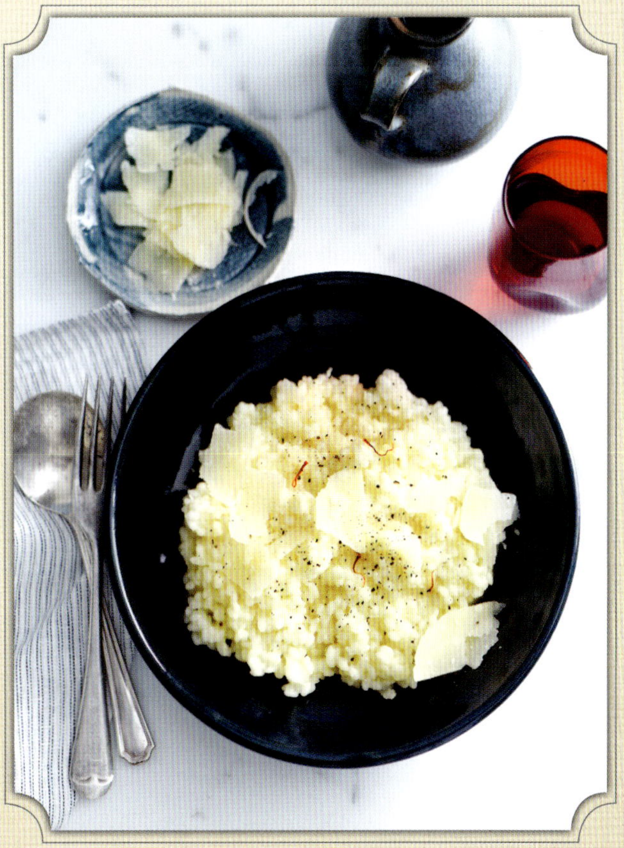

CHAPTER 6
ROASTS & BAKES

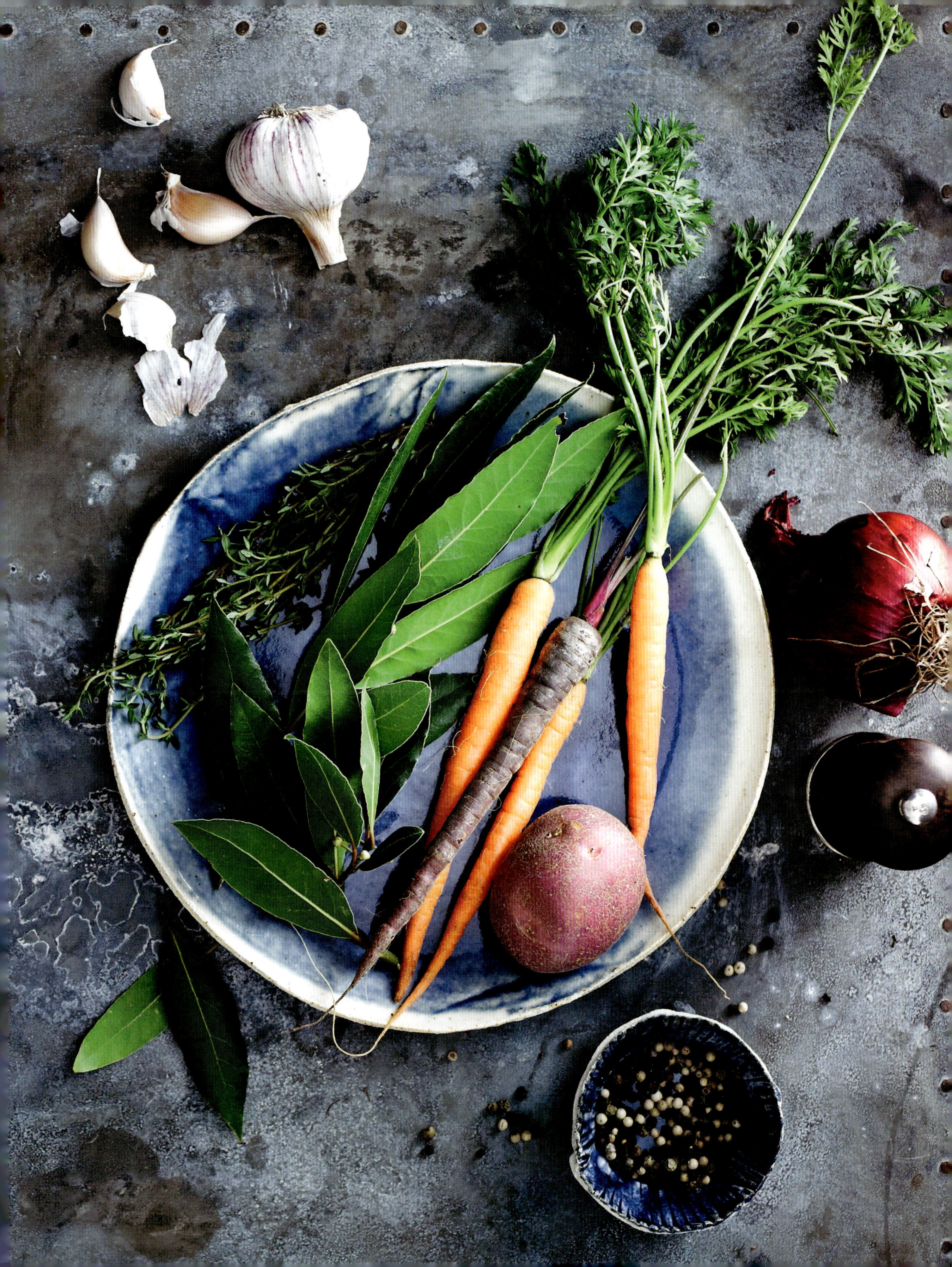

CLASSIC ROAST CHICKEN
and Gravy

PREP + COOK TIME 1 HOUR 45 MINUTES / SERVES 4

We've used a classic French technique for roasting our chicken to keep it moist and succulent. First, the chicken is cooked upside down to allow juices into the leaner breast meat, before finishing it the right-way up to brown and crisp the skin.

50g (1½ ounces) butter, softened
1 clove garlic, crushed
1.4kg (2¾-pound) whole chicken
3 medium brushed potatoes (sebago) (500g), quartered lengthways
3 medium carrots (320g), halved lengthways, then halved widthways
2 medium white onions (285g), cut into wedges
1 tablespoon olive oil
1 tablespoon plain (all-purpose) flour
1½ cups (375ml) salt-reduced chicken stock

1. Preheat oven to 220°C/400°F.
2. Combine butter and garlic in a small bowl; season. Rinse chicken under cold water; pat dry inside and out with paper towel. Starting from neck end of breast, carefully separate skin from flesh of chicken without tearing the skin. Using your fingers, spread garlic butter evenly under skin to cover chicken breasts. Tie legs together with kitchen string.
3. Toss vegetables and oil together in a flameproof roasting pan; season. Push vegetables to outer sides of dish; place chicken in the centre, breast-side down. Roast 20 minutes. Turn chicken breast-side up, turn vegetables, baste both with pan juices. Roast a further 40 minutes, basting during cooking.
4. To test if chicken is cooked, pierce the thickest part of the thigh with a skewer. If the juices run clear, it's cooked, if they're a little pink, return to oven for 5-10 minutes, then test again. Transfer chicken and vegetables to a platter; cover with foil.
5. To prepare the gravy, pour pan juices from baking dish into a small jug. Discard fat from surface of pan juices; reserve juices. Sprinkle flour into same baking dish; cook, stirring, until well browned. Gradually add reserved pan juices and stock, stirring with a wire whisk until gravy boils and thickens. Strain gravy into a jug.
6. Serve chicken with vegetables and gravy.

SERVING SUGGESTION Serve with green beans.

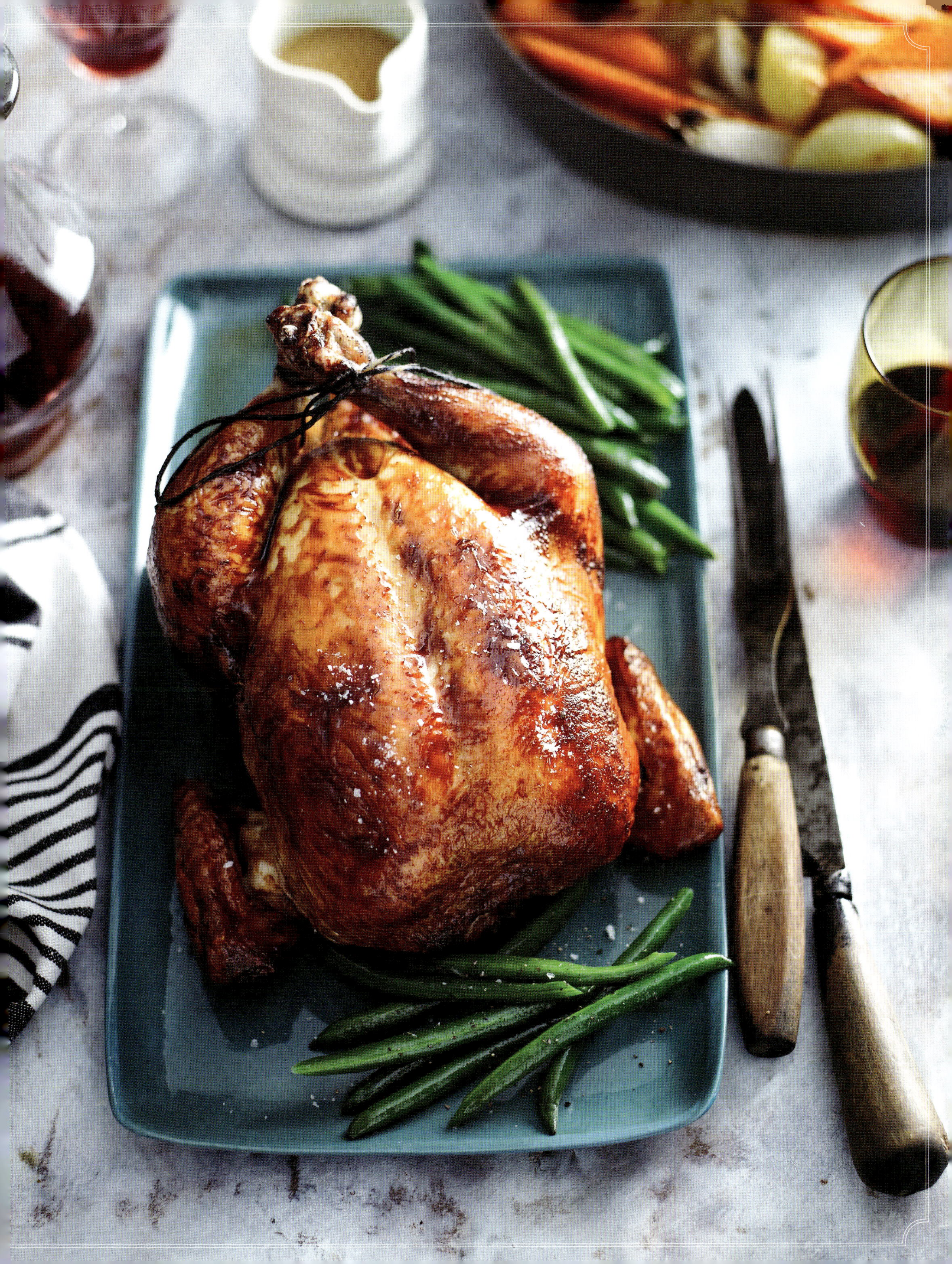

LEMON AND GARLIC LAMB RACK
with Roasted Zucchini

LEMON AND GARLIC LAMB RACK
with Roasted Zucchini

PREP + COOK TIME *1 HOUR* **SERVES** *4*

2 tablespoons olive oil
3 x 4 cutlet neck-end lamb racks (1.2kg)
12 baby new potatoes (600g)
2 medium lemons (280g), quartered
1 medium bulb garlic (70g), unpeeled, cloves separated
4 small zucchini (360g), halved lengthways
1 tablespoon fresh lemon thyme leaves

1. Preheat oven to 200°C/400°F.
2. Heat half the oil in a large frying pan; cook lamb, turning on all sides for 5 minutes or until browned all over. Transfer lamb to a roasting dish; season. Add potatoes, lemon and garlic to dish; drizzle with remaining oil.
3. Roast lamb 25 minutes for medium-rare or until cooked as desired. Remove lamb from pan; rest, covered with foil, 15 minutes.
4. Meanwhile, add zucchini to potatoes in dish; toss to combine. Increase oven to its hottest setting; roast potato mixture for 20 minutes or until tender and golden. Add thyme; toss to combine.
5. Serve lamb with roasted vegetables and lemon.

TIP The neck-end lamb racks are a cheaper alternative to the traditional racks of lamb.

SERVING SUGGESTION Serve with baby (dutch) carrots.

ROAST BEEF RUMP
with Red Wine Gravy

PREP + COOKING TIME *1 HOUR 40 MINUTES* **SERVES** *8*

1 tablespoon port
2 tablespoons wholegrain mustard
1½ tablespoons worcestershire sauce
2.5kg (5-pound) piece beef rump (corner piece)
1 cup (250ml) dry red wine
1½ cups (375ml) water
40g (1½ ounces) butter
2 tablespoons plain (all-purpose) flour
1½ cups (375ml) beef stock

1. Preheat oven to 220°C/425°F.
2. Combine port, mustard and 1 tablespoon of the worcestershire sauce in a small bowl; rub over beef.
3. Place beef on a wire rack in a flameproof baking dish. Combine ½ cup of the wine and ½ cup of the water; pour into dish. Roast 10 minutes.
4. Reduce oven to 160°C/325°F; roast a further 1 hour for medium or until cooked as desired. Add extra water if the pan juices evaporate. Transfer beef to a platter; cover to keep warm while making the gravy. Drain pan juices into a small heatproof bowl.
5. Melt butter in the same flameproof dish over a medium heat, add flour; cook, stirring, until well browned. Gradually stir in remaining wine, then stock, reserved pan juices and remaining worcestershire sauce; cook, stirring, until gravy boils and thickens slightly. Strain into a jug.
6. Serve beef with gravy.

TIP Carving well-rested roast beef should be easy if you have a large, sharp carving or a chef's knife. Carve across the grain of the beef at a consistent angle. Gently remove any string as you carve.

SERVING SUGGESTION Serve with roast potatoes and peas.

(PHOTOGRAPH PAGE 182)

ROAST BEEF RUMP
with Red Wine Gravy
(RECIPE PAGE 181)

SLOW-ROASTED
Lamb Shoulder

(RECIPE PAGE 184)

SLOW-ROASTED Lamb Shoulder

PREP + COOK TIME 4 HOURS SERVES 4

1.3kg (2¾-pound) lamb shoulder with the shank on
2 tablespoons olive oil
1kg (2 pounds) potatoes, cut into thin wedges
2 medium onions (300g), sliced thinly
4 anchovy fillets, chopped finely
2 whole garlic bulbs
3 sprigs fresh rosemary
2 tablespoons lemon juice
1 cup (250ml) chicken stock
1 cup (250ml) water or dry white wine
¼ cup fresh dill sprigs

1. Preheat oven to 180°C/350°F. Rub lamb all over with salt and freshly ground black pepper.
2. Heat a flameproof roasting pan over medium-high heat. Add oil, then lamb; cook, turning for 5 minutes or until lamb is well browned all over. Turn off the heat; remove lamb from pan.
3. Layer potato, onion and anchovies in the base of the same roasting pan, seasoning with salt and freshly ground pepper between layers. Cut garlic bulbs in half widthways; place on potatoes.
4. Place lamb on top of potatoes; sprinkle with rosemary and lemon juice. Pour combined stock and the water over potatoes. Cover dish tightly with two layers of foil. Roast for 1½ hours. Reduce oven to 160°C/325°F; remove foil, roast a further 1½-2 hours or until meat falls easily from the bone.
5. Cover lamb with foil; rest 20 minutes before serving. Serve lamb scattered with dill.

(PHOTOGRAPH PAGE 183)

ROAST LEG OF LAMB with Mustard and Herbs

PREP + COOK TIME 2 HOURS SERVES 6

4 medium potatoes (800g), peeled, cut into wedges
1 medium red onion (170g), cut into wedges
1½ cups (375ml) chicken stock
1½ tablespoons dijon mustard
3 cloves garlic, crushed
2 anchovies, chopped finely
2 teaspoons finely grated lemon rind
2kg (4-pound) leg of lamb
½ cup coarsely chopped fresh flat-leaf parsley
2 tablespoons coarsely chopped fresh oregano
¼ cup (60ml) olive oil
1 medium lemon (140g), cut into wedges

1. Preheat oven to 180°C/350°F.
2. Place potato and onion in an oiled roasting pan with stock.
3. Combine mustard, garlic, anchovies and rind in a small bowl. Rub mustard mixture over lamb. Place lamb on top of potato and onion.
4. Roast lamb and vegetables for 1½ hours or until lamb is cooked as desired. Remove lamb from pan; rest, covered, 15 minutes.
5. Meanwhile, increase oven to 250°C/475°F; roast vegetables a further 15 minutes or until browned.
6. Serve lamb and vegetables topped with herbs, drizzled with oil.

ROAST LEG OF LAMB
with Mustard and Herbs

ROAST TURKEY
with Roasted Almond Stuffing

PREP + COOK TIME 4 HOURS 15 MINUTES **SERVES** 8

5kg (15-pound) turkey
60g (2 ounces) butter, melted
1 litre (4 cups) salt-reduced chicken stock, approximately
⅓ cup (50g) plain (all-purpose) flour

ROASTED ALMOND STUFFING
80g (2½ ounces) butter
2 medium onions (300g), chopped finely
2 cloves garlic, crushed
350g (11 ounces) minced (ground) turkey
1¼ cups (100g) flaked almonds, roasted
½ cup finely chopped fresh flat-leaf parsley
2 teaspoons finely grated lemon rind
¼ cup (60ml) lemon juice
3 cups (200g) stale breadcrumbs

1. Make roasted almond stuffing.
2. Preheat oven to 180°C/350°F.
3. Discard neck from turkey. Rinse turkey under running cold water. Pat dry inside and out with paper towel. Fill turkey cavities with stuffing. Tie turkey legs together with kitchen string; tuck the wings under. Place turkey on an oiled rack in a large flameproof roasting pan. Brush turkey all over with half the butter; sprinkle with salt. Pour 2 cups of the stock into the pan.
4. Cover roasting pan tightly with two layers of greased foil. Roast turkey for 2 hours. Remove foil, brush with remaining butter.
5. Roast turkey, uncovered, for a further 1½ hours or until browned and cooked through. Add water to the pan during cooking to prevent juices burning, if necessary. Remove turkey from pan; cover with foil. Rest in a warm place for 15 minutes before carving.
6. Meanwhile, pour juices from roasting pan into a jug; stand for a few minutes or until fat has risen to surface. Skim off fat and return 2 tablespoons to pan. Discard remaining fat. Top up pan juices with chicken stock to 3 cups. Place roasting pan over medium heat; add flour, cook, stirring, until browned. Gradually add reserved pan juice mixture; cook, stirring, until mixture boils and thickens. Season to taste. Strain gravy into a heatproof jug.
7. Serve turkey with gravy.

ROASTED ALMOND STUFFING
Heat butter in a small frying pan over low heat; cook onion and garlic, stirring, for 5 minutes or until softened. Transfer to a large bowl. Add turkey, almonds, parsley, rind, juice and half the breadcrumbs; mix well. Season. Add remaining breadcrumbs; fold to combine.

SERVING SUGGESTION Serve with roasted baby (dutch) heirloom carrots in rosemary and thyme.

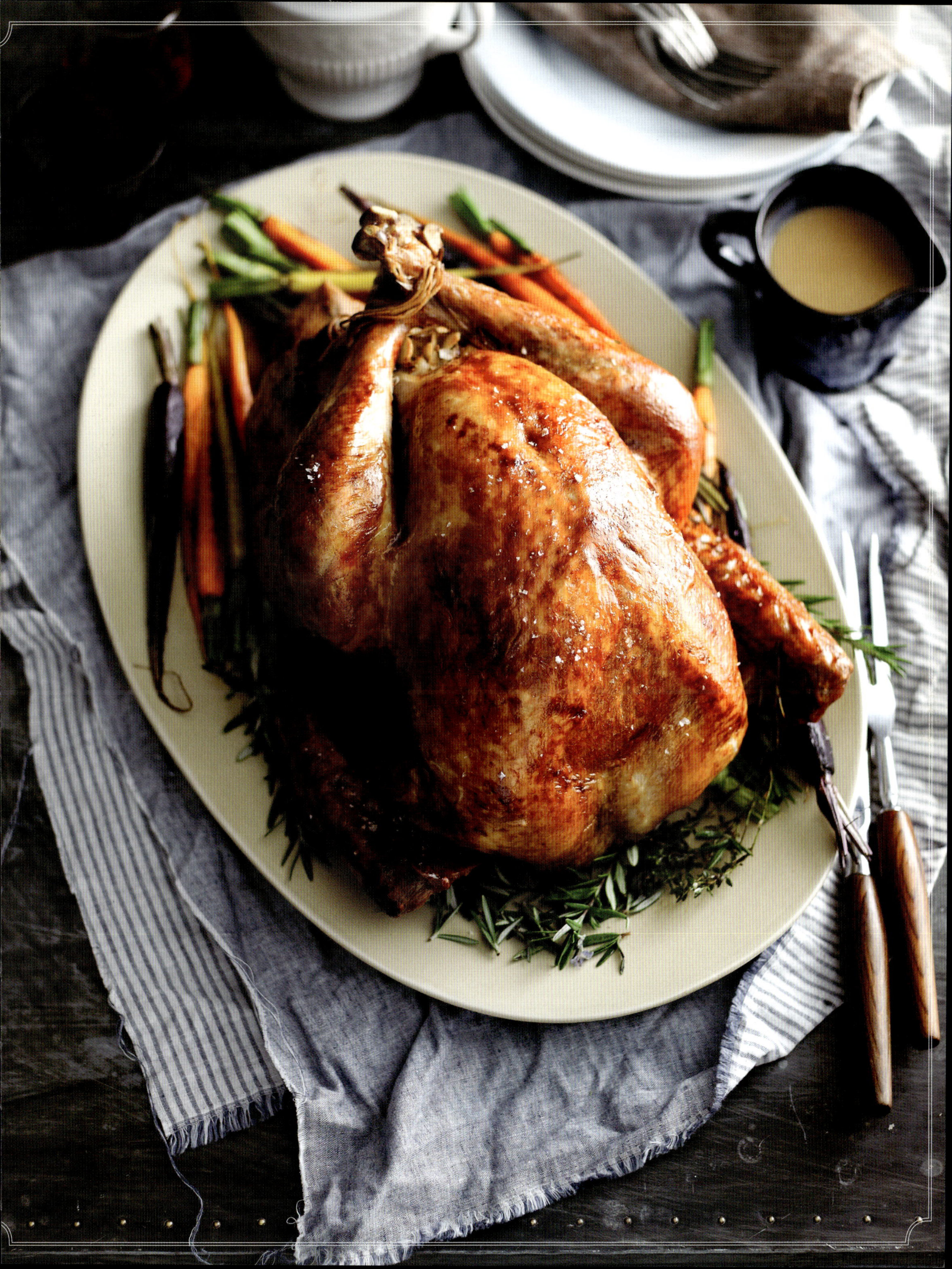

ROAST PORK LOIN
with Nam Jim

PREP + COOK TIME *1 HOUR 30 MINUTES* **SERVES 8**

3kg (6-pound) boneless loin of pork, rind on
1 tablespoon olive oil
1 tablespoon coarse cooking (kosher) salt

NAM JIM
3 cloves garlic
3 large green chillies, seeded, chopped coarsely
2 coriander (cilantro) roots
2 tablespoons fish sauce
2 tablespoons grated palm sugar
3 french shallots (25g), chopped
¼ cup (60ml) lime juice

1. Preheat oven to 240°C/475°F.
2. Lie pork flat, flesh-side down, on a chopping board. Score rind with a very sharp knife, vertically cutting into the fat but not into the meat.
3. Dry rind well with paper towel then tie the pork at 5cm (2-inch) intervals with kitchen string. Rub pork with oil then salt, massaging into the rind.
4. Place pork on a roasting rack in a roasting pan. Stand at room temperature for 30 minutes.
5. Roast pork 30 minutes or until rind blisters. Reduce oven to 180°C/350°F; roast a further 45 minutes to 1 hour or until cooked through. Rest, uncovered, 15 minutes.
6. Make nam jim.
7. Serve pork with nam jim.

NAM JIM
Blend or process ingredients until smooth.

TIP To barbecue the pork instead, preheat a barbecue to the highest heat setting (very hot). Place pork on a roasting rack in a disposable aluminium roasting pan. Place on the barbecue over indirect heat and cook, with the hood down, for 30 minutes or until the rind blisters. Reduce heat to low and cook for a further 45-60 minutes, or until cooked through. Rest, uncovered, 15 minutes.

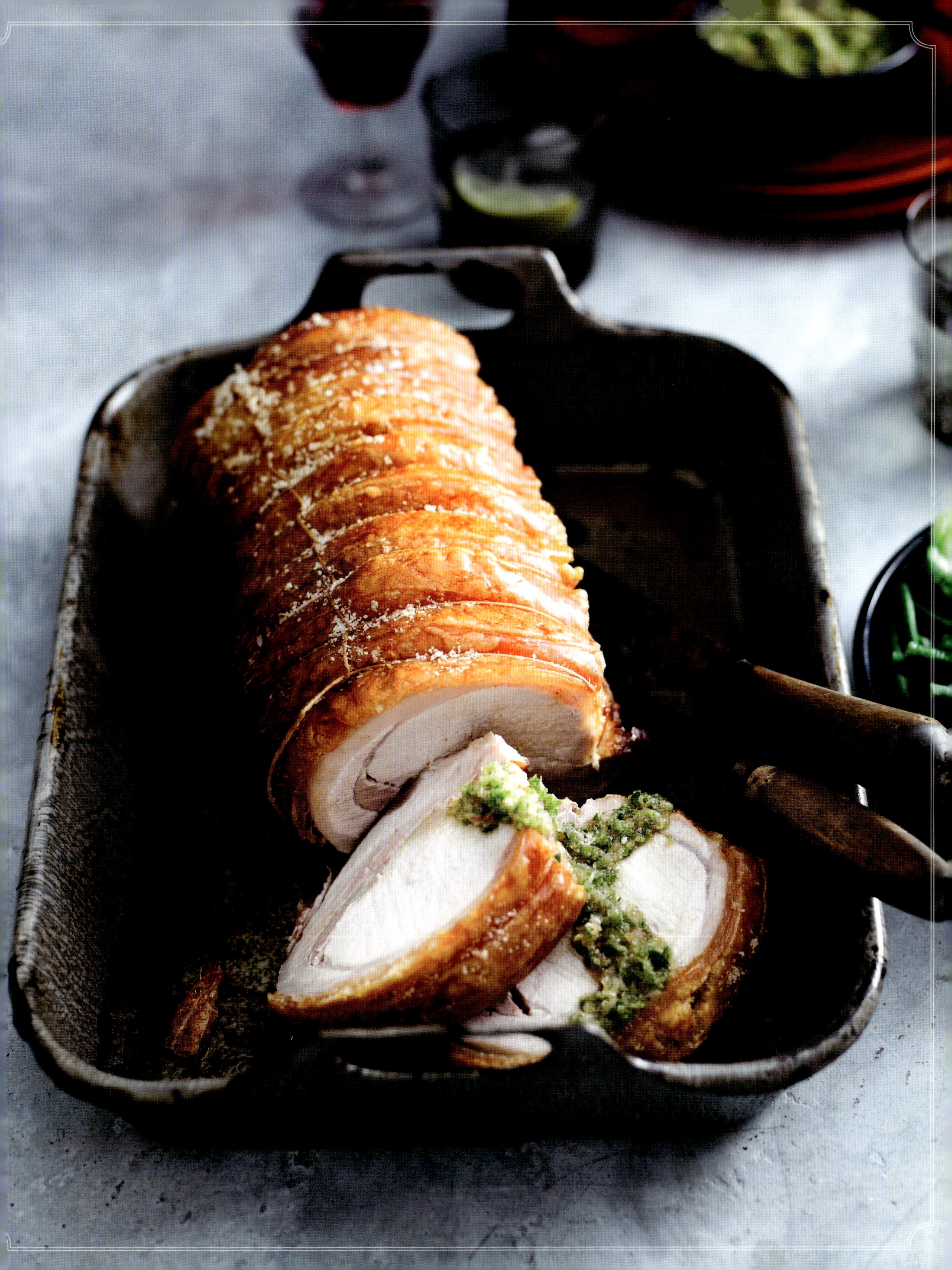

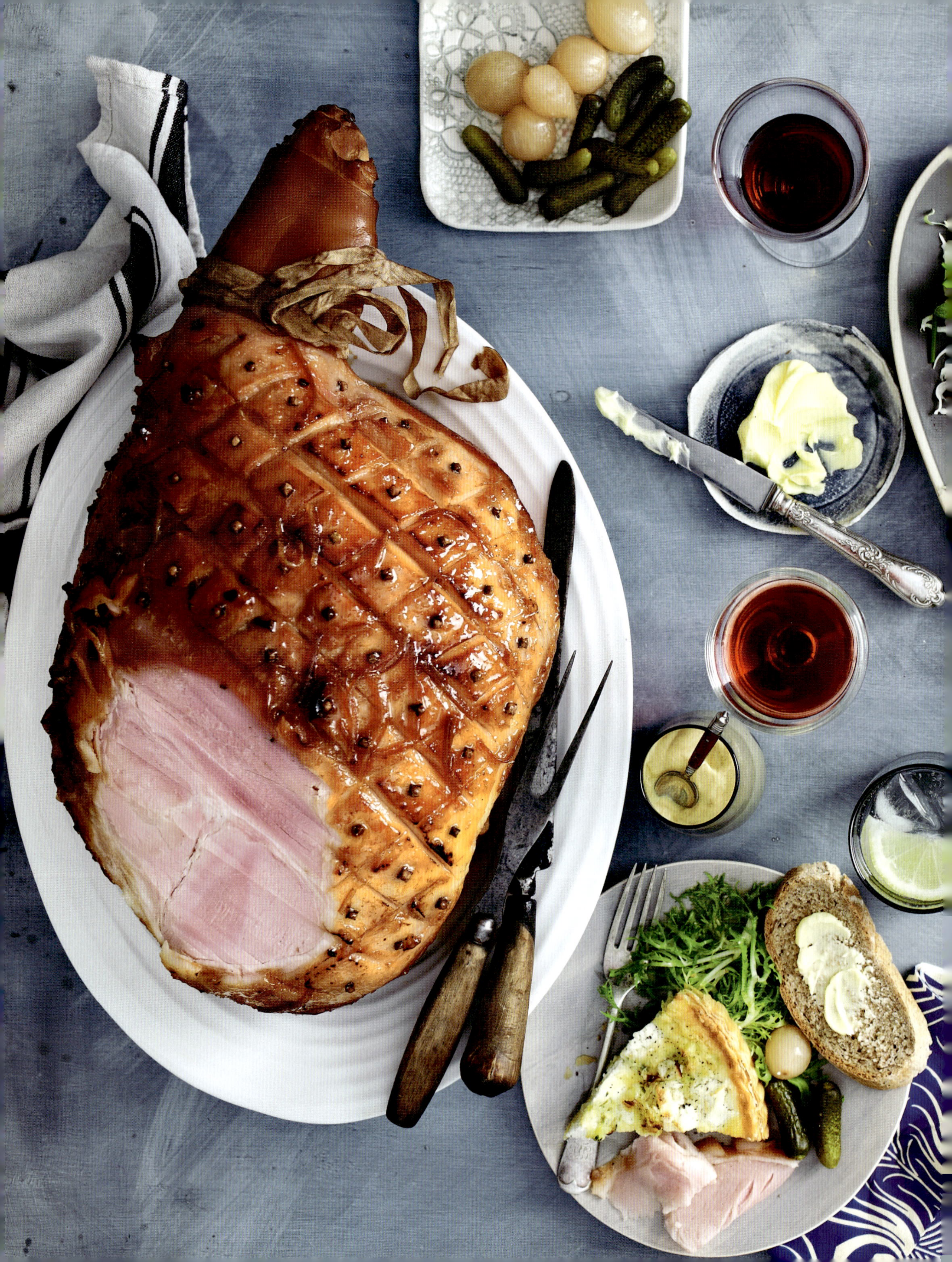

CASUAL BRUNCH

BLOOD ORANGE MARMALADE
Glazed Ham

(RECIPE PAGE 192)

GOAT'S CHEESE
and Leek Tart

(RECIPE PAGE 120)

AVOCADO, BACON
and Cabbage Salad

(RECIPE PAGE 30)

SOURDOUGH RYE
Bread

(RECIPE PAGE 328)

TROPICAL FRUIT
with Rosewater Syrup

(RECIPE PAGE 214)

BLOOD ORANGE
Marmalade Glazed Ham

PREP + COOK TIME 2 HOURS 20 MINUTES **SERVES** 20

9kg (20 pound) cooked leg of ham
whole cloves, to decorate

BLOOD ORANGE MARMALADE GLAZE
350g (11 ounces) blood orange marmalade
¼ cup (55g) brown sugar
¼ cup (60ml) orange juice

1. Preheat oven to 180°C/350°F. Cut through the rind of the ham about 10cm (4-inches) from the shank end of the leg.
2. To remove the rind, run your thumb around the edge of the rind, just under the skin. Start pulling the rind from the widest edge of the ham; continue to pull the rind carefully away from the fat up to the cut. Remove the rind completely (reserved rind can be used to cover the cut surface of the ham to keep it moist during storage).
3. Using a sharp knife, score across the fat very lightly at about 3cm (1¼-inch) intervals, cutting just through the surface of the top fat. Don't cut too deeply or the fat will spread apart during cooking. Score in the opposite direction to form a diamond pattern.
4. Make blood orange marmalade glaze.
5. Line a large roasting pan with overlapping sheets of baking paper (this will make cleaning the dish easier). Place ham on a wire rack in the pan. Brush ham well with the glaze; cover shank end with foil.
6. Bake ham 40 minutes; decorate with cloves. Bake for a further 40 minutes or until browned all over, brushing occasionally with glaze during cooking.
7. Serve ham warm or cold.

BLOOD ORANGE MARMALADE GLAZE
Stir ingredients in a small saucepan over low heat until sugar is dissolved.

TIPS To carve the ham, cut a small slice from underneath the ham so it sits flat (if you don't have a ham stand). About 3cm (1¼-inches) from the rind of the shank end, make a cut at an angle. Remove the wedge. Cut several thin slices right down to the bone, parallel to the second cut.
Carved ham is suitable to freeze for up to 1 month (ham will become saltier if frozen longer).

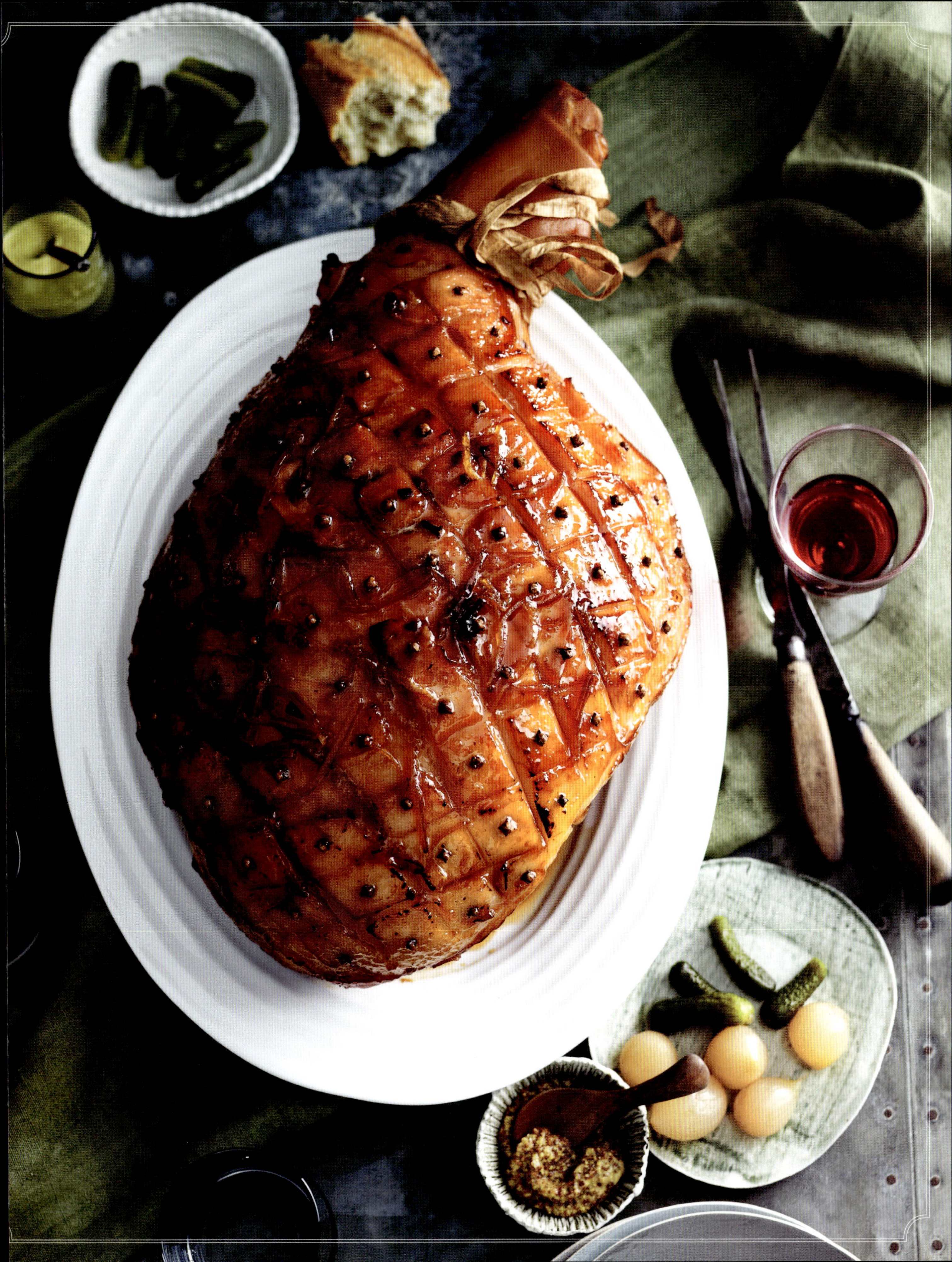

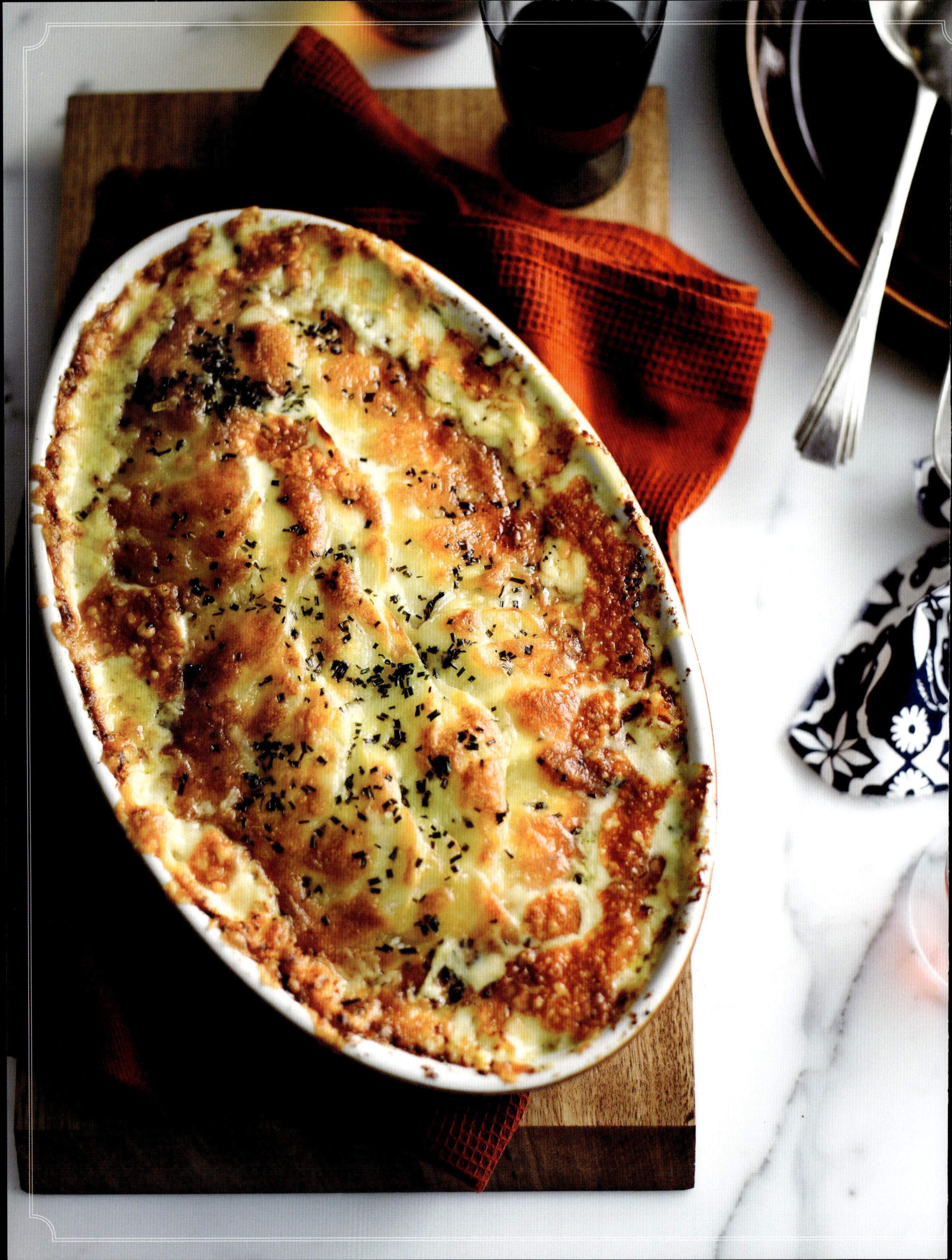

Up until the 18th century, potatoes were banned for fear that they caused leprosy, until Antoine Augustine-Parmentier won over Louis XVI with his repertoire of dishes. The modern-day potato bake has evolved from a dish created at this time.

POTATO BAKE

PREP + COOK TIME 55 MINUTES SERVES 6

2 teaspoons olive oil
1 medium brown onion (150g), sliced thinly
6 slices pancetta (90g), chopped coarsely
1 cup (250ml) pouring cream
½ cup (120g) sour cream
2 tablespoons finely chopped chives
1kg (2 pounds) sebago potatoes, cut into 3mm (⅛-inch) thick slices
1 cup (120g) coarsely grated cheddar

1. Preheat oven to 200°C/400°F. Grease a 2-litre (8-cup) ovenproof dish.
2. Heat oil in a medium frying pan over medium heat; cook onion and pancetta, stirring, until onion softens and pancetta is crisp.
3. Combine cream, sour cream and chives in a jug.
4. Layer a third of the potato slices over base of the dish; sprinkle with half the pancetta mixture. Pour a third of the cream mixture over pancetta mixture; sprinkle with a third of the cheese. Repeat layering, finishing with cheese.
5. Bake 40 minutes or until browned. Stand 10 minutes before serving.

SERVING SUGGESTION Serve with roast beef, chicken or veal and steamed green beans.

MIDDLE EASTERN MEATLOAF

PREP + COOK TIME *1 HOUR* **SERVES** *6*

2 tablespoons extra virgin olive oil
¾ cup (150g) fine burghul (crushed wheat)
1 medium onion (150g), quartered
500g (1 pound) lean minced (ground) lamb
1 teaspoon sea salt
½ teaspoon freshly ground black pepper
1 teaspoon ground cinnamon
2 tablespoons pine nuts
1 cup lightly packed fresh flat-leaf parsley leaves
1 teaspoon sumac

SPICED ONIONS
¼ cup (60ml) extra virgin olive oil
3 medium brown onions (450g), sliced
½ teaspoon ground cinnamon
pinch ground allspice
2 tablespoons toasted pine nuts

1 Preheat oven to 180°C/350°F. Oil a 24cm (9½-inch) springform tin, line base with baking paper. Spread 1 tablespoon of the oil over the base.
2 Rinse burghul in a fine sieve under cold water; drain well.
3 Process onion until chopped finely. Add lamb, salt, pepper, cinnamon and burghul; process until a thick paste forms. Press lamb mixture over base of tin. Brush with remaining oil. Sprinkle with pine nuts; press lightly into the surface.
4 Bake meatloaf 30 minutes or until cooked through.
5 Meanwhile, make spiced onions.
6 Top meatloaf with spiced onions, parsley and sumac.

SPICED ONIONS
Heat oil in a medium frying pan over medium heat; cook onion, covered, for 15 minutes. Uncover; cook, stirring occasionally, for a further 10 minutes or until onion is soft. Add spices and season; cook, stirring, until fragrant. Stir in pine nuts.

TIP This recipe is a twist on a classic Middle Eastern baked kibbeh, where a mixture of minced lamb, burghul and spices is baked in a rectangular dish and the top scored in a diamond pattern.

SERVING SUGGESTION Serve with a cucumber and tomato salad.

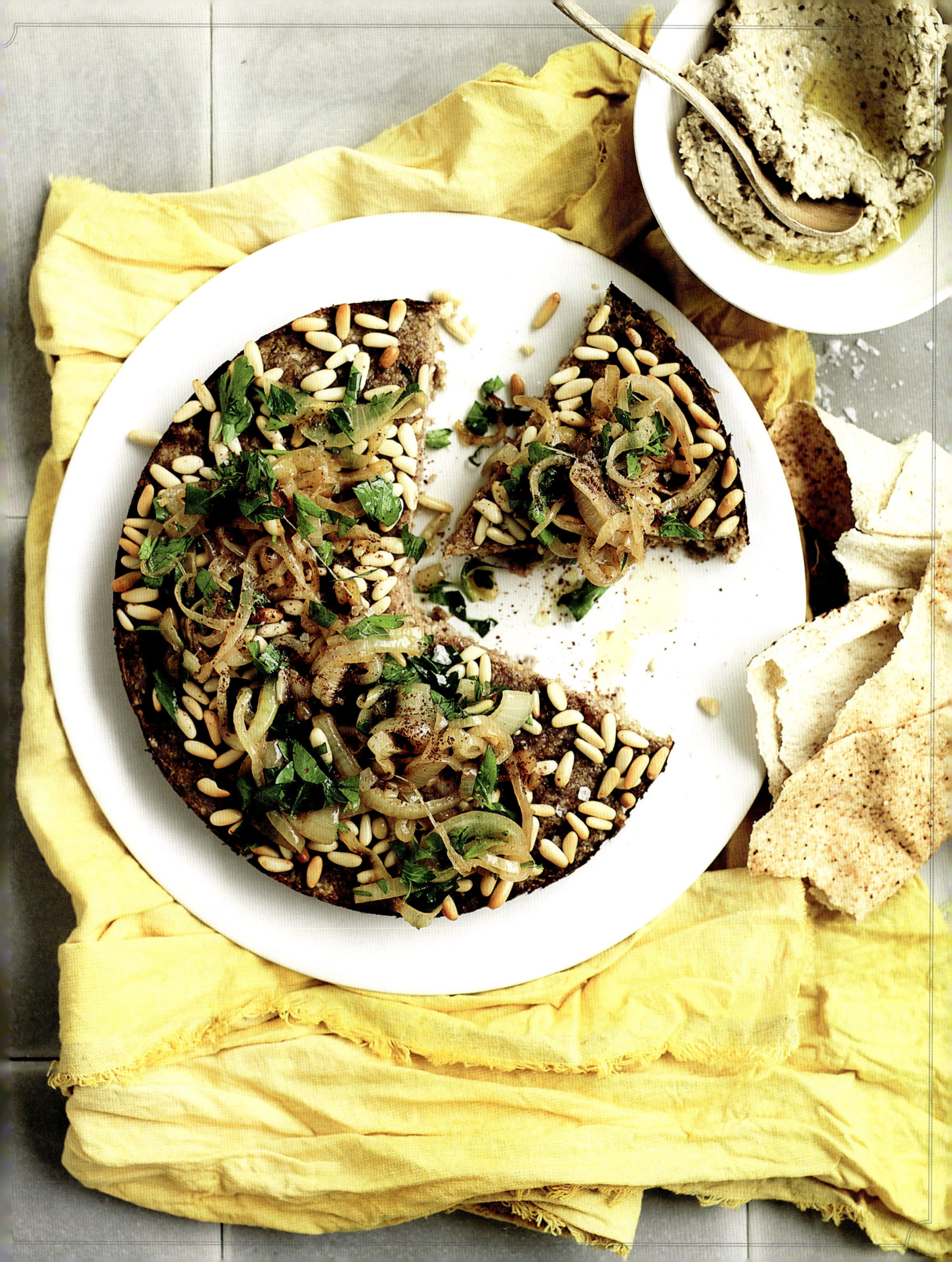

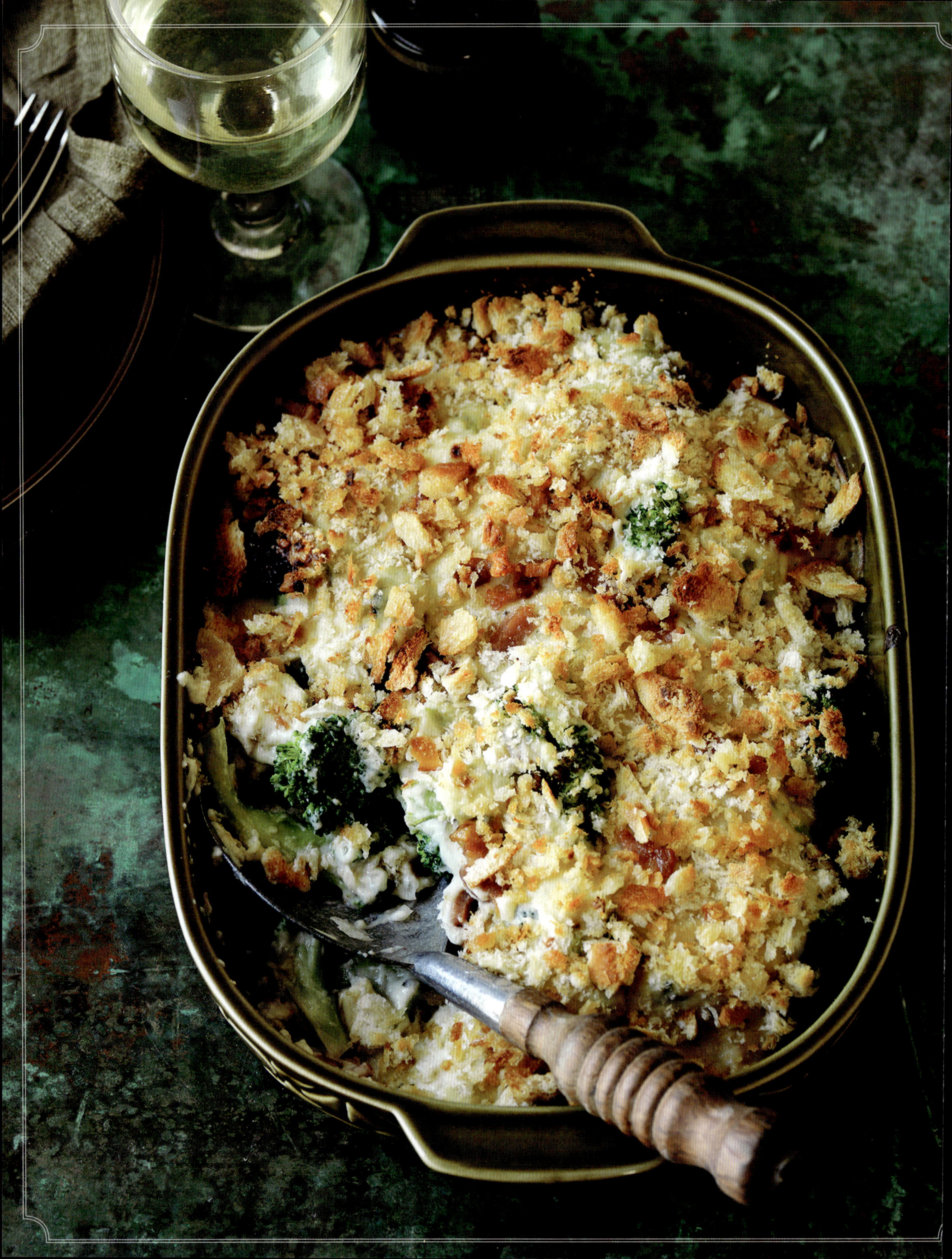

BROCCOLI PANCETTA
and Blue Cheese Gratin

PREP + COOK TIME *50 MINUTES* **SERVES** *6 AS A SIDE DISH*

1 large head broccoli (500g), cut into florets, stalks peeled, sliced
150g (4½-ounce) piece pancetta, diced
1 small brown onion (80g), chopped finely
2 tablespoons plain (all-purpose) flour
2 teaspoons mustard powder
2 cups (500ml) milk
120g (4 ounces) gorgonzola, crumbled
¾ cup (50g) coarse stale breadcrumbs

1. Boil, steam or microwave broccoli until just bright green but still firm; drain. Place in a greased shallow 1.5-litre (6-cup) ovenproof dish.
2. Preheat oven to 190°C/375°F.
3. Heat a medium saucepan over medium heat; cook pancetta, stirring, occasionally, for 10 minutes or until fat is rendered and pancetta crisp. Remove from pan with a slotted spoon. Scatter pancetta over broccoli.
4. Cook onion in same pan over medium heat, stirring for 3 minutes or until translucent. Add flour and mustard powder; stir for 30 seconds. Gradually add milk, stirring continuously until mixture boils and thickens slightly.
5. Remove from heat; stir in cheese and season with freshly ground black pepper to taste until cheese melts. Pour sauce over broccoli, top with breadcrumbs.
6. Bake for 20 minutes until browned lightly.

TIP Pancetta and gorgonzola (blue cheese) both contain naturally occurring monosodium glutamates, a flavour known as 'umami', which is defined as one of the five basic tastes, along with sweet, salt, sour and bitter. Ingredients with a umami quality have the ability to enhance the flavours they are paired with, giving food like broccoli, a very moreish taste.

POTATO, OLIVE AND
Capsicum Frittata

PREP + COOK TIME *30 MINUTES* **SERVES 4**

---

1 cured chorizo sausage (170g), sliced thickly on the diagonal
500g (1 pound) desiree potatoes, cut into 3cm (1¼-inch) cubes
1 tablespoon olive oil
8 eggs
½ cup (125ml) pouring cream
2 tablespoons finely chopped fresh flat-leaf parsley
½ cup (120g) drained char-grilled red capsicum (bell pepper), cut into strips
¼ cup (40g) pitted black olives

1. Cook chorizo in a 18cm (7¼-inch) (base measure) ovenproof frying pan over high heat until crisp; remove from pan. Wipe pan clean with paper towel.
2. Meanwhile, boil, steam or microwave potatoes 5 minutes or until just tender; drain.
3. Heat oil in same pan; cook potato, stirring, until golden all over.
4. Meanwhile, whisk eggs and cream in a large jug until combined. Stir in parsley; season.
5. Add chorizo to pan with capsicum and olives. Pour egg mixture over ingredients; cook, over low heat, 6 minutes or until base and side of egg is set.
6. Meanwhile, preheat grill (broiler).
7. Place frittata under grill for 5 minutes or until just set (see tips). Turn frittata onto large board; cut into wedges to serve. If you like, top with rocket (arugula) leaves.

TIPS You need a frying pan with a heatproof handle for this recipe. If the handle of your pan is not heatproof, wrap it in two layers of foil.
Grill the frittata about 15cm (6 inches) below the heat element.
Store cooled frittata on a plate, covered in plastic wrap in the refrigerator, for up to 2 days.

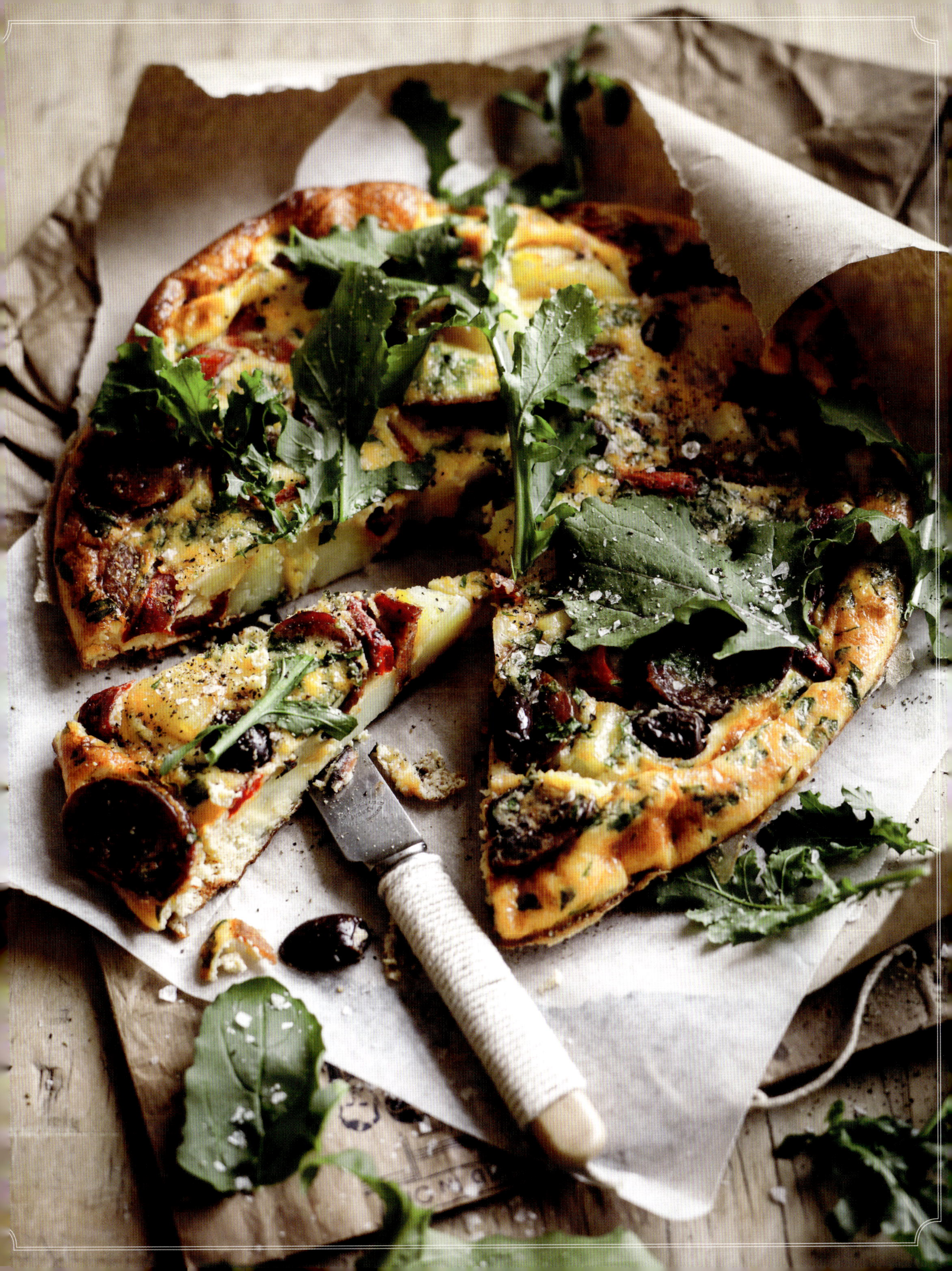

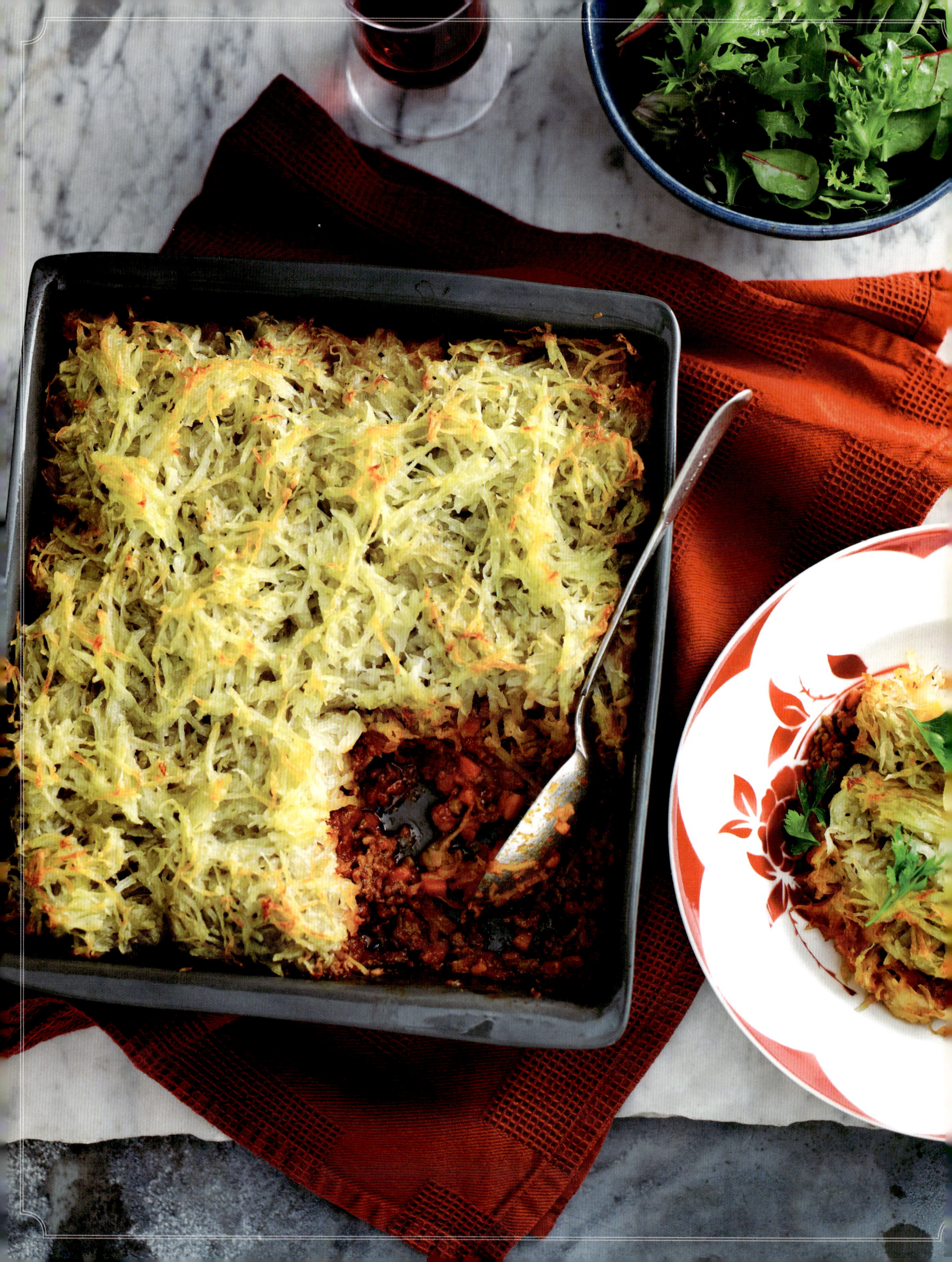

RÖSTI COTTAGE PIE

PREP + COOK 1 HOUR 45 MINUTES SERVES 6

2 tablespoons olive oil
2 large brown onion (400g), chopped finely
4 medium carrots (480g), chopped finely
2 trimmed celery sticks (200g), chopped finely
3 cloves garlic, crushed
1kg (2 pounds) minced (ground) beef
¼ cup (60ml) tomato paste
½ cup (125ml) dry red wine
800g (1½ pounds) canned diced tomatoes
1 bay leaf
1kg (2 pounds) sebago potatoes
100g (3 ounces) butter, melted
2 tablespoons fresh flat-leaf parsley leaves

1. Heat oil in a large saucepan over medium heat; cook onion, carrot, celery and garlic, stirring for 5 minutes or until beginning to soften.
2. Increase heat to high, add beef; cook, breaking up with a wooden spoon, for 8 minutes or until browned. Add tomato paste and wine; simmer until wine evaporates. Add tomatoes and bay leaf, season; simmer for 45 minutes or until sauce has thickened.
3. Transfer beef mixture to a 6cm (2½-inch) deep, 2 litre (8-cup) ovenproof dish.
4. Preheat oven to 200°C/400°F.
5. Peel, then coarsely grate potatoes into a large bowl. Place potato in a clean tea towel; squeeze out as much liquid as possible. Return potato to bowl; stir in butter, season. Spread potato mixture over beef mixture.
6. Bake pie for 50 minutes or until rösti top is golden. Serve pie topped with parsley.

TIPS You can add your favourite spices to the beef mixture during cooking.
You could use desiree potatoes instead of sebago.

SERVING SUGGESTION Serve with a mixed leaf salad.

SELF-SAUCING MEATLOAF

PREP + COOK TIME *1 HOUR 25 MINUTES (+ STANDING)* **SERVES** *6*

6 slices white bread, crusts removed
½ cup (125ml) milk
500g (1 pound) minced (ground) beef
250g (8 ounces) sausage meat
1 medium red capsicum (bell pepper) (200g), chopped finely
1 large brown onion (200g), chopped finely
¼ cup (60ml) barbecue sauce
1 egg, beaten lightly
¼ cup finely chopped fresh flat-leaf parsley
400g (12½ ounces) canned diced tomatoes
125g (4 ounces) cherry tomatoes, halved

1. Preheat oven to 200°C/400°F. Line a shallow oven tray with baking paper.
2. Combine bread and milk in a medium bowl; stand 2 minutes. Lightly squeeze bread to remove excess milk; discard excess milk.
3. Place bread, beef, sausage meat, capsicum, onion, sauce, egg and parsley in a large bowl. Season. Using your hands, mix until well combined.
4. Line base of a loaf pan with baking paper, extending the paper 5cm (2 inches) over long sides. Press mixture firmly into pan. Turn meatloaf out onto oven tray; remove loaf pan and discard lining paper. Spoon half the combined canned and cherry tomatoes over meatloaf.
5. Bake meatloaf for 30 minutes. Top with remaining tomatoes (some will fall onto the paper); bake for a further 20 minutes or until cooked through. Stand 10 minutes before cutting.

TIP If you prefer, use minced lamb instead of beef.

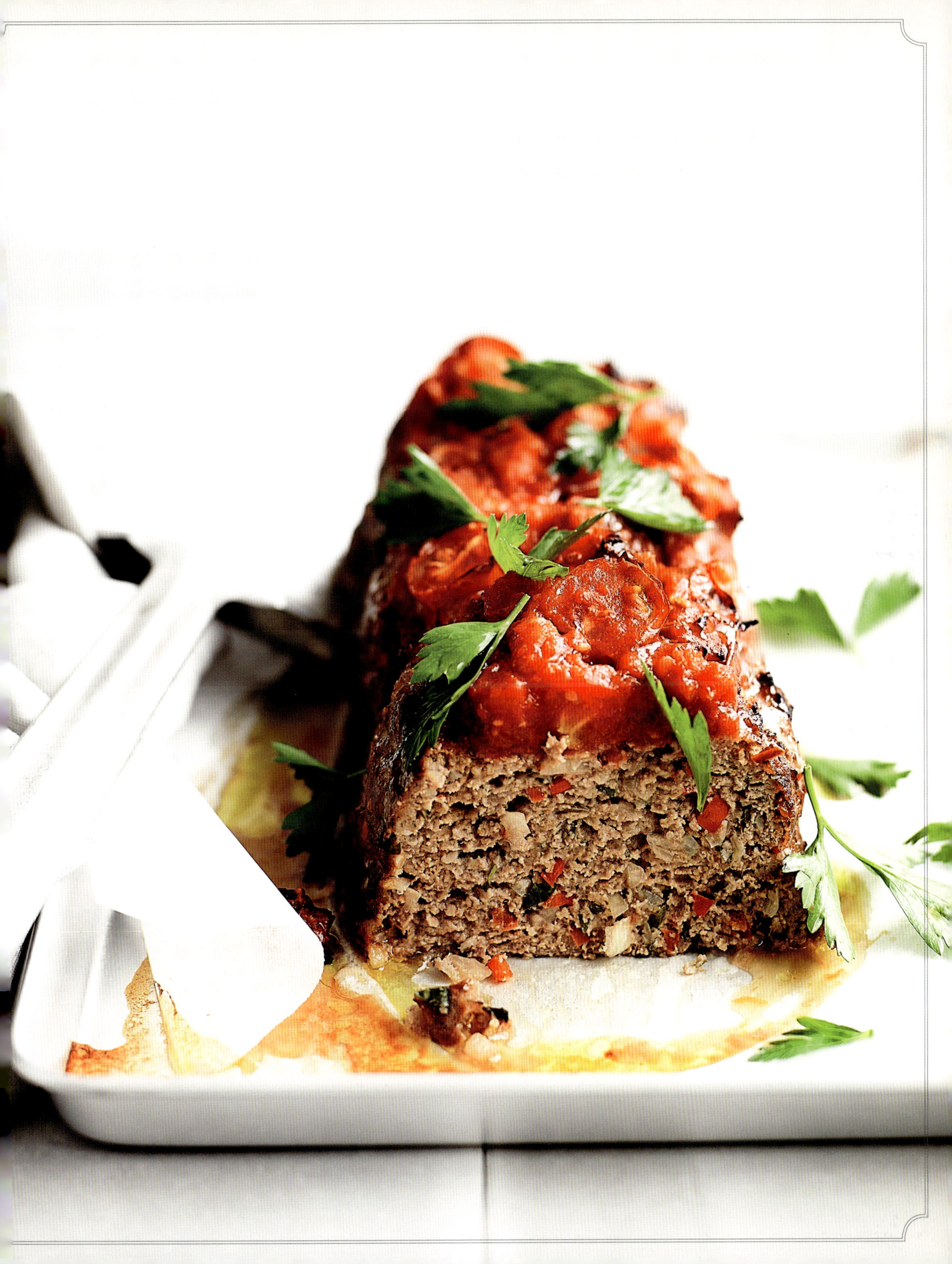

CHAPTER 7
PUDDINGS & DESSERTS

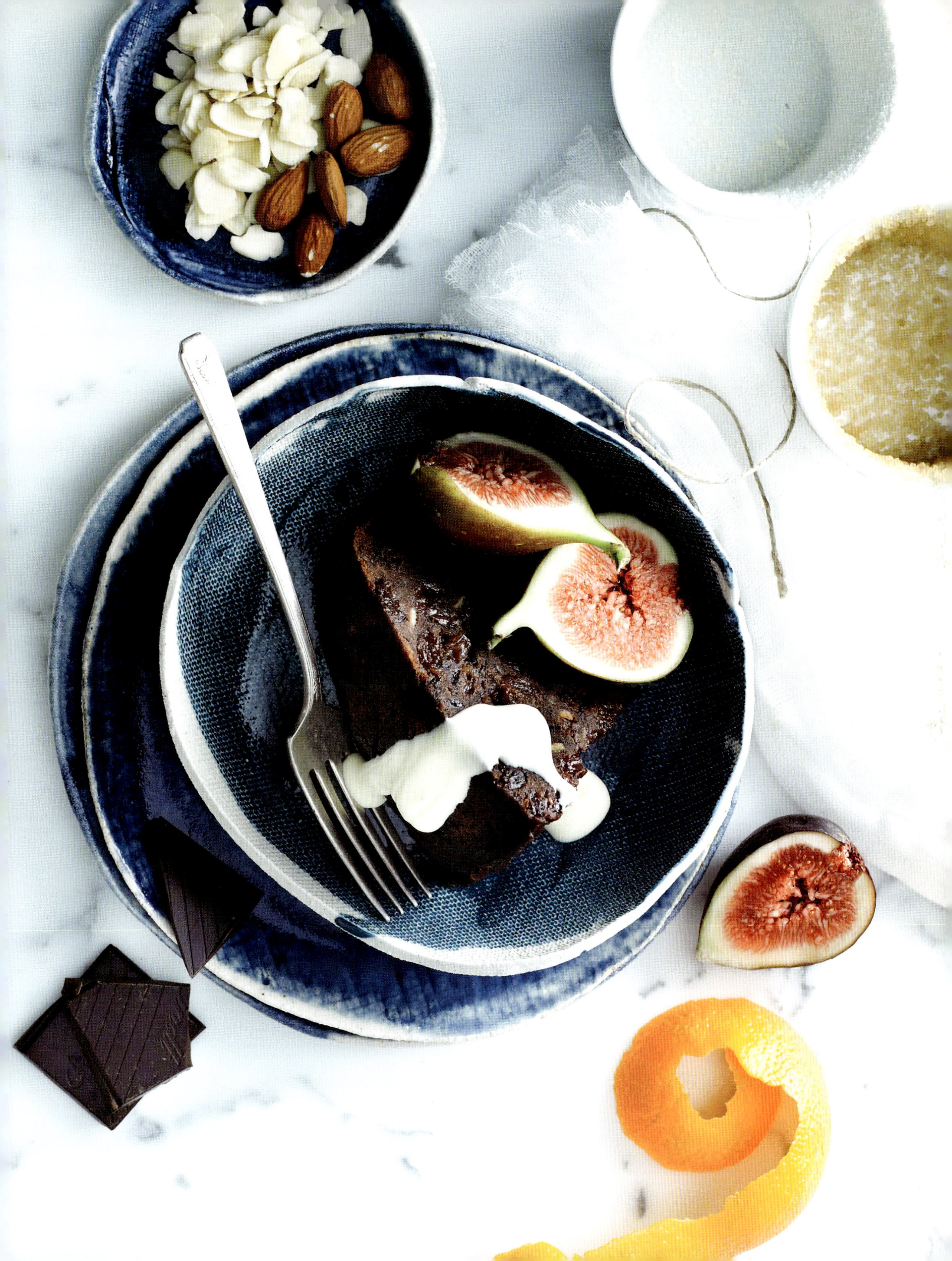

CHOCOLATE PARFAIT
with Orange Salad

PREP + COOK TIME *30 MINUTES (+ FREEZING)* **SERVES** *8*

Parfait, meaning 'perfect' in French, describes the wonderfully light texture of this frozen chocolate dessert. Make sure you use a chocolate with at least 70% cocoa solids to get the best chocolate taste. Start the recipe a day ahead.

⅔ cup (150 g) caster (superfine) sugar
⅔ cup (160ml) water
200g (6½ ounces) dark chocolate (70% cocoa), chopped finely
5 egg yolks
300ml (½ pint) thickened (heavy) cream
¾ cup (185g) mascarpone cheese
1 tablespoon brandy
1 cup (80g) natural flaked almonds, toasted
2 teaspoons dutch cocoa

ORANGE SALAD
3 medium oranges (720g)
1 tablespoon honey

1. Line base and sides of an 8cm x 22cm (3¼-inch x 9-inch) terrine or loaf pan with baking paper, extending the paper 5cm (2 inches) over long sides.
2. Stir sugar and the water in a small saucepan over medium heat, without boiling, until sugar dissolves. Bring to the boil; boil, uncovered, without stirring, for 3 minutes. Remove from heat; add chocolate, stir until melted and syrup is smooth.
3. Beat egg yolks in a small bowl with an electric mixer for 3 minutes or until pale. Gradually pour in chocolate syrup, beating constantly until mixture is cool.
4. Beat cream and mascarpone in a medium bowl with an electric mixer until soft peaks form. Fold chocolate syrup, brandy and half the almonds into cream mixture. Pour mixture into pan. Cover; freeze overnight or until firm.
5. Make orange salad.
6. Turn out parfait; top with remaining almonds. Dust with sifted cocoa. Serve sliced with orange salad.

ORANGE SALAD
Remove rind and white pith from oranges. Working with one at a time, hold an orange over a medium bowl, remove segments by cutting down between each side of the membrane and segment. Place segments in a medium bowl. Squeeze juice from the orange membrane. Drizzle with honey.

TIP Dutch cocoa has an alkali added to it to neutralise its acidity and make it more soluble. It has a richer flavour and darker colour than regular cocoa powder. It is available from specialty food stores and some supermarkets.

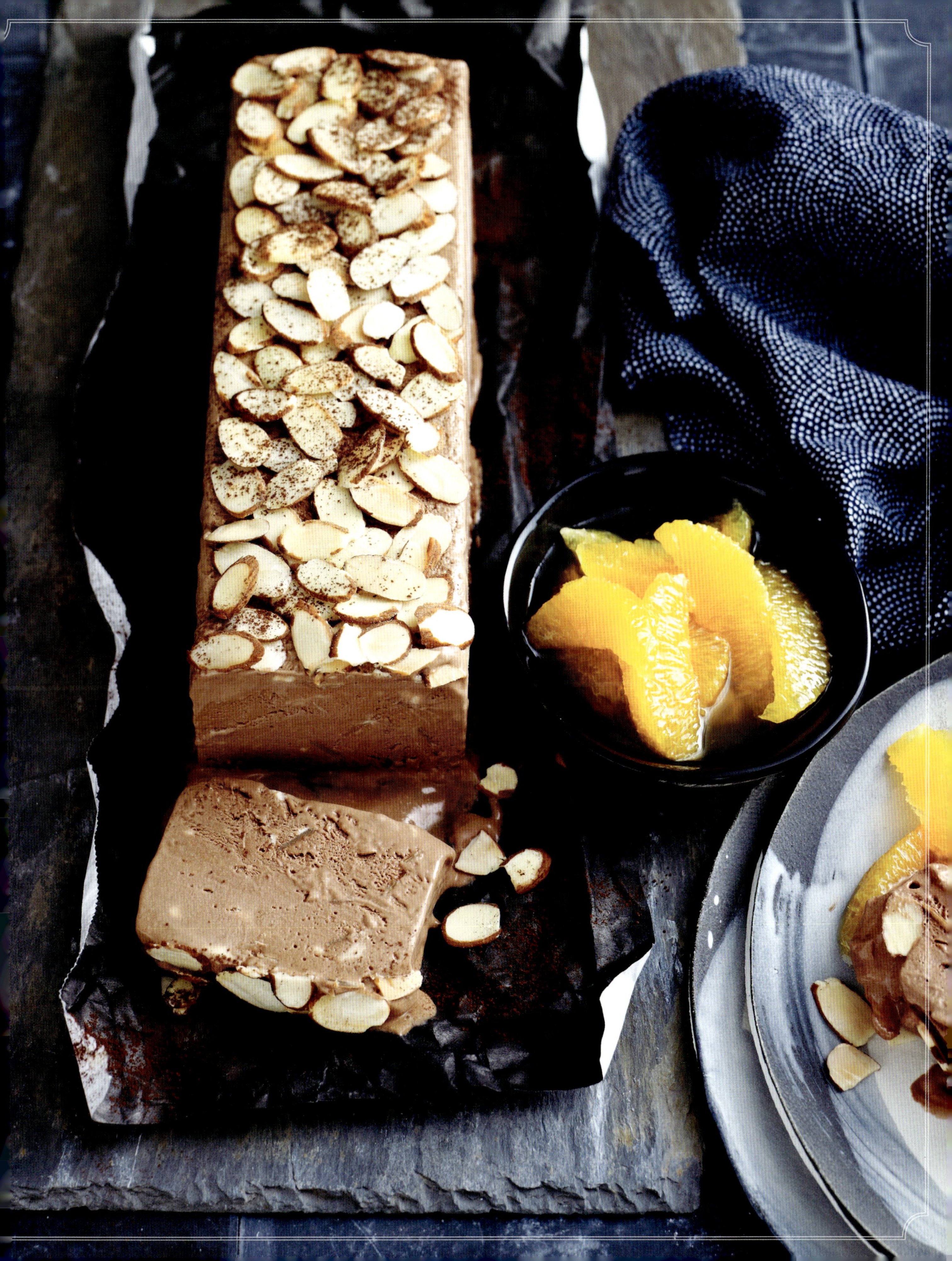

BAKED PEARS
with Chocolate Sauce

BAKED PEARS
with Chocolate Sauce

PREP + COOK TIME 1 HOUR SERVES 4

4 ripe medium beurre bosc pears (1kg), peeled, halved lengthways
¼ cup (90g) golden syrup or honey
25g (¾ ounce) butter, chopped
50g (1½ ounces) dark chocolate, chopped
½ cup (125ml) cream
4 scoops vanilla ice-cream

1. Preheat oven 200°C/400°F. Line an ovenproof dish, large enough to fit pears in a single layer, with baking paper.
2. Remove core from pears with a small spoon. Place pears, cut-side up in dish; drizzle with golden syrup, then dot with butter.
3. Bake pears for 45 minutes, turning and basting occasionally or until soft.
4. Meanwhile, combine chocolate and cream in a small heavy-based saucepan; stir over low heat until combined. Remove from heat.
5. Serve pears and ice-cream drizzled with some of the pear cooking liquid and chocolate sauce.

ROASTED PEACH
and Nectarine Compote

PREP + COOK TIME 30 MINUTES SERVES 8

6 medium peaches (900g)
6 medium nectarines (750g)
2 vanilla beans, split lengthways
½ cup (110g) firmly packed brown sugar
12 cardomom pods, bruised
1 cup (250ml) water

1. Preheat oven to 200°C/400°F.
2. Halve peaches and nectarines; remove stones. Place fruit, cut-side down, into two ceramic baking dishes.
3. Scrape seeds from vanilla beans into a small saucepan, then add pods. Add sugar, cardomom and the water; stir over low heat until sugar dissolves. Bring to the boil. Pour immediately over fruit.
4. Roast fruit 10 minutes; turn fruit over, roast a further 5 minutes or until soft. Cool. Peel away skin.
5. Serve hot or refrigerate, covered, until chilled.

SERVING SUGGESTION Serve with thick (double) cream, ice-cream or halva and pistachio yoghurt.

(PHOTOGRAPH PAGE 212)

ROASTED PEACH
and Nectarine Compote
(RECIPE PAGE 211)

TROPICAL FRUIT
with Rosewater Syrup

(RECIPE PAGE 214)

TROPICAL FRUIT with Rosewater Syrup

PREP + COOK TIME *20 MINUTES (+ COOLING & REFRIGERATION)*
SERVES *4*

¼ cup (55g) white (granulated) sugar
½ cup (125ml) water
2 tablespoons lime juice
¼ teaspoon rosewater
1 large mango (600g), chopped
1 large red papaya (650g), chopped
12 lychees (300g), peeled
2 passionfruit

1. Stir sugar and the water in a small saucepan over medium heat, without boiling, until sugar dissolves. Bring to the boil. Reduce heat; simmer, for 5 minutes. Pour into a heatproof jug or bowl. Cool.
2. Stir juice and rosewater into syrup; refrigerate until cold.
3. Just before serving, divide fruit into serving bowls; drizzle with syrup.

TIP You can use pineapple or even watermelon instead of the papaya if you prefer. You could also use 4 cardamom pods and a cinnamon quill instead of the rosewater.

(PHOTOGRAPH PAGE 213)

LEMON DELICIOUS Pudding

PREP + COOK TIME *1 HOUR* **SERVES** *6*

80g (2½ ounces) butter, softened
3 teaspoons finely grated lemon rind
½ cups (110g) caster (superfine) sugar
3 eggs, separated
¼ cup (35g) self-raising flour
1⅔ cups (400ml) milk
⅓ cup (80ml) lemon juice
2 teaspoons icing (confectioners') sugar

1. Preheat oven to 180°C/350°F. Grease a 1.5-litre (6-cup) ovenproof dish; place on an oven tray.
2. Beat butter, rind and sugar in a small bowl with an electric mixer until pale. Beat in egg yolks, one at a time, until thick. Stir in flour, milk and juice until well combined.
3. Beat egg whites in a small bowl with an electric mixer until firm peaks form; lightly fold into lemon mixture, in two batches. Pour mixture into dish.
4. Bake pudding for 35 minutes or until golden and just firm to the touch. Serve immediately dusted with sifted icing sugar.

SERVING SUGGESTION Serve with cream.

LEMON DELICIOUS
Pudding

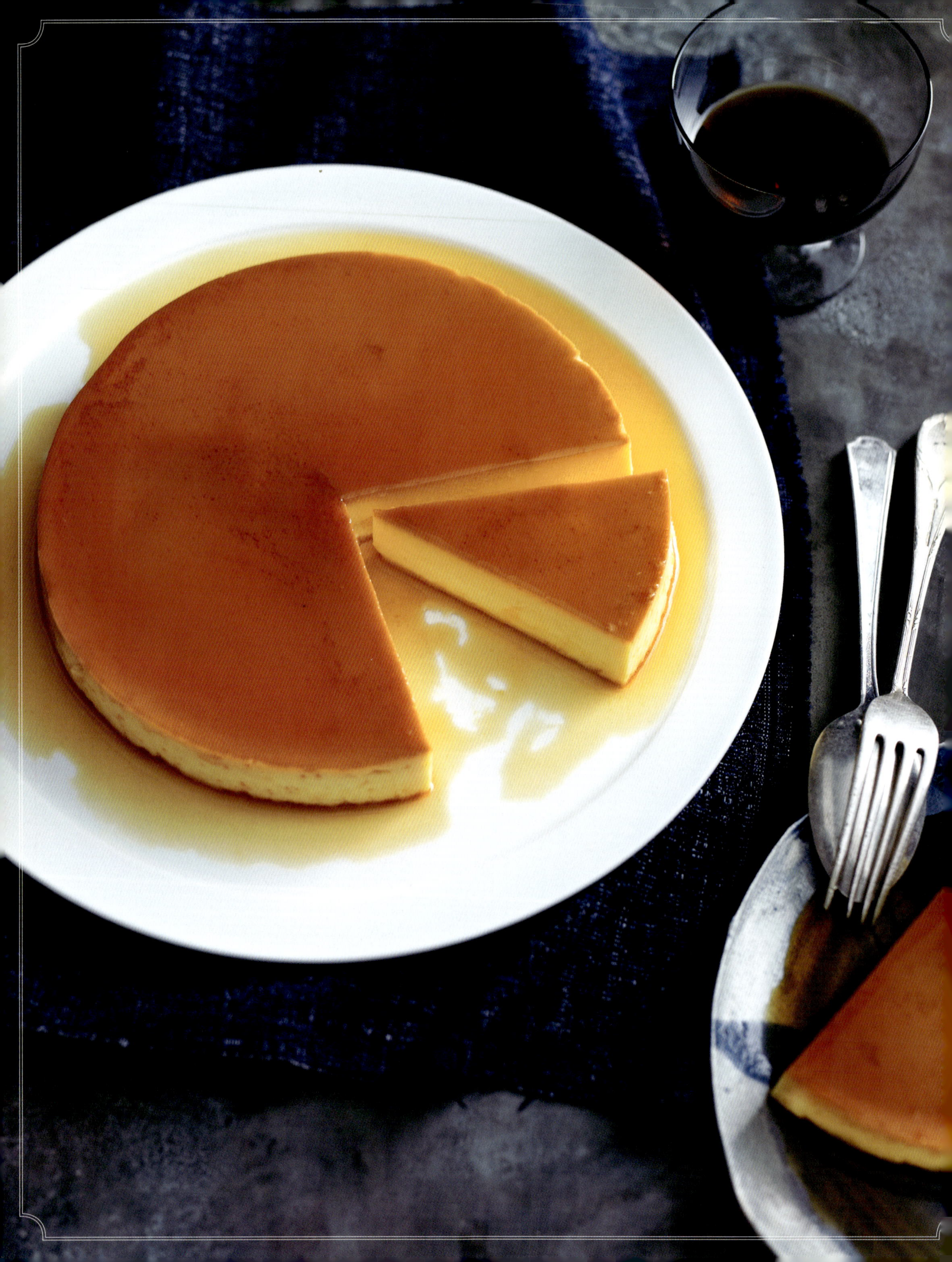

CRÈME CARAMEL

PREP + COOK TIME *1 HOUR (+ REFRIGERATION)* **SERVES** *8*

Start this recipe the day before.

¾ cup (165g) caster (superfine) sugar
½ cup (125ml) water
6 eggs
2 teaspoons vanilla extract
⅓ cup (75g) caster (superfine) sugar, extra
1¾ cups (430ml) milk
300ml (½ pint) pouring cream

1. Preheat oven to 160°C/325°F.
2. Stir sugar and the water in a small saucepan over medium heat, without boiling, until sugar dissolves. Brush the side of the pan with a wet pastry brush to remove any undissolved sugar crystals. Bring to the boil; boil without stirring until mixture is a dark golden caramel colour. Taking care, immediately pour caramel into a deep 20cm (8-inch) round cake pan.
3. Whisk eggs, extract and extra sugar in a large heatproof bowl or jug.
4. Stir milk and cream in a medium saucepan; bring to the boil. Whisking continuously, pour hot milk mixture into egg mixture. Strain mixture through a sieve into the cake pan.
5. Place cake pan in a medium roasting pan; pour enough boiling water into the roasting pan to come halfway up the side of the cake pan.
6. Bake 35 minutes or until set. Remove cake pan from water; cool. Cover; refrigerate overnight.
7. Using your fingers, gently ease the crème caramel away from the side of the pan. Place a platter with a lip over the pan, then quickly invert.

TIP To clean the saucepan you've just made caramel in, fill with water and place back on the stove for a few minutes until the water dissolves the caramel. Or, just leave the pan, filled with water, overnight to dissolve the toffee.

ULTIMATE BERRY TRIFLE

PREP + COOK TIME *45 MINUTES (+ REFRIGERATION)* **SERVES** *8*

1½ tablespoons (21g) powdered gelatine
½ cup (125ml) cold water
2⅔ cups (660ml) raspberry cranberry juice
8 large sponge finger biscuits (160g), cut in half lengthways
1½ tablespoons orange-flavoured liqueur
500g (1 pound) strawberries, sliced thickly
250g (8 ounces) raspberries
125g (4 ounces) blueberries
⅓ cup fresh mint leaves

MASCARPONE MIXTURE
3 eggs, separated
2 teaspoons vanilla bean paste or extract
½ cup (110g) caster (superfine) sugar
500g (1 pound) mascarpone cheese
1 tablespoon orange-flavoured liqueur

1. Sprinkle gelatine over the water in a small bowl; stand 3 minutes. Microwave gelatine mixture on MEDIUM (50%) for 20 seconds or until dissolved (or stand in pan of simmering water until dissolved). Cool slightly.
2. Combine gelatine mixture and juice in a large jug. Pour mixture into a 2.5-litre (10-cup) serving dish. Refrigerate 1½ hours or until almost set.
3. Make mascarpone mixture.
4. Brush cut-side of sponge fingers with liqueur; arrange on jelly, breaking any sponge fingers into smaller pieces as needed to fit dish. Scatter half the strawberries and half the raspberries onto sponge fingers; spoon mascarpone mixture over berries. Cover with plastic wrap; refrigerate several hours or until firm.
5. Just before serving, top trifle with the remaining strawberries and raspberries, then blueberries and mint leaves.

MASCARPONE MIXTURE
Beat egg yolks, paste and half the sugar in a small bowl with an electric mixer until fluffy. Place mascarpone and liqueur in a large bowl; stir with a wooden spoon until well combined. Gently fold egg yolk mixture into mascarpone mixture. Beat egg whites and remaining sugar in a clean small bowl with an electric mixer until soft peaks form. Gently fold egg white mixture into mascarpone mixture.

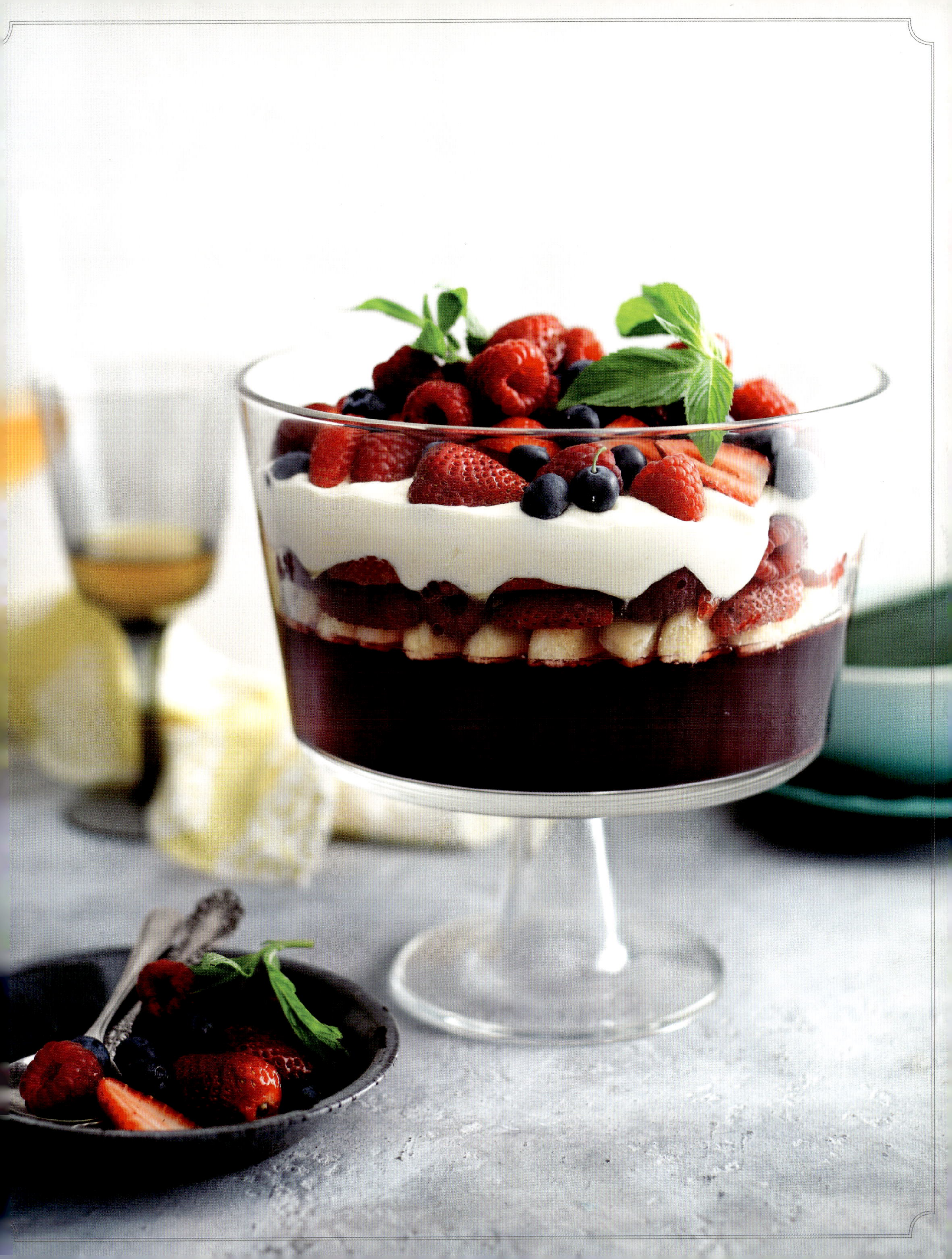

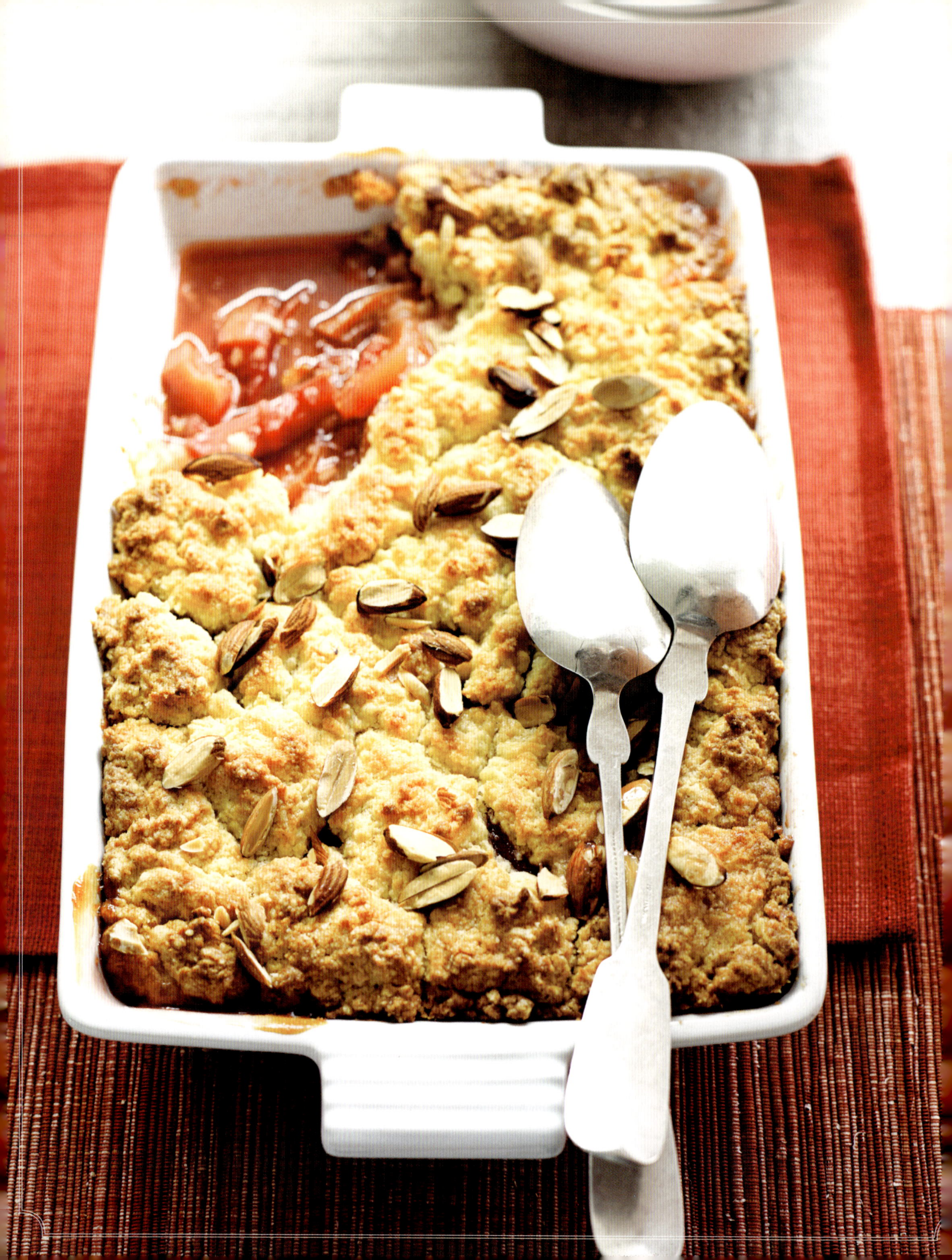

QUINCE AND RHUBARB *Cobbler*

PREP + COOK TIME *4 HOURS* **SERVES** *8*

4 medium quinces (1.4kg)
2 cups (440g) caster (superfine) sugar
3 cups (750ml) water
1 strip lemon rind
6 trimmed stems rhubarb (375g), cut into 5cm (2-inch) lengths
2 tablespoons lemon juice
2 tablespoons almonds, sliced thickly

TOPPING
1½ cups (225g) self-raising flour
⅓ cup (75g) caster (superfine) sugar
large pinch salt
150g (4½ ounces) butter, chopped
¼ cup (60ml) buttermilk
1 teaspoon vanilla extract

1. Peel and core quinces; cut each quince into six or eight wedges.
2. Stir sugar, the water and rind in a large saucepan over low heat until sugar dissolves; bring to the boil. Add quince. Reduce heat to low; simmer, covered, 1 hour. Uncover; simmer, stirring occasionally, 1½ hours or until quince is tender and syrup is rosy-pink in colour.
3. Preheat oven to 180°C/350°F. Grease a 2-litre (8-cup) ovenproof dish.
4. Using a slotted spoon, remove quince from syrup; place in dish with rhubarb. Add juice and enough syrup to quince mixture to almost cover fruit.
5. Make topping; drop teaspoonfuls of topping over hot fruit, sprinkle with almonds.
6. Bake cobbler 1 hour or until top is browned.

TOPPING
Sift flour, sugar and salt into a large bowl; rub in butter with fingertips. Make a well; add combined buttermilk and extract. Use a butter knife to "cut" milk mixture through dry ingredients to a soft, sticky dough.

SERVING SUGGESTION Serve with vanilla ice-cream, thick (double) cream or custard.

CHOCOLATE LOVE POTS

PREP + COOK TIME *25 MINUTES (+ REFRIGERATION)* **SERVES 6**

Tantalising and devilishly chocolatey this very adult-tasting dessert is quick and easy to make for any special occasion. Make sure you use chocolate with 70% cocoa solids to get the best results.

200g (6½ ounces) dark chocolate (70% cocoa)
30g (1 ounce) butter, softened
3 eggs, separated
300ml (½ pint) thickened (heavy) cream
1½ tablespoons dutch cocoa
12 pieces almond bread (60g)

1. Melt chocolate in a medium heatproof bowl over a medium saucepan of simmering water (don't let the water touch the bottom of the bowl). Remove the bowl from heat; stir in butter until smooth. Fold in egg yolks. Transfer mixture to a large bowl.
2. Beat cream in a small bowl with an electric mixer until soft peaks form.
3. Beat egg whites in another small bowl with electric mixer until soft peaks form.
4. Fold cream into chocolate mixture, then fold in egg whites, in two batches. Spoon mixture into six 1¼-cup (310ml) cups or glasses. Refrigerate 3 hours or overnight.
5. Just before serving, dust with cocoa; serve with almond bread.

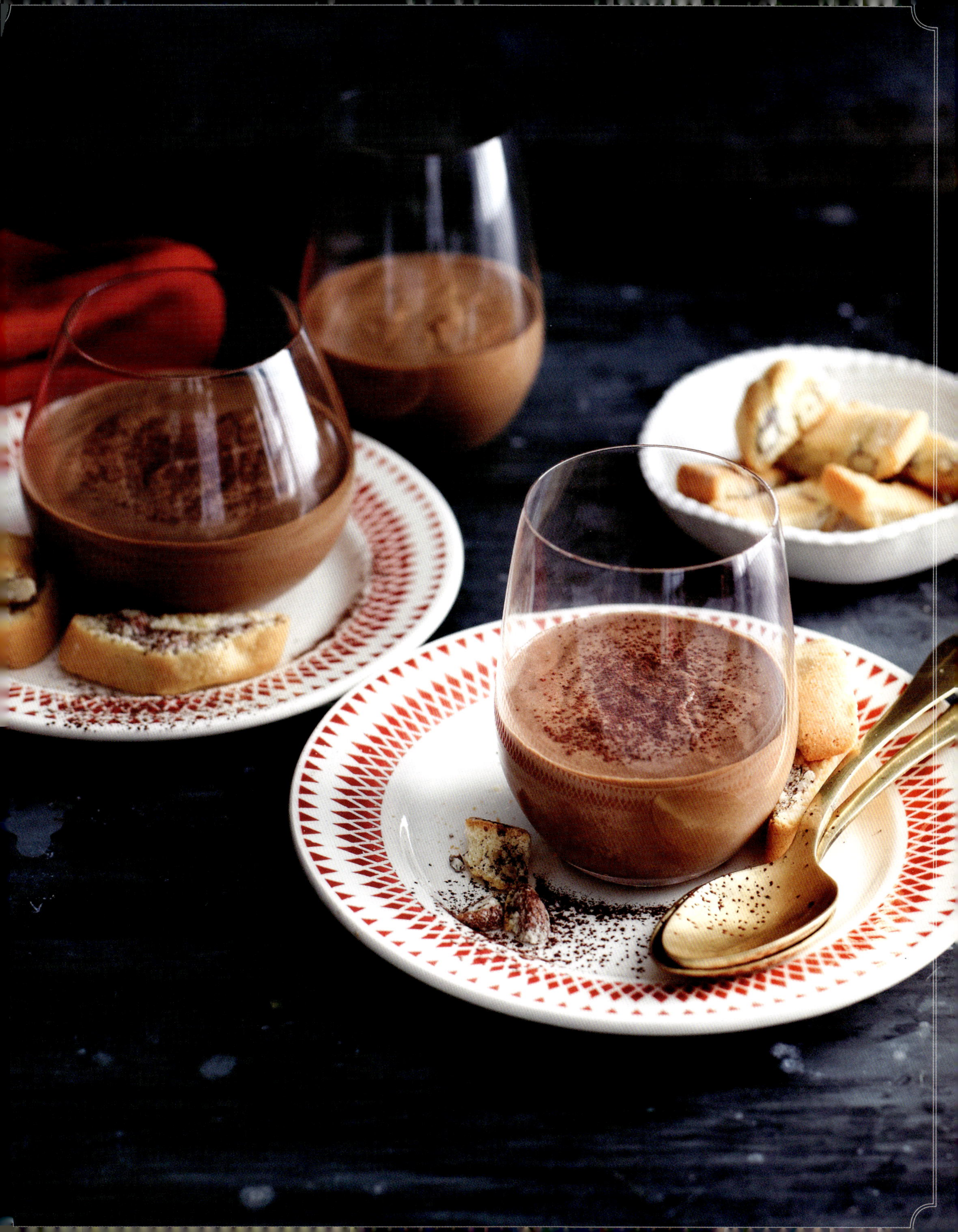

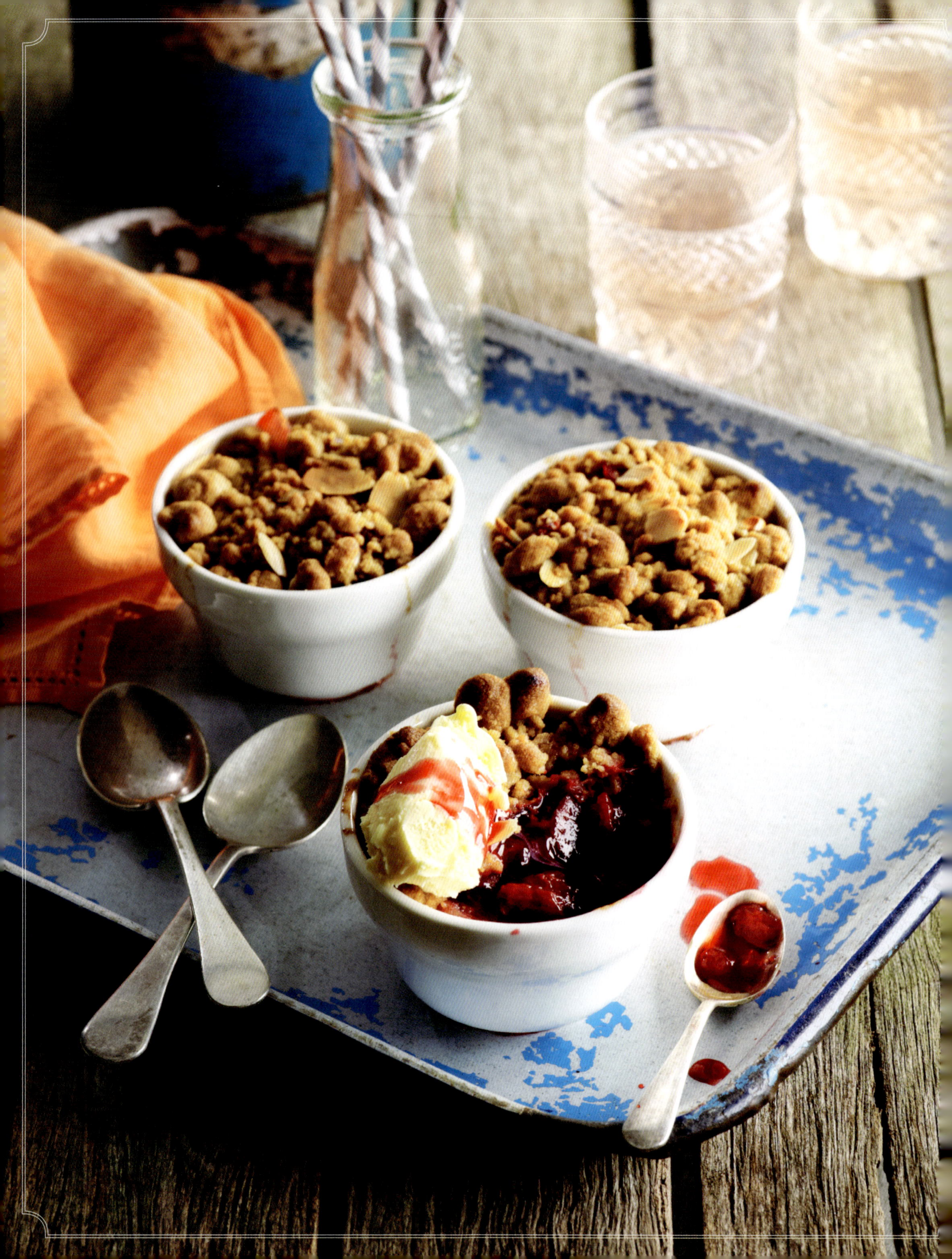

SPICED PLUM AND APPLE
Crumble

PREP + COOK TIME 1 HOUR SERVES 6

500g (1 pound) apples
¾ cup (165g) caster (superfine) sugar
2 tablespoons water
700g (1½ pounds) red-fleshed plums
1 cup (150g) plain (all-purpose) flour
½ cup (110g) firmly packed brown sugar
1 teaspoon mixed spice
125g (4 ounces) cold unsalted butter, chopped finely
¼ cup (20g) flaked almonds

1 Preheat oven to 200°C/400°F.
2 Peel and core apples; cut into chunks. Place apple in a large saucepan with caster sugar and the water; cook, stirring, over medium heat, until sugar dissolves. Cover; cook a further 10 minutes or until apple is just tender.
3 Quarter plums, discard stone. Stir into apples; cook, covered, 5 minutes or until plums are soft but still hold their shape.
4 Remove fruit from syrup with a slotted spoon; transfer to a 1.25-litre (5-cup) ovenproof dish. Reserve syrup.
5 Combine flour, brown sugar and mixed spice in a large bowl. Rub in butter with your fingertips until the mixture resembles breadcrumbs and starts to clump together. Add almonds; fold through mixture. Sprinkle crumble over fruit.
6 Bake for 30 minutes or until golden and bubbling. Serve crumble warm, drizzled with reserved syrup, if you like.

TIPS We used pink lady apples in this recipes, as they tend to hold their shape well.
You can keep any unused syrup for another time, to serve over ice-cream and fresh berries.

SERVING SUGGESTION Serve with thick (double) cream or vanilla ice-cream

NEW YORK-STYLE CHEESECAKE

PREP + COOK TIME *2 HOURS 30 MINUTES (+ REFRIGERATION)* **SERVES** *12*

250g (8 ounces) plain sweet biscuits
125g (4 ounces) butter, melted
750g (1½ pounds) cream cheese, softened
2 teaspoons finely grated orange rind
1 teaspoon finely grated lemon rind
1 cup (220g) caster (superfine) sugar
3 eggs
¾ cup (180g) sour cream
¼ cup (60ml) lemon juice

SOUR CREAM TOPPING
1 cup (240g) sour cream
2 tablespoons caster (superfine) sugar
2 teaspoons lemon juice

1. Process biscuits until fine crumbs form. Add butter, process until combined. Press biscuit mixture over base and side of a 24cm (9½-inch) springform pan. Place on an oven tray; refrigerate 30 minutes.
2. Preheat oven to 180°C/350°F.
3. Beat cream cheese, rinds and sugar in a medium bowl with an electric mixer until smooth. Beat in eggs, one at a time, then sour cream and juice. Pour filling into pan.
4. Bake cheesecake 1¼ hours; remove from oven. Cool 15 minutes.
5. Meanwhile, make sour cream topping.
6. Spread topping over cheesecake. Bake a further 20 minutes; cool in oven with the door ajar. Refrigerate cheesecake 3 hours or overnight, before serving.

SOUR CREAM TOPPING
Combine ingredients in a small bowl until smooth.

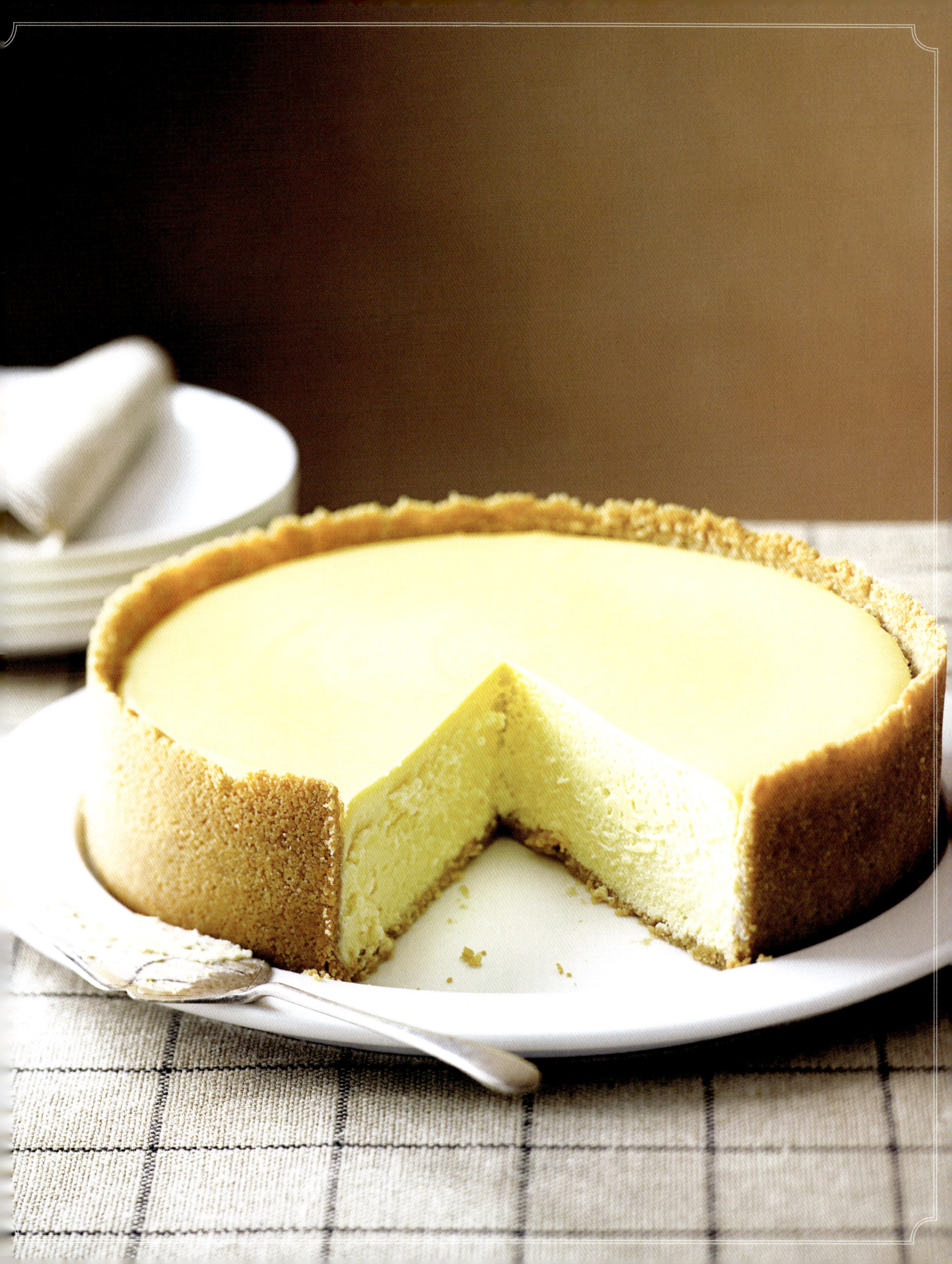

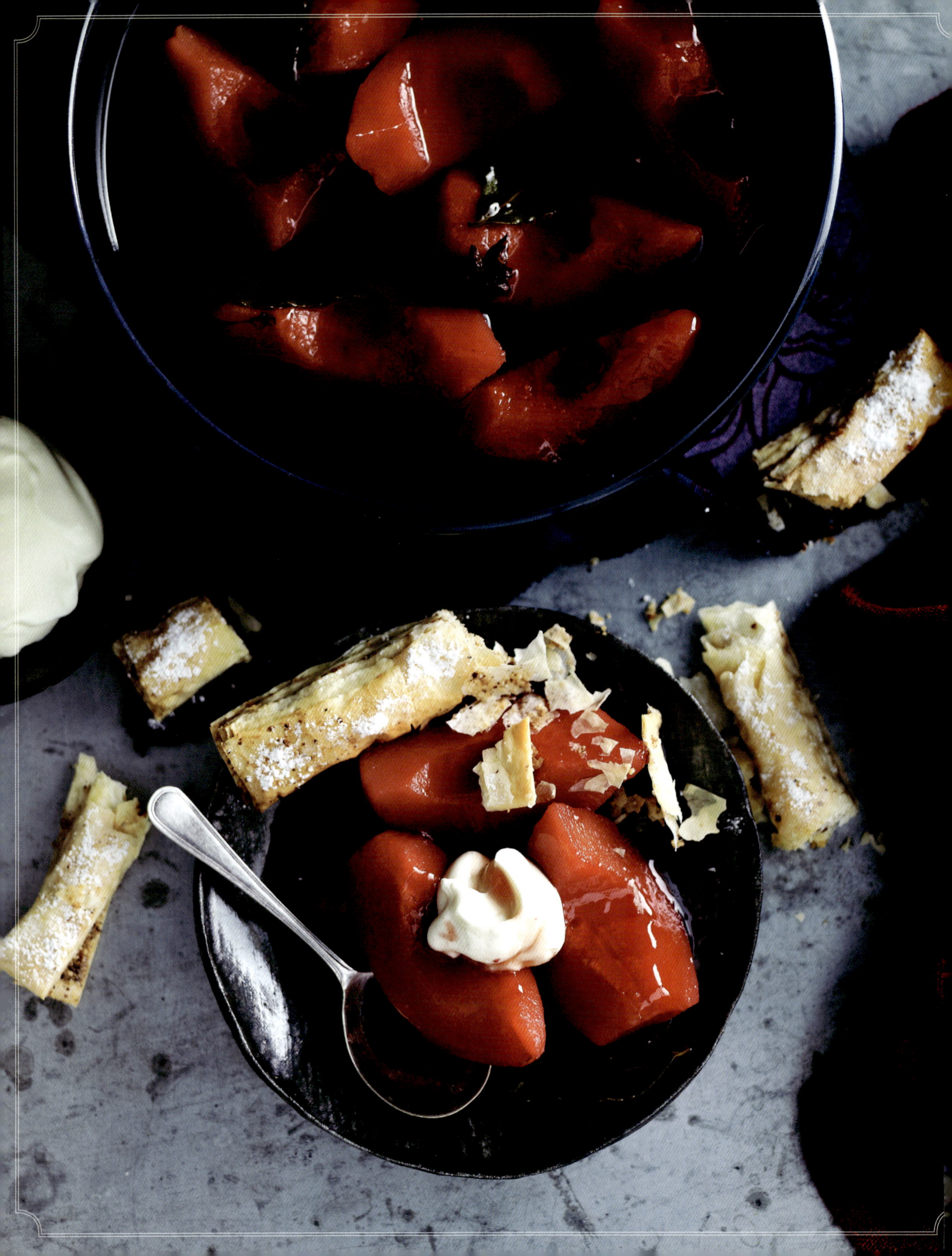

SLOW-POACHED QUINCE
with Fillo Fingers

PREP + COOK TIME *4 HOURS* **SERVES** 6

Quince are a winter fruit, that in their raw state are inedibly bitter, but when they are cooked slowly with sugar and spices a wonderful alchemy results, transforming the flesh to a fragrant and rosy hue. Once cooked they store well.

1½ cup (330g) caster (superfine) sugar
½ cup (175g) honey
3 bay leaves
3 star anise
2 cups (500ml) red wine
2.25 litres (9 cups) water
6 large quinces (2.4kg)

FILLO FINGERS
4 sheets fillo pastry
60g (2 ounces) unsalted butter, melted
2 tablespoons ground hazelnut
1 tablespoon icing (confectioners') sugar

1 Stir sugar, honey, bay leaves, star anise, red wine and the water in a large saucepan over medium heat until sugar dissolves.
2 Peel quinces, cut into quarters (or eighths depending on their size); remove cores. Add quince to syrup; cook over medium heat until syrup comes to a simmer. Simmer, covered, over low heat for 3½ hours or until quince is soft and rosy-coloured.
3 Strain half the poaching liquid into a medium saucepan; simmer 40 minutes until syrupy and reduced by half.
4 Meanwhile, preheat oven to 150°C/300°F. Line an oven tray with baking paper.
5 To make fillo fingers, place one sheet of pastry on the bench. Brush with a little of the butter; top with remaining sheet of pastry, brushing with more butter. Fold layered pastry in half widthways. Brush with butter; fold in half widthways again. Brush with a little more butter; sprinkle with half the ground hazelnuts. Fold in half once more and brush with butter. Cut the rectangle into four long strips; place on tray. Repeat process with remaining ingredients to make another four pastry fingers.
6 Bake fillo fingers 10 minutes or until golden. Dust with sifted icing sugar.
7 Serve quince with syrup and fillo fingers.

TIP Quince will keep in their syrup in the fridge for up to 1 month.

SERVING SUGGESTION Serve with vanilla ice-cream, double (thick) cream or yoghurt.

CLASSIC PAVLOVA
Baked on a Plate

PREP + COOK TIME *1 HOUR 45 MINUTES (+ COOLING)* **SERVES** *8*

This clever marshmallow-textured pavlova is cooked directly on the platter it's served on, which eliminates the risk of breaking the fragile meringue when transferring it. Simply make sure the platter is sturdy, ovenproof and has no decorative or metallic embellishments.

10g (½ ounce) butter, melted
2 teaspoons cornflour (cornstarch)
5 egg whites
1¼ cups (275g) caster (superfine) sugar
1 tablespoon cornflour (cornstarch), extra
1½ cups (375ml) thickened (heavy) cream
250g (8 ounces) strawberries, halved
1 large mango (600g), sliced thinly
⅓ cup (80ml) passionfruit pulp

1. Preheat oven to 150°C/300°F. Grease a 29cm (11¾-inch) round ovenproof platter or cake stand with butter, leaving a 3cm (1¼-inch) border. Sift cornflour over the greased area.
2. Beat egg whites in a large bowl with an electric mixer until soft peaks form. Gradually add sugar, beating until dissolved between additions, scraping down the side of the bowl occasionally, or until thick and glossy. Using a large metal spoon or spatula, fold in extra sifted cornflour.
3. Pile meringue into the centre of the plate. Using a metal spatula or the back of a spoon, spread the meringue into a 23cm (9¼-inch) round, making a shallow well in the centre.
4. Reduce oven to 100°C/200°F.
5. Bake pavlova in the lower half of the oven for 1½ hours or until dry and crisp. Turn off the oven; cool in oven with door ajar.
6. Beat cream in a small bowl with an electric mixer until soft peaks form.
7. Top pavlova with cream, strawberries, mango and passionfruit.

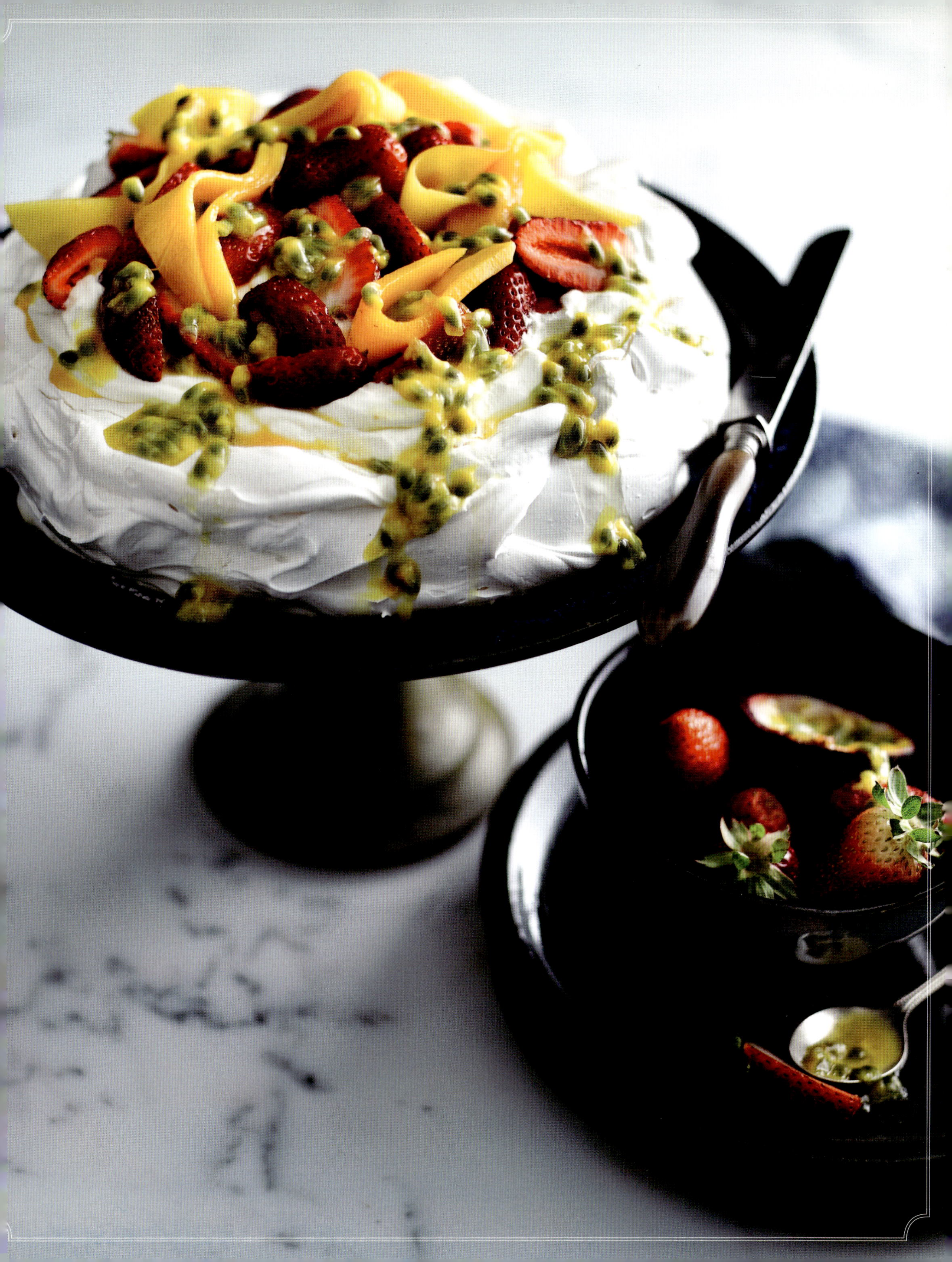

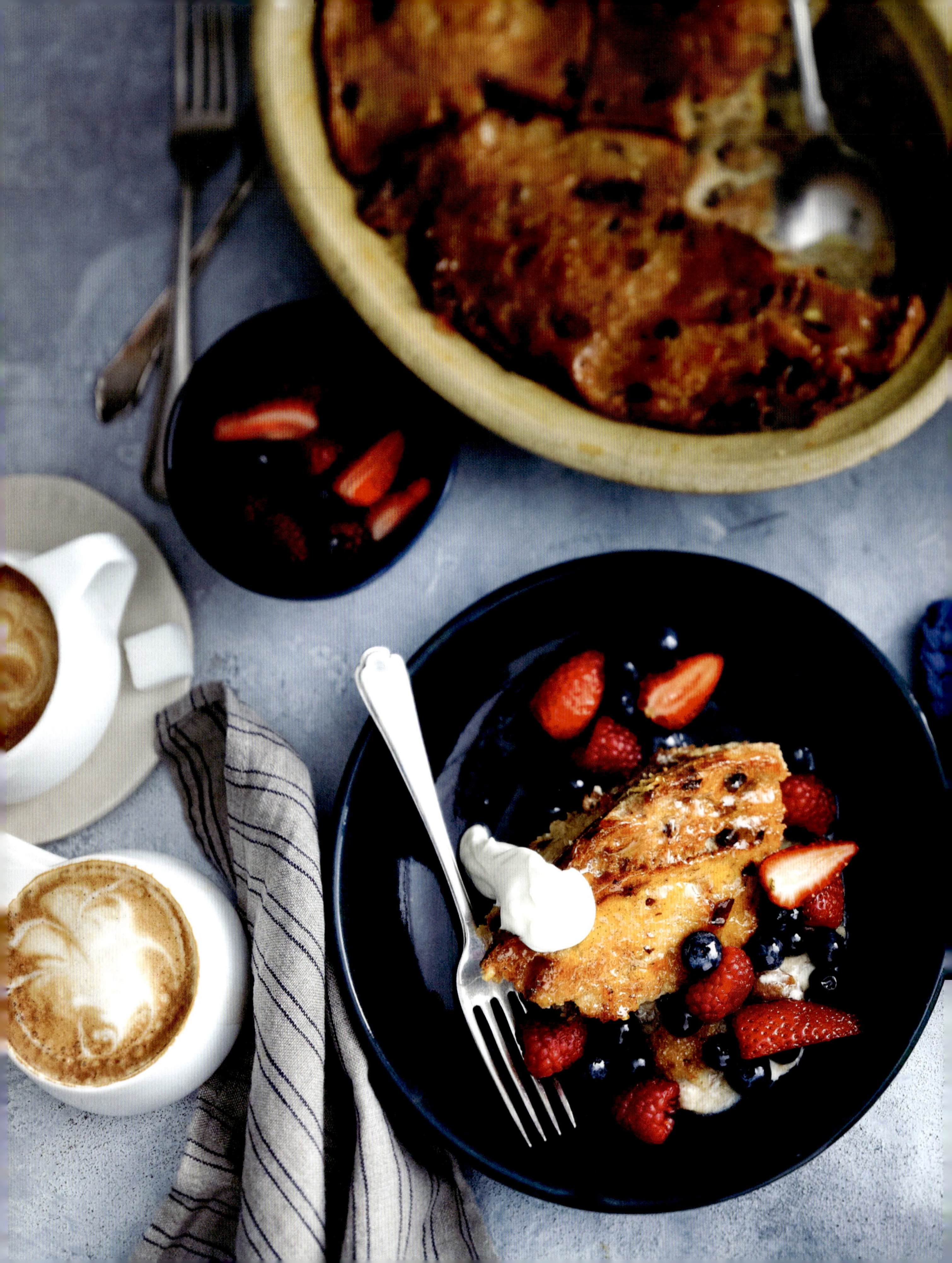

WINTER MENU

PUMPKIN RAVIOLI
with Sage Butter

(RECIPE PAGE 62)

MEDITERRANEAN
Fish Soup

(RECIPE PAGE 23)

PANETTONE CUSTARD PUDDING
with Macerated Fruit

(RECIPE PAGE 235)

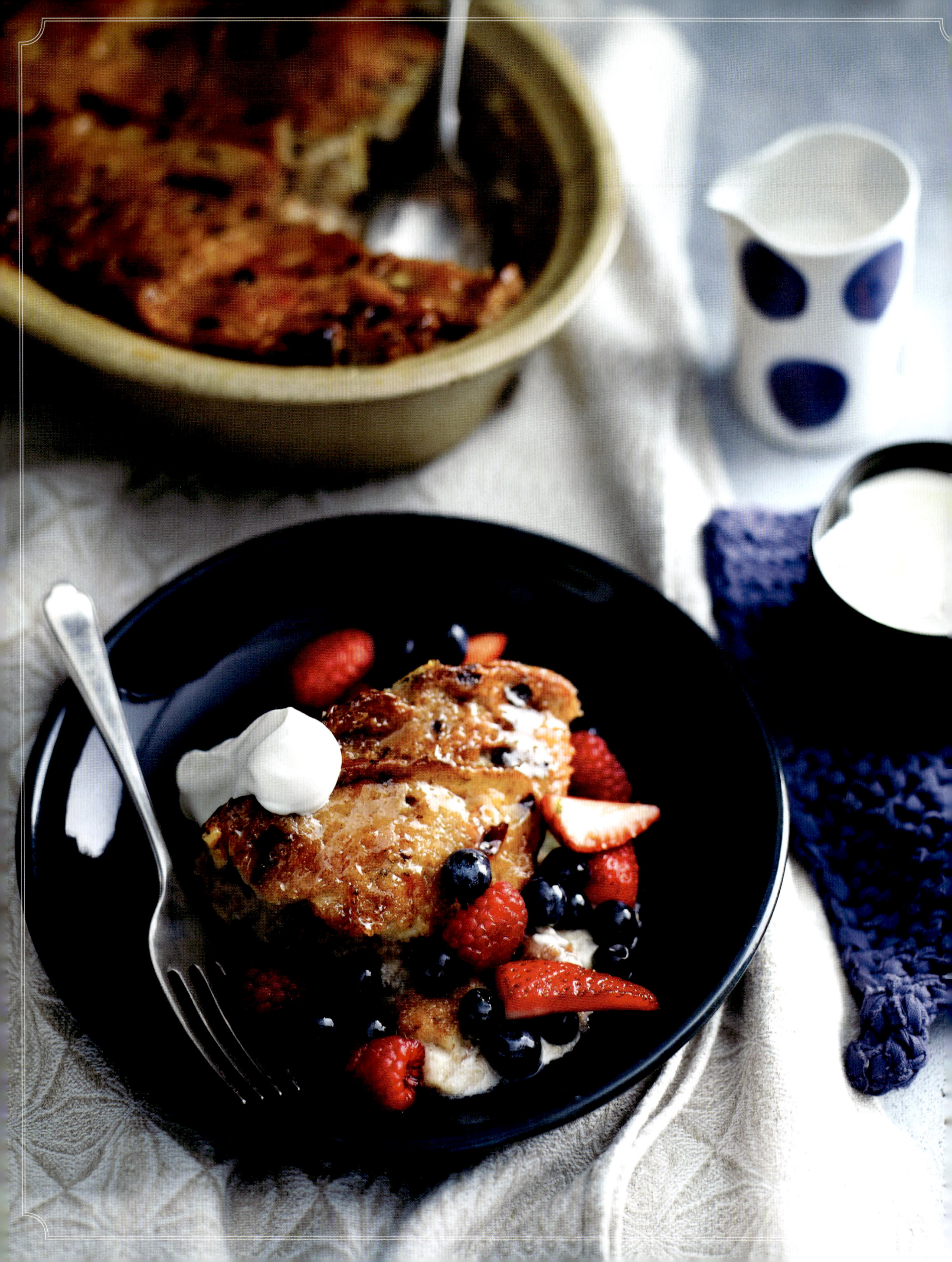

PANETTONE CUSTARD PUDDING
with Macerated Fruit

PREP + COOK TIME 1 HOUR 45 MINUTES SERVES 8

½ x 500g (1 pound) panettone
90g (3 ounces) soft butter
3 cups (750ml) milk
300ml (½ pint) thickened (heavy) cream
½ cup (110g) caster (superfine) sugar
1 teaspoons finely grated orange rind
4cm (1½-inch) piece vanilla bean, split lengthways
4 eggs
2 egg yolks
1 tablespoon apricot jam
1 tablespoon orange-flavoured liqueur

MACERATED FRUIT
200g (6½ ounces) raspberries
250g (8 ounces) strawberries, halved
200g (6½ ounces) blueberries
1 medium mango (430g), chopped
2 tablespoons caster (superfine) sugar
¼ cup (60ml) orange-flavoured liqueur

SOURED CREAM
½ cup (125ml) thickened (heavy) cream
⅓ cup (80g) sour cream
1 tablespoons icing (confectioners') sugar

1. Preheat grill (broiler).
2. Cut panettone into 1cm (½-inch) slices. Place under grill until lightly toasted on both sides. While panettone is hot, spread with butter, then cut into fingers. Place toast fingers in a criss-cross pattern in a shallow 1.5-litre (6-cup) ovenproof dish.
3. Stir milk, cream, sugar, rind and vanilla bean in a saucepan, over medium heat until sugar dissolves; bring almost to the boil. Remove from heat. Cover; stand 10 minutes. Strain mixture through a sieve into a heatproof jug.
4. Preheat oven to 180°C/350°F.
5. Whisk eggs and egg yolks in a medium bowl; gradually whisk in milk mixture. Pour custard over panettone. Place dish in a large baking dish; add enough boiling water to the baking dish to come halfway up the sides of the ovenproof dish.
6. Bake pudding 1 hour or until browned lightly and set. Remove pudding dish from baking dish.
7. Meanwhile, make macerated fruit, then make soured cream.
8. Brush hot pudding with combined jam and liqueur; serve warm or cold with fruit and soured cream.

MACERATED FRUIT
Combine ingredients in a large bowl.

SOURED CREAM
Beat thickened cream in a small bowl with an electric mixer until soft peaks form. Add sour cream and sifted icing sugar, beat briefly until soft peaks form again.

TIP Panettone are easy to find around Christmas time, at other times they may not be as readily available. You can use brioche instead, adding a handful of sultanas, or thick-cut fruit bread.

FROZEN MANGO
Macadamia Crunch

PREP TIME *30 MINUTES (+ FREEZING & STANDING)* **SERVES 8**

100g (3 ounces) brandy snap biscuits
2 tablespoons finely chopped toasted macadamia nuts
20g (¾ ounce) butter, melted
2 large mangoes (1.2kg)
1 tablespoon caster (superfine) sugar
1 tablespoon lime juice
400g (12½ ounces) fresh ricotta
¾ cup (165g) caster (superfine) sugar, extra
300g (9½ ounces) sour cream
2 medium mangoes (860g), sliced, extra
2 limes, sliced thinly

1. Grease a 14cm x 22cm (5½-inch x 9-inch) loaf pan; line base and sides with two layers of foil, extending the foil 10cm (4-inch) over edge of pan.
2. Blend or process biscuits until they become fine crumbs; transfer to a medium bowl. Stir in nuts and butter until combined. Using your hands, press biscuit mixture lightly over base of pan. Cover; freeze 20 minutes or until firm.
3. Meanwhile, slice cheeks from mangoes; discard skin and seed. Blend or process mango, sugar and juice until smooth. Transfer to a medium bowl.
4. Blend or process ricotta and extra sugar until smooth. Add sour cream; blend or process until just combined.
5. Drop alternate spoonfuls of mango mixture and ricotta mixture over biscuit base in pan; using a butter knife, gently swirl the mixtures. Cover; freeze overnight or until firm.
6. Turn frozen mixture out of the pan onto a platter or board; remove foil lining. Decorate with extra mango slices and lime. Stand 15 minutes before serving.

TIP Instead of brandy snaps, you could use ginger snap, butternut snap or honey snap biscuits.

Puddings & Desserts

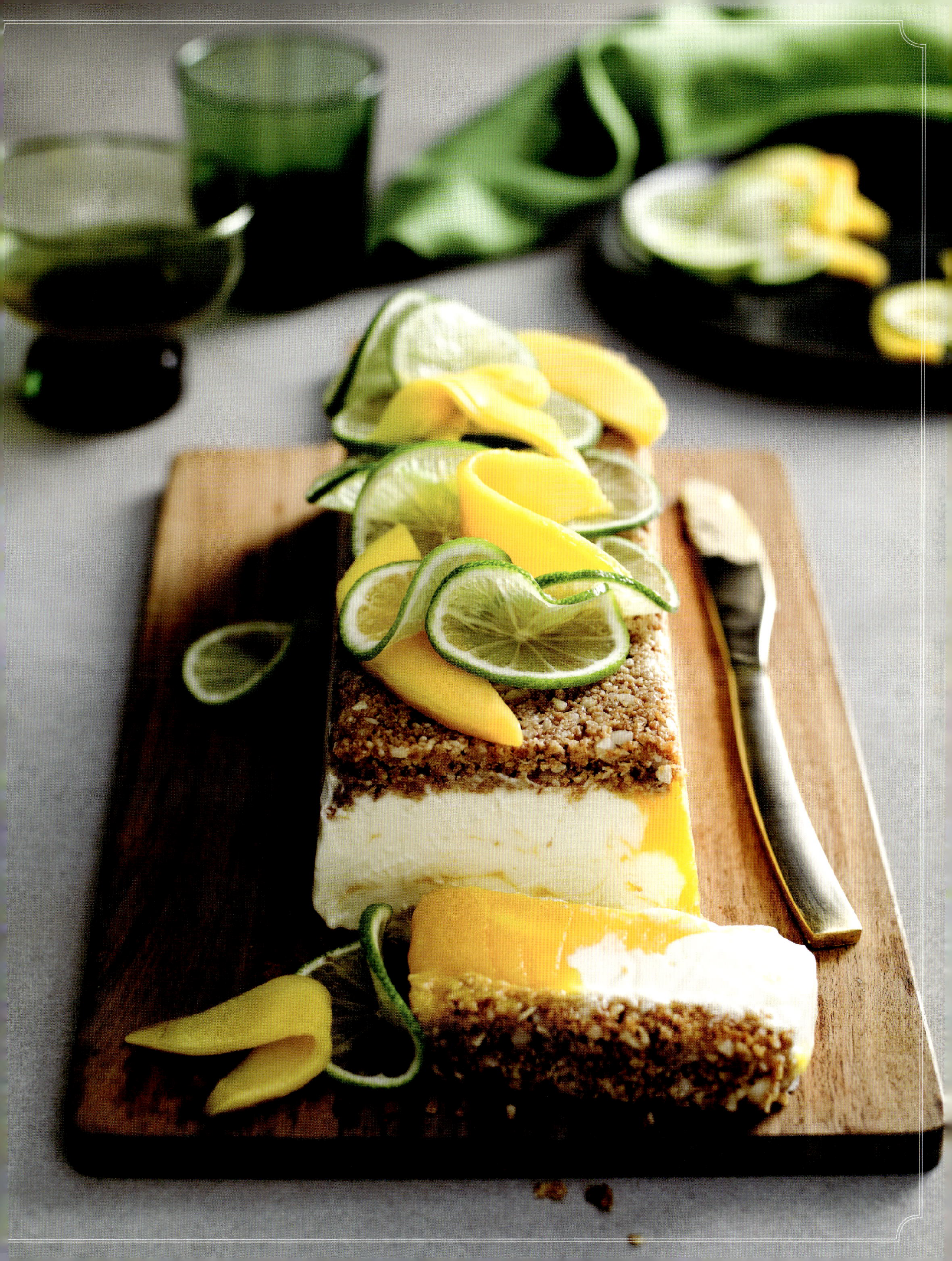

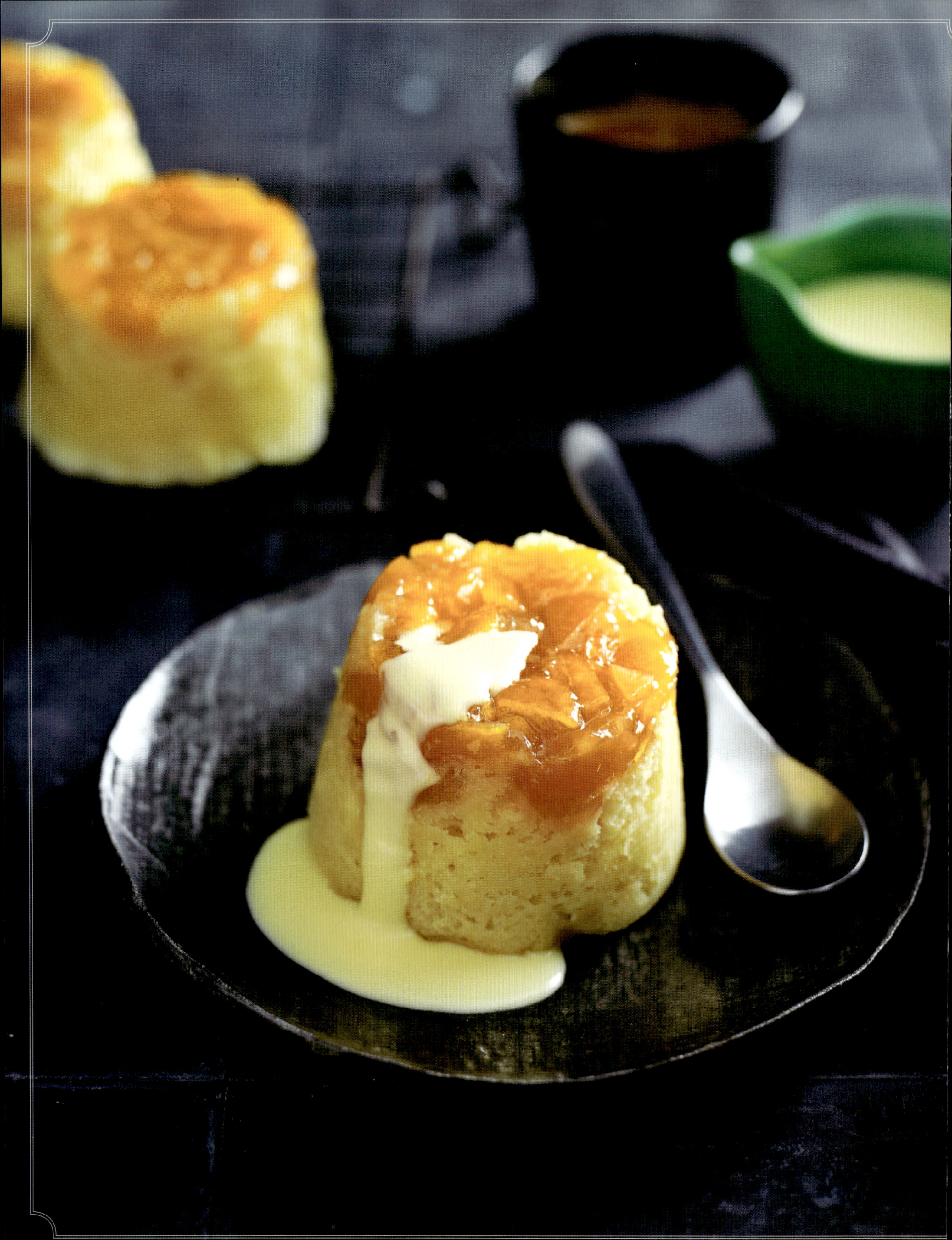

MANDARIN JAM Puddings

PREP + COOK TIME 2 HOURS SERVES 6

125g (4 ounces) butter, softened, chopped
1 teaspoon vanilla extract
½ cup (110g) caster (superfine) sugar
2 eggs
2 cups (300g) self-raising flour
½ cup (125ml) milk

MANDARIN JAM
4 small mandarins (350g), unpeeled, chopped coarsely
2 cups (500ml) water
1 cup (220g) caster (superfine) sugar

CUSTARD
¾ cup (180ml) pouring cream
¾ cup (180ml) milk
4 egg yolks
¼ cup (55g) caster (superfine) sugar
2 tablespoons orange-flavoured liqueur

1. Preheat oven to 180°C/350°F. Grease and line the base and side of six 1-cup (250ml) metal diarole moulds.
2. Make mandarin jam.
3. Beat butter, extract and sugar in a small bowl with an electric mixer until thick and creamy. Beat in eggs one at a time. Transfer mixture to a medium bowl; stir in sifted flour and milk, in two batches.
4. Spoon mandarin jam into moulds, top with pudding mixture; tap moulds gently to level mixture. Cover each mould with greased foil, secure with string. Place moulds in a large roasting pan; pour enough boiling water into the pan to come one-third of the way up sides of the moulds.
5. Bake puddings 40 minutes or until a skewer inserted into the centre comes out clean.
6. Meanwhile, make custard.
7. Turn hot puddings out onto individual plates, serve with warm custard.

MANDARIN JAM
Place mandarin and the water in a medium saucepan; simmer, uncovered, stirring occasionally, for 1 hour or until mandarin is tender. Add sugar; stir until sugar dissolves. Simmer over medium heat for 10 minutes or until mixture is the consistency of soft jam.

CUSTARD
Bring cream and milk almost to the boil in a medium saucepan. Meanwhile, whisk egg yolks and sugar in a medium bowl until thick and creamy; gradually whisk in hot milk mixture. Return mixture to same pan; stir over low-medium heat until mixture thickens enough to coat the back of the spoon (do not allow to boil). Stir in liqueur.

CLASSIC CHOCOLATE
Self-saucing Pudding

PREP + COOK TIME 1 HOUR 10 MINUTES **SERVES** 6

---

1 cup (150g) self-raising flour
¼ cup (25g) cocoa powder
½ cup (110g) firmly packed brown sugar
½ cup (125ml) milk
1 egg
60g (2 ounces) butter, melted, cooled
⅓ cup (35g) cocoa powder, extra
½ cup (110g) firmly packed brown sugar, extra
1¾ cups (430ml) boiling water

1. Preheat oven to 180°C/350°F. Grease a 1.5-litre (6-cup) ovenproof dish; place on a baking-paper-lined oven tray (to catch any drips).
2. Sift flour and cocoa into a medium bowl; stir in sugar, breaking up any lumps.
3. Whisk milk, egg and butter in a jug; pour mixture into dry ingredients, whisking to form a smooth batter. Pour mixture into dish; smooth the surface.
4. Combine sifted extra cocoa and extra sugar in a small bowl; sprinkle evenly over pudding batter. Gently pour the water over mixture.
5. Bake pudding 50 minutes or until centre is firm.

TIP We used a round dish 17cm (6¾ inches) in diameter and 8cm (3¼ inches) deep. A wider, shallower dish could also be used, but the cooking time should be reduced by 5-10 minutes.

SERVING SUGGESTION Serve dusted with sifted cocoa powder and with cream or vanilla ice-cream.

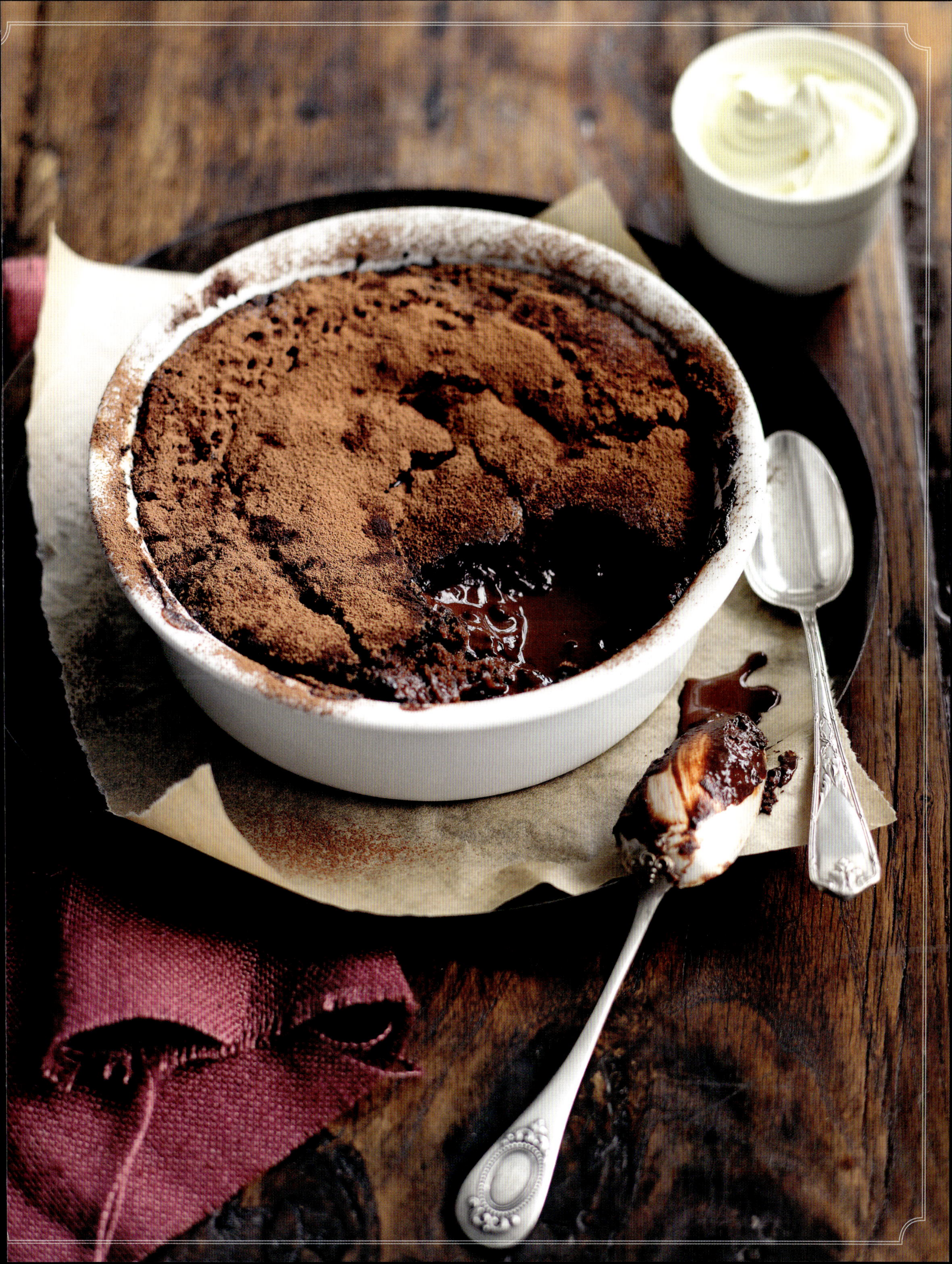

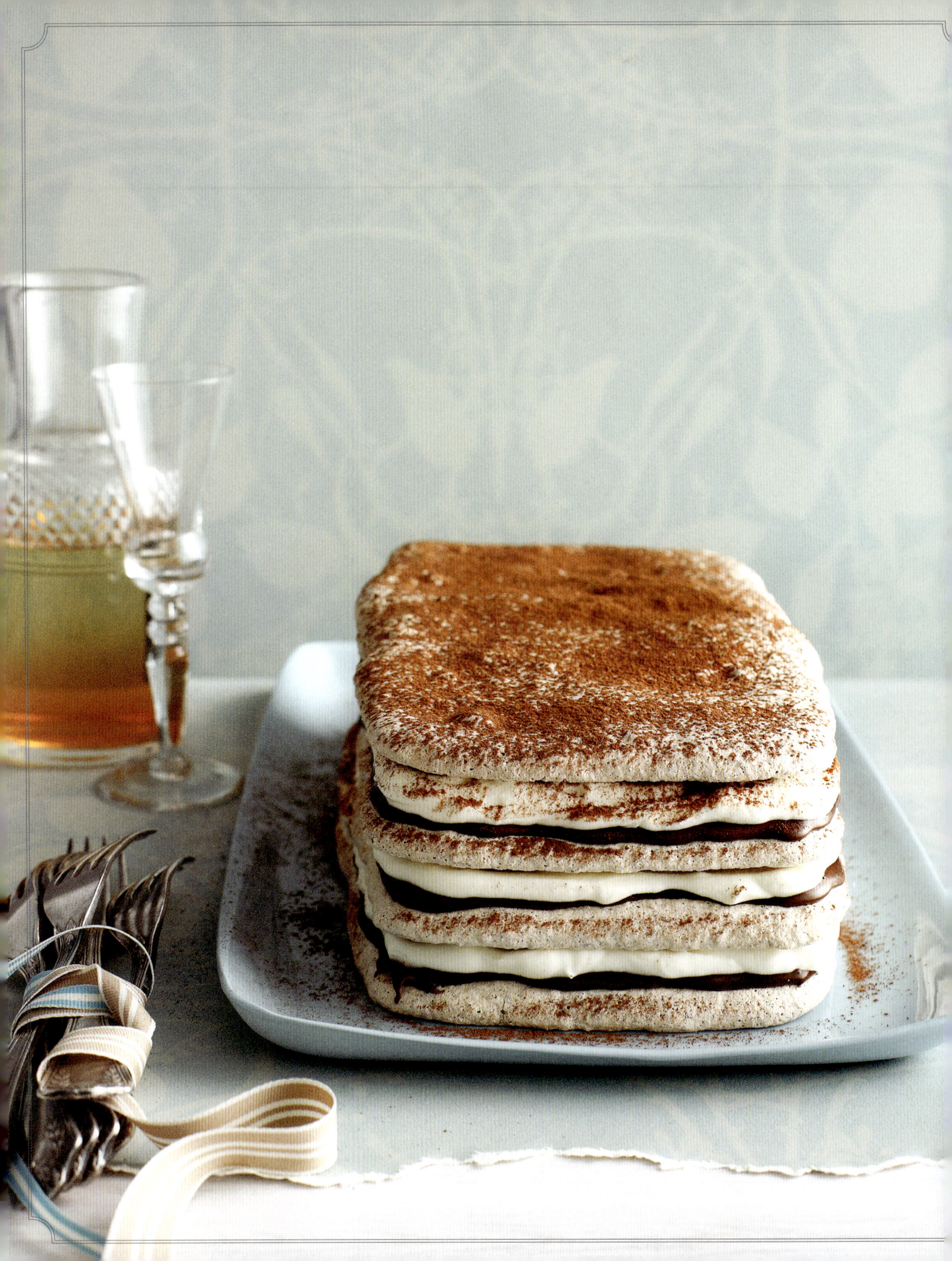

CHOCOLATE HAZELNUT *Torte*

PREP + COOK TIME *1 HOUR* **SERVES** *10*

5 egg whites
1¼ cups (275g) caster (superfine) sugar
1½ cups (150g) ground hazelnuts
600ml (1 pint) thickened (heavy) cream
1 cup (320g) chocolate hazelnut spread
1 teaspoon dutch cocoa

1. Preheat oven to 160°C/325°F. Line two large oven trays with baking paper. Using a pencil, mark two 12cm x 25cm (4¾-inch x 10-inch) rectangles on each tray. Turn the baking paper over so the pencil marks are facing down.
2. Beat egg whites in a medium bowl with an electric mixer until soft peaks form. Gradually add sugar, beat until dissolved. Fold in ground hazelnuts.
3. Spread one quarter of the mixture evenly over each outlined rectangle. Bake, swapping trays halfway through cooking, for 40 minutes or until crisp. Cool on trays.
4. Beat cream in a medium bowl with an electric mixer until soft peaks form.
5. Place chocolate hazelnut spread in a small bowl. Microwave on HIGH (100%) for 20 seconds or until it becomes a soft, spreadable consistency. Spread chocolate spread evenly over three of the meringue rectangles.
6. Place one of the chocolate-topped meringue rectangles on a platter. Spread with one-third of the cream. Repeat layering with remaining chocolate-topped meringue rectangles and cream. Top with remaining plain meringue rectangle. Serve dusted with cocoa.

TIP This torte will keep in the refrigerator, covered, for up to 2 days. In fact, it cuts better after a day or so of standing.

Puddings & Desserts

STICKY DATE
Pudding

PREP + COOK TIME *1 HOUR 15 MINUTES* **SERVES** *10*

1¾ cups (300g) dates, chopped coarsely
1½ cups (375ml) boiling water
1 teaspoon bicarbonate of soda (baking soda)
90g (3 ounces) butter, softened
1¼ cups (250g) brown sugar
3 eggs, beaten lightly
1½ cups (225g) self-raising flour
⅓ cup (40g) walnuts
⅓ cup (40g) pecans

CARAMEL SAUCE
1 cup (200g) firmly packed brown sugar
300ml (½ pint) pouring cream
100g (3 ounces) butter, chopped coarsely

1. Preheat oven to 180°C/350°F. Grease a 22cm (9-inch) round cake pan; line base and side with baking paper.
2. Combine dates and the water in a medium heatproof bowl. Stir in soda; stand 5 minutes.
3. Process date mixture with butter and sugar until smooth. Add egg and flour; process until just combined. Spread mixture into pan; sprinkle evenly with nuts.
4. Bake pudding 1 hour or until a skewer inserted into the centre comes out clean. Stand pudding in pan 10 minutes before turning, top-side up, onto a wire rack.
5. Make caramel sauce.
6. Brush top of hot pudding with ¼ cup of caramel sauce. Serve pudding with remaining sauce.

CARAMEL SAUCE
Stir ingredients in a medium saucepan over medium-low heat, without boiling, until sugar dissolves. Simmer, stirring, 3 minutes.

TIPS Both the pudding and the sauce can be made a day ahead. Store separately, covered, in the fridge. The pudding can also be frozen for up to 3 months. Defrost and warm individual slices in the microwave for about 30 seconds.
The caramel sauce may separate when stored in the fridge overnight. Don't worry, simply reheat in a small saucepan or in the microwave, whisking until the sauce is smooth again.

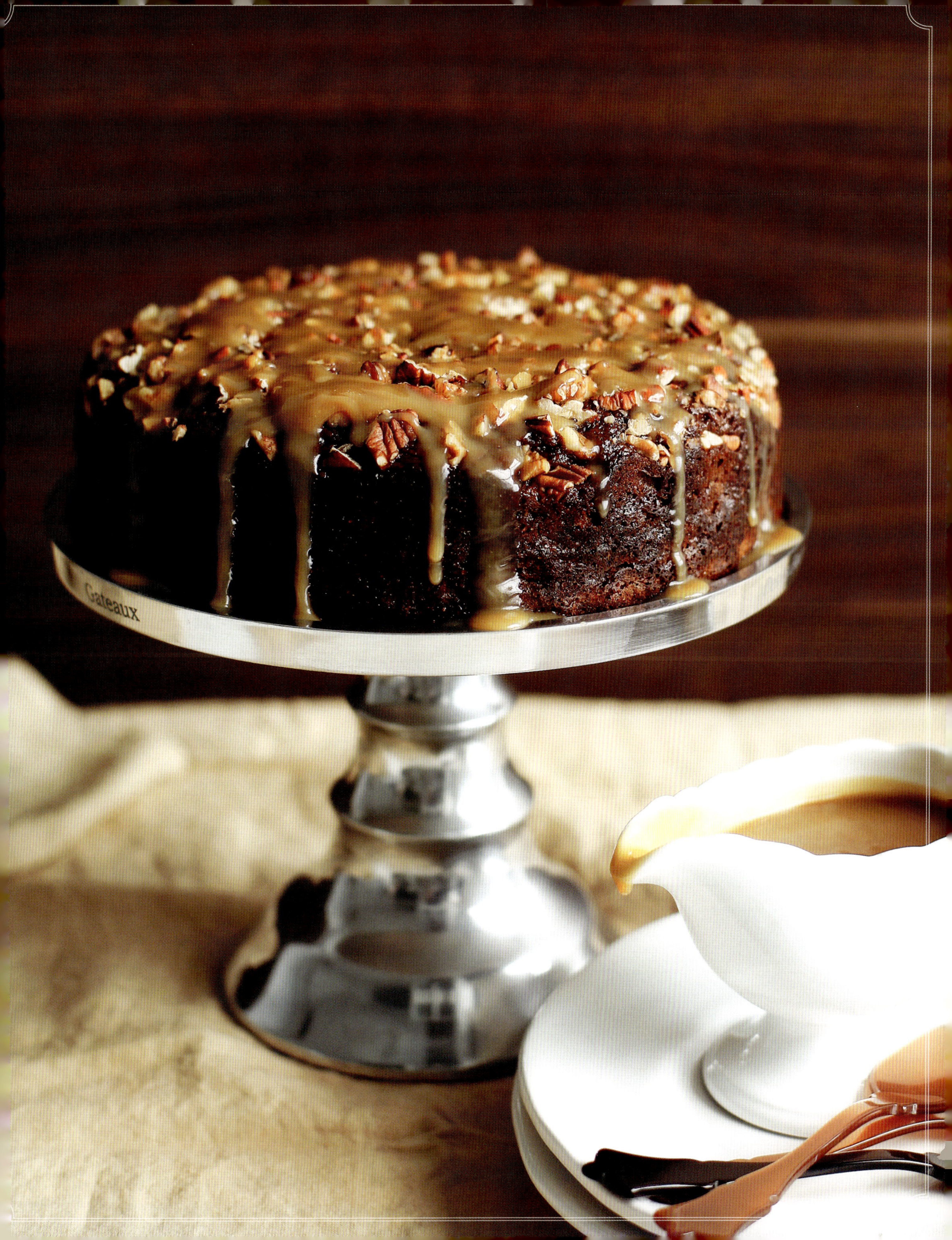
Gateaux

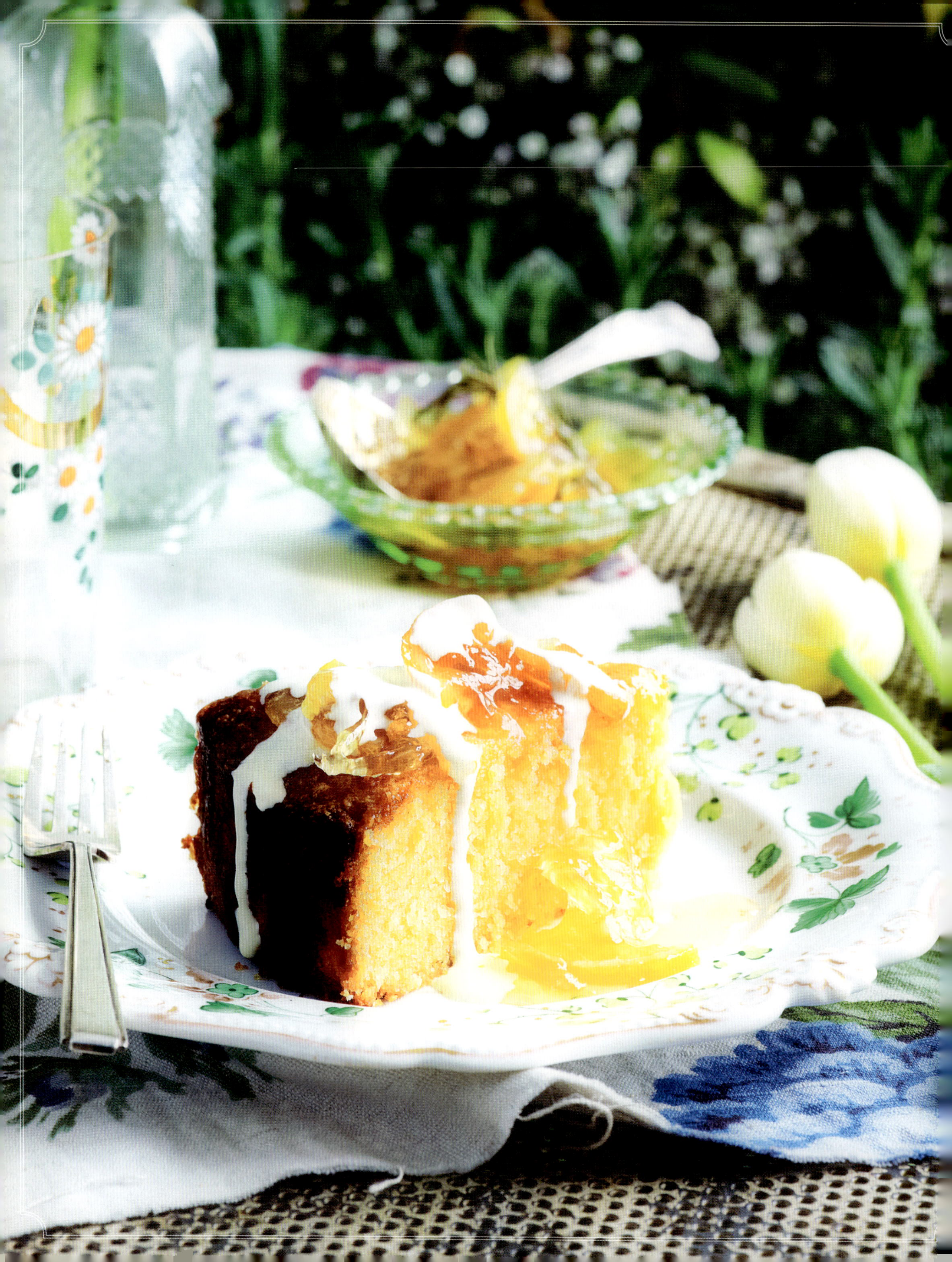

LEMON POLENTA CAKE
with Lemon Compote

PREP + COOK TIME 3 HOURS 25 MINUTES (+ COOLING) SERVES 8

200g (6½ ounces) butter, softened
1 cup (220g) caster (superfine) sugar
3 eggs
2 cups (250g) ground almonds
½ cup (85g) instant polenta
1 teaspoon baking powder
1 tablespoon finely grated lemon rind
½ cup (125ml) lemon juice
1½ teaspoons orange blossom water

LEMON COMPOTE
2 medium lemons (280g), sliced thinly
1 cup (220g) caster (superfine) sugar
2 sprigs fresh rosemary
1 cup (250ml) water

1. Preheat oven to 150°C/300°F.
2. Make lemon compote.
3. Increase oven to 180°C/350°F. Grease a 20cm (8-inch) round cake pan; line base and side with baking paper.
4. Beat butter and sugar in a small bowl with an electric mixer until pale and creamy. Beat in eggs, one at a time. Stir in ground almonds, polenta and baking powder; then stir in rind, juice and orange blossom water. Spread mixture into pan; smooth the surface.
5. Bake cake 1 hour or until a skewer inserted in the centre comes out clean. Cool cake in pan.
6. Serve cake topped with lemon compote.

LEMON COMPOTE
Cut lemon slices into quarters; remove seeds. Layer quarters in a medium non-metalic baking dish. Place sugar, rosemary and the water in a small saucepan; stir over a low heat until sugar is dissolved. Bring to the boil. Reduce heat; simmer 1 minute. Pour syrup over lemon quarters. Cover surface of lemon mixture with baking paper, then cover the dish with foil. Bake 30 minutes. Remove foil and paper; bake a further 30 minutes or until syrup is thick and lemons are caramelised. Cool.

TIP Orange blossom water, also called orange flower water, is a concentrated flavouring made from orange blossoms. It is available from Middle Eastern food stores, delicatessens and some supermarkets.

SERVING SUGGESTION Serve with cream.

BLOOD ORANGE SORBET
and Ice-cream Slice

PREP + COOK TIME *25 MINUTES (+ CHURNING & FREEZING)* **SERVES** *8*

---

1 cup (220g) caster (superfine) sugar
1 cup (250ml) water
1 cup (250ml) strained blood orange juice
2 litre (8 cups) vanilla ice-cream
2 medium blood oranges (320g), segmented
2 medium oranges (480g), segmented

1. Stir sugar and the water in a small saucepan over low heat, without boiling, until sugar dissolves. Bring to the boil; boil 1 minute. Remove from heat, cool to room temperature.
2. Combine 1 cup (250ml) of the syrup (reserve remaining syrup) and the juice in a medium jug; refrigerate until cold.
3. Churn mixture in an ice-cream machine, following manufacturer's instructions, until firm. (Or, pour mixture into a shallow, freezer-proof container; freeze until just set. Chop mixture, process until combined.)
4. Line base and two long sides of an 11cm x 25cm (4½-inch x 10-inch) loaf pan (inside top measure) with baking paper, extending the paper 5cm (2-inches) over the sides.
5. Spread sorbet over base of pan; smooth the surface. Cover; freeze several hours or until mixture is firm.
6. Meanwhile, place vanilla ice-cream in the refrigerator for 30 minutes to soften slightly. Spoon ice-cream over sorbet; smooth top. Cover; freeze several hours or overnight, until firm.
7. Combine blood orange and orange segments with ¼ cup (60ml) of the remaining syrup in a medium bowl. Cover; refrigerate until required.
8. To serve, rub outside of pan with a warm, damp cloth. Invert pan, remove paper, cut into slices. Serve with orange segments in syrup.

TIPS If blood oranges are not available, you can use 1 pink grapefruit instead.
Packaged blood orange juice is available from the the refrigerated section at most major supermarkets.

VARIATION For a lime sorbet (also pictured), make the syrup as in step 1, using 1¼ cups (275g) caster sugar and 1¼ cups (310ml) water. Use 1½ cups (375ml) of the syrup and ½ cup (125ml) strained lime juice for the sorbet in step 2.

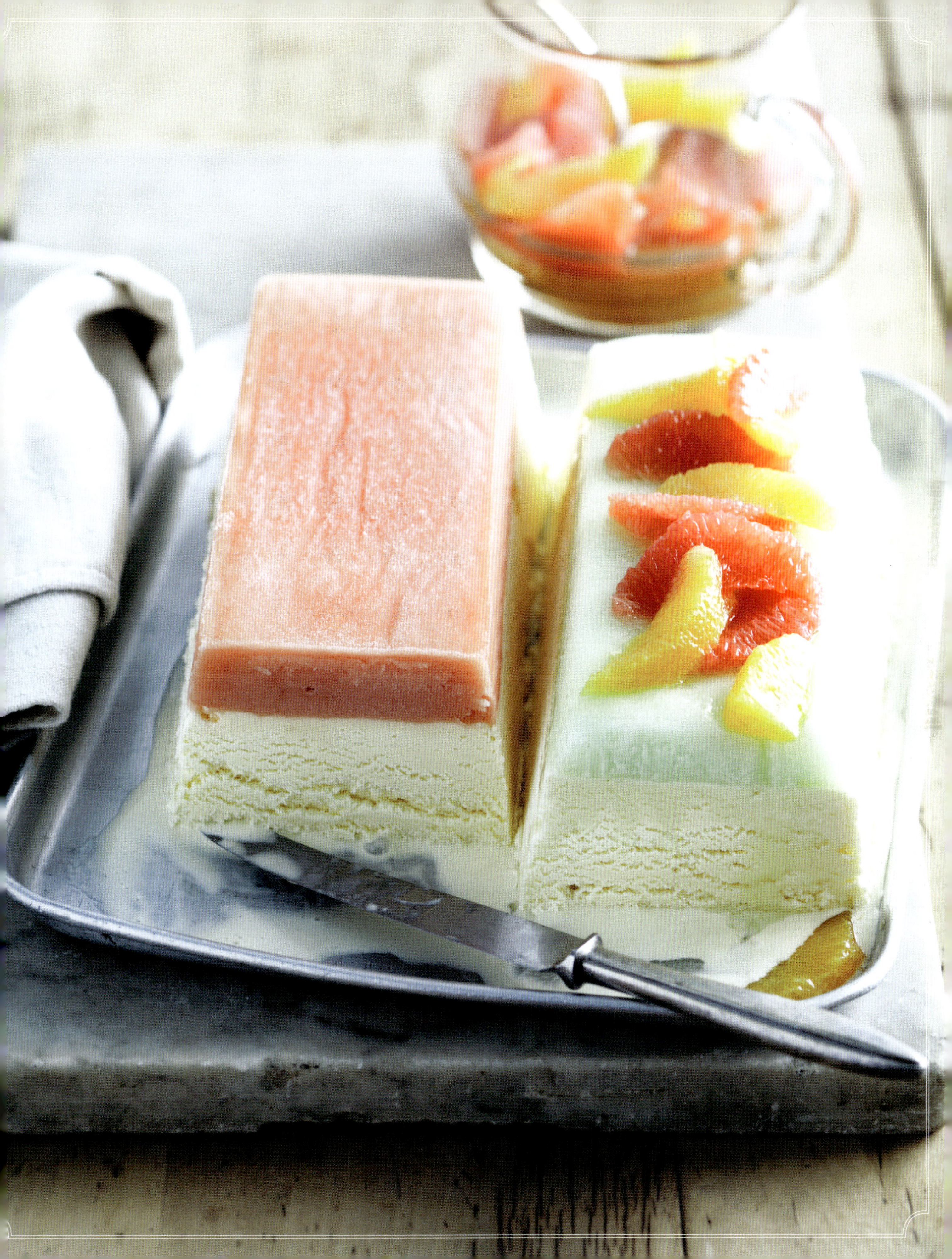

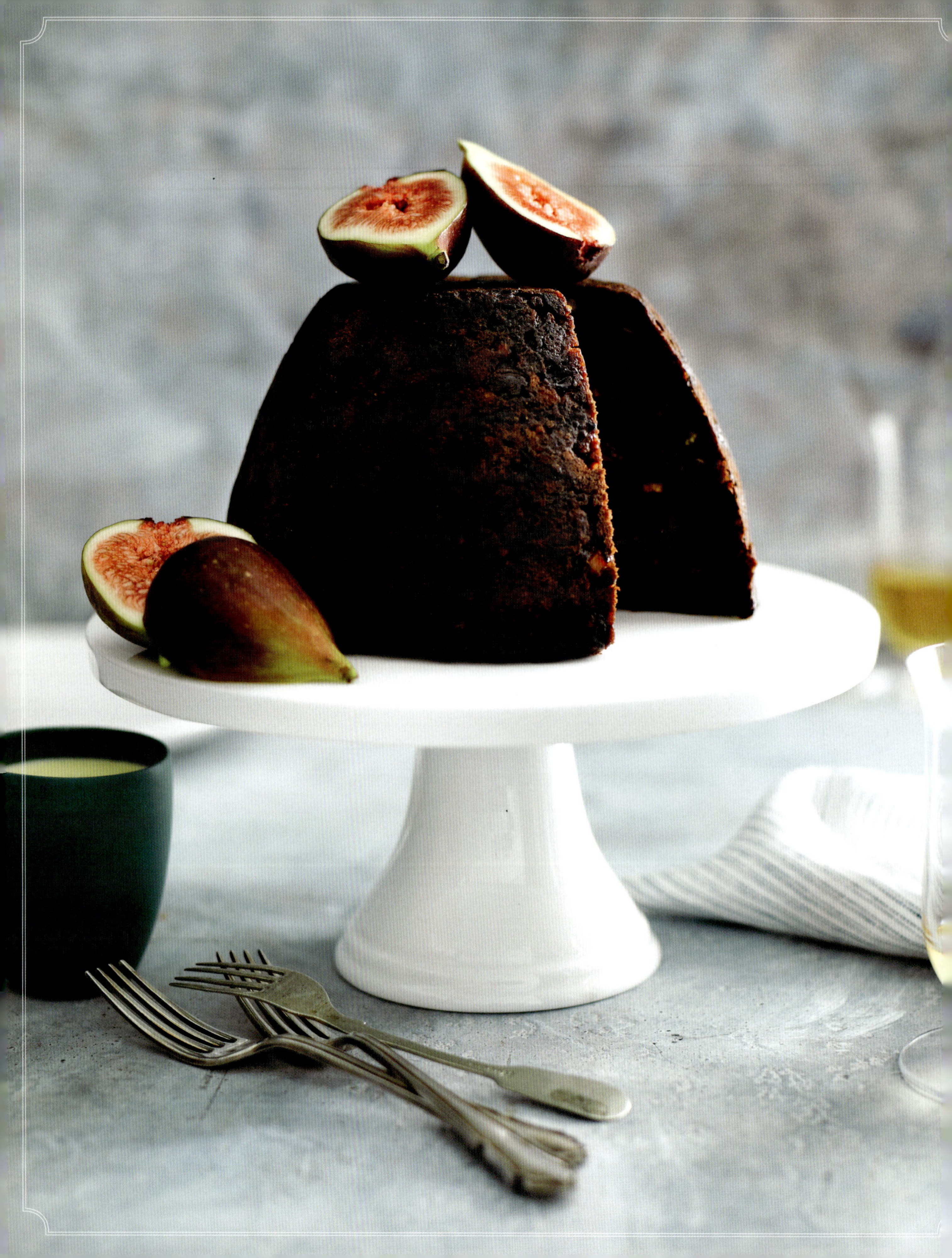

PRESSURE-COOKER CHRISTMAS PUDDING
with Ice-cream Sauce

PREP + COOK TIME 1 HOUR 40 MINUTES (+ COOLING) SERVES 8

3 cups (500g) mixed dried fruit
¾ cups (140g) finely chopped prunes
¾ cup (125g) finely chopped raisins
¾ cup (180ml) water
1 cup (220g) firmly packed dark brown sugar
125g (4 ounces) butter, chopped coarsely
½ teaspoon bicarbonate of soda (baking soda)
3 eggs, beaten lightly
3 cups (210g) stale breadcrumbs
¾ cup (110g) self-raising flour
2 tablespoons cocoa powder
2 teaspoons mixed spice
1 teaspoon ground cinnamon
⅓ cup (80ml) dark rum

1 Wash combined fruit under cold water; drain. Combine fruit, the water, sugar and butter in a medium saucepan. Stir over heat until butter melts and sugar dissolves; bring to the boil. Reduce heat; simmer 5 minutes. Transfer mixture to a large heatproof bowl, stir in soda; cool.

2 Stir eggs, breadcrumbs, sifted dry ingredients and rum into the fruit mixture.

3 Grease a 1.5-litre (6-cup) pudding steamer or basin; line base with a round of baking paper. Spoon mixture into steamer; secure with steamer lid. If steamer or basin does not have a lid, place a sheet of foil on bench, top with a sheet of baking paper. Fold a 5cm (2-inch) pleat crossways through both layers. Place sheet, baking paper-side down, over basin; secure around basin with string. Make a handle using excess string tied across the top. Trim away excess foil and paper, leaving about 4cm (1½-inches). Crush remaining foil around string to help form a good seal.

4 Place pressure cooker steamer basket in 8-litre (32-cup) pressure cooker; add 2 cups water to the pressure cooker. Place pudding steamer on a tea towel; using tea towel lower steamer into basket in cooker. Fold tea towel overhang over top of steamer; secure lid of cooker. Bring cooker to high pressure. Reduce heat to stabilise pressure; cook 1½ hours.

5 Release pressure using quick release method; remove lid. Remove steamer from cooker; stand 10 minutes before turning out.

TIP If you have an electric pressure cooker, you won't need to reduce the heat to stabilise the pressure; your cooker will automatically stabilise itself. Always check the manufacturer's instructions before use.

SERVING SUGGESTION Serve with ice-cream sauce (recipe page 252) and fresh figs or cherries.

ICE-CREAM SAUCE

PREP + COOK TIME 15 MINUTES SERVES 8

1 cup (250ml) vanilla ice-cream
2 teaspoons cornflour (cornstarch)
2 teaspoons water
¾ cup (180ml) thickened (heavy) cream
2 tablespoons icing (confectioners') sugar
2 tablespoons brandy

1 Melt ice-cream in a medium saucepan over a low heat. Stir in blended cornflour and the water until it boils and thickens. Transfer to a medium bowl.
2 Beat cream in a small bowl with an electric mixer until soft peaks form. Fold cream, sifted icing sugar and brandy into ice-cream mixture.
3 Serve sauce with pressure-cooker Christmas pudding (recipe page 251) at room temperature.

TIPS You need to use a good-quality ice-cream for best results. Don't use the reduced-fat variety. You can flavour the sauce with grated nutmeg.

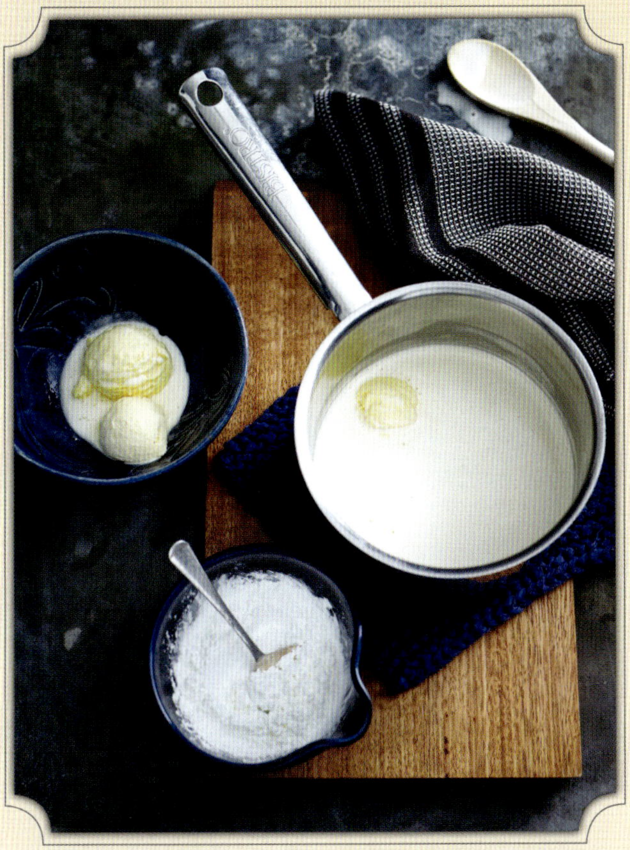
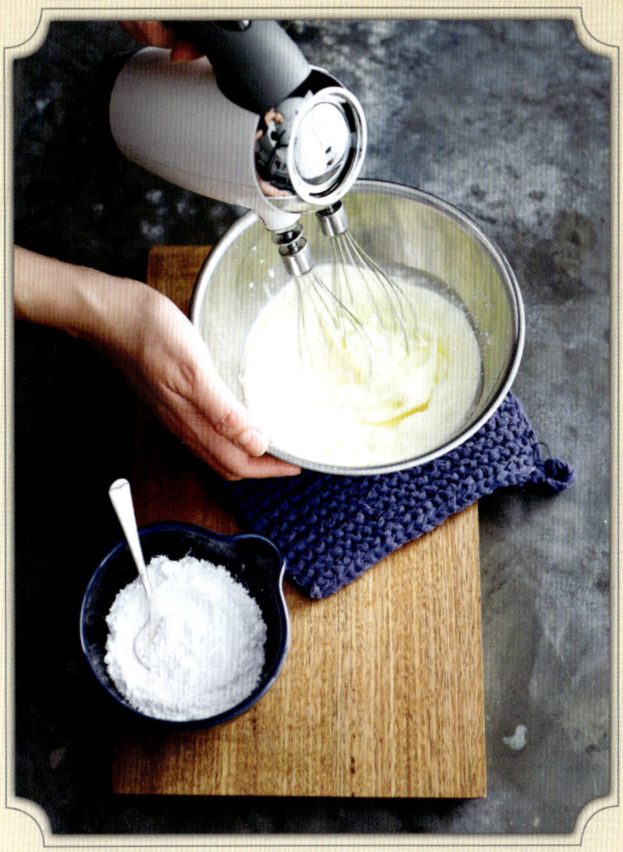
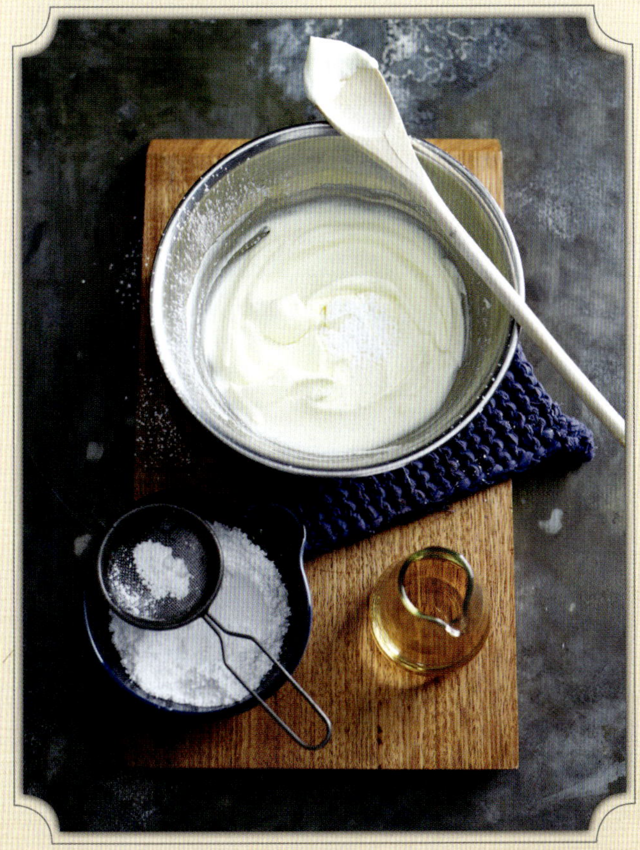
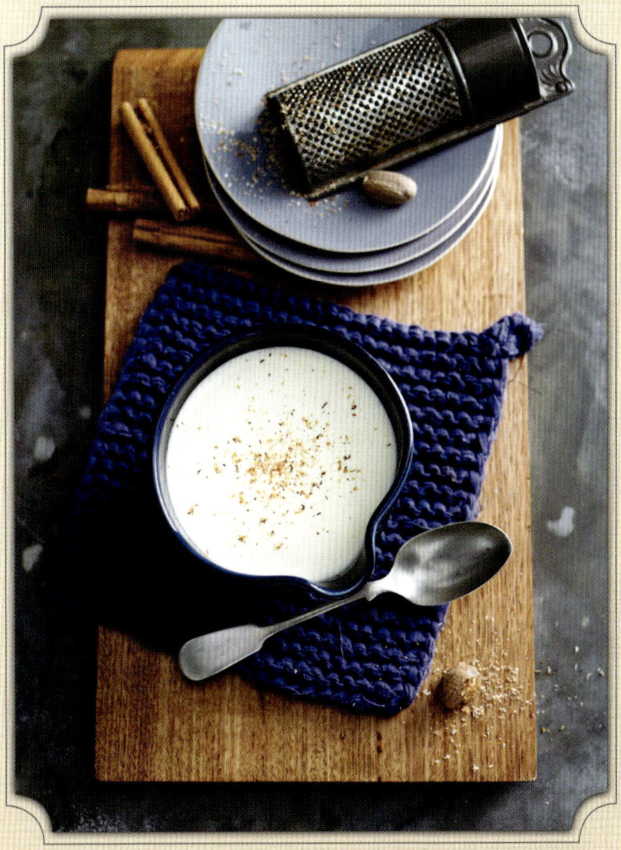

CHAPTER 8
CAKES & CUPCAKES

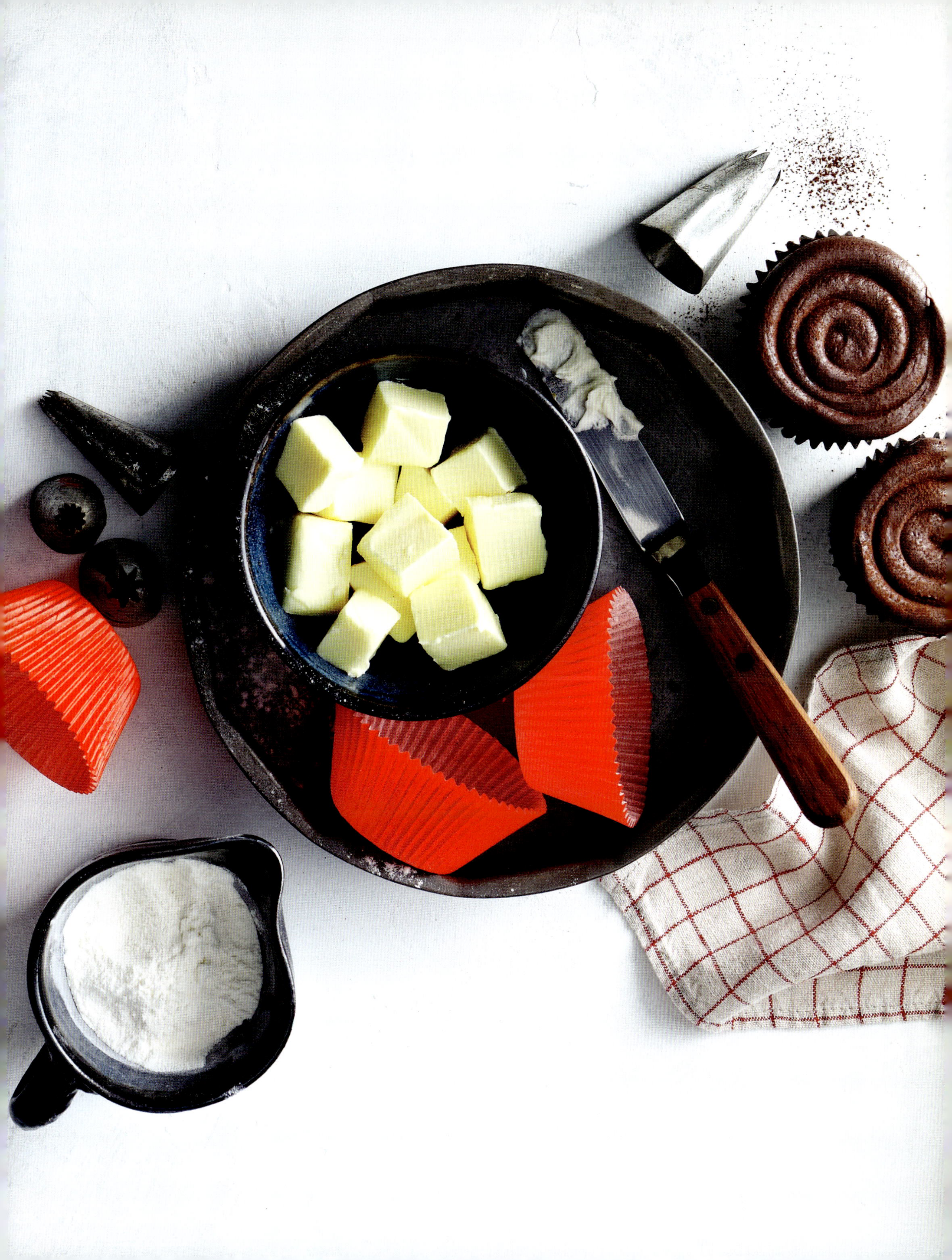

FEATHERLIGHT SPONGE

PREP + COOK TIME *40 MINUTES (+ STANDING)* SERVES *10*

Of the hundreds of sponge cake recipes created in the Test Kitchen, this heirloom recipe from the family of Cathie and Wendy Lonnie wins our vote hands down, as our best ever.

4 eggs
¾ cup (165g) caster (superfine) sugar
⅔ cup (150g) wheaten cornflour (cornstarch)
¼ cup (30g) custard powder
1 teaspoon cream of tartar
½ teaspoon bicarbonate of soda (baking soda)
300ml (½ pint) thickened (heavy) cream
1 teaspoon vanilla extract
¼ cup (80g) strawberry jam
250g (8 ounces) strawberries, sliced thinly
125g (4 ounces) strawberries, extra, halved

ICING
1 cup (160g) icing (confectioners') sugar
10g (½ ounce) butter, softened
1½ tablespoons milk, approximately

1. Preheat oven to 200°C/400°F. Grease two deep 22cm (9-inch) round cake pans; lightly flour the pans with a little plain flour and shake out the excess.
2. Beat eggs and sugar in a small bowl with an electric mixer, 7 minutes, until thick and creamy (see tips). Transfer mixture to a large bowl.
3. Sift dry ingredients twice onto a piece of baking paper. Sift flour mixture a third time evenly onto egg mixture. Using a balloon whisk or large metal spoon, quickly and lightly fold flour mixture through egg mixture until incorporated. Pour mixture evenly into pans; tilt pans to spread mixture to the edge.
4. Bake sponges 20 minutes or until they spring back when pressed lightly in the centre. Turn sponges immediately, top-side up, onto baking-paper-covered wire racks. Cool.
5. Beat cream and extract in a small bowl with an electric mixer until firm peaks form.
6. Place one sponge on a cake stand or plate, spread with jam and cream; top with sliced strawberries.
7. Make icing.
8. Turn remaining sponge top-side down on lined wire rack; spread with warm icing. Place on other sponge. Stand 15 minutes or until icing is set. Top with extra strawberries.

ICING
Sift icing sugar into a medium heatproof bowl; stir in butter and enough milk to form a firm paste. (Add the milk gradually, as just a small amount can alter the consistency.) Place bowl over a medium saucepan of simmering water; stir until icing is a pouring consistency.

TIPS Aluminium cake pans are the best to use for sponge cakes as they conduct the heat. Avoid black coated pans.
Using a small bowl when beating the eggs and sugar in step 2 will maximise volume. To test when the mixture is thick and creamy, turn off mixer then lift the beaters – the mixture should form thick ribbons. Before baking, tap the sponge on the base of the pan with your fingers to remove large air pockets. This recipe is best made on the day of serving. The sponge can be filled several hours before.

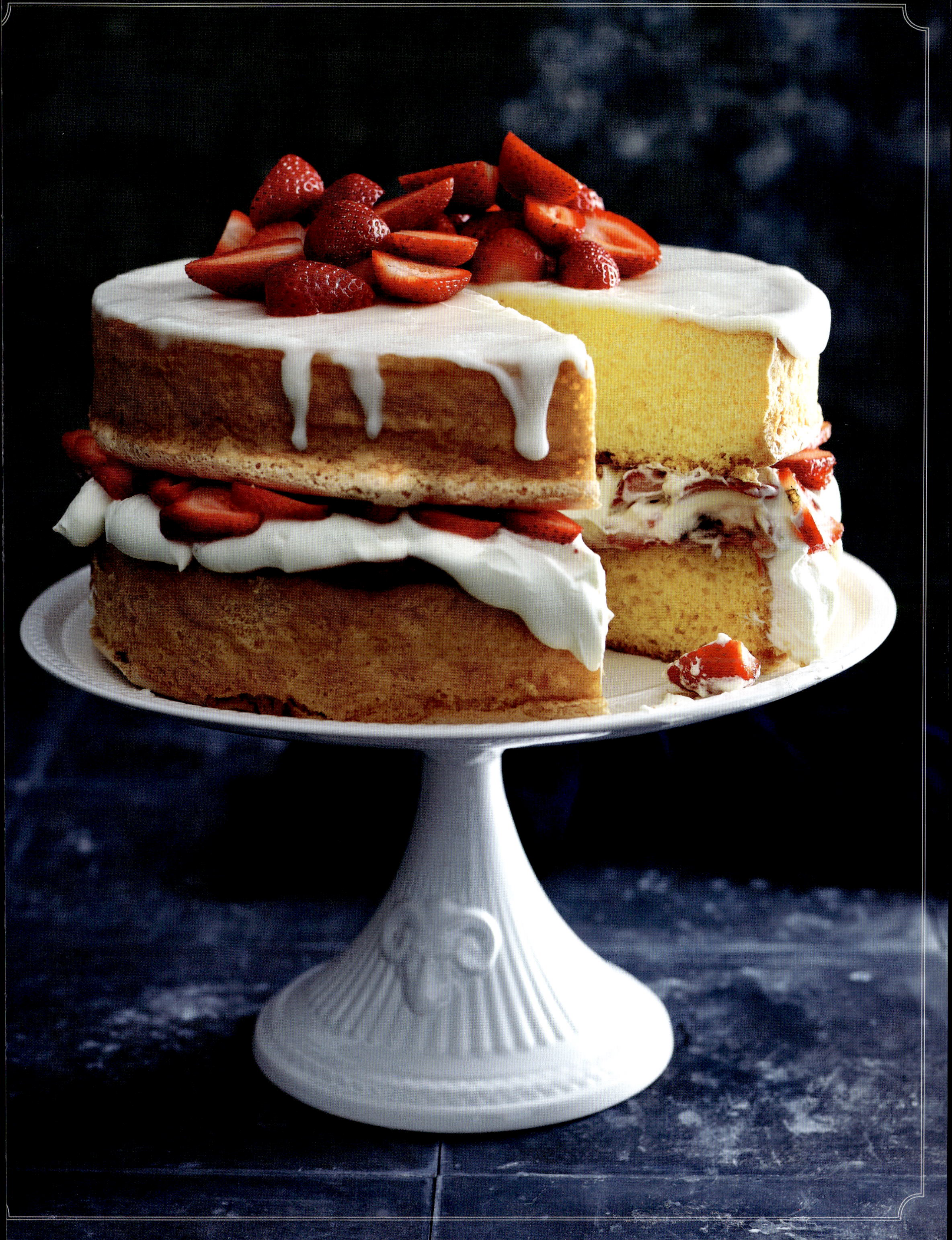

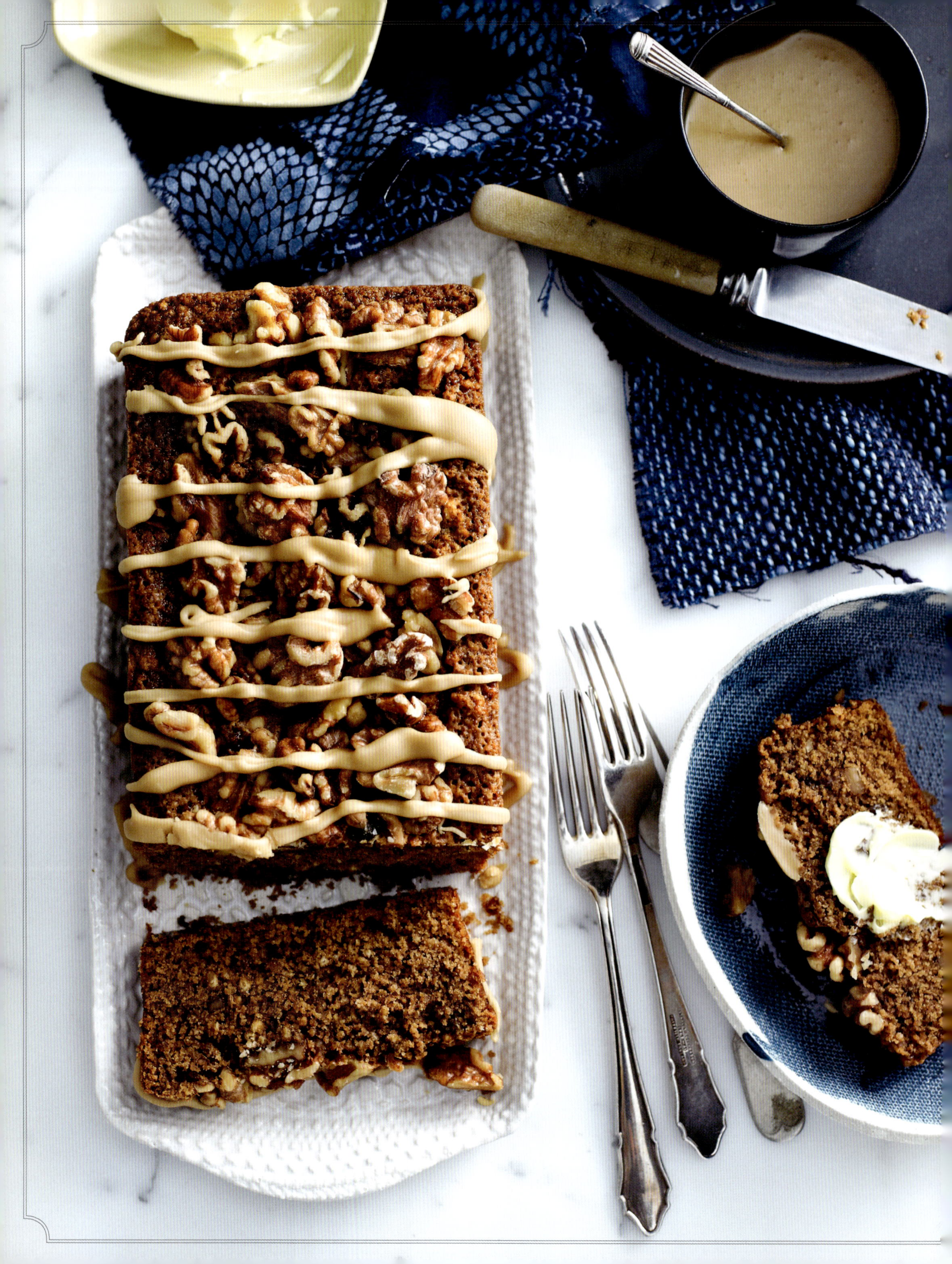

COFFEE WALNUT LOAF

PREP + COOK TIME *1 HOUR 10 MINUTES* **SERVES** *12*

125g (4 ounces) butter, chopped
1 cup (220g) raw caster (superfine) sugar
½ cup (125ml) milk
2 tablespoons instant coffee granules
1½ cups (150g) toasted whole walnuts
1⅓ cups (200g) self-raising flour
2 teaspoons ground cinnamon
2 eggs, beaten lightly

COFFEE ICING
2 teaspoons instant coffee granules
1 tablespoon boiling water
1 cup (160g) icing (confectioners') sugar
10g (½ ounce) soft butter

1. Preheat oven to 160°C/325°F. Grease and line a 11cm x 25cm (4½-inch x 10-inch) loaf pan (top measurement).
2. Stir butter, sugar, milk and coffee in a small saucepan over low heat until melted. Remove from heat.
3. Chop half the walnuts. Sift flour and cinnamon into a medium bowl; stir in eggs, butter mixture and chopped walnuts. Pour mixture into pan.
4. Bake loaf 15 minutes. Top loaf with remaining walnuts; bake a further 30 minutes or until a skewer inserted in the centre comes out clean. Turn loaf, top-side up, onto a wire rack. Cool.
5. Make coffee icing.
6. Drizzle icing over loaf; stand until set.

COFFEE ICING
Combine coffee and the water in a small jug. Sift icing sugar into a small heatproof bowl; stir in butter and enough of the coffee mixture to form a firm paste. Place bowl over a small saucepan of simmering water; stir until icing is a thin consistency.

TIP When testing a cake to see if it is done, don't insert a skewer through a crack, as it will give you an inaccurate reading.

SERVING SUGGESTION Serve sliced with buttter.

MISSISSIPPI MUD CAKE

PREP + COOK TIME *1 HOUR 30 MINUTES* **SERVES** *9*

This recipe was given to us by a long-gone Sydney restaurant of the 1980s called Jo-Jos. It's a great recipe, not too muddy, just right – and possibly our most-requested recipe of all time.

250g (8 ounces) butter, chopped
150g (4½ ounces) dark (semi-sweet) chocolate, chopped coarsely
2 cups (440g) white (granulated) sugar
1 cup (250ml) hot water
⅓ cup (80ml) whisky
1 tablespoon instant coffee granules
1½ cups (225g) plain (all-purpose) flour
¼ cup (35g) self-raising flour
¼ cup (25g) cocoa powder
2 eggs, beaten lightly
1 tablespoon cocoa powder, extra

1. Preheat oven to 160°C/350°F. Grease a 23cm (9-inch) square cake pan; line base and sides with baking paper.
2. Stir butter, chocolate, sugar, the water, whisky and coffee in a medium saucepan over low heat until mixture is smooth. Cool.
3. Stir sifted flours and cocoa into chocolate mixture, then egg. Pour mixture into pan.
4. Bake cake 1¼ hours or until a skewer inserted into the centre comes out with moist crumbs attached. Stand in pan 10 minutes; turn, top-side up, onto a wire rack to cool.
5. Serve dusted with extra cocoa; top with berries, if you like.

TIP You can use orange-, coffee- or hazelnut-flavoured liqueur instead of the whisky. You can also omit the alcohol completely and use the same quantity of water, milk or orange juice instead.

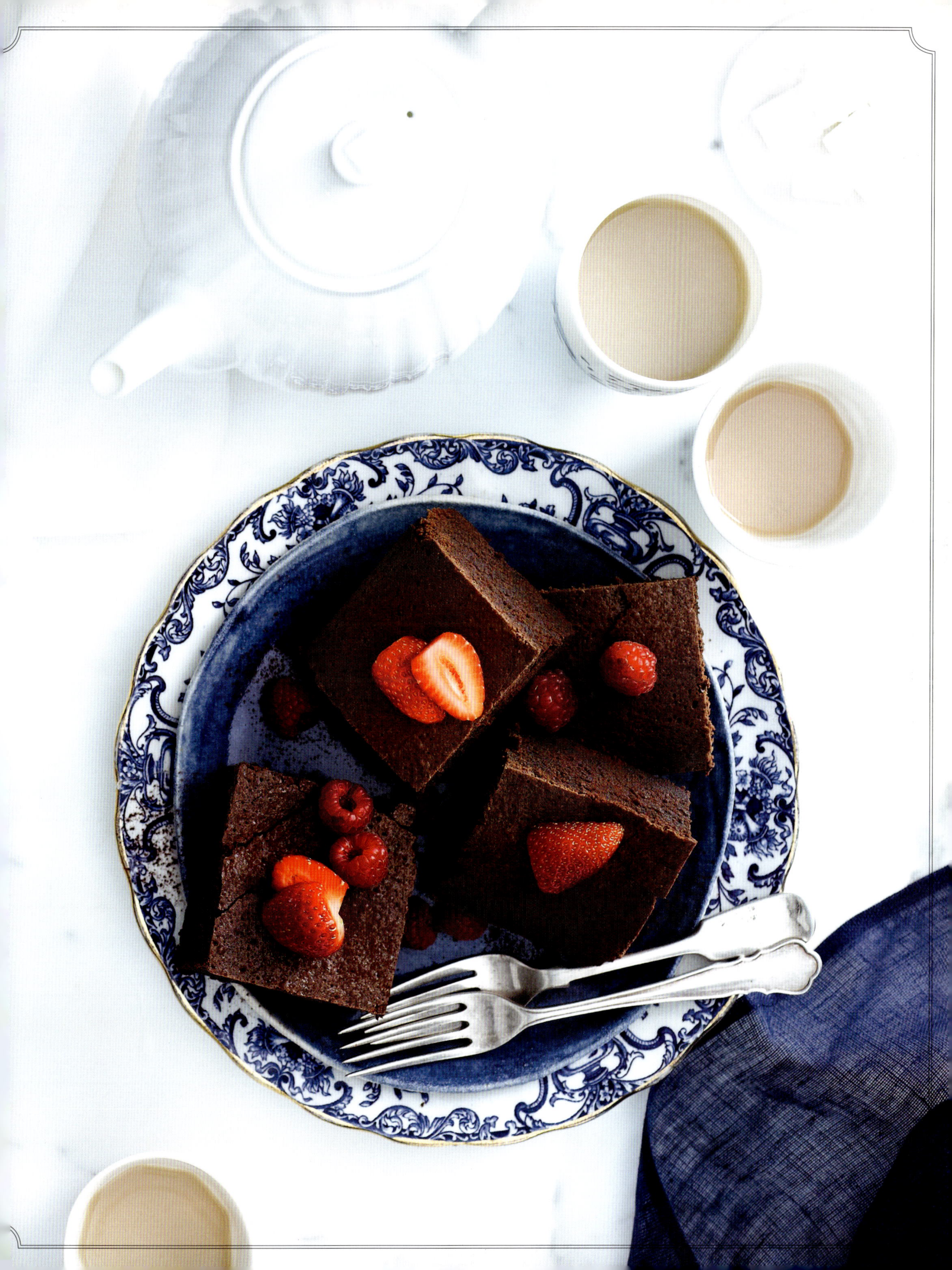

ALMOND BERRY
Sugar Cakes

PREP + COOK TIME *45 MINUTES* **MAKES** *8*

185g (6 ounces) butter, softened
2 teaspoons vanilla extract
1 cup (220g) caster (superfine) sugar
3 eggs
½ cup (60g) ground almonds
1 cup (150g) self-raising flour
½ cup (75g) plain (all-purpose) flour
½ cup (125ml) milk
1 cup (150g) frozen raspberries
⅓ cup (25g) flaked almonds
1 tablespoon demerara sugar

1. Preheat oven to 180°C/350°F. Line eight holes from two 6-hole (¾-cup/180ml) texas muffin pans with paper cases.
2. Beat butter, extract and sugar in a small bowl with an electric mixer until light and fluffy. Beat in eggs one at a time. Fold in ground almonds, combined sifted flours and milk, in two batches. Gently fold in half the raspberries.
3. Spoon mixture into paper cases; top with remaining raspberries, then flaked almonds and sugar.
4. Bake cakes 35 minutes or until a skewer inserted into the centre comes out clean. Turn onto a wire rack to cool.

TIP Many domestic ovens brown unevenly so don't be afraid to open the door (after halfway through the cooking time) to turn the pans around and avoid any of the oven's hot spots.

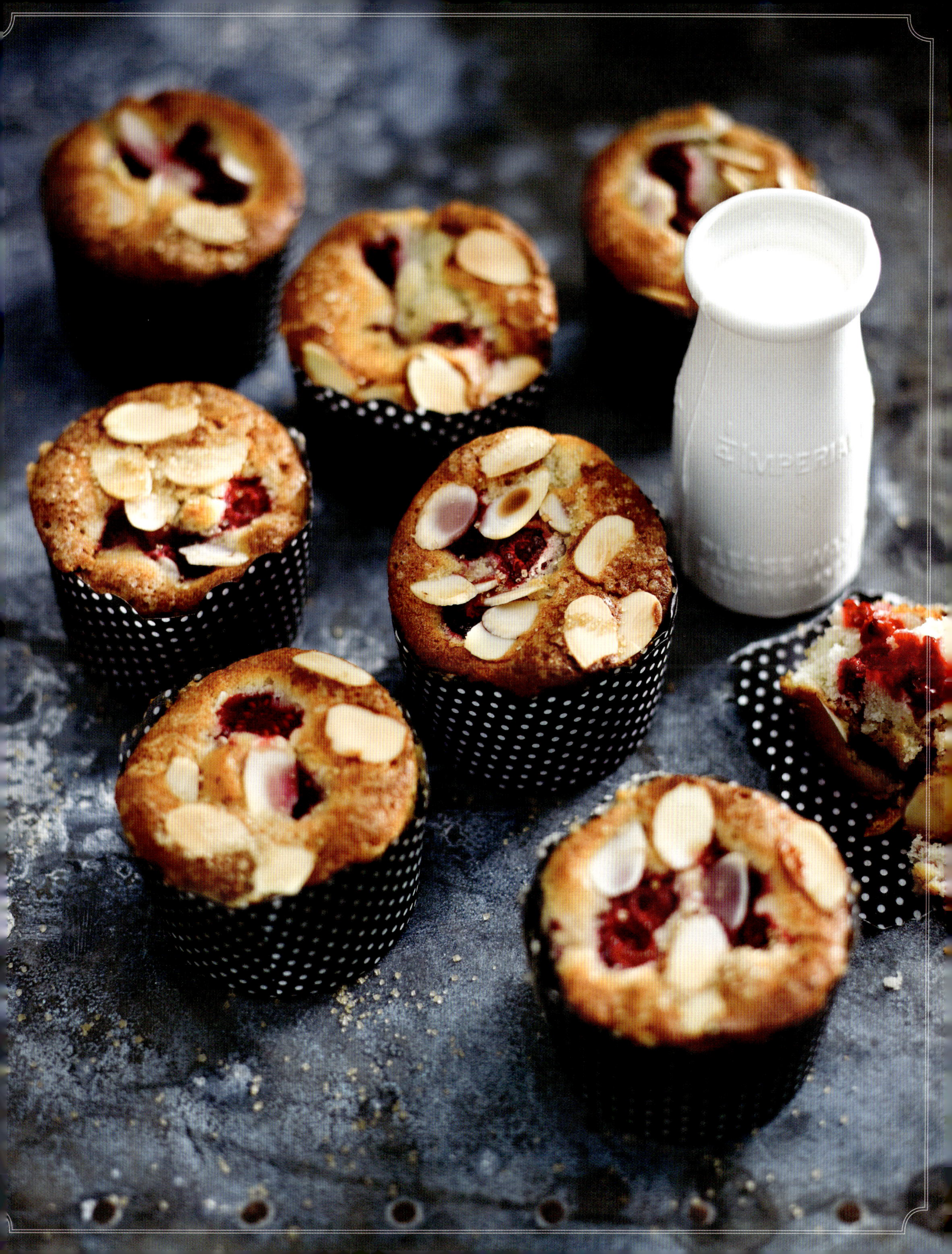

APRICOT
Upside-down Cakes

APRICOT Upside-down Cakes

PREP + COOK TIME 40 MINUTES **MAKES** 12

1 tablespoon brown sugar
12 canned apricot halves in syrup, drained
2 eggs
¾ cup (150g) firmly packed brown sugar, extra
¾ cup (90g) ground almonds
1 teaspoon vanilla extract
⅓ cup (50g) wholemeal self-raising flour
½ cup (125ml) skim milk
¼ cup (80g) apricot conserve, warmed

1. Preheat oven to 180°C/350°F. Grease a 12-hole (⅓-cup/80ml) muffin pan; line each base with baking paper.
2. Sprinkle sugar equally into pan holes; place one apricot half, cut-side down, on base of each hole.
3. Beat eggs and extra sugar in a medium bowl with an electric mixer until light and fluffy. Stir in ground almonds, extract, flour and milk. Spoon mixture into pan holes.
4. Bake cakes 20 minutes or until a skewer inserted into the centre comes out clean. Stand cakes in pan 5 minutes, before turning onto a wire rack. Brush apricot conserve over hot cakes. Serve cakes warm or at room temperature.

TIP You can use canned pears instead of the apricots, and ground hazelnuts instead of almonds.

HAZELNUT PLUM and Sour Cherry Cake

PREP + COOK TIME 1 HOUR 20 MINUTES **SERVES** 12

125g (4 ounces) butter, softened
1 teaspoon vanilla extract
1¼ cups (275g) firmly packed brown sugar
3 eggs
¾ cup (110g) plain (all-purpose) flour
¾ cup (110g) self-raising flour
½ cup (125ml) milk
½ cup (50g) ground hazelnuts
6 small plums (270g), halved, stones removed
¼ cup (40g) drained sour cherries
¼ cup (35g) roasted, peeled hazelnuts, chopped coarsely

1. Preheat oven to 160°C/325°F. Grease 20cm x 30cm (8-inch x 12-inch) slice pan; line base and long sides with baking paper, extending the paper 5cm (2 inches) over sides.
2. Beat ingredients in a medium bowl with an electric mixer on low speed until just combined. Increase speed to medium, beat until mixture is smooth and changed to a paler colour (1 to 2 minutes).
3. Spread mixture into pan. Top with plums, cherries and nuts.
4. Bake cake 1 hour or until a skewer inserted into the cake part comes out clean. Cool cake in pan.

(PHOTOGRAPH PAGE 266)

HAZELNUT PLUM
and Sour Cherry Cake
(RECIPE PAGE 265)

SIX LAYER
Chocolate Cake

(RECIPE PAGE 268)

SIX LAYER
Chocolate Cake

PREP + COOK TIME 1 HOUR 20 MINUTES SERVES 16

350g (11 ounces) butter, softened
2 teaspoons vanilla extract
3 cups (660g) caster (superfine) sugar
8 eggs, separated
1½ cups (225g) self-raising flour
½ cup (50g) cocoa powder
1½ cups (375ml) buttermilk

CHOCOLATE ICING
600g (1¼ pounds) dark chocolate (70% cocoa), melted
375g (12 ounces) butter, melted
¾ cup (120g) icing (confectioners') sugar

1. Preheat oven to 180°C/160°F. Grease two deep 20cm (8-inch) round cake pans; line bases with baking paper.
2. Beat butter, extract and sugar in a large bowl with an electric mixer until light and fluffy. Beat in egg yolks, one at a time, until just combined. Stir in sifted dry ingredients and buttermilk.
3. Beat egg whites in a clean large bowl with an electric mixer until soft peaks form; fold into cake mixture, in two batches. Divide mixture into pans.
4. Bake cakes 1 hour or until a skewer inserted into the centre comes out clean. Cool cakes in pans.
5. Make chocolate icing; reserve half the icing to cover top and side of cake.
6. Split cakes into three layers; place one layer on a plate, spread with one-fifth of the icing. Repeat layering with cake and icing, finishing with a cake layer. Spread reserved icing over top and side.

CHOCOLATE ICING
Whisk chocolate and butter together in a medium bowl; whisk in sifted icing sugar. Cool icing to room temperature; whisk until thickened and spreadable.

(PHOTOGRAPH PAGE 267)

RASPBERRY YOGHURT
Loaf Cake

PREP + COOK TIME 1 HOUR 30 MINUTES SERVES 12

This delicious loaf is low in fat and sugar making it perfect for those watching their diet.

½ cup (125g) reduced-fat dairy-free spread
¾ cup (165g) firmly packed brown sugar
2 eggs
1¼ cups (200g) wholemeal self-raising flour
½ cup (140g) low-fat yoghurt
100g (3 ounces) frozen raspberries

CREAM CHEESE FROSTING
80g (2½ ounces) light cream cheese
⅓ cup (55g) icing (confectioners') sugar
1 teaspoon lemon juice

1. Preheat oven to 180°C/350°F. Grease an 11cm x 25cm (4½-inch x 10-inch) loaf pan (inside top measure); line base and two long sides with baking paper.
2. Beat spread and sugar in a medium bowl with an electric mixer until light and fluffy. Beat in eggs, one at a time, until just combined. Stir in flour, yoghurt and raspberries. Spread mixture into pan.
3. Bake cake 1 hour or until a skewer inserted into the centre comes out clean. Stand cake in pan 10 minutes before turning, top-side up onto a wire rack to cool.
4. Meanwhile, make cream cheese frosting.
5. Spread cake with frosting.

CREAM CHEESE FROSTING
Stir ingredients in a small bowl until smooth.

RASPBERRY YOGHURT
Loaf Cake

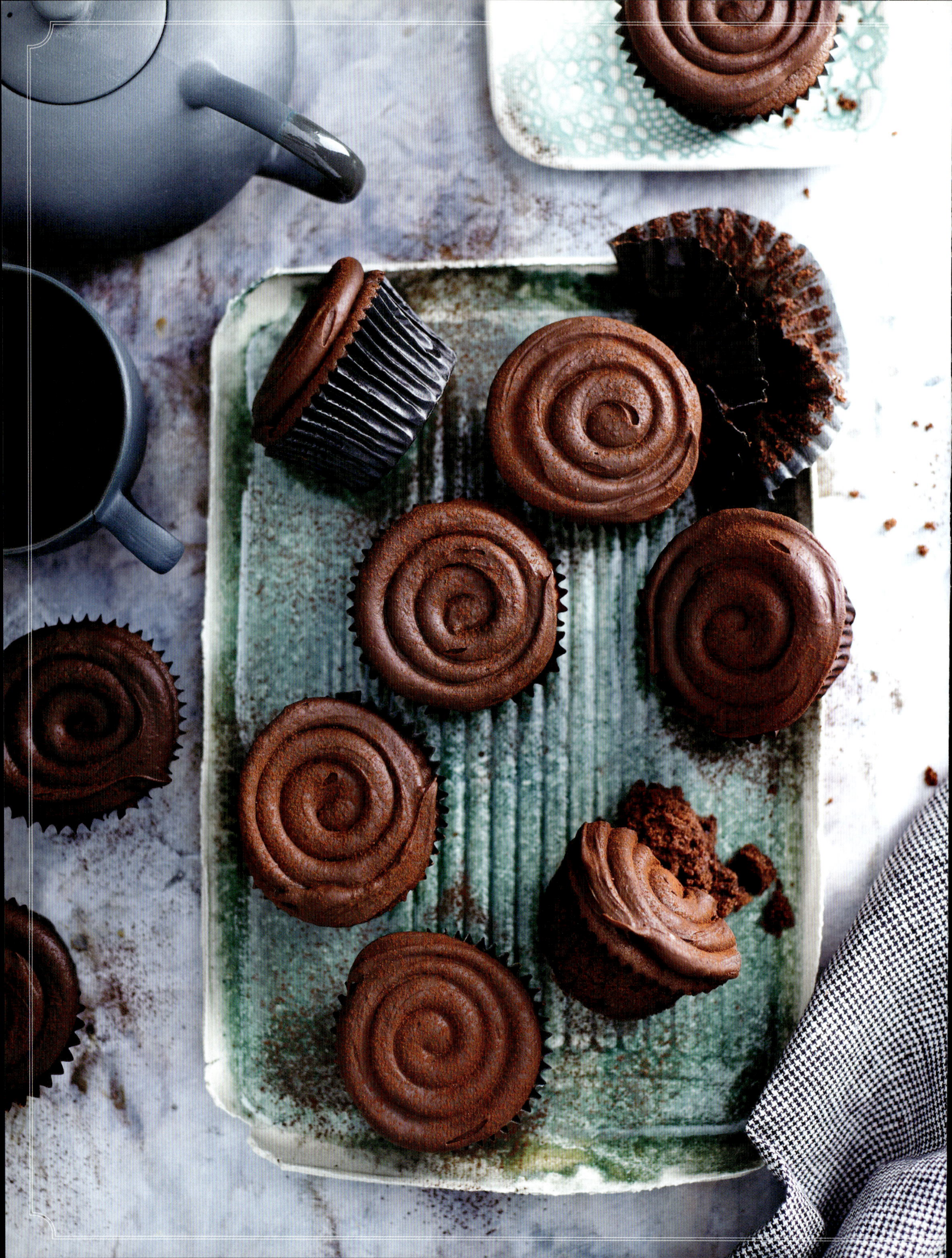

RICH CHOCOLATE
Cupcakes

PREP + COOK TIME 1 HOUR 50 MINUTES MAKES 30

¾ cup (75g) cocoa powder
¾ cup (180ml) boiling water
250g (8 ounces) butter, softened
2¼ cups (500g) caster (superfine) sugar
1 teaspoon vanilla extract
4 eggs
2 cups (300g) self-raising flour
½ cup (75g) plain (all-purpose) flour
½ teaspoon bicarbonate of soda (baking soda)
300ml (½ pint) buttermilk

CHOCOLATE GANACHE

150g (4½ ounces) dark chocolate (70% cocoa), chopped
100g (3 ounces) milk chocolate, chopped
90g (3 ounces) butter, chopped

1. Preheat oven to 160°C/325°F. Line 30 holes from three 12-hole (⅓-cup/80ml) muffin pans with paper cases.
2. Whisk cocoa and the water in a small heatproof bowl until smooth; cool.
3. Beat butter, sugar and extract in a medium bowl with an electric mixer until light and fluffy. Beat in eggs, one at a time, until just combined. Transfer mixture to a large bowl. Stir in combined sifted flours and soda, and buttermilk, in two batches. Stir in cocoa mixture. Spoon mixture into paper cases.
4. Bake cakes 25 minutes or until a skewer inserted into the centre comes out clean. Cool on wire racks.
5. Meanwhile, make chocolate ganache.
6. Spoon ganache into a piping bag fitted with a plain tube. Pipe ganache onto cupcakes in a spiral. If you like, dust with a little cocoa powder.

CHOCOLATE GANACHE

Stir ingredients in a medium heatproof bowl over a medium saucepan of simmering water (don't allow bowl to touch water) until melted and smooth. Remove bowl from pan; stand, stirring occasionally until thickened and of a spreadable consistency.

CITRUS BUTTER CAKE

PREP + COOK TIME *1 HOUR 45 MINUTES* **SERVES** *12*

250g (8 ounces) butter, softened, chopped
1 tablespoon finely grated orange rind
1 tablespoon finely grated lemon rind
1½ cups (330g) caster (superfine) sugar
4 eggs
1½ cups (225g) self-raising flour
½ cup (75g) plain (all-purpose) flour
½ cup (125ml) orange juice
¼ cup (60ml) lemon juice

CANDIED CITRUS
1 cup (220g) caster (superfine) sugar
½ cup (125ml) water
1 medium orange (240g), sliced thinly
1 medium lime (75g), sliced thinly

GLACÉ ICING
2 cups (320g) icing (confectioners') sugar
¼ cup (60ml) boiling water

1 Preheat oven to 160°C/350°F. Grease a deep 22cm (9-inch) round cake pan; line base and side with baking paper.
2 Beat butter, rinds and sugar in a large bowl with an electric mixer until light and fluffy. Beat in eggs, one at a time. Fold in sifted flours and juices, in two batches. Spread mixture into pan.
3 Bake cake 1 hour 10 minutes or until a skewer inserted into the centre comes out clean. Stand cake in pan 10 minutes before turning, top-side up, onto a wire rack to cool.
4 Meanwhile, make candied citrus.
5 Make glacé icing.
6 Drizzle cold cake with icing. Just before serving, top with candied citrus slices.

CANDIED CITRUS
Stir sugar and the water in a large frying pan over low heat, without boiling, until sugar dissolves. Add orange and lime slices; bring to the boil. Reduce heat to low; simmer, 15 minutes, turning slices occasionally. Remove from heat, cool slices on a wire rack.

GLACÉ ICING
Sift icing sugar into a medium bowl; add the water, stir until smooth.

TIPS You will need about 2 oranges and 1 lemon for the cake.
This cake will keep in an airtight container at room temperature for up to 4 days. The cake, without the filling and glaze, is suitable to freeze.

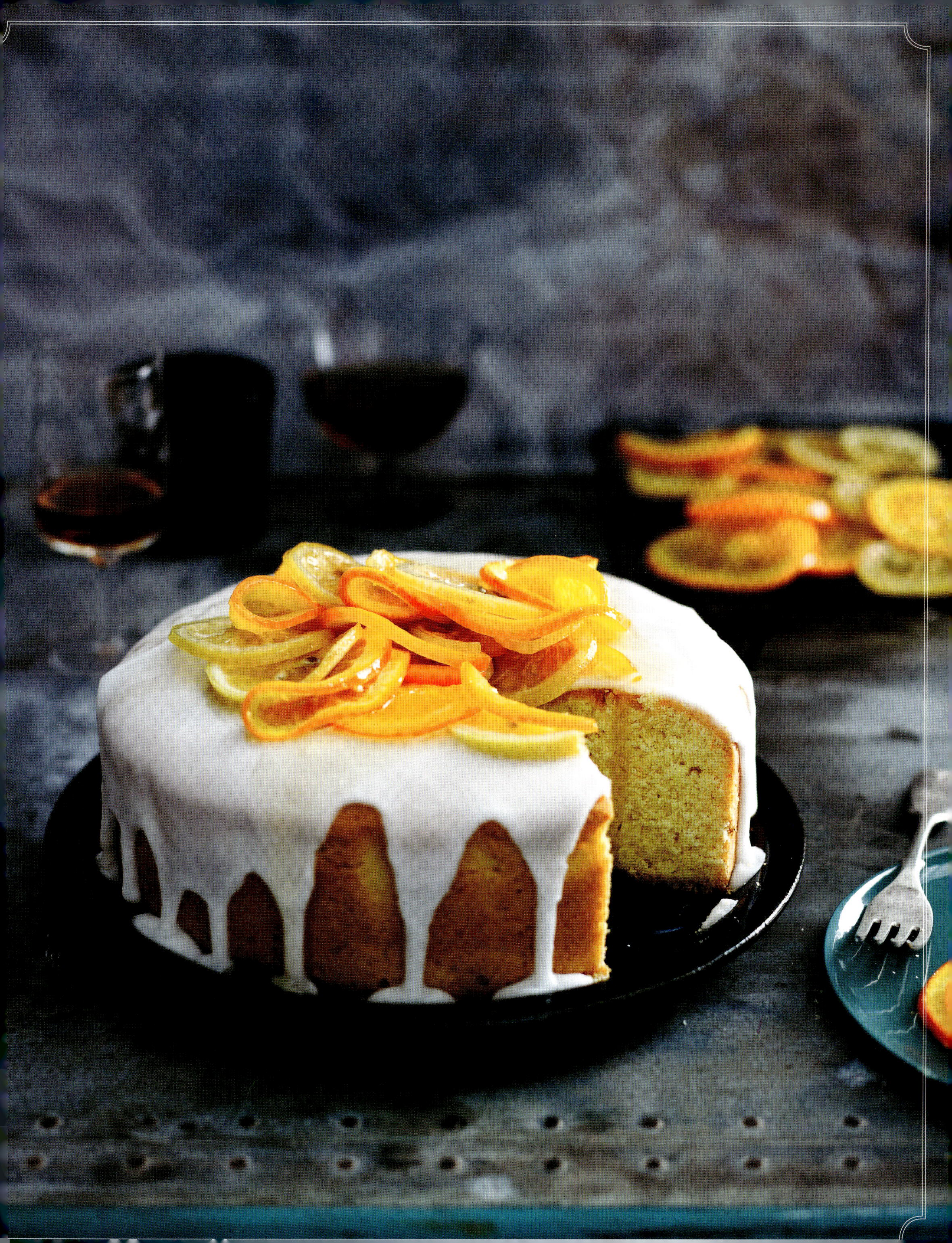

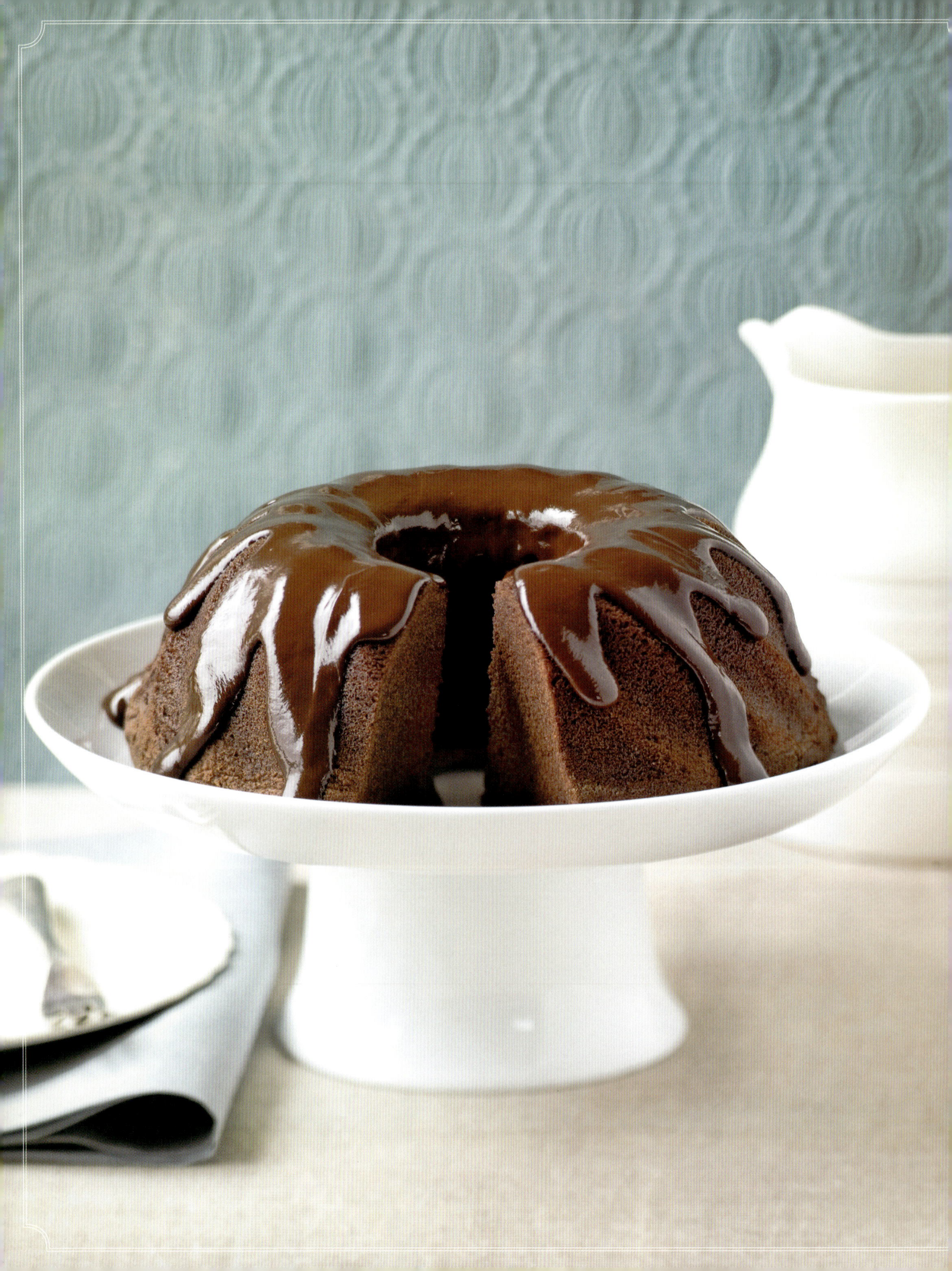

CHOCOLATE Sour Cream Cake

PREP + COOK TIME *1 HOUR 25 MINUTES* **SERVES** *8*

Cake baking doesn't get any easier than this one-bowl cake recipe. Just make sure not to beat the ingredients for too long, to achieve the best texture.

125g (4 ounces) butter, softened
1 teaspoon vanilla extract
1¼ cups (275g) caster (superfine) sugar
3 eggs
¼ cup (35g) plain (all-purpose) flour
¾ cup (110g) self-raising flour
½ cup (50g) cocoa powder, sifted
½ cup (125ml) milk
¼ cup (60g) sour cream

SOUR CREAM GANACHE
150g (4½ ounces) dark (semi-sweet) chocolate, chopped coarsely
½ cup (120g) sour cream
1–2 tablespoons boiling water (optional)

1. Preheat oven to 160°C/325°F. Grease a 21cm (8½-inch) bundt pan well.
2. Beat cake ingredients in a medium bowl on low speed with an electric mixer until just combined. Increase speed to medium, beat until smooth and changed to a paler colour. Add sour cream, beat until just combined. Spread mixture into pan.
3. Bake cake 1 hour or until a skewer inserted into the centre comes out clean. Stand cake in pan 5 minutes before turning, top-side up on to a wire rack to cool.
4. Meanwhile, make sour cream ganache.
5. Drizzle ganache over cold cake.

SOUR CREAM GANACHE
Stir chocolate and sour cream in a medium heatproof bowl over a medium saucepan of simmering water (don't let water touch base of bowl), stirring occasionally, until smooth and chocolate has melted. If ganache becomes too thick, add enough of the water to thin it down.

TIP Bundt pans have a tendency to stick, so use melted butter and a pastry brush to grease pans evenly, paying particular attention to any joins in the pan and the tube.

LITTLE WHITE CHOCOLATE *Lamingtons*

PREP + COOK TIME *1 HOUR 20 MINUTES* **MAKES** *32*

250g (8 ounces) butter, softened, chopped
1 teaspoon almond extract
1⅓ cups (300g) caster (superfine) sugar
4 eggs
1 cup (150g) plain (all-purpose) flour
⅔ cup (100g) self-raising flour
1 cup (120g) ground almonds
3 cups (210g) shredded coconut

WHITE CHOCOLATE ICING
1¾ cups (260g) white chocolate Melts
1 cup (250ml) milk
5½ cups (880g) icing (confectioners') sugar

1. Preheat oven to 180°C/350°F. Grease a 20cm x 30cm (8-inch x 12-inch) slice pan; line base and two opposite sides with a strip of baking paper.
2. Beat butter, extract, sugar and eggs in a large bowl with an electric mixer until light and fluffy. Stir in sifted flours and ground almonds, in two batches. Spread mixture into pan; smooth surface.
3. Bake cake 35 minutes or until cake springs back when touched lightly in the centre. Stand cake 5 minutes before turning onto a wire rack to cool. Cut cake into 32 pieces. Cool.
4. Make white chocolate icing.
5. Using a fork, dip cake pieces, one at a time, into icing until completely coated; drain off excess icing. Toss in coconut until well coated. Place lamingtons on baking-paper-lined wire racks; stand until icing is set.

WHITE CHOCOLATE ICING
Stir chocolate Melts and milk in a small saucepan over low heat until smooth. Transfer mixture to a large bowl; stir in sifted icing sugar until smooth.

TIP If the icing thickens during dipping, soften by placing the bowl in hot water, or microwave on HIGH (100%) for about 20 seconds.

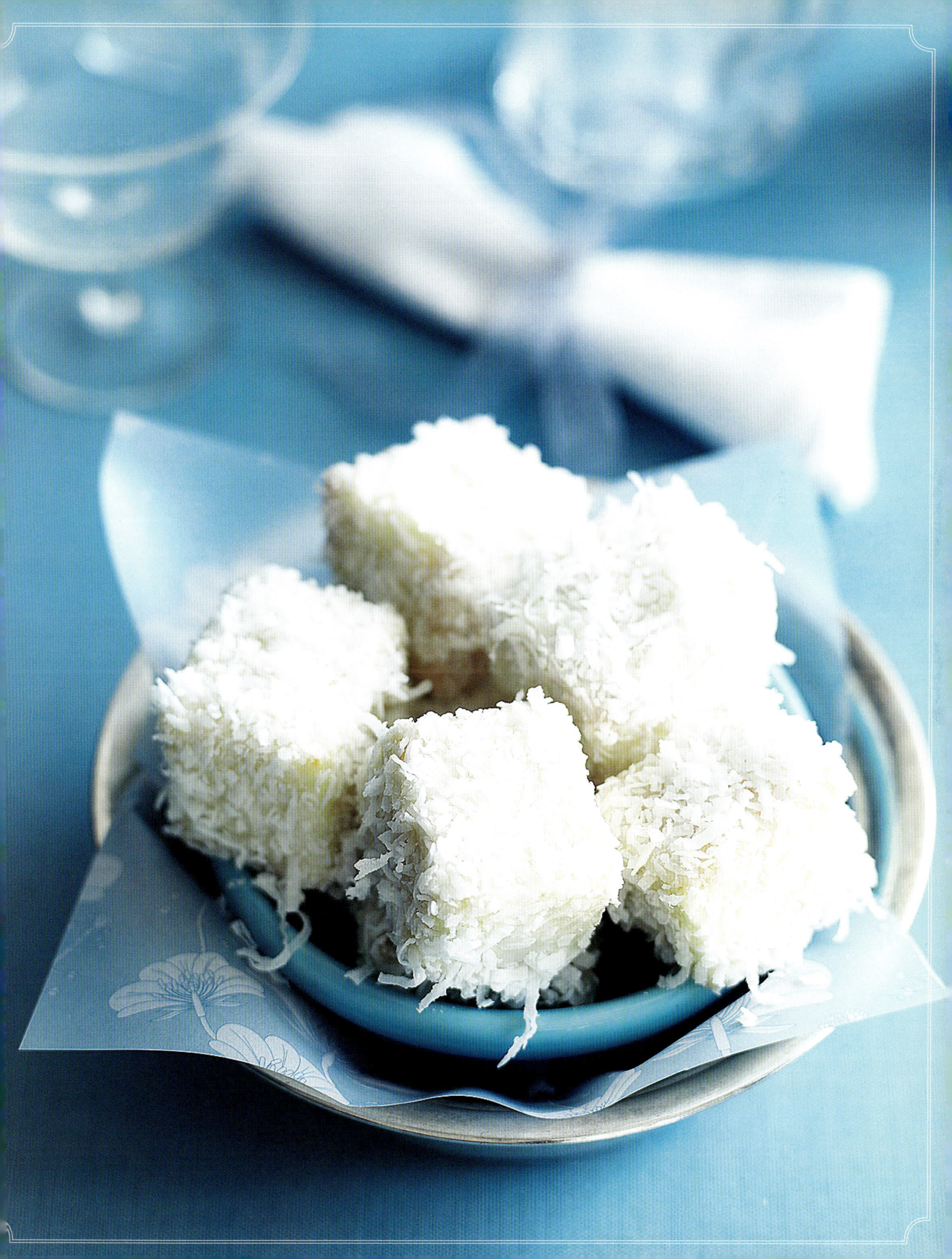

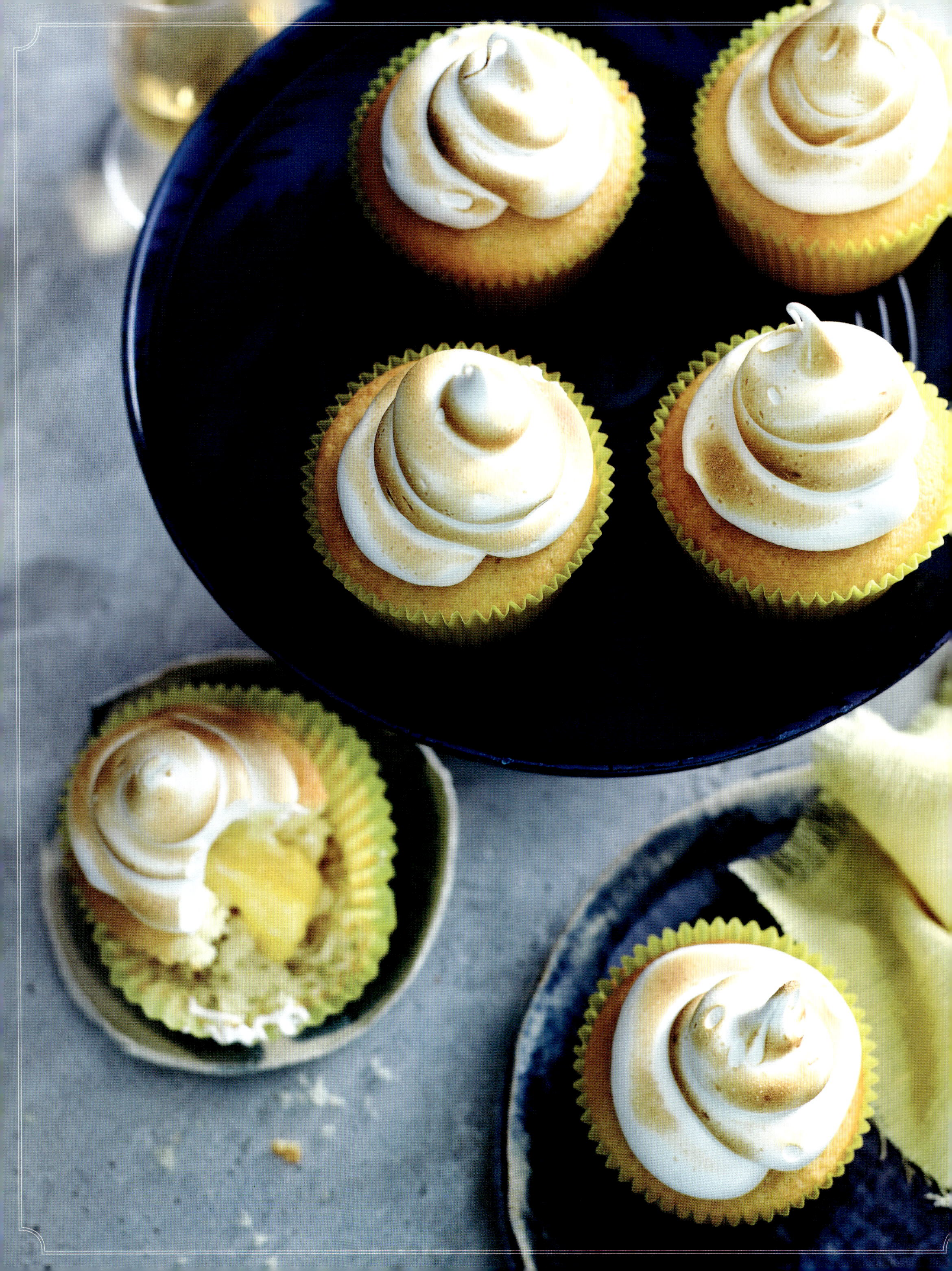

LEMON MERINGUE
Cupcakes

PREP + COOK TIME *1 HOUR 10 MINUTES (+ REFRIGERATION)* **MAKES** *12*

125g (4 ounces) butter, softened
2 teaspoons finely grated lemon rind
⅔ cup (150g) caster (superfine) sugar
2 eggs
¾ cup (60g) desiccated coconut
1¼ cups (185g) self-raising flour
⅓ cup (80ml) milk

LEMON CURD
4 egg yolks
⅓ cup (75g) caster (superfine) sugar
1 teaspoon finely grated lemon rind
⅓ cup (80ml) lemon juice
40g (1½ ounces) butter

MERINGUE
4 egg whites
1 cup (220g) caster (superfine) sugar

1. Make lemon curd.
2. Preheat oven to 180°C/350°F. Line 12-hole (⅓-cup/80ml) muffin pan with paper cases.
3. Beat butter, rind, sugar and eggs in a small bowl with an electric mixer until light and fluffy. Stir in coconut, then sifted flour and milk. Spoon mixture into cases; smooth surface.
4. Bake cakes 20 minutes or until a skewer inserted into the centre comes out clean. Cool on wire racks. Increase oven to 220°C/425°F.
5. Cut a 2cm (¾-inch) deep hole in the centre of each cake, fill with lemon curd; discard tops.
6. Make meringue.
7. Spoon meringue into a piping bag fitted with a 1cm (½-inch) plain tube. Pipe meringue on cakes; place on an oven tray. Bake 5 minutes or until meringue is browned lightly.

LEMON CURD
Place ingredients in a small heatproof bowl over a small saucepan of simmering water; stir constantly, until mixture thickens slightly. Remove from heat. Cover surface of curd with plastic wrap; refrigerate until cold.

MERINGUE
Beat ingredients in a small bowl with an electric mixer until thick and glossy.

PASSIONFRUIT MERINGUE *Cake*

PREP + COOK TIME *1 HOUR* **SERVES** *8*

125g (4 ounces) butter
1 teaspoon vanilla extract
1¾ cup (385g) caster (superfine) sugar
2 eggs
¾ cup (110g) self-raising flour
2 tablespoons plain (all-purpose) flour
⅓ cup (80ml) milk
4 egg whites
½ teaspoon cream of tartar
1 teaspoon caster (superfine) sugar, extra

PASSIONFRUIT CREAM
300ml (½ pint) thickened (heavy) cream
250g (8 ounces) mascarpone cheese
2 tablespoons passionfruit pulp
2 tablespoons icing (confectioners') sugar

1. Preheat oven 180°C/350°F. Grease two 22cm (9-inch) round springform pans; line base and side of pans with baking paper.
2. Beat butter, extract and ¾ cup of the sugar in a small bowl with an electric mixer until light and fluffy. Beat in eggs, one at a time. Transfer mixture to a large bowl; fold in combined sifted flours and milk, in two batches. Spread mixture evenly into pans.
3. Beat egg whites and cream of tartar in a small bowl with an electric mixer until soft peaks form. Gradually add remaining sugar, beating until dissolved between additions, or until thick and glossy. Spread meringue over cake mixture in pans. In one pan, smooth the meringue flat; in the other pan, use the back of a spoon, to peak the meringue, then sprinkle with extra sugar.
4. Bake cakes 30 minutes or until cooked when tested. Cool in pans.
5. Meanwhile, make passionfruit cream.
6. Place flat-meringue-topped cake on a platter; spread with passionfruit cream. Place other cake, meringue side-up, on top.

PASSIONFRUIT CREAM
Beat cream in a small bowl with an electric mixer until soft peaks form. Combine mascarpone, passionfruit pulp and icing sugar in a medium bowl; fold in whipped cream.

TIPS Invert the base of the springform pans before clipping securely so that they are flat – this makes it easier to remove the cake from the bases.
You will need about 3 passionfruit for this recipe.
The cakes can be made a day ahead. Assemble cake several hours before serving.

SERVING SUGGESTION Serve topped with fresh passionfruit pulp.

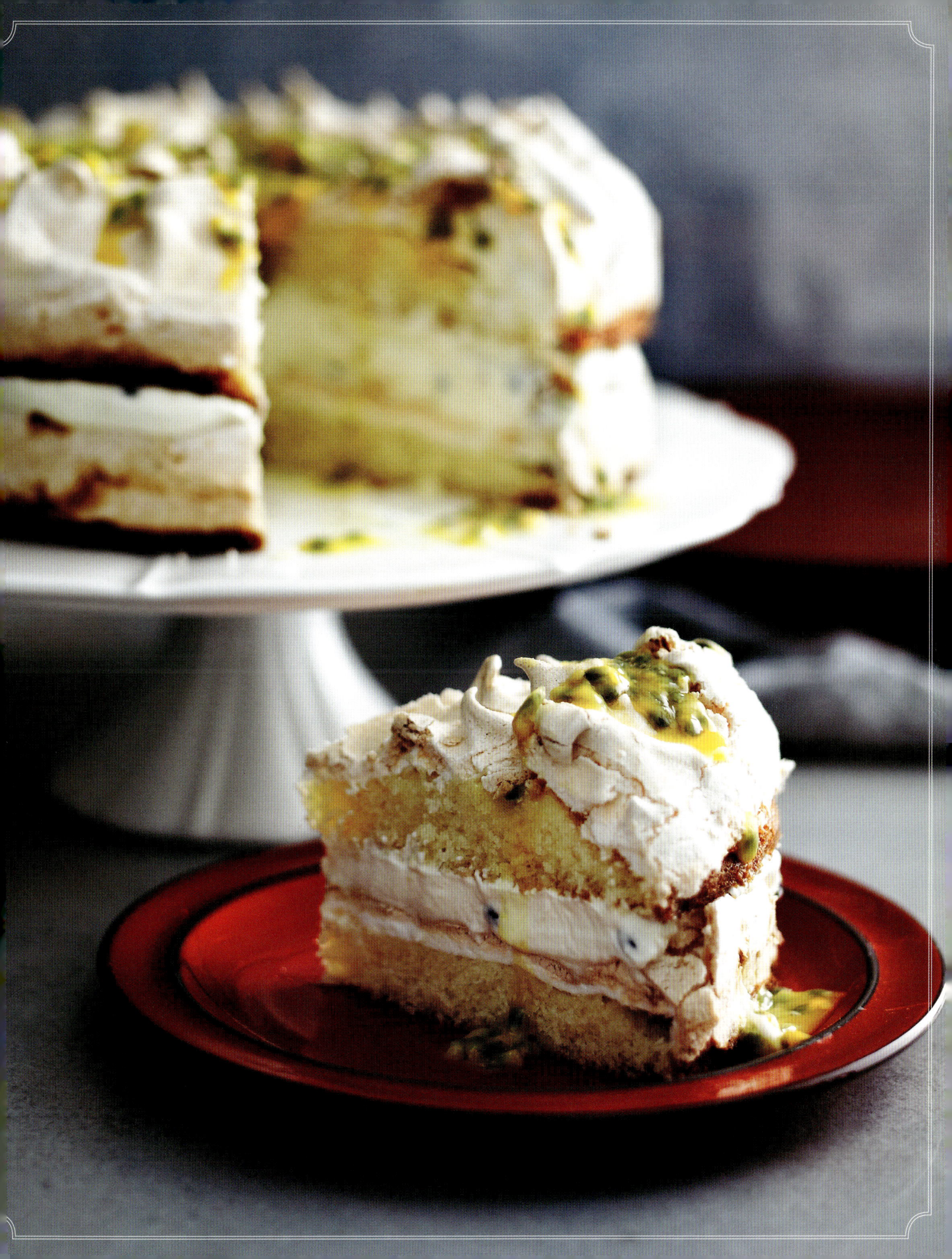

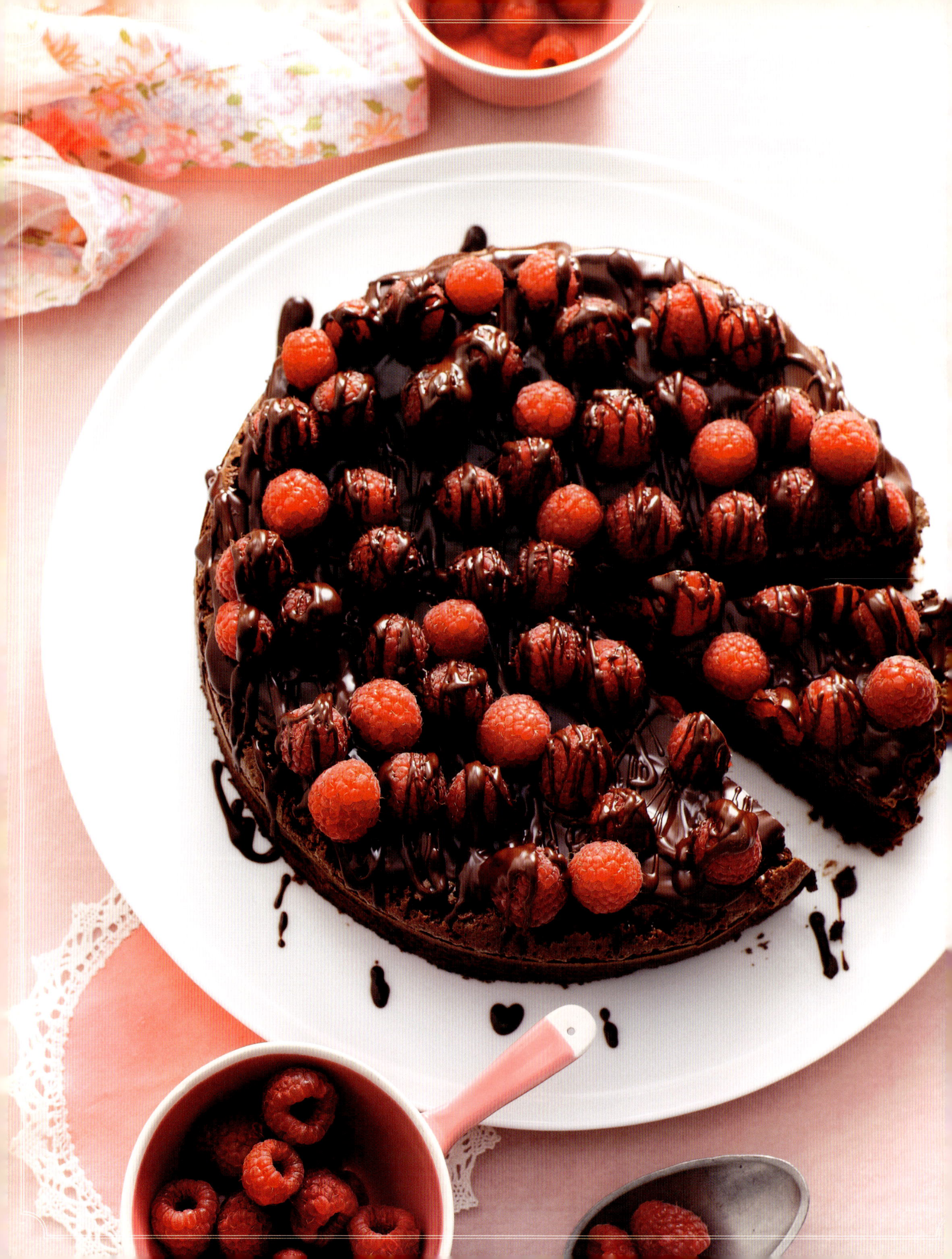

CHOCOLATE
and Raspberry Cake

PREP + COOK TIME 1 HOUR 45 MINUTES (+ STANDING) SERVES 12

⅓ cup (35g) cocoa powder
⅓ cup (80ml) hot water
150g (4½ ounces) dark (semi-sweet) chocolate, chopped coarsely
150g (4½ ounces) butter, chopped
1⅓ cups (300g) firmly packed brown sugar
1 cup (125g) ground almonds
4 eggs, separated
240g (7½ ounces) raspberries

CHOCOLATE GANACHE
200g (6½ ounces) dark (semi-sweet) chocolate, chopped coarsely
⅔ cup (160ml) thickened (heavy) cream

1. Preheat oven to 180°C/350°F. Grease a deep 22cm (9-inch) round cake pan; line base and side with baking paper.
2. Blend cocoa powder with the water in a small bowl until smooth.
3. Stir chocolate and butter in a large heatproof bowl over a large saucepan of simmering water until melted. Remove bowl from heat; stir in cocoa mixture, sugar, ground almonds and egg yolks.
4. Beat egg whites in a clean small bowl with an electric mixer until soft peaks form; fold into chocolate mixture, in two batches. Pour into pan.
5. Bake cake 1¼ hours or until a skewer inserted into the centre comes out with moist crumbs attached. Stand cake in pan 15 minutes before turning, top-side up, onto a wire rack to cool.
6. Meanwhile, make chocolate ganache.
7. Pour three-quarters of the ganache over cake (spread to cover top if necessary), top with raspberries; drizzle with remaining ganache. Stand at room temperature until set.

CHOCOLATE GANACHE
Stir ingredients in a small saucepan over low heat until smooth.

POPPY SEED CUPCAKES
with Orange Frosting

PREP + COOK TIME 1 HOUR MAKES 12

125g (4 ounces) butter, softened
1 teaspoon vanilla extract
1¼ cups (275g) caster (superfine) sugar
3 eggs
¾ cup (110g) plain (all-purpose) flour
¾ cup (110g) self-raising flour
½ cup (125ml) milk
2 teaspoons finely grated orange rind
¼ cup (40g) poppy seeds
1 medium orange (240g)

ORANGE FROSTING
150g (4½ ounces) cream cheese, softened
75g (2½ ounces) butter, softened
2 cups (320g) icing (confectioners') sugar
2 teaspoons finely grated orange rind

1. Preheat oven to 180°C/350°F. Line a 12-hole (⅓-cup/80ml) pan with paper cases.
2. Beat cake ingredients in a medium bowl on low speed with an electric mixer until just combined. Increase speed to medium, beat until mixture is smooth and changed to a paler colour. Spoon mixture into paper cases.
3. Bake cakes 25 minutes or until a skewer inserted into the centre comes out clean. Stand cakes in pan 2 minutes before turning, top-side up, onto a wire rack to cool.
4. Make orange frosting.
5. Peel large pieces of rind from orange, without removing any of the white pith. Cut rind into long, thin strips.
6. Spread frosting onto cooled cakes; top with strips of rind and, if you like, sprinkle with a little extra poppy seeds.

ORANGE FROSTING
Beat cream cheese and butter in a small bowl with an electric mixer until smooth. Gradually beat in sifted icing sugar; stir in rind.

TIP You can use a zesting tool to make the thin strips of orange rind.

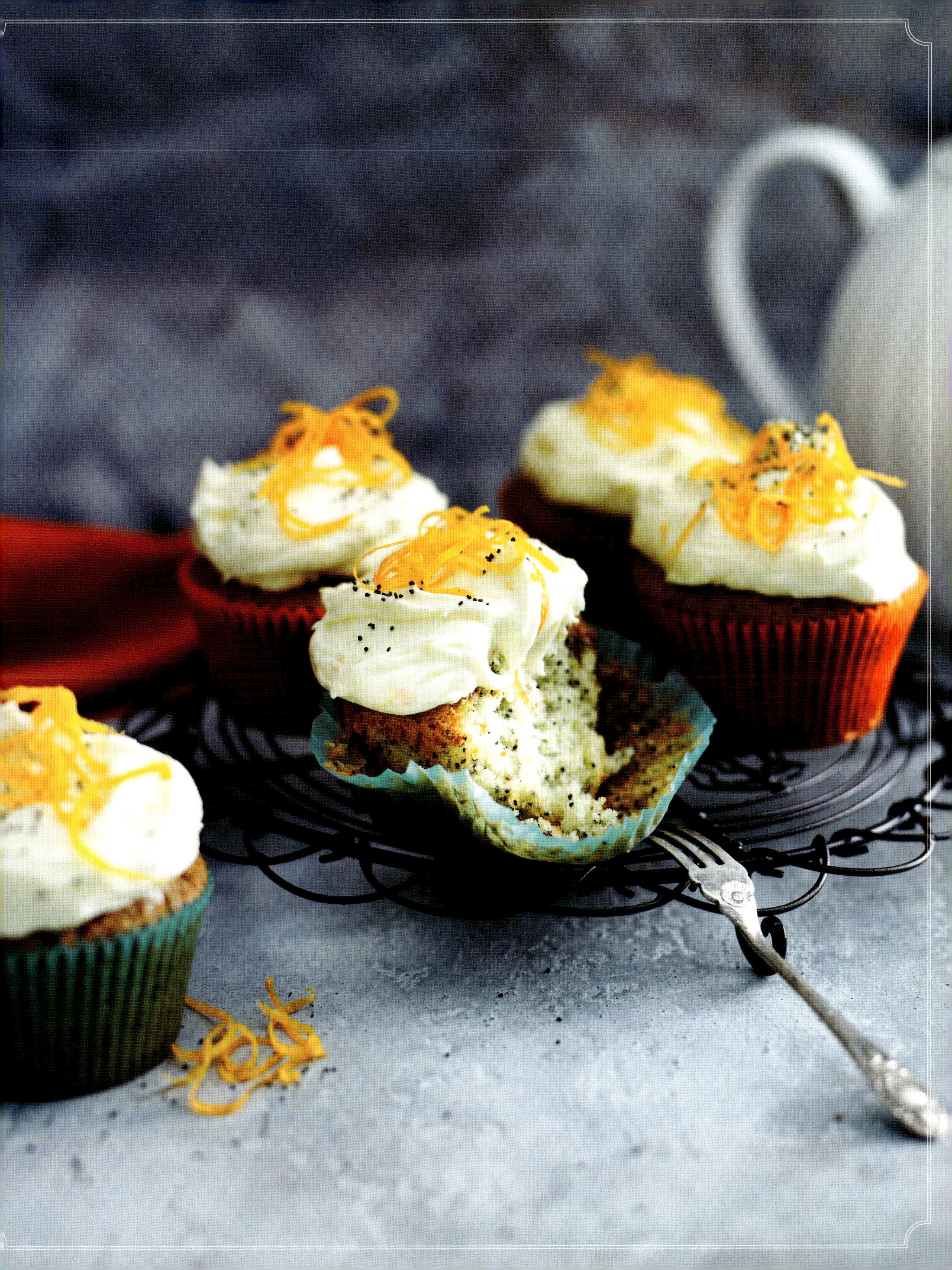

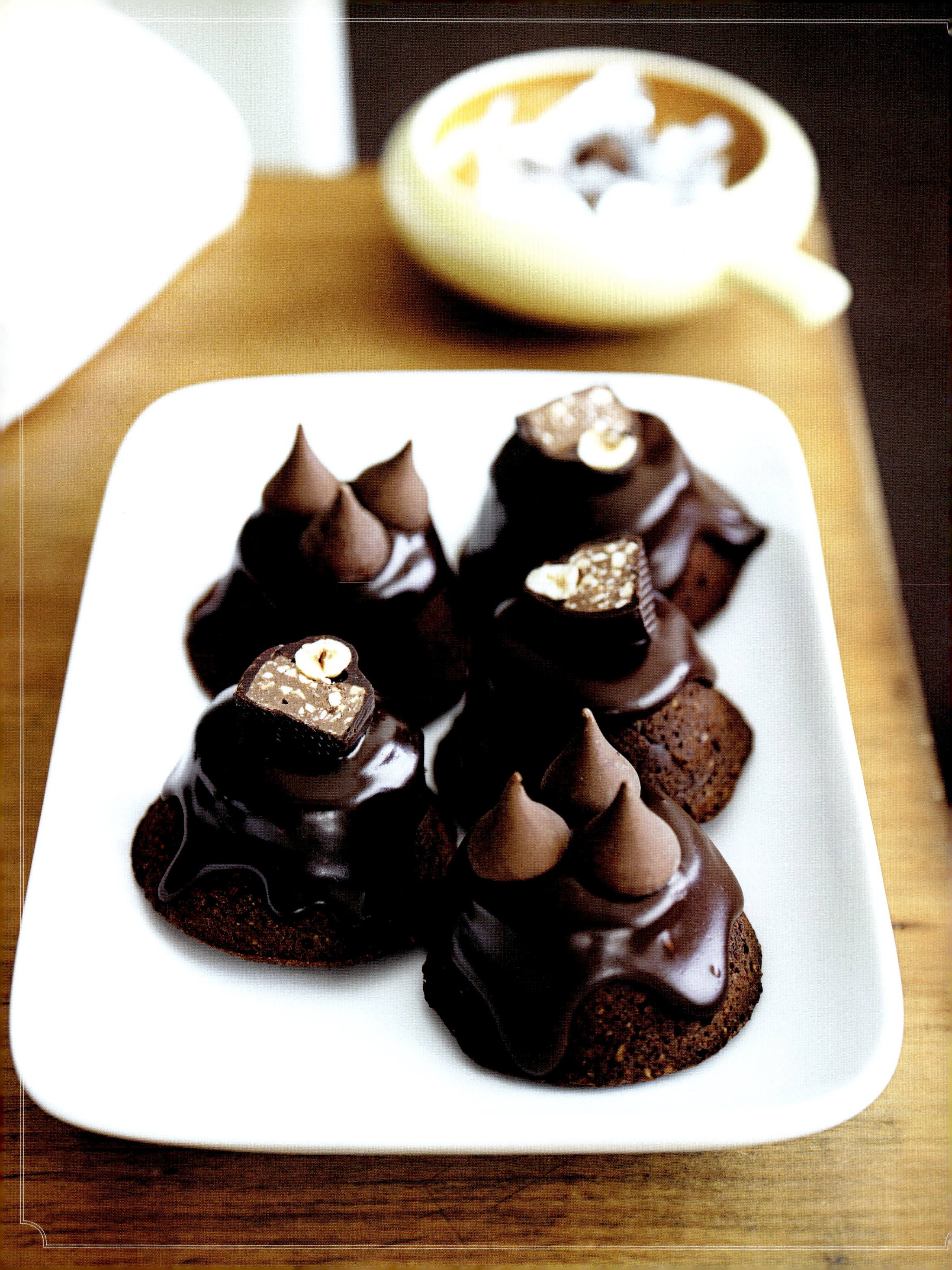

LITTLE CHOCOLATE
Hazelnut Cakes

PREP + COOK TIME *1 HOUR 10 MINUTES (+ COOLING)* **MAKES** *18*

250g (8 ounces) butter, softened
1 cup (220g) caster (superfine) sugar
6 eggs, separated
300g (9½ ounces) dark (semi-sweet) chocolate (70% cocoa solids), melted
2 cups (220g) ground hazelnuts
1 tablespoon hazelnut-, chocolate- or coffee-flavoured liqueur
1 teaspoon vanilla extract
chocolates, to decorate (see tip)

CHOCOLATE GANACHE
200g (6½ ounces) dark (semi-sweet) chocolate, chopped coarsely
100g (3 ounces) butter, chopped

1. Preheat oven to 180°C/350°F. Grease 18 holes from two 12-hole (⅓-cup/80ml) muffin pans.
2. Beat butter and sugar in a small bowl with an electric mixer until light and fluffy. Beat in egg yolks, one at a time. Transfer mixture to a large bowl, stir in cooled chocolate, then fold in ground hazelnuts, liqueur and extract.
3. Beat egg whites in a clean small bowl with an electric mixer until soft peaks form. Fold egg white into chocolate mixture, in two batches. Spoon mixture into pan holes.
4. Bake cakes 25 minutes or until a skewer inserted into the centre comes out with moist crumbs attached. Stand cakes in pans 5 minutes before turning, onto a wire rack to cool.
5. Make chocolate ganache.
6. Pour a little chocolate ganache over each cake; decorate tops with chocolates. Stand at room temperature until set.

CHOCOLATE GANACHE
Combine chocolate and butter in a heatproof bowl over a pan of barely simmering water, stirring occasionally, until smooth and glossy. Remove from heat; stand 30 minutes or until thickened slightly.

TIPS To decorate the cake you can use halved chocolates, choc chips, or even slice up your favourite chocolate bar.
Un-iced cakes can be made four days ahead; store covered in an airtight container at room temperature. Ice cakes on the day of serving.

BANANA CARAMEL
Layer Cake

PREP + COOK TIME 1 HOUR 25 MINUTES SERVES 8

185g (6 ounces) butter, softened
1¼ cups (275g) caster (superfine) sugar
2 teaspoons vanilla extract
3 eggs
1¼ cups mashed banana
2¼ cups (335g) self-raising flour
½ teaspoon bicarbonate of soda (baking soda)
⅓ cup (80ml) milk
500g (1 pound) mascarpone cheese
½ cup (125ml) thickened (heavy) cream
380g (12 ounces) canned caramel top 'n' fill, chilled
1 large banana (230g), sliced thinly
1 tablespoon boiling water

1. Preheat oven to 180°C/350°F. Grease a 24cm (9½-inch) bundt pan well; dust with flour, shake out excess.
2. Beat butter, sugar and extract in a small bowl with an electric mixer until light and fluffy. Beat in eggs, one at a time. Beat in mashed banana. Transfer mixture to a large bowl. Stir in sifted flour and soda, then milk. Spread mixture into pan.
3. Bake cake, on lower shelf in oven, for 30 minutes. Cover loosely with baking paper; bake for a further 10 minutes or until a skewer inserted into the cake comes out clean. Stand cake in pan 10 minutes before turning, top-side up, onto a wire rack to cool.
4. Beat mascarpone and cream in a small bowl with an electric mixer until soft peaks form.
5. Split cold cake into three layers. Whisk caramel in a small bowl. Spread bottom layer of cake with one-third of the caramel, then half the mascarpone mixture and half the banana slices. Repeat next layer with half the remaining caramel, remaining mascarpone mixture and remaining banana slices. Replace top of cake.
6. Whisk remaining caramel with the water; drizzle over top of cake.

TIPS Bundt pans have a tendency to stick, so use melted butter and a pastry brush to grease the pan evenly, paying particular attention to any joins in the pan and the tube.
You will need about 2 large overripe bananas (460g) for the amount of mashed banana.

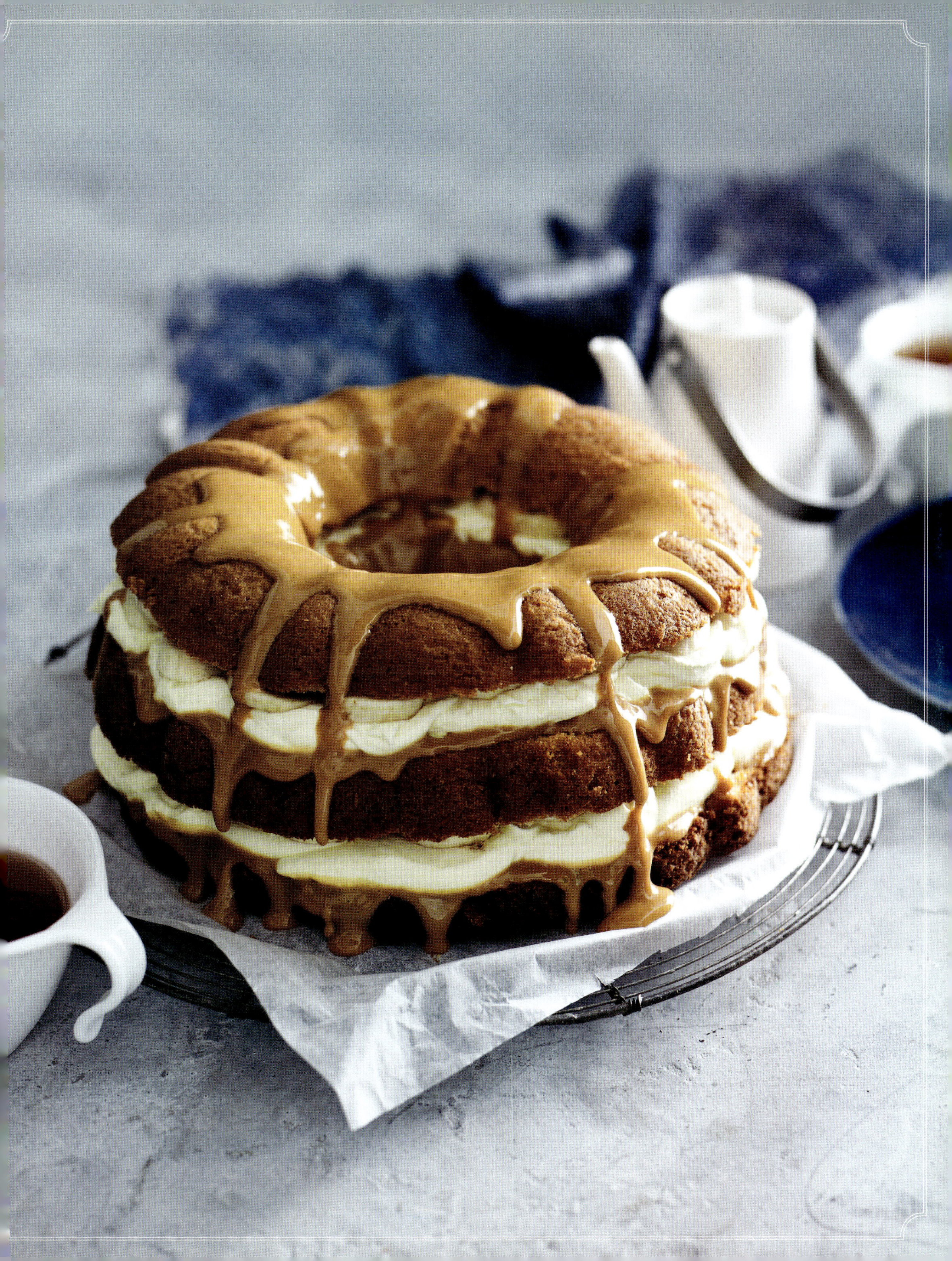

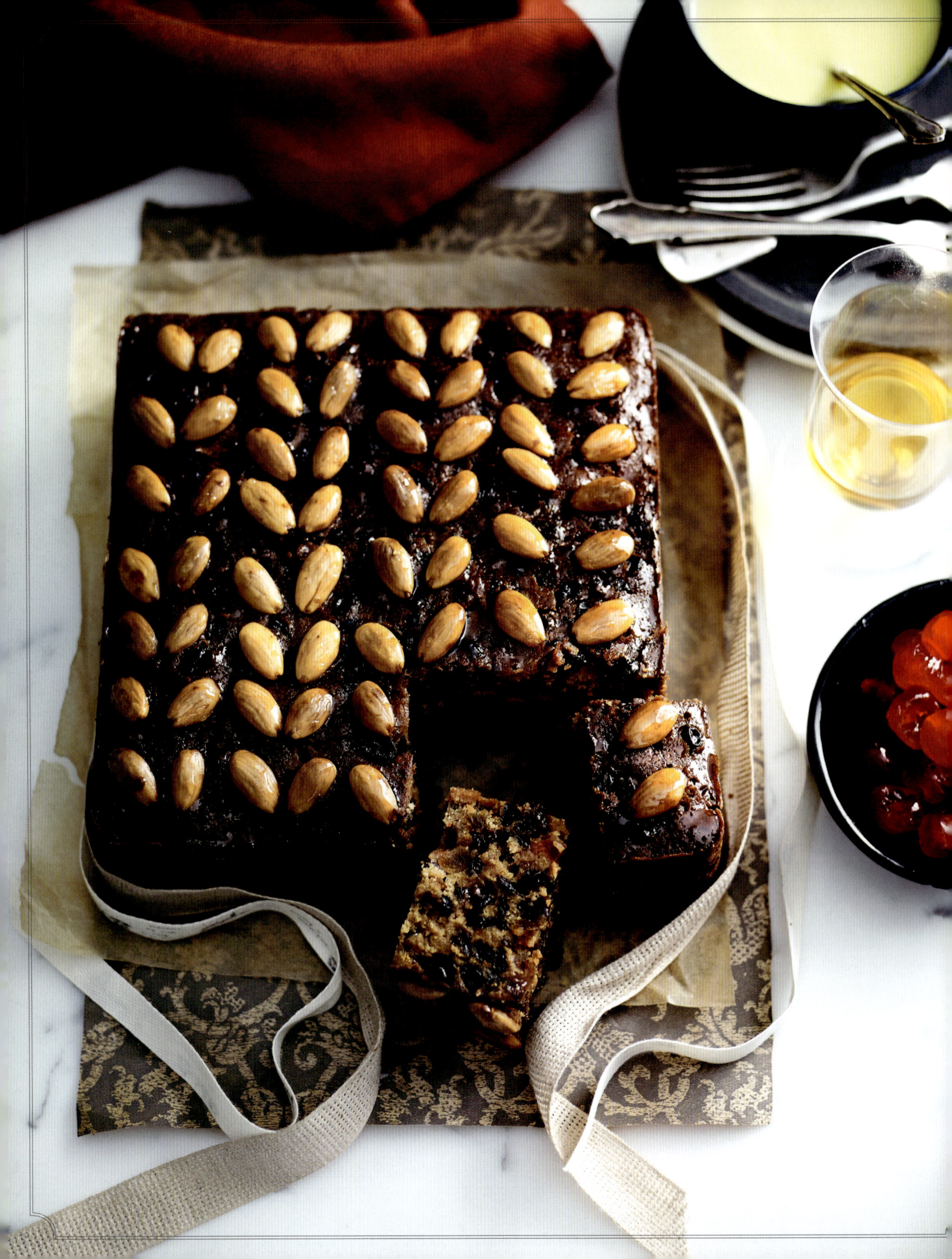

RICH FRUIT CAKE

PREP + COOK TIME *3 HOURS 30 MINUTES (+ COOLING)* **SERVES** *16*

500g (1 pound) sultanas
250g (8 ounces) raisins, chopped
125g (4 ounces) currants
125g (4 ounces) quartered glacé cherries
125g (4 ounces) glacé peaches, chopped
⅓ cup (80ml) orange juice
2 tablespoons marmalade
½ cup (125ml) rum
250g (8 ounces) butter, softened
1 cup (220g) firmly packed dark brown sugar
1 teaspoon finely grated orange rind
1 teaspoon finely grated lemon rind
4 eggs
2 cups (300g) plain (all-purpose) flour
2 teaspoons mixed spice
¾ cup (120g) blanched whole almonds
¼ cup (60ml) rum, extra
2 tablespoons honey
2 tablespoons boiling water

1. Preheat oven to 150°C/300°F. Line a deep 20cm (8-inch) square cake pan with two layers of brown paper and two layers of baking paper, extending the papers 5cm (2 inches) over the sides.
2. Combine all fruit, juice, marmalade and rum in a large bowl.
3. Beat butter, sugar and rinds in a small bowl with an electric mixer until combined. Beat in eggs, one at a time, until just combined.
4. Stir butter mixture into fruit mixture, then stir in sifted flour and spice. Spread mixture into pan; decorate top with almonds.
5. Bake cake 3 hours or until a skewer inserted into the centre comes out clean. Brush top of cake with extra rum. Cover hot cake, in pan, tightly with a clean tea towel; cool overnight.
6. Before serving, stir honey and the water in a small bowl until smooth. Brush over top of cake.

TIP This fruit cake can be made up to 12 months ahead; store in an airtight container at room temperature. If the weather is humid, keep the container in the fridge or freezer.

AFTERNOON TEA

RASPBERRY AND PASSIONFRUIT
Mile-high Layer Cake

(RECIPE PAGE 294)

LEMON MERINGUE
Cupcakes

(RECIPE PAGE 279)

CHOCOLATE
French Macaroons

(RECIPE PAGE 312)

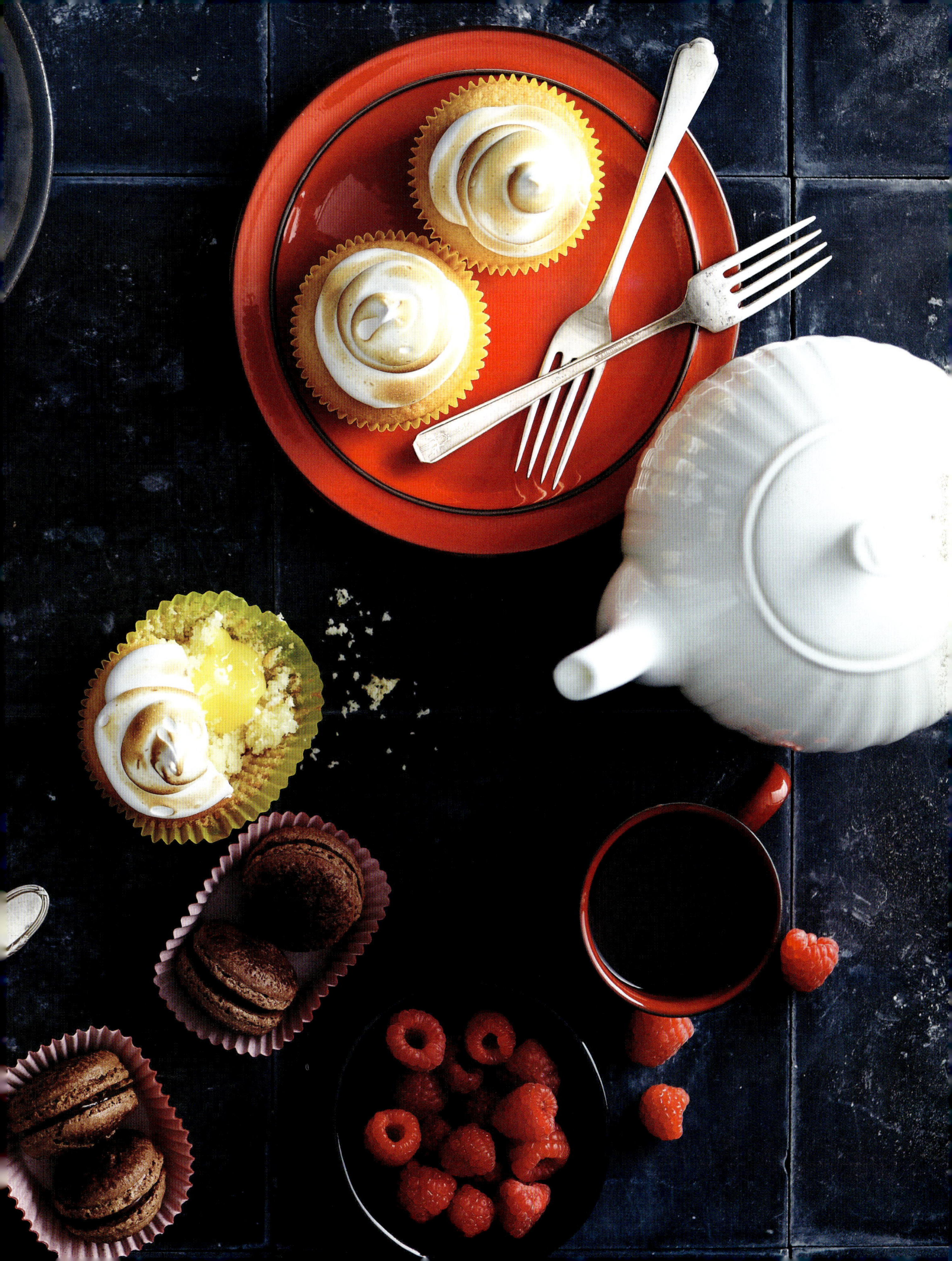

RASPBERRY AND PASSIONFRUIT
Mile-high Layer Cake

PREP + COOK TIME 1 HOUR 50 MINUTES SERVES 12

250g (8 ounces) butter, softened
2 cups (440g) caster (superfine) sugar
1 teaspoon vanilla extract
4 eggs
2 cups (300g) plain (all-purpose) flour
¼ cup (35g) self-raising flour
¾ cup (180ml) milk
600g (1¼ pounds) raspberries

PASSIONFRUIT CREAM
600ml (1 pint) thickened (heavy) cream
2 tablespoons icing (confectioners') sugar
⅓ cup (80ml) passionfruit pulp

MERINGUE FROSTING
⅔ cup (150g) caster (superfine) sugar
1 tablespoon glucose syrup
2 tablespoons water
3 egg whites
1 tablespoon caster (superfine) sugar, extra

1. Preheat oven to 160°C/325°F. Grease three 20cm (8-inch) round sandwich pans; line each base with baking paper.
2. Beat butter, sugar and vanilla in a large bowl with an electric mixer until light and fluffy. Beat in eggs, one at a time. Fold in sifted flours and milk, in two batches. Divide mixture evenly into pans.
3. Bake cakes 35 minutes or until a skewer inserted into the centre comes out clean. Stand cakes in pans 5 minutes before turning, top-side down, onto wire racks to cool.
4. Meanwhile, make passionfruit cream.
5. Split cold cakes in half. Spread one cake layer with one-fifth of the passionfruit cream, top with one-sixth of the raspberries, then with another cake layer. Repeat layering, finishing with a cake layer.
6. Make meringue frosting.
7. Spread frosting all over top and side of cake; top cake with remaining raspberries.

PASSIONFRUIT CREAM
Beat cream in a small bowl with an electric mixer until soft peaks form. Stir in sifted icing sugar and passionfruit.

MERINGUE FROSTING
Stir sugar, glucose and the water in a small saucepan over medium heat until sugar dissolves. Bring to the boil; boil 3 minutes or until syrup reaches 116°C on a sugar thermometer (or when a teaspoon of syrup, dropped into a cup of cold water, forms a soft ball when mixture is gathered up and rolled between fingers). Remove from heat to allow bubbles to subside. Meanwhile, beat egg whites in a small bowl with an electric mixer until soft peaks form; beat in extra sugar until dissolved. While motor is operating, pour in hot syrup in a thin steady stream; beat on high speed for 5 minutes or until mixture is thick.

TIP You can make the cake a day ahead. Complete the recipe to the end of step 5 then refrigerate for several hours or overnight. Cover cake with meringue frosting 3 hours before serving.

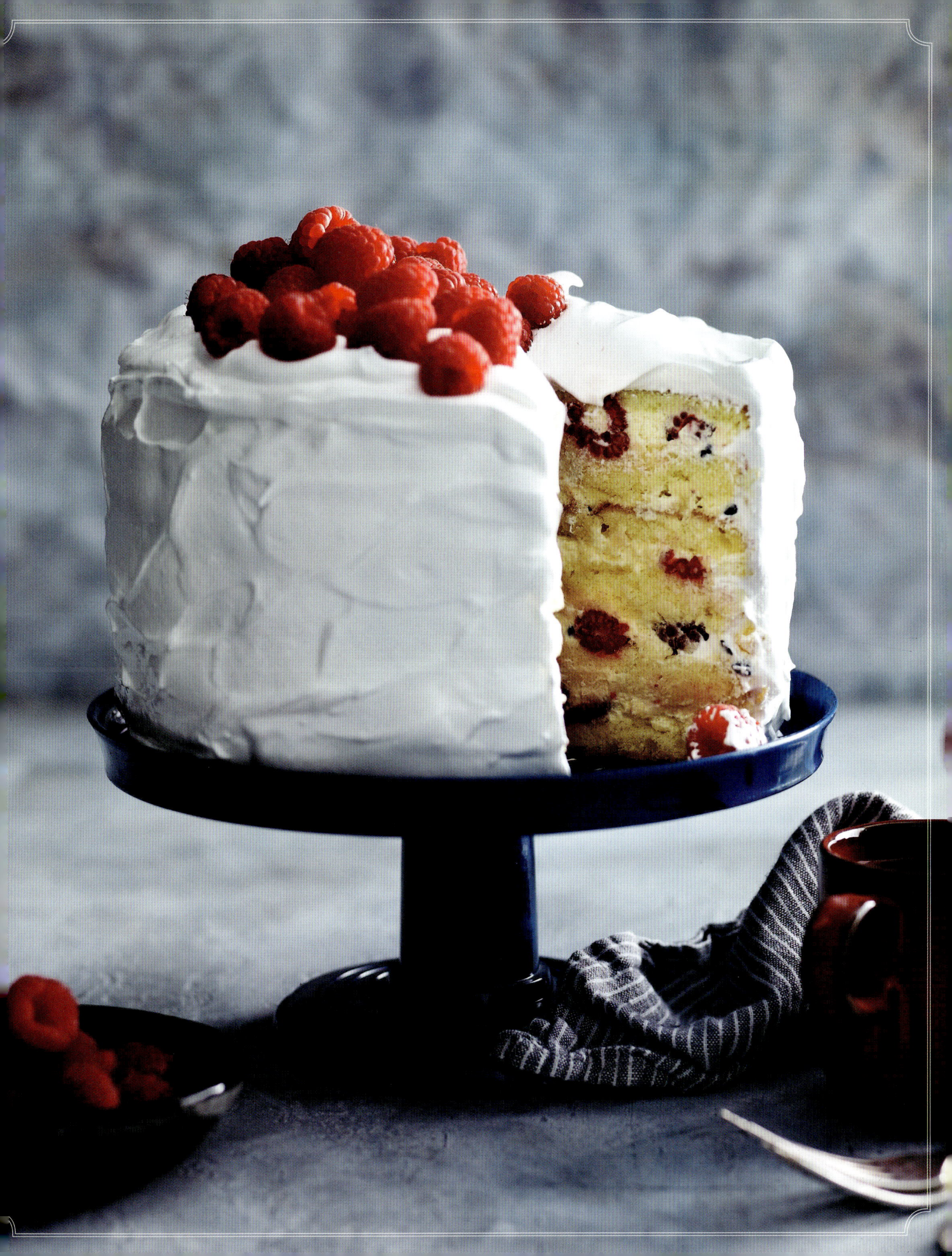

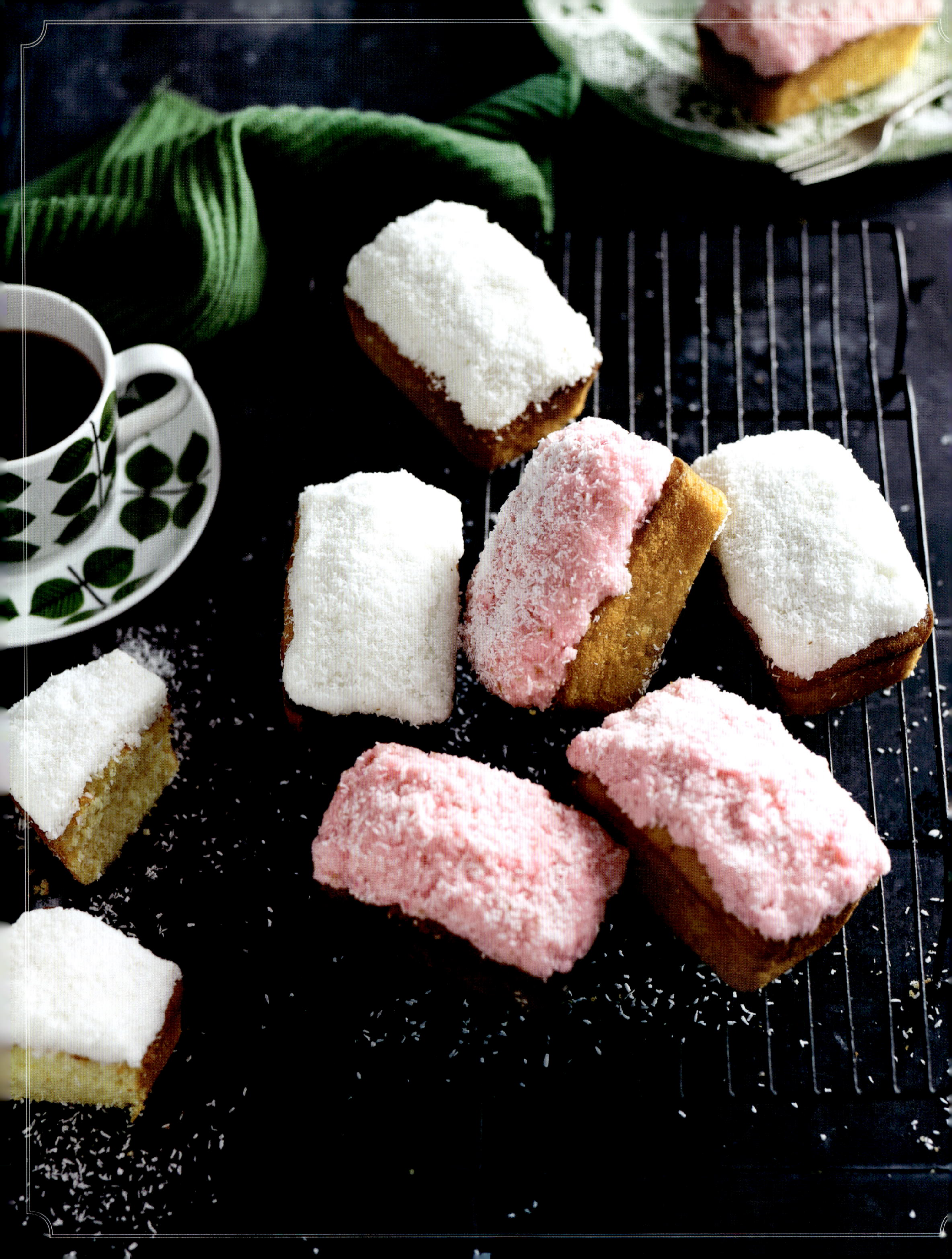

MOIST COCONUT CAKE
with Coconut Ice Frosting

PREP + COOK TIME *1 HOUR 15 MINUTES (+ COOLING)* **MAKES** *8*

125g (4 ounces) butter, softened
½ teaspoon coconut extract
1 cup (220g) caster (superfine) sugar
2 eggs
1½ cups (225g) self-raising flour
½ cup (40g) desiccated coconut
250g (8 ounces) extra-light sour cream
⅓ cup (80ml) milk

COCONUT ICE FROSTING
2 cups (320g) icing (confectioners') sugar
1⅓ cups (110g) desiccated coconut
2 egg whites, beaten lightly
1 tablespoon water
pink food colouring

1. Preheat oven to 180°C/350°F. Grease an 8-hole (½-cup/125ml) petite loaf pan; line each base with baking paper.
2. Beat butter, extract and sugar in a small bowl with an electric mixer until light and fluffy. Beat in eggs, one at a time. Transfer mixture to a large bowl. Stir in sifted flour, coconut, sour cream and milk, in two batches, until smooth. Spread mixture into pan.
3. Bake cakes 25 minutes or until a skewer inserted into the centre comes out clean. Stand cakes in pan 10 minutes before turning, top-side up, onto a wire rack to cool.
4. Meanwhile, make coconut ice frosting.
5. Spread half the cakes with pink frosting and remaining cakes with white frosting.

COCONUT ICE FROSTING
Stir sifted icing sugar, coconut, egg whites and the water in a medium bowl until well combined. Divide frosting in half; tint one half pink.

TIP You can make this cake in a deep 22cm (9-inch) round cake pan. Grease, then line the base of the pan with baking paper. Follow the recipe as directed; bake for 50 minutes.

Cakes & Cupcakes

RICH CHOCOLATE
Roulade

PREP + COOK TIME *30 MINUTES (+ COOLING & REFRIGERATION)* **SERVES 8**

This flourless cake is rich but surprisingly light. This also means it can crack slightly when rolled – but that's proof it is flourless.

200g (6½ ounces) dark (semi-sweet) chocolate, chopped coarsely
¼ cup (60ml) hot water
1 teaspoon instant coffee granules
4 eggs, separated
½ cup (110g) caster (superfine) sugar
1 tablespoon caster (superfine) sugar, extra
300ml (½ pint) thickened (heavy) cream
150g (4½ ounces) raspberries
2 tablespoons dutch cocoa

1. Preheat oven to 180°C/350°F. Grease a 25cm x 30cm (10-inch x 12-inch) swiss roll pan; line base and long sides with baking paper, extending the paper 5cm (2 inches) over the sides.
2. Stir chocolate, the water and coffee in a medium heatproof bowl over a medium saucepan of simmering water (don't let water touch base of bowl) until chocolate melts.
3. Beat egg yolks and sugar in a small bowl with an electric mixer 5 minutes or until thick and creamy. Stir egg mixture into chocolate mixture.
4. Beat egg whites in a clean small bowl with an electric mixer until soft peaks form. Gently fold egg white into chocolate mixture, in two batches. Spread mixture into pan.
5. Bake cake 12 minutes or until top is firm to touch.
6. Sprinkle top of cake evenly with extra sugar; cover with a large piece of baking paper, then an upside-down wire rack. Carefully invert cake onto paper-covered rack; peel away the lining paper. Cool.
7. Beat cream in a small bowl with an electric mixer until firm peaks form. Spread cream over cake, scatter evenly with raspberries. Using paper as a guide, roll up from one long side. Refrigerate at least 30 minutes. Before serving, dust with cocoa; if you like, top with some more raspberries.

TIPS If the roulade is cracked or badly shaped, refrigerate it for a few hours or until it is firm, then gently press the sides of the roll into a round shape. It can also be wrapped firmly in plastic wrap to keep its shape.
The roulade can be made a day ahead and rolled 6 hours before serving. Keep it covered with plastic wrap in the refrigerator.

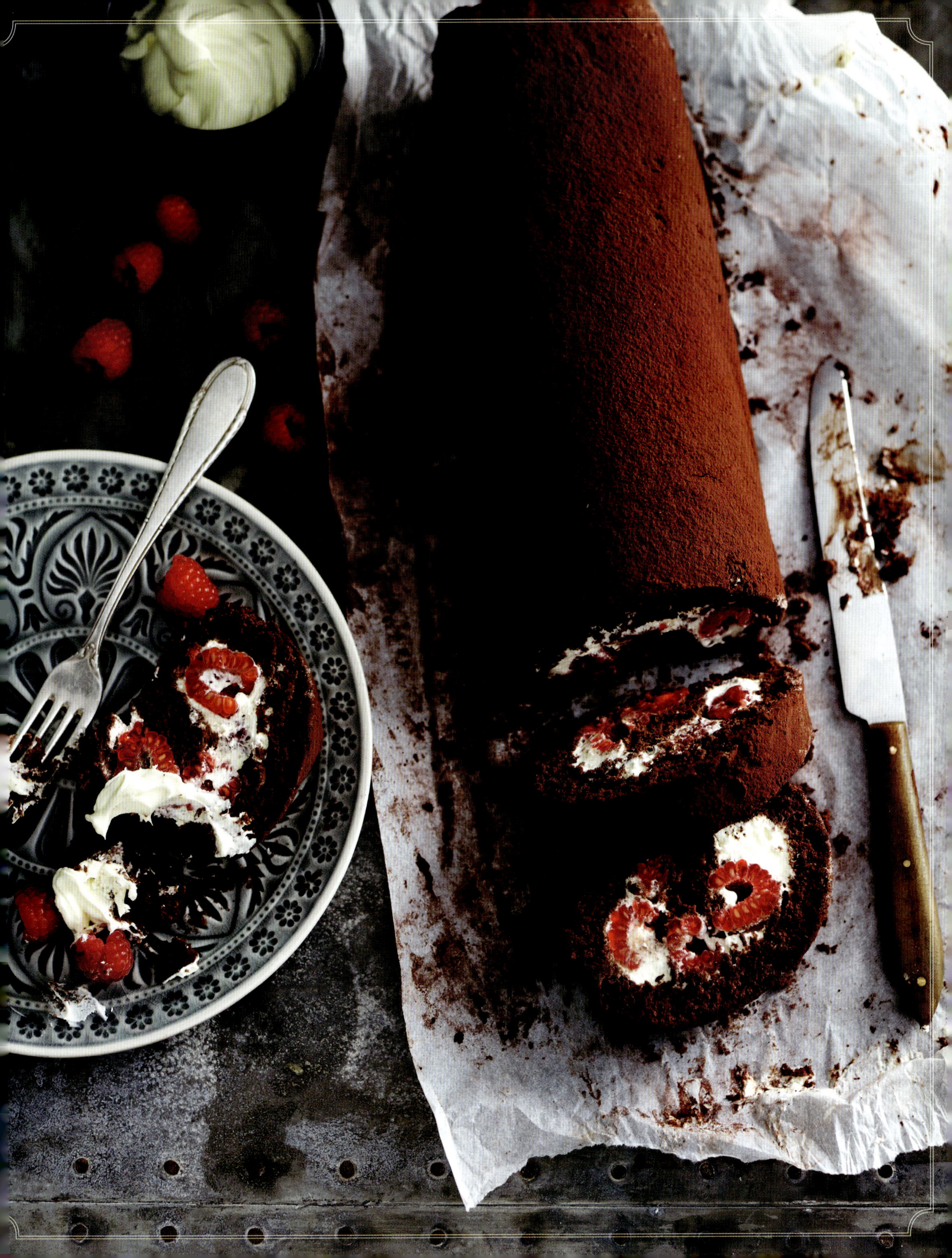

CHAPTER 9
BISCUITS & SLICES

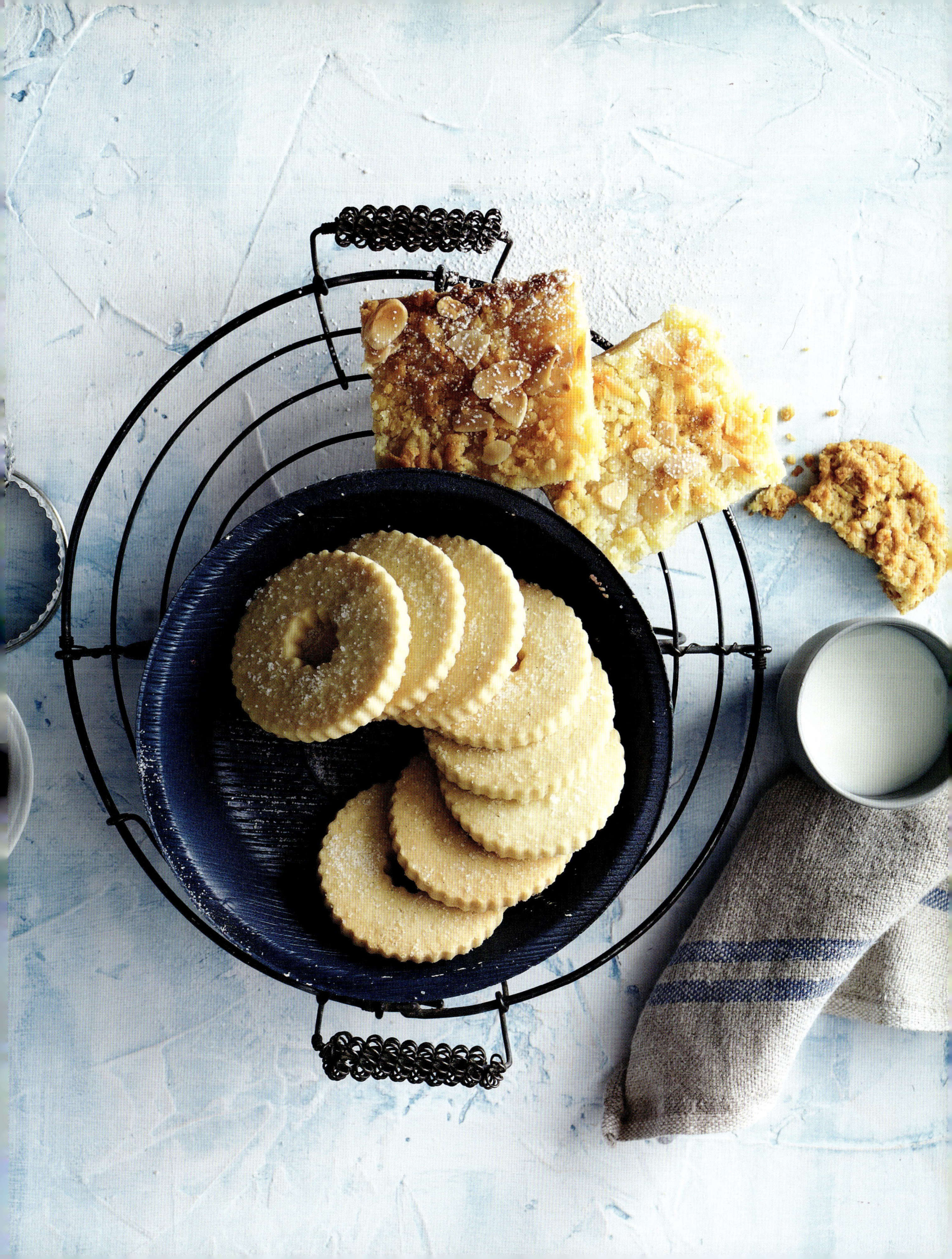

VANILLA SHORTBREAD

PREP + COOK TIME *1 HOUR 10 MINUTES* MAKES *48*

This is a really lovely shortbread; buttery-tasting with a lovely crumbly shortness to it. You can have fun with the shapes, using your favourite cutters to theme them for any occasion you like or to give as a gift.

500g (1 pound) butter, softened
¾ cup (165g) caster (superfine) sugar
¼ cup (60g) vanilla bean dusting sugar
1 teaspoon vanilla extract
4½ cups (675g) plain (all-purpose) flour
½ cup (75g) rice flour
2 tablespoons white (granulated) sugar

1 Beat butter, caster sugar, dusting sugar and extract in a large bowl with an electric mixer until pale and fluffy. Stir in sifted flours; press mixture together to form a firm dough. Knead gently on a floured surface until smooth. Divide dough in half. Wrap each in plastic wrap; refrigerate 30 minutes.
2 Preheat oven to 150°C/300°F. Grease oven trays.
3 Roll one dough half between two sheets of baking paper until 1cm (½-inch) thick. Using a 6cm (2½-inch) round fluted cutter, cut out rounds from dough; from each round, cut a hole in the centre with a 1.5cm (¾-inch) fluted cutter. Re-roll scraps and repeat until all the dough has been used.
4 Place rounds on oven trays, sprinkle with white sugar. Repeat with remaining half of dough.
5 Bake shortbread 30 minutes or until a pale straw colour. Stand on trays for 5 minutes; transfer to a wire rack to cool.

TIP To give as a gift, thread ribbon through centre of the shortbread and tie into a ring. Or, you can hang shortbread from your Christmas tree.

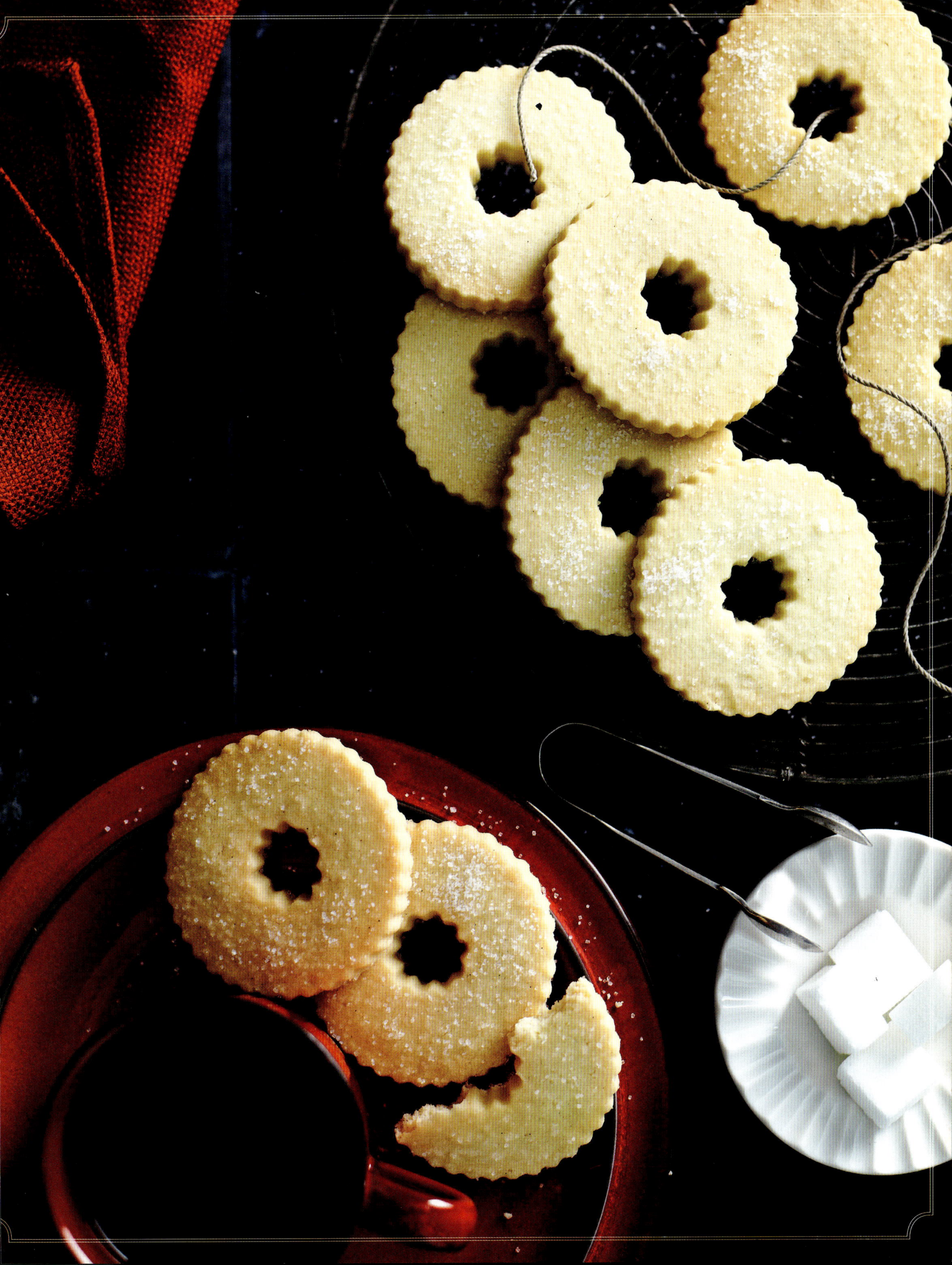

MACADAMIA
Anzac Biscuits

MACADAMIA Anzac Biscuits

PREP + COOK TIME *40 MINUTES* **MAKES** *32*

125g (4 ounces) butter, chopped
2 tablespoons golden syrup or treacle
½ teaspoon bicarbonate of soda (baking soda)
2 tablespoons boiling water
1 cup (90g) rolled oats
1 cup (150g) plain (all-purpose) flour
1 cup (220g) firmly packed brown sugar
¾ cup (60g) desiccated coconut
½ cup (65g) finely chopped macadamia nuts
½ cup (45g) finely chopped glacé ginger

1. Preheat oven to 180°C/350°F. Grease oven trays; line with baking paper.
2. Stir butter and syrup in a medium saucepan over low heat until smooth. Stir in combined soda and the water, then remaining ingredients.
3. Roll level tablespoons of mixture into balls; place 5cm (2 inches) apart on oven trays, then flatten slightly.
4. Bake biscuits 15 minutes or until golden. Cool biscuits on trays.

TIPS Make sure you use rolled oats rather than quick-cooking oats as they will produce a different result.
These biscuits can be stored in an airtight container for up to 1 week.

CARAMEL GINGER Crunchies

PREP + COOK TIME *1 HOUR* **MAKES** *45*

2 cups (300g) plain (all-purpose) flour
½ teaspoon bicarbonate of soda (baking soda)
1 teaspoon ground cinnamon
2 teaspoons ground ginger
1 cup (220g) caster (superfine) sugar
125g (4 ounces) cold butter, chopped
1 egg
1 teaspoon golden syrup or treacle
2 tablespoons finely chopped glacé ginger
45 wrapped hard caramels

1. Preheat oven to 180°C/350°C. Grease oven trays; line with baking paper.
2. Process sifted dry ingredients with butter until mixture is crumbly. Add egg, golden syrup and ginger; process until ingredients come together. Knead dough on a floured surface until smooth.
3. Roll round teaspoons of mixture into balls; place 3cm (1¼ inches) apart on trays.
4. Bake biscuits 13 minutes; place a caramel on top of each hot biscuit. Bake a further 6 minutes or until caramel begins to melt. Cool biscuits on trays.

(PHOTOGRAPH PAGE 306)

CARAMEL
GINGER
CRUNCHIES
(RECIPE PAGE 305)

PEANUT BUTTER COOKIES

(RECIPE PAGE 308)

PEANUT BUTTER *Cookies*

PREP + COOK TIME *45 MINUTES* **MAKES** *18*

We trawled though all our peanut butter cookie recipes from over the years before narrowing our selection down to three, which we taste-tested, side-by-side. This was voted the winner for peanut taste and crisp chewy texture.

60g (2 ounces) butter
½ cup (130g) smooth peanut butter
½ cup (110g) caster (superfine) sugar
½ cup (110g) firmly packed brown sugar
1 egg
1 cup (140g) roasted unsalted peanuts, chopped coarsely
40g (1½-ounce) chocolate-coated honeycomb bar, chopped coarsely
1 cup (150g) self-raising flour

1. Preheat oven to 180°C/350°F. Grease three oven trays; line each with baking paper.
2. Beat butter, peanut butter and sugars in a small bowl with an electric mixer until pale and fluffy. Beat in egg until just combined. Stir in peanuts and honeycomb, then sifted flour.
3. Roll 1½ tablespoons of mixture into balls; place 3cm (1¼ inches) apart on trays. Flatten mixture slightly, pushing any nuts or honeycomb back into mixture if they fall out.
4. Bake biscuits 15 minutes or until lightly browned. Cool on tray.

(PHOTOGRAPH PAGE 307)

CHOCOLATE *Caramel Slice*

PREP + COOK TIME *50 MINUTES (+ REFRIGERATION)*
MAKES *24 PIECES*

½ cup (75g) plain (all-purpose) flour
⅓ cup (35g) cocoa powder
½ cup (110g) caster (superfine) sugar
1 cup (80g) desiccated coconut
125g (4 ounces) unsalted butter, melted
1 teaspoon vanilla extract
1 egg
125g (4 ounces) butter, chopped, extra
2 x 395g (12½ ounces) canned sweetened condensed milk
⅓ cup (115g) golden syrup or treacle

1. Preheat oven to 180°C/350°F. Grease a 18cm x 26cm (7¼-inch x 10½-inch) slice pan; line base with baking paper, extending the paper 5cm (2-inches) over the long sides.
2. Sift flour and cocoa into a medium bowl. Stir in sugar and coconut; make a well in the centre. Stir in melted butter, vanilla and egg until combined. Spoon mixture into pan; using the back of a spoon, press evenly over the base. Cover with a sheet of baking paper, press down firmly until even and smooth. Refrigerate 15 minutes.
3. Meanwhile, stir extra chopped butter, condensed milk and syrup in a medium saucepan over low heat until combined. Pour over chocolate base.
4. Bake slice 25 minutes or until the top is toffee-coloured; cool. Refrigerate.
5. Dust the top with a little extra cocoa, if you like, before cutting into squares.

CHOCOLATE
Caramel Slice

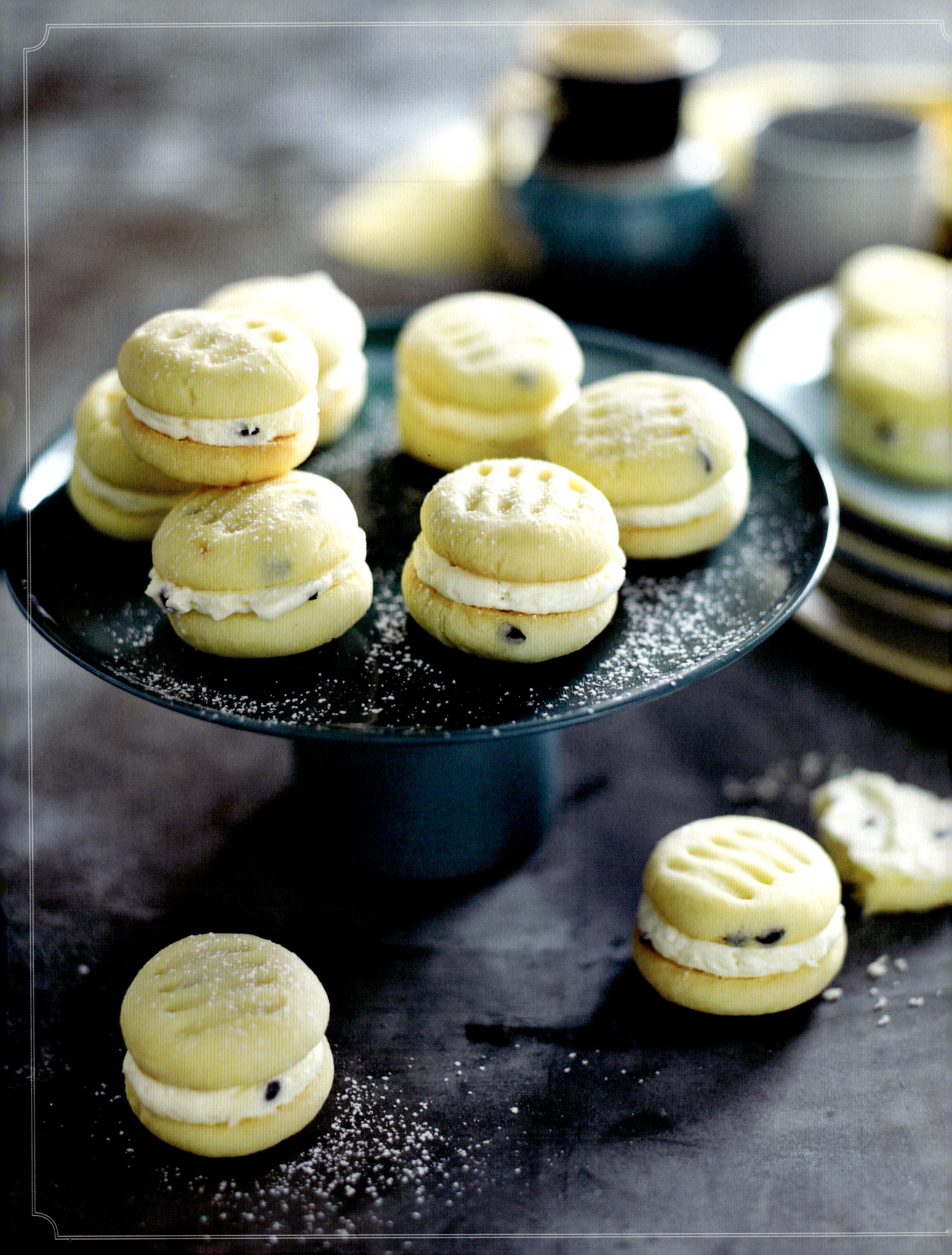

PASSIONFRUIT
Melting Moments

PREP + COOK TIME 1 HOUR   MAKES 25

3 passionfruit
250g (8 ounces) butter, softened
1 teaspoon vanilla extract
½ cup (80g) icing (confectioners') sugar
1⅔ cups (250g) plain (all-purpose) flour
½ cup (75g) cornflour (cornstarch)

PASSIONFRUIT BUTTER CREAM
80g (2½ ounces) butter, softened
⅔ cup (110g) icing (confectioners') sugar

1. Preheat oven to 160°C/325°F. Grease three oven trays; line with baking paper.
2. Spoon pulp from passionfruit into a fine sieve over a small bowl. Press down with the back of the spoon to extract 1 tablespoon juice for the passionfruit butter cream; reserve juice.
3. Beat butter, vanilla and sifted icing sugar with an electric mixer until pale. Stir in combined sifted flours, in two batches; stir in passionfruit pulp.
4. With floured hands, roll 2 level teaspoons of mixture into balls. Place on trays 3cm (1¼ inches) apart. Dip a fork into a little extra flour, press biscuits to flatten lightly.
5. Bake biscuits for 15 minutes or until pale straw in colour. Stand biscuits on trays 5 minutes before transferring to wire racks to cool.
6. Meanwhile, make passionfruit butter cream.
7. Sandwich biscuits with a teaspoon of passionfruit butter cream. Dust with a little extra sifted icing sugar, if you like.

PASSIONFRUIT BUTTER CREAM
Beat butter and sifted icing sugar in a small bowl with an electric mixer until pale and fluffy. Beat in reserved passionfruit juice.

TIP The biscuits can be made a week ahead. Store in an airtight container. Sandwich biscuits with butter cream close to serving.

CHOCOLATE
French Macaroons

PREP + COOK TIME *50 MINUTES (+ STANDING)* **MAKES 16**

3 egg whites
2 tablespoons caster (superfine) sugar
few drops almond extract (optional)
185g (6 ounces) icing (confectioners') sugar
1 tablespoon cocoa powder
1 cup (120g) ground almonds
1 teaspoon cocoa powder, extra

DARK CHOCOLATE GANACHE
150g (4½ ounces) dark (semi-sweet) chocolate, chopped coarsely
⅓ cup (80ml) pouring cream

1. Preheat oven to 150°C/300°F. Grease two oven trays; line with baking paper.
2. Beat egg whites in a small bowl with an electric mixer until soft peaks form. Beat in caster sugar until it dissolves. Transfer mixture to a large bowl. Fold in extract, combined sifted icing sugar, cocoa, and ground almonds, in two batches.
3. Spoon mixture into a large piping bag fitted with a 1.5cm (¾-inch) plain tube. Pipe 4cm (1½-inch) rounds, 2cm (¾ inch) apart, onto trays. Tap trays on bench to spread macaroons slightly. Flatten peaks lightly with a damp finger. Dust with extra cocoa. Stand for 30 minutes.
4. Bake macaroons 20 minutes or until dry to touch. Stand macaroons on trays 5 minutes; transfer to a wire rack to cool.
5. Meanwhile, make dark chocolate ganache.
6. Sandwich macaroons together with ganache.

DARK CHOCOLATE GANACHE
Stir chocolate and cream in a small heatproof bowl over a small saucepan of simmering water (don't let water touch base of bowl) until chocolate is melted. Cover; refrigerate until mixture is of a spreadable consistency.

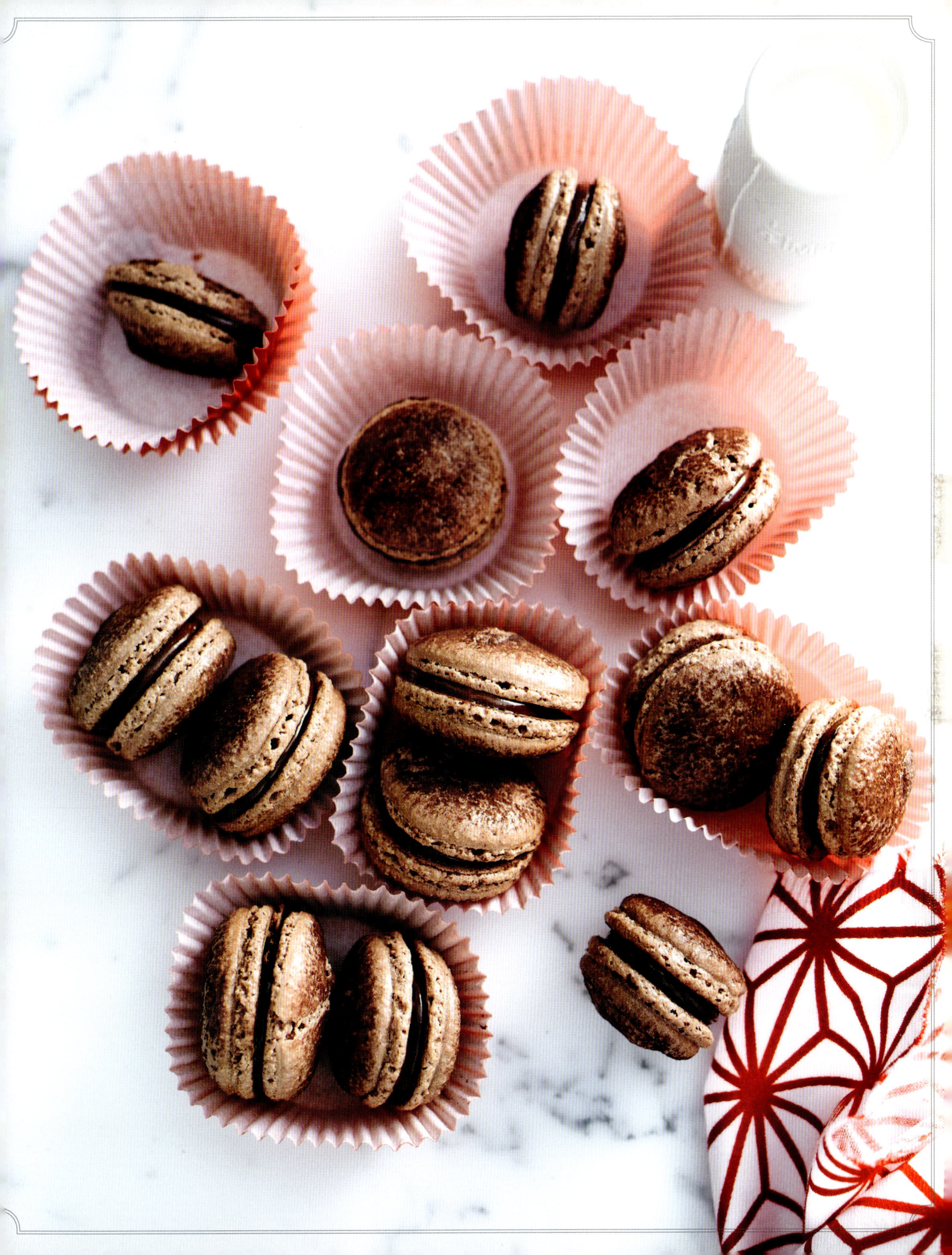

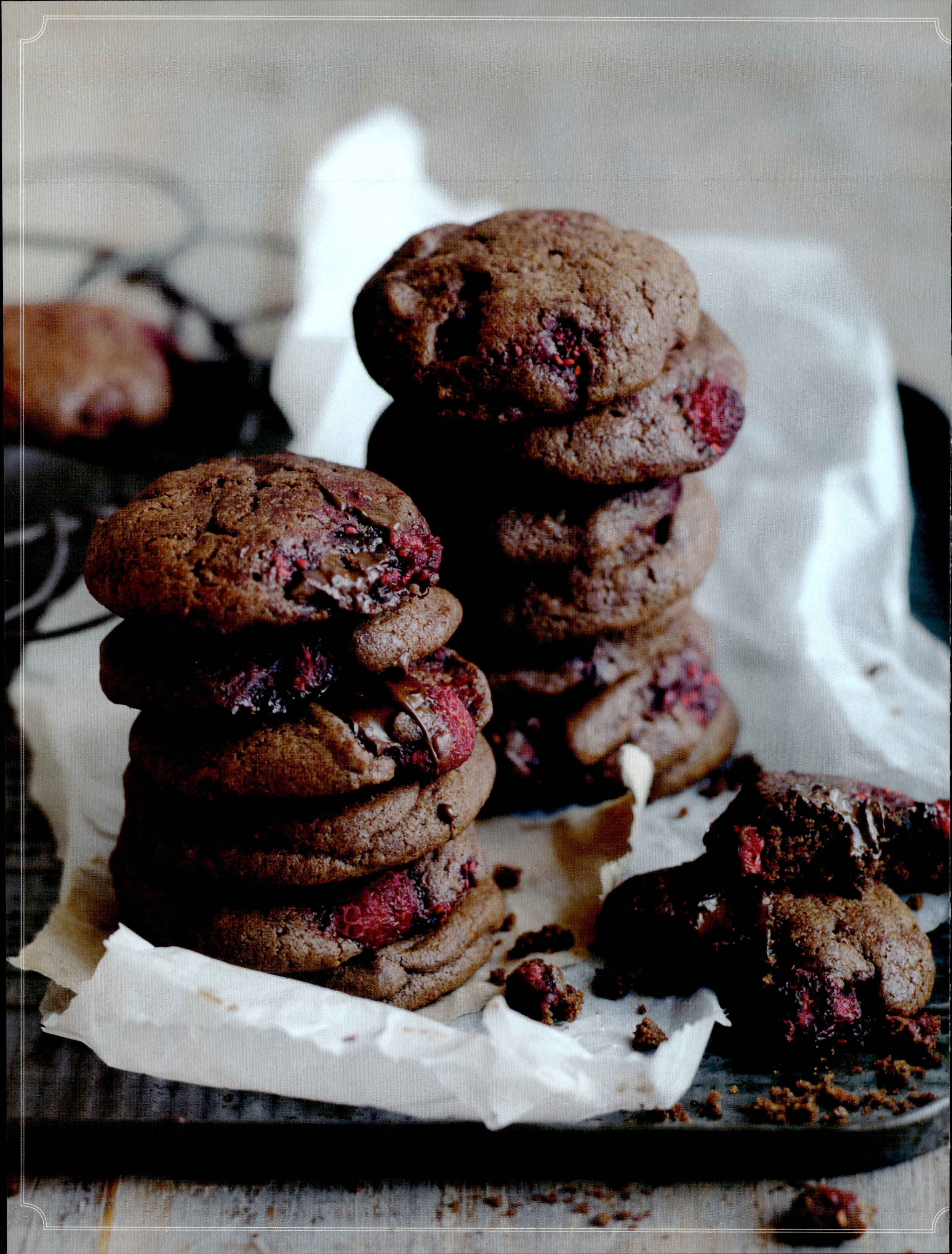

CHOCOLATE CHUNK
and Raspberry Cookies

PREP + COOK TIME 35 MINUTES MAKES 28

125g (4 ounces) butter, softened
¾ cup (165g) firmly packed brown sugar
1 egg
1 teaspoon vanilla extract
1 cup (150g) plain (all-purpose) flour
¼ cup (35g) self-raising flour
⅓ cup (35g) cocoa powder
½ teaspoon bicarbonate of soda (baking soda)
90g (3 ounces) dark (semi-sweet) chocolate, chopped coarsely
125g (4 ounces) frozen raspberries

1 Preheat oven to 180°C/350°F. Grease oven trays; line with baking paper.
2 Beat butter, sugar, egg and extract in a small bowl with an electric mixer until combined. Stir in sifted flours, cocoa and soda, in two batches, then stir in chocolate and raspberries.
3 Using damp hands, drop level tablespoons of mixture 5cm (2 inches) apart onto trays; flatten into 4cm (1½-inch) rounds.
4 Bake cookies for 15 minutes or until a biscuit can be pushed gently without breaking. Stand cookies on trays for 5 minutes before transferring to a wire rack to cool.

TIP Cookies will keep refrigerated in an airtight container for up to 1 week.

LEMON BUTTER
Almond Slice

PREP + COOK TIME 1 HOUR 10 MINUTES (+ REFRIGERATION & COOLING) MAKES 16 PIECES

250g (8 ounces) butter, softened, chopped
2 teaspoons vanilla extract
1¼ cups (275g) caster (superfine) sugar
⅔ cup (80g) ground almonds
2 cups (300g) plain (all-purpose) flour
½ cup (40g) flaked almonds

LEMON BUTTER

1 teaspoon finely grated lemon rind
⅔ cup (160ml) strained lemon juice
1⅓ cups (300g) caster (superfine) sugar
250g (8 ounces) unsalted butter, chopped
4 eggs, beaten lightly, strained

1. Make lemon butter.
2. Preheat oven to 200°C/400°F. Grease a 26cm x 32cm (10½-inch x 12¾-inch) swiss roll pan; line base and two long sides with baking paper, extending the paper 5cm (2 inches) over sides.
3. Beat butter, vanilla and sugar in a small bowl with an electric mixer until light and fluffy; transfer to a large bowl. Add ground almonds and sifted flour; mix well using hands.
4. Press two-thirds of the pastry evenly over base of pan. Wrap remaining pastry in plastic wrap; refrigerate.
5. Bake base 12 minutes or until browned lightly. Cool 10 minutes.
6. Spread lemon butter over base. Crumble reserved pastry over lemon butter; top with flaked almonds.
7. Bake slice 25 minutes or until browned. Cool in pan. Refrigerate until cold. Remove from pan; cut into 16 pieces. If you like, dust with a little sifted icing (confectioners') sugar before serving.

LEMON BUTTER

Stir ingredients in a medium heavy-based saucepan over very low heat for 10 minutes or until thickened (do not allow to boil or the mixture will curdle). Pour mixture into a medium heatproof bowl; cover surface with plastic wrap. Refrigerate several hours or until thick and cold.

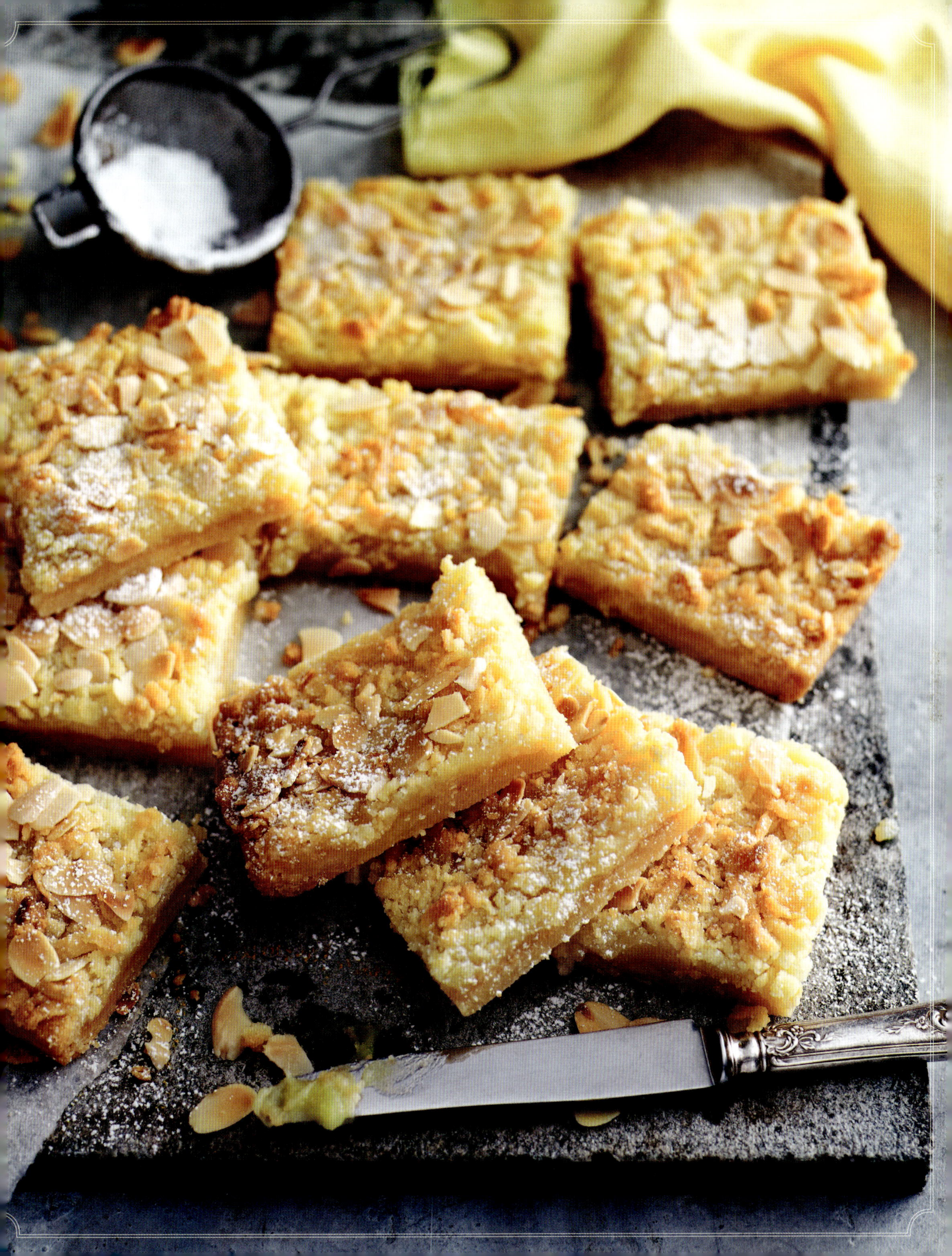

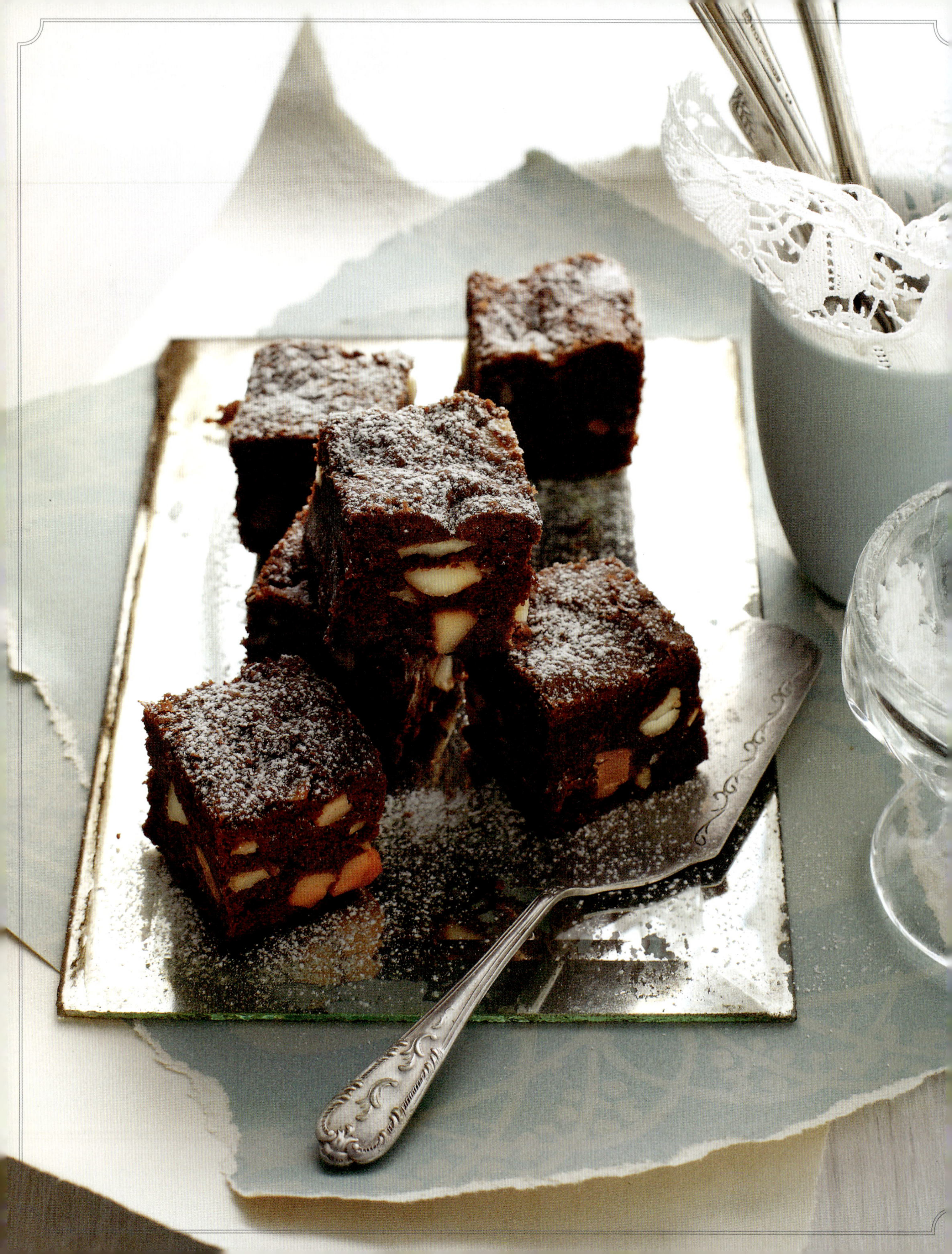

OVER-THE-TOP CHOCOLATE
and Macadamia Brownies

PREP + COOK TIME 1 HOUR MAKES 25 PIECES

275g (9 ounces) dark (semi-sweet) chocolate, chopped finely
150g (4½ ounces) butter, chopped
⅔ cup (150g) caster (superfine) sugar
2 eggs, beaten lightly
1 cup (150g) plain (all-purpose) flour
½ cup (75g) self-raising flour
⅔ cup (90g) unsalted macadamias, lightly roasted, chopped coarsely
100g (3 ounces) milk chocolate, chopped coarsely
100g (3 ounces) dark (semi-sweet) chocolate, extra, chopped coarsely
2 teaspoons icing (confectioners') sugar

1. Preheat oven to 170°C/325°F. Grease a 20cm (8-inch) square shallow cake pan; line base with baking paper.
2. Stir chocolate and butter in a medium saucepan over low heat until smooth. Remove from heat.
3. Stir in sugar, then egg. Fold in combined sifted flours, followed by macadamias, milk chocolate and extra dark chocolate. Spread mixture into pan.
4. Bake 35 minutes or until a skewer inserted into the centre comes out with moist crumbs. Cool in pan.
5. Dust with sifted icing sugar; cut into small pieces.

TIP These brownies will only be as good as the chocolate used. The more cocoa solids in the chocolate you use, the more intense the chocolate taste will be. Aim for a dark chocolate containing anywhere between 50–70% cocoa solids. Chocolate with a lower cocoa solid percentage means that more sugar and fat has been added.

SLICE-AND-BAKE
Butter Biscuits

PREP + COOK TIME 1 HOUR 30 MINUTES (+ REFRIGERATION)   MAKES 48

250g (8 ounces) butter
1¼ cups (200g) icing (confectioners') sugar
2 teaspoons vanilla extract
2 cups (300g) plain (all-purpose) flour
½ cup (75g) rice flour
⅓ cup (50g) cornflour (cornstarch)
2 tablespoons milk

1. Beat butter, icing sugar and vanilla in a large bowl with an electric mixer until pale and fluffy. Stir in combined sifted flours, in two batches, then milk until mixed well.
2. Divide mixture in half. Knead each half on a floured surface until smooth; roll halves into 25cm (10-inch) logs. Wrap each log in baking paper; refrigerate 1 hour or until firm. (If you are not intending to bake biscuits within 2 days, wrap them in foil and keep in the freezer.)
3. Preheat oven to 160°C/325°F. Grease oven trays.
4. Cut logs into 1cm (½-inch) slices; place rounds 3cm (1¼-inches) apart on oven trays.
5. Bake biscuits for 20 minutes or until pale golden. Stand on trays 20 minutes, before transferring to wire racks to cool.

TIP These biscuits will keep in an airtight container for up to 1 week.

VARATIONS

ORANGE AND POPPY SEED Omit vanilla extract and beat 1 tablespoon finely grated orange rind with the butter and icing sugar; add 1½ tablespoons poppy seeds with combined sifted flours.

PECAN AND CINNAMON Add 1 teaspoon ground cinnamon to sifted flours and stir in 1 cup (100g) roasted chopped pecans. Sprinkle biscuits with 2 tablespoons cinnamon sugar before baking.

M&M'S Stir in 230g (7 ounces) M&M's mini baking bits with combined sifted flours.

LEMON AND PISTACHIO Omit vanilla and beat 1 tablespoon finely grated lemon rind with butter and icing sugar, then stir in ¾ cup (110g) roasted chopped pistachios with combined sifted flours.

Biscuits & Slices

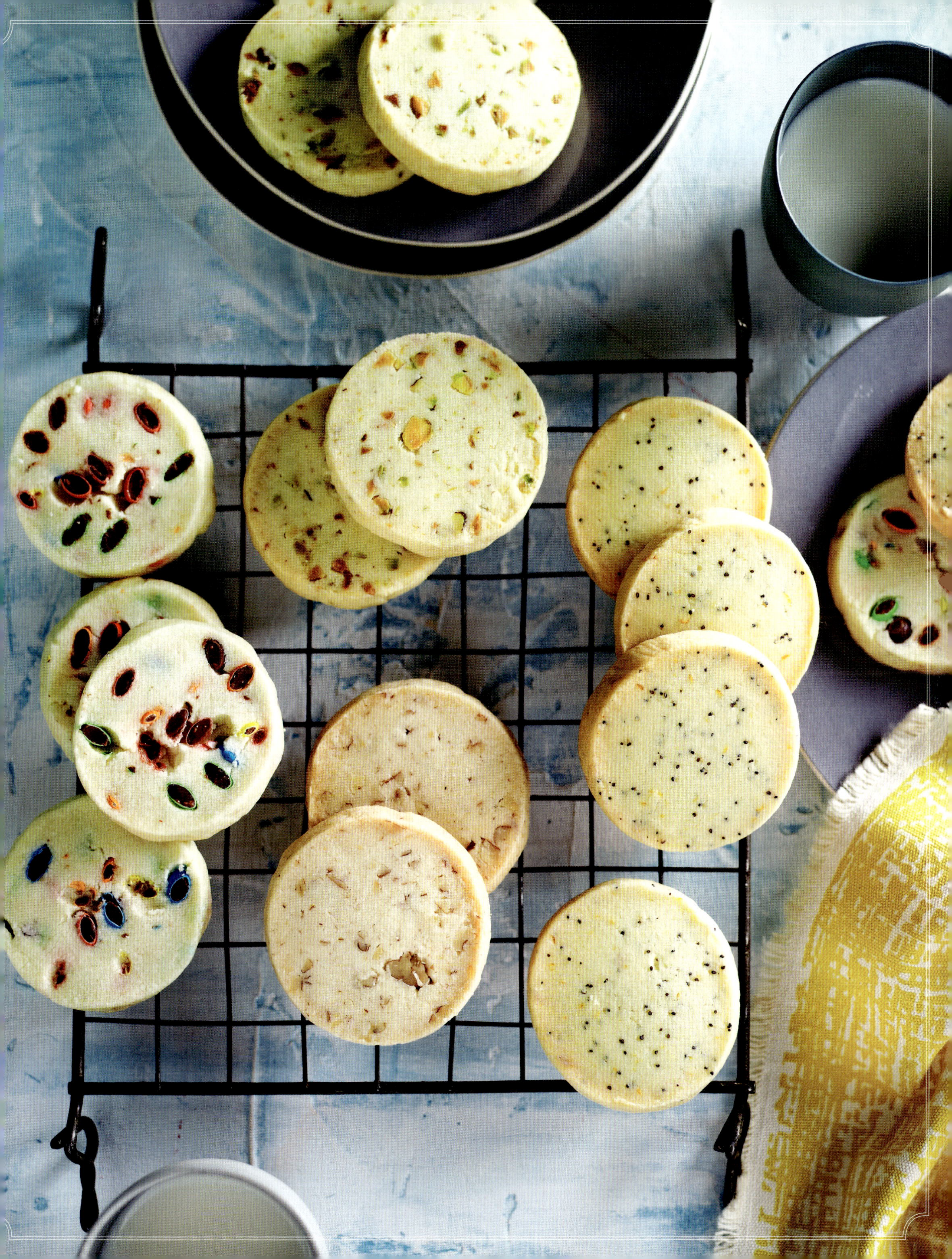

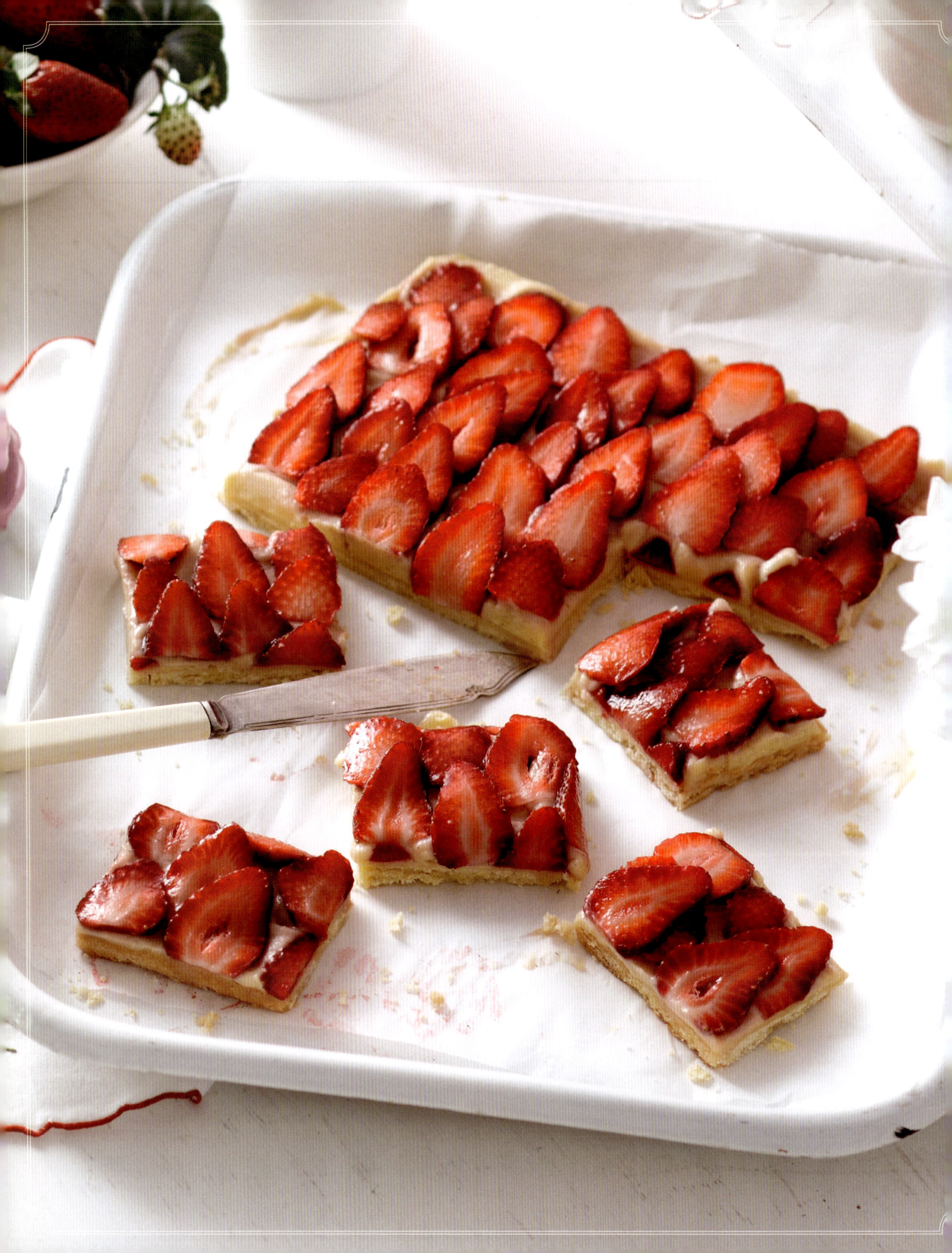

STRAWBERRY CUSTARD
Slice

PREP + COOK TIME *40 MINUTES (+ REFRIGERATION)* **MAKES** *15 PIECES*

In Australia we're lucky to have two seasons for strawberries. In summer they come from Victoria and in winter from Queensland. Outside of these two seasons the flavour may not be as good and the strawberries often have white tops and lack sweetness.

⅔ cup (160ml) milk
½ cup (125ml) pouring cream
1 vanilla bean
4 egg yolks
¼ cup (55g) caster (superfine) sugar
2 tablespoons cornflour (cornstarch)
1¼ cups (185g) plain (all-purpose) flour
¼ cup (40g) icing (confectioners') sugar
125g (4 ounces) unsalted butter, chopped coarsely
2 teaspoons iced water, approximately
250g (8 ounces) strawberries, sliced thinly
2 tablespoons raspberry jam, warmed, strained

1. Grease 20cm x 30cm (8-inch x 12-inch) slice pan; line base and long sides with baking paper, extending the paper 5cm (2 inches) over sides.
2. Combine milk and cream in a medium saucepan. Split vanilla bean; scrape seeds into pan with bean. Bring cream mixture almost to the boil. Whisk 3 of the egg yolks, caster sugar and cornflour in a small bowl until combined. Discard vanilla bean from cream mixture; gradually whisk hot cream mixture into egg mixture. Return to pan; cook, whisking, until custard boils and thickens. Cool.
3. Meanwhile, process flour, icing sugar and butter until crumbly. Add remaining egg yolk and enough of the water until ingredients cling together. Knead dough on a floured surface until smooth. Press dough over base of pan; prick all over with a fork. Cover with plastic wrap; refrigerate 30 minutes.
4. Preheat oven to 200°C/400°F.
5. Bake base 15 minutes or until browned lightly; cool.
6. Spread custard over base; top with strawberries. Brush strawberries with jam; refrigerate 1 hour before cutting.

RICH CHOCOLATE
Almond Slice

PREP + COOK TIME *1 HOUR 10 MINUTES* (+ REFRIGERATION) **MAKES** *24 PIECES*

150g (4½ ounces) dark (semi-sweet) chocolate, chopped coarsely
3 egg whites
¾ cup (165g) caster (superfine) sugar
1 cup (110g) ground almonds
2 tablespoons plain (all-purpose) flour

TOPPING
200g (6½ ounces) dark (semi-sweet) chocolate, chopped coarsely
125g (4 ounces) butter, chopped
⅓ cup (75g) caster (superfine) sugar
3 egg yolks
1 tablespoon brandy (optional)

1. Preheat oven to 180°C/350°F. Grease a 20cm x 30cm (8-inch x 12-inch) slice pan; line base and two long sides with baking paper, extending the paper 5cm (2 inches) over the edges.
2. Stir chocolate in a small heatproof bowl over a small saucepan of simmering water (don't let water touch base of bowl) until melted. Spread chocolate over base of pan. Refrigerate 10 minutes or until set.
3. Beat egg whites in a small bowl with an electric mixer until soft peaks form; gradually add sugar, beating until dissolved between additions. Fold in ground almonds and flour. Spread mixture over chocolate base.
4. Bake 20 minutes or until firm; cool 20 minutes.
5. Make topping; spread over slice.
6. Bake 15 minutes or until set; cool. Refrigerate until firm. Before serving, dust with cocoa; cut into squares.

TOPPING
Stir chocolate in a small heatproof bowl over a small saucepan of simmering water (don't let the water touch the base of the bowl) until melted. Beat butter, sugar, egg yolks and brandy in a small bowl with an electric mixer until sugar dissolves. Add chocolate, stir until smooth.

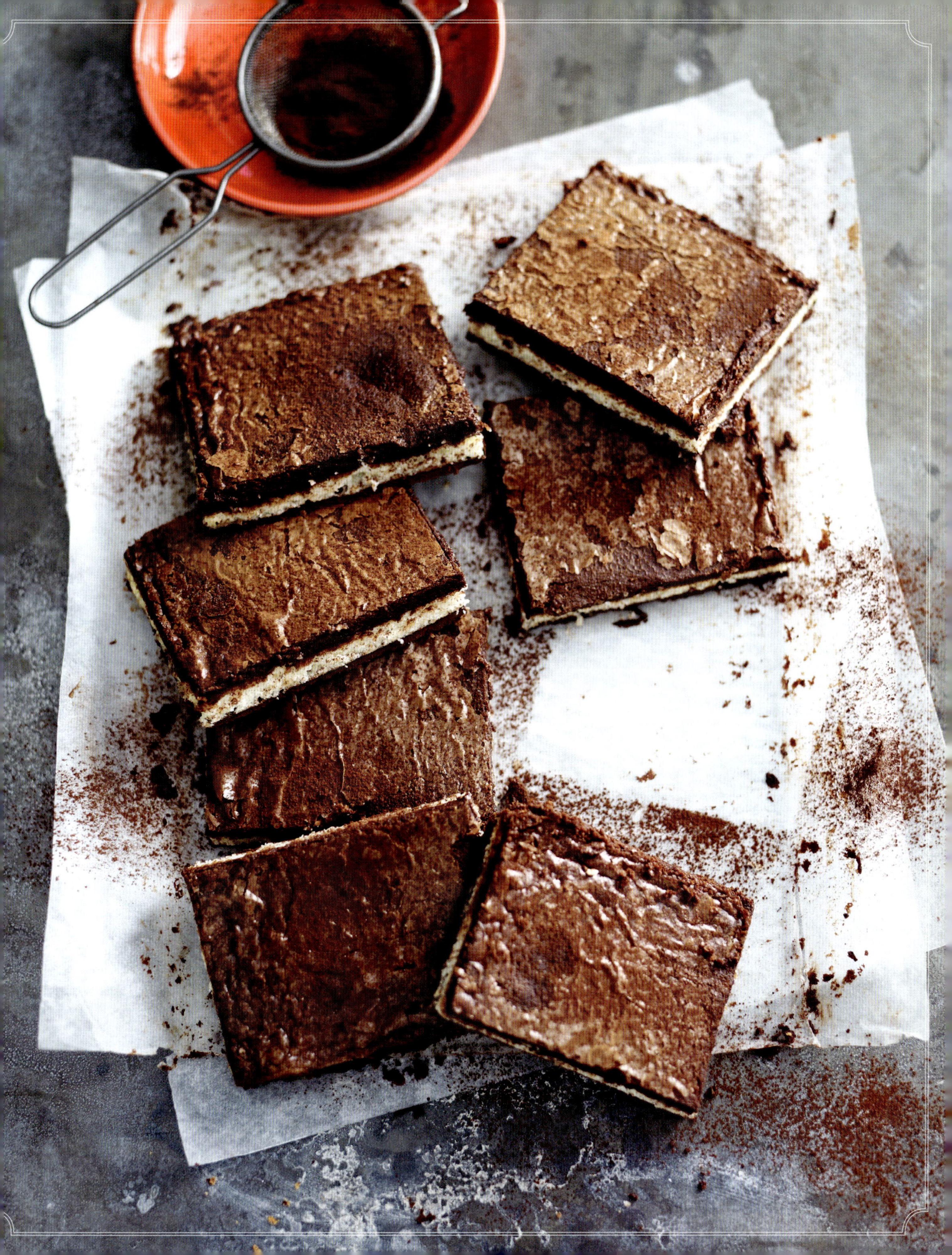

CHAPTER 10
BREADS & SCONES

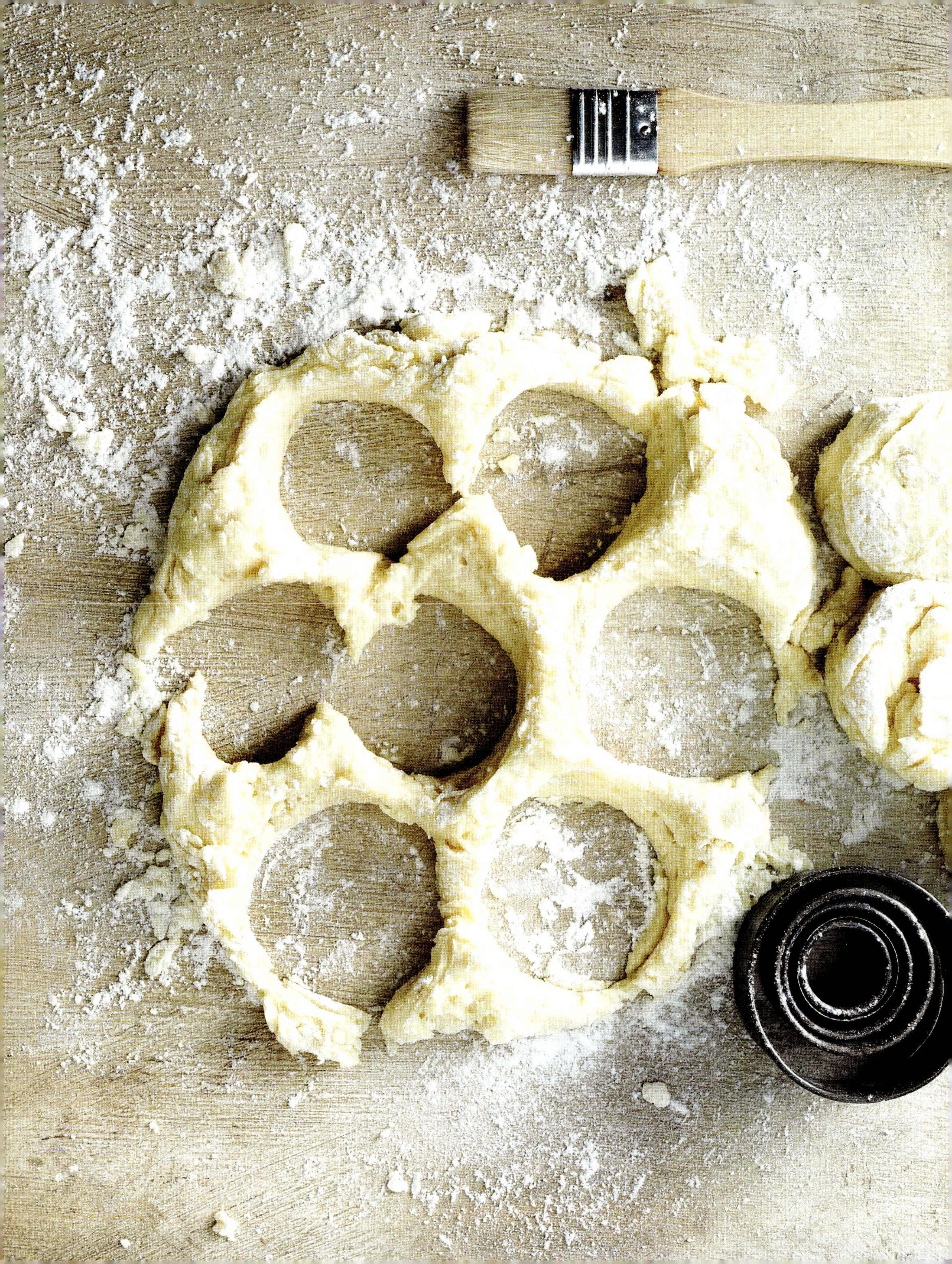

SOURDOUGH RYE BREAD

PREP + COOK TIME *1 HOUR 15 MINUTES (+ STANDING)* **MAKES** *2 LOAVES*

This recipe first appeared in the September 1975 issue of The Australian Women's Weekly, in a decade when sourdough bread was not commonplace, showing The Weekly was well and truly ahead of its time. You will need to start the recipe 3 days ahead; however the end result is well worth the effort. And once you've got your sourdough starter it will keep in good condition for 2 weeks.

4 teaspoons (14g) dried yeast
1 tablespoon brown sugar
4¾ cups (675g) plain (all-purpose) flour
3 cups (750ml) lukewarm water
1 tablespoon caraway seeds
4 cups (375g) rye flour
3 teaspoons fine salt
2 tablespoons olive oil
2 tablespoons plain (all-purpose) flour, extra

SOURDOUGH STARTER
2 teaspoon (7g) dried yeast
1 teaspoon caster (superfine) sugar
1¼ cups (310ml) lukewarm water
1½ cups (225g) plain (all-purpose) flour

1. Make sourdough starter 3 days ahead.
2. To make the bread on the third day, stir yeast with 1 teaspoon of the sugar and 1 teaspoon of the plain flour in a small bowl. Add ½ cup of the water, stand in a warm place for 15 minutes or until mixture starts to bubble.
3. Sift remaining flours and sugar with salt into a large bowl; return hulls in sifter to flour. Stir in caraway seeds. Make a well in the centre of the dry ingredients. Combine yeast mixture, remaining lukewarm water, oil and ¼ cup of the sourdough starter. Add to dry ingredients; mix to form a dough. You may need an extra ¼-½ cup lukewarm water, if the mixture is too dry; this is because flour varies in its moisture content.
4. Turn the dough onto a floured surface; knead for 8 minutes or until smooth and elastic. Place in a large oiled bowl. Cover; stand in a warm place for 30 minutes or until doubled in size. Punch dough down with your fist. Turn onto a floured surface.
5. Divide dough in half. Shape each portion on a well-floured surface into a 7cm x 30cm (2¾-inch x 12-inch) oval-shaped loaf. Gently lift each onto a lightly oiled oven tray. (You may need to place them diagonally on the trays to fit.) Cover trays with clean tea towels; stand in a warm place 15 minutes or until dough has risen.
6. Meanwhile, preheat oven to 250°C/480°F.
7. Dust a little extra flour over the top of each loaf. Using a small, sharp knife, cut seven shallow slashes, about 3.5cm (1½-inches) apart, across the top.
8. Bake bread 30 minutes or until hollow sounding when tapped on the base. Transfer to wire racks to cool.

SOURDOUGH STARTER
Combine yeast, sugar and the water in a large bowl. Cover; stand 10 minutes or until bubbling. Add sifted flour; stir to combine. Cover; stand, unrefrigerated, for 2 days before using. After 2 days the starter should have a pleasant mild sour smell and have small bubbles on the surface – a sign that it's active.

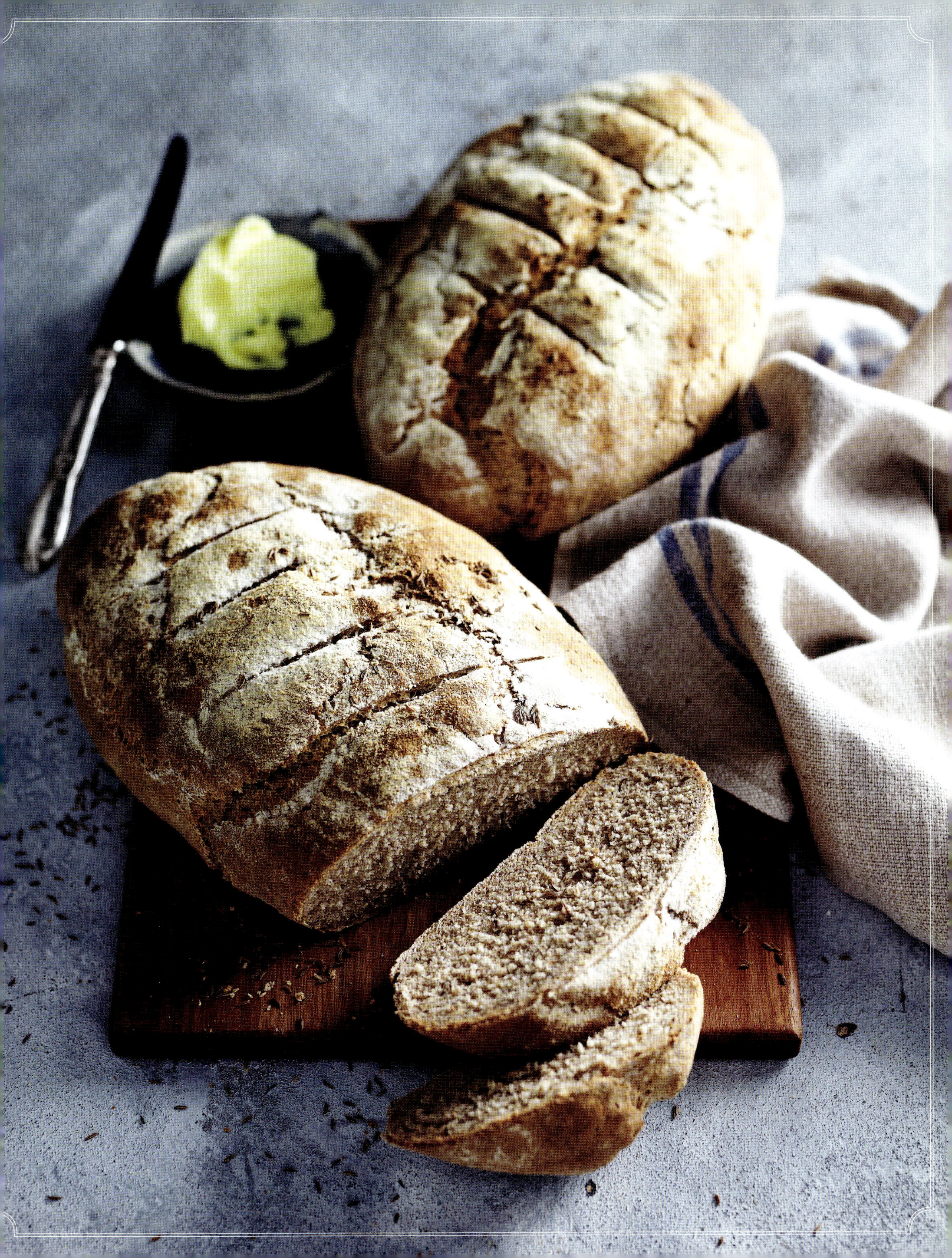

OLIVE AND ROSEMARY
Quick Bread

QUINOA AND SEED
Cheese Damper

OLIVE AND ROSEMARY
Quick Bread

PREP + COOK TIME *40 MINUTES* **MAKES** *12 PIECES*

3 cups (450g) self-raising flour
½ teaspoon salt
75g (2½ ounces) butter, chopped
1 tablespoon finely chopped fresh rosemary
¾ cup (115g) kalamata olives, pitted, halved
¾ cup (180ml) buttermilk
½ cup (125ml) water, approximately
1 tablespoon buttermilk, extra
1 tablespoon fresh rosemary sprigs, extra
6 kalamata olives, pitted, halved, extra

1. Preheat oven to 220°C/400°F. Grease a 23cm (9-inch) square cake pan.
2. Sift flour and salt into a large bowl. Using your fingertips, rub in butter until mixture resembles coarse breadcrumbs; add rosemary and olives. Stir in buttermilk and enough of the water to make a soft, sticky dough.
3. Knead dough on a floured surface until smooth; using your hands, press into a 22cm (8¾-inch) square shape. Using a sharp knife, cut dough into 12 equal pieces; place pieces slightly apart in pan. Brush tops with the extra buttermilk; top with the extra rosemary sprigs and olives.
4. Bake bread 30 minutes or until golden. Stand in pan 5 minutes before turning out on a wire rack.

QUINOA AND SEED
Cheese Damper

PREP + COOK TIME *1 HOUR 5 MINUTES (+ STANDING)*
MAKES *12 SLICES*

¼ cup (50g) red quinoa
½ cup (125ml) boiling water
3 cups (450g) self-raising flour
2 teaspoons sea salt
40g (1½ ounces) butter, chopped
¼ cup (50g) roasted buckwheat
2 tablespoons linseeds
2 tablespoons pepitas (pumpkin seeds)
¾ cup (90g) grated vintage cheddar
½ cup (125ml) milk
¾ cup (180ml) water, approximately

1. Place quinoa in a small heatproof bowl; cover with the boiling water. Stand 20 minutes. Drain well.
2. Preheat oven to 180°C/350°F. Flour a large oven tray.
3. Place flour and salt in a large bowl; rub in butter. Stir in quinoa, buckwheat, linseeds, pepitas and cheddar. Stir in milk and enough of the water to mix to a soft dough. Knead dough on a floured surface until smooth.
4. Place dough on the tray; press into a 16cm (6½-inch) round. Brush with a little extra water or milk; sprinkle with a little extra flour. Cut a 1cm (½-inch) deep cross in top of dough.
5. Bake damper 50 minutes or until golden brown and sounds hollow when tapped on the base.

TIP Damper is best made on the day of serving, or reheat, wrapped in foil, in the oven for 15 minutes or until warmed through.

SERVING SUGGESTION Serve with soup or butter and golden syrup.

FLATBREADS WITH ROASTED PEPPERS
and Zucchini

PREP + COOK TIME 40 MINUTES (+ STANDING) MAKES 4

2 teaspoons (7g) dry yeast
1 teaspoon caster (superfine) sugar
1 cup (250ml) lukewarm water
2½ cups (375g) 00 flour, bread flour or plain (all-purpose) flour
2 teaspoons salt
¼ cup (60ml) extra virgin olive oil
2 medium brown onions (300g), sliced thinly
285g (9 ounces) bottled piquillo wood-roasted small whole peppers
2 cloves garlic, sliced thinly
1 medium green zucchini (120g), peeled thinly lengthways into ribbons
1 tablespoon fresh oregano leaves

1. Combine yeast, sugar and the water in a medium bowl of an electric mixer. Stand in a warm place 10 minutes or until bubbly.
2. Add flour, salt and 1 tablespoon of the oil to the bowl; mix with a dough hook on knead setting 8 minutes or until smooth and elastic. Cover dough; stand in a warm place 30 minutes or until doubled in size.
3. Meanwhile, heat 1 tablespoon of the oil in a large frying pan over medium heat; cook onion, stirring, 5 minutes, or until soft.
4. Preheat oven to 240°C/475°F. Oil two large oven trays.
5. Punch down dough with your fist. Knead dough on a floured surface until smooth. Divide dough into four equal portions. Roll dough on floured surface into 30cm (12-inch) ovals; place on trays.
6. Drain peppers; pat dry, cut into quarters. Divide onion between bases; top with peppers, garlic and zucchini. Brush zucchini with remaining oil; season.
7. Bake flatbread 10 minutes or until bases are golden and crisp. Sprinkle with oregano; serve immediately.

TIPS An electric mixer with a dough hook or hooks takes the hard work out of preparing the dough. If you don't have a mixer with a dough hook, knead the dough by hand on a floured surface for 10 minutes by pulling and stretching the dough at every quarter turn.
Flatbreads are best served freshly baked.

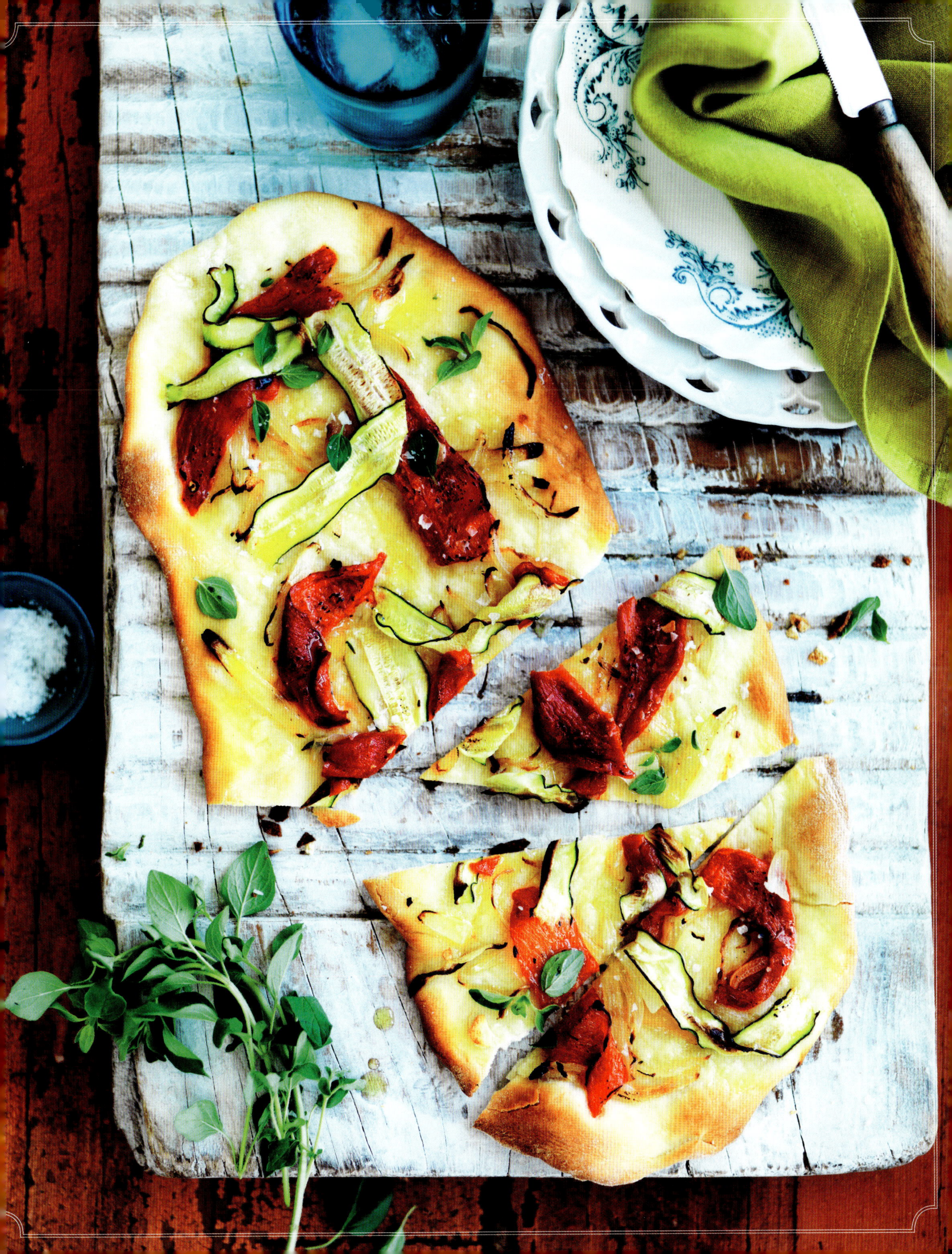

AMERICAN CHEESE
Scones

PREP + COOK TIME 30 MINUTES MAKES 20

1⅔ cups (250g) self-raising flour
½ teaspoon salt
20g (¾ ounce) butter
1 egg
½ cup (125ml) milk
½ cup (60g) extra sharp cheddar, grated finely
30g (1 ounce) butter, melted, extra
½ teaspoon mustard powder
pinch of cayenne pepper

1. Preheat oven to 220°C/425°F. Grease an oven tray.
2. Sift flour and salt in a medium bowl; rub in butter with your fingertips. Whisk egg and milk together; pour over dry ingredients. Use a flat-bladed knife to cut the milk mixture through the flour mixture to make a soft dough.
3. Turn dough onto a floured surface; knead lightly, folding over once. Roll out gently until 3cm (1¼ inches) thick; cut into 4cm (1½-inch) rounds. Place rounds on tray so they are just touching. Re-roll scraps; cut into rounds.
4. Stir cheddar, melted butter, mustard and cayenne over low heat until cheddar starts to melt. Spoon cheese mixture over scones.
5. Bake scones 15 minutes or until tops are golden and sound hollow when tapped. Place, top-side up, onto a wire rack.

TIP It is best to grate the cheese yourself as pre-grated cheese behaves differently on heating.

HOT MARMALADE
Scones

PREP + COOK TIME 40 MINUTES MAKES 16

3 cups (450g) self-raising flour
pinch salt
40g (1½ ounces) butter
¼ cup (55g) caster (superfine) sugar
1 teaspoon grated orange rind
1 teaspoon grated lemon rind
2 eggs
1 cup (250ml) buttermilk
½ cup (170g) orange marmalade
1 tablespoon honey
1 teaspoon grated orange rind, extra

1. Preheat oven to 220°C/425°F. Grease a 22cm (9-inch) square cake pan.
2. Sift flour and salt into a medium bowl; rub in butter with your fingertips. Add sugar and grated rinds. Whisk egg and buttermilk together until just combined; pour over dry ingredients. Use a flat-bladed knife to cut the milk mixture through the flour mixture to make a soft dough.
3. Turn dough onto a floured surface; divide into two portions. Using your hands, flatten each portion into a 22cm (9-inch) square. Thinly spread marmalade on one square, place second square on top. Using a floured knife, cut into 16 squares. Place squares, just touching, in pan.
4. Bake scones 20 minutes or until tops are golden and sound hollow when tapped. Place, top-side up, onto a wire rack.
5. Heat honey in a small saucepan over low heat until runny; stir in extra rind. Brush glaze over scones.

AMERICAN CHEESE
Scones

HOT MARMALADE
Scones

CHOC-CHIP
Hot Cross Buns

PREP + COOK TIME 1 HOUR (+ STANDING) **MAKES** 20

4 teaspoons (14g) dry yeast
⅓ cup (75g) caster (superfine) sugar
1 cup (250ml) warm milk
4 cups (600g) plain (all-purpose) flour
1 teaspoon mixed spice
1 teaspoon ground cinnamon
½ teaspoon salt
80g (2½ ounces) butter, chopped
1½ cups (185g) dark choc bits
1 egg, beaten lightly
⅓ cup (80ml) warm water, approximately

FLOUR PASTE
¼ cup (35g) plain (all-purpose) flour
1 tablespoon sifted cocoa powder
2 teaspoons caster (superfine) sugar
¼ cup (60ml) cold water, approximately

GLAZE
1 tablespoon caster (superfine) sugar
1 teaspoon powdered gelatine
1 tablespoon water

1. Whisk yeast with 1 tablespoon of the sugar and milk in a small bowl until yeast dissolves. Cover; stand in a warm place 10 minutes or until yeast mixture is frothy.
2. Sift flour, spices and salt into a large bowl; rub in butter with your fingertips. Stir in remaining sugar, chocolate chips, yeast mixture, egg and enough of the water to make a soft dough. Cover bowl with oiled plastic wrap; stand in a warm place 1 hour or until mixture has doubled in size.
3. Turn dough onto a floured surface; knead 10 minutes or until smooth and elastic. Divide into 20 portions. One at a time, place hand over a portion of dough and, using a circular motion, roll into a ball. Place balls, almost touching, on a large greased oven tray. Stand in a warm place 20 minutes or until almost doubled in size.

4 Preheat oven to 220°C/400°F.
5 Make flour paste by sifting flour, cocoa and sugar into a small bowl; gradually stir in enough of the water to make a smooth, thick paste. Place paste into a piping bag fitted with a small plain tube; pipe crosses onto buns.
6 Bake buns 20 minutes or until they sound hollow when tapped.
7 Meanwhile, make glaze.
8 Transfer buns to a wire rack; brush hot buns with hot glaze.

GLAZE
Stir ingredients in a small saucepan over low heat, without boiling, until dissolved.

TIPS To help with proving on a cold day, preheat your oven to 100°C/200°F. Open the oven door and place a chopping board on the door. Place the bowl of yeast mixture in step 1 on the chopping board – this will serve as a 'warm place' to activate the yeast. You can also do this to prove the bowl of kneaded dough in step 2.
To make a quick piping bag, snip the corner off a resealable plastic bag.

BANANA Caramel Scrolls

PREP + COOK TIME 1 HOUR (+ STANDING)   MAKES 10

¼ cup (60ml) freshly brewed espresso coffee
⅓ cup (55g) sultanas
60g (2 ounces) butter, softened, extra
¾ cup (165g) firmly packed brown sugar
1 teaspoon ground cinnamon
2½ cups (375g) self-raising flour
1 teaspoon baking powder
1 tablespoon caster (superfine) sugar
1 cup (100g) roasted walnuts, chopped coarsely
60g (2 ounces) cold butter, chopped finely
1 small overripe banana (140g)
1 egg
⅔ cup (160ml) buttermilk
140g (4½ ounces) canned caramel top 'n' fill

1. Combine hot coffee and sultanas in a heatproof bowl; stand 1 hour. Drain well; discard coffee. Pat sultanas dry on paper towel.
2. Preheat oven to 190°C/375°F. Line a large oven tray with baking paper.
3. Using your fingertips, rub softened butter, brown sugar and cinnamon together in a small bowl.
4. Process flour, baking powder, caster sugar and three-quarters of the walnuts until nuts are finely ground. Add cold butter; process until mixture resembles breadcrumbs. Add to a large bowl.
5. Mash banana in a small bowl; you will need ⅓ cup. Whisk egg and buttermilk into mashed banana. Pour banana mixture over dry ingredients. Using a flat-bladed knife, cut banana mixture through flour mixture to make a soft dough.
6. Roll dough on a piece of well-floured baking paper into a 25cm x 32cm (10-inch x 12¾-inch) rectangle. Scatter sugar mixture and sultanas over dough. Using paper as a guide, roll up dough from one long edge. Flouring a sharp serrated knife, between each cut, cut roll into 10 pieces. Using your hands, reshape slices slightly so they are round, rather than oval. Place slices, cut-side up, 4cm (1½ inches) apart on tray.
7. Bake scrolls 25 minutes or until golden and risen. Immediately brush top and side of each scroll with caramel; scatter with remaining chopped walnuts. Cool 10 minutes before serving.

TIPS If the roll feels too soft to slice, place it in the freezer for 10 minutes to firm up.
These scrolls are best eaten on the day of making.

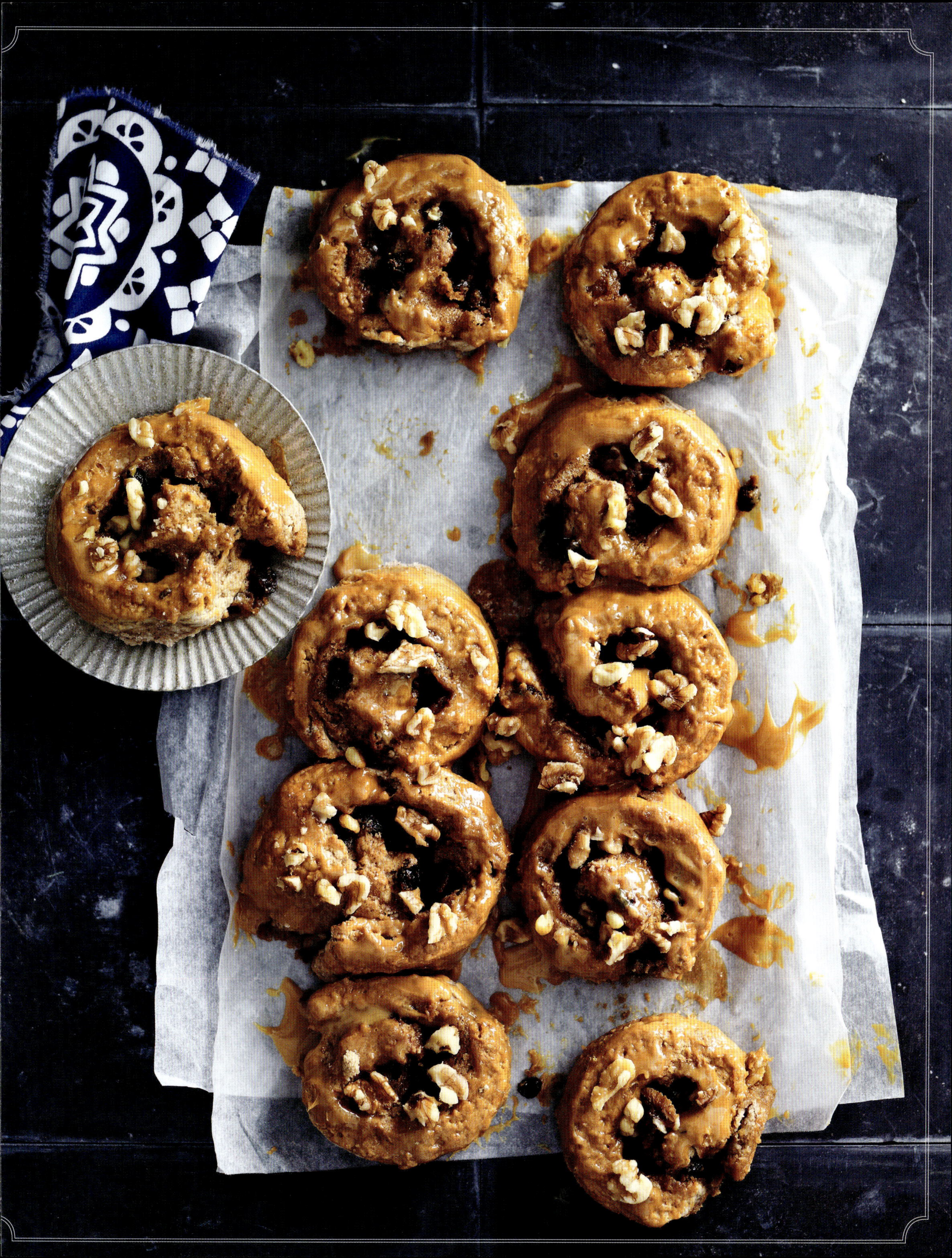

GLOSSARY

ALMONDS
blanched brown skins removed.
flaked paper-thin slices.
ground also known as almond meal.
slivered small pieces cut lengthways.

BACON SLICES also known as rashers.

BAKING PAPER also called parchment paper or baking parchment; a silicone-coated paper primarily used for lining baking pans and oven trays so cakes and biscuits won't stick, making removal easy.

BAKING POWDER a raising agent consisting mainly of two parts cream of tartar to one part bicarbonate of soda (baking soda).

BASIL
sweet the most common type of basil; used extensively in Italian dishes and one of the main ingredients in pesto.
thai also called horapa; different from sweet basil in both look and taste, having smaller leaves and purplish stems. It has a slight aniseed taste and is one of the identifying flavours of Thai food.

BEANS
cannellini small white bean similar in appearance and flavour to other *phaseolus vulgaris* varieties (great northern, navy or haricot). Available dried or canned.
green also known as french or string beans, this long thin fresh bean is consumed in its entirety once cooked.
kidney medium-sized red bean, slightly floury in texture yet sweet in flavour; sold dried or canned, it's found in bean mixes.

BEETROOT (BEETS) also called red beets; firm, round root vegetable.

BICARBONATE OF SODA (BAKING SODA) a raising agent.

BLOOD ORANGE a virtually seedless citrus fruit with blood-red-streaked rind and flesh; sweet, non-acidic, salmon-coloured pulp and juice having slight strawberry or raspberry overtones. The juice can be drunk straight or used in cocktails, sauces, sorbets and jellies; can be frozen for use in cooking when the growing season finishes. The rind is not as bitter as an ordinary orange.

BRIOCHE French in origin; a rich, yeast-leavened, cake-like bread made with butter and eggs. Available from cake or specialty bread shops.

BUCKWHEAT a herb in the same plant family as rhubarb; not a cereal so it is gluten-free. Available as flour; ground (cracked) into coarse, medium or fine granules (kasha) and used similarly to polenta; or groats, the whole kernel sold roasted as a cereal product.

BUK CHOY also called bok choy, pak choi, chinese white cabbage or chinese chard; has a fresh, mild mustard taste. Use stems and leaves, stir-fried or braised.

BUTTER we use salted butter unless stated otherwise; 125g is equal to 1 stick (4 ounces). Unsalted or "sweet" butter has no salt added.

BUTTERMILK originally the term given to the slightly sour liquid left after butter was churned from cream, today it is made from no-fat or low-fat milk to which specific bacterial cultures have been added. Despite its name, it is actually low in fat.

CAPERS the grey-green buds of a warm climate (Mediterranean) shrub, sold either dried and salted or pickled in a vinegar brine; tiny young ones, called baby capers, are also available both in brine or dried in salt. Their pungent taste adds piquancy to a tapenade, sauces and condiments.

CAPSICUM (BELL PEPPER) also called pepper. Comes in many colours: red, green, yellow, orange and purplish-black. Be sure to discard seeds and membranes before use.

CARAMEL TOP 'N' FILL a canned milk product consisting of condensed milk that has been boiled to a caramel.

CARDAMOM a spice native to India; can be purchased in pod, seed or ground form. Has a distinctive aromatic, sweetly rich flavour.

CELERIAC (CELERY ROOT) tuberous root with knobbly brown skin, white flesh and a celery-like flavour. Keep peeled celeriac in acidulated water to stop it discolouring. It can be grated and eaten raw in salads; used in soups and stews; boiled and mashed like potatoes; or sliced thinly and deep-fried as chips.

CHAR SIU SAUCE a Chinese barbecue sauce made from sugar, water, salt, fermented soya bean paste, honey, soy sauce, malt syrup and spices. Found at most supermarkets.

CHEESE
cheddar the most common cow-milk tasty cheese; should be aged, hard and have a pronounced bite.
cream commonly called philadelphia or philly; a soft cow-milk cheese, its fat content ranges from 14% to 33%.
fetta Greek in origin; a crumbly textured goat- or sheep-milk cheese having a sharp, salty taste. Ripened and stored in salted whey; particularly good cubed and tossed into salads.
goat's made from goat's milk, has an earthy, strong taste. Available in soft, crumbly and firm textures, in various shapes and sizes, and sometimes rolled in ash or herbs.
gorgonzola a creamy Italian blue cheese with a mild, sweet taste; good as an accompaniment to fruit or used to flavour sauces (especially pasta).
mascarpone an Italian fresh cultured-cream product made in much the same way as yogurt. Whiteish to creamy yellow in colour, with a buttery-rich, luscious texture. Soft, creamy and spreadable, it is used in Italian desserts and as an accompaniment to fresh fruit.

mozzarella soft, spun-curd cheese; originating in southern Italy where it was traditionally made from water-buffalo milk. Now generally made from cow's milk, it is the most popular pizza cheese because of its low melting point and elasticity when heated.
parmesan also called parmigiano; is a hard, grainy cow-milk cheese originating in Italy. Reggiano is the best variety.
ricotta a soft, sweet, moist, white cow-milk cheese with a low fat content and a slightly grainy texture. The name roughly translates as "cooked again" and refers to ricotta's manufacture from a whey that is itself a by-product of other cheese making.

CHICKEN
breast fillet breast halved, skinned and boned.
drumsticks leg with skin and bone intact.
thigh skin and bone intact.
thigh cutlets thigh with skin and centre bone intact; sometimes found skinned with bone intact.
thigh fillets the skin and bone removed.

CHILLI
available in many types and sizes. Use rubber gloves when seeding and chopping fresh chillies as they can burn your skin. Removing membranes and seeds lessens the heat level.
cayenne pepper dried, long, thin-fleshed, extremely hot, ground red chilli.
green any unripened chilli; also some particular varieties that are ripe when green, such as jalapeño, habanero, poblano or serrano.
long red available both fresh and dried; a generic term used for any moderately hot, thin, long (6-8cm/2¼-3¼-inch) chilli.

CHOCOLATE
choc bits also known as chocolate chips or chocolate morsels; available in milk, white and dark chocolate. Made of cocoa liquor, cocoa butter, sugar and an emulsifier, these hold their shape in baking and are ideal for decorating.
dark (semi-sweet) also called luxury chocolate; made of a high percentage of cocoa liquor and cocoa butter, and little added sugar. Unless stated otherwise, we use dark chocolate in this book as it's ideal for use in desserts and cakes.
Melts small discs of compounded milk, white or dark chocolate ideal for melting and moulding.
milk most popular eating chocolate, mild and very sweet; similar in make-up to dark with the difference being the addition of milk solids.
white contains no cocoa solids but derives its sweet flavour from cocoa butter. Very sensitive to heat.

CIABATTA
in Italian, the word means slipper, the traditional shape of this popular crisp-crusted, open-textured white sourdough bread. A good bread to use for bruschetta.

CINNAMON
available in sticks (or quills) and ground into powder; used as a sweet, fragrant flavouring in sweet and savoury foods.

COCOA POWDER also known as cocoa; dried, unsweetened, roasted and ground cocoa beans (cacao seeds).
dutch cocoa is treated with an alkali to neutralise its acids. It has a reddish-brown colour, a mild flavour and easily dissolves in liquids.

COCONUT
cream obtained commercially from the first pressing of the coconut flesh alone, without the addition of water; the second pressing (less rich) is sold as coconut milk. Available in cans and cartons at most supermarkets.
desiccated concentrated, dried, unsweetened and finely shredded coconut flesh.
essence synthetically produced from flavouring, oil and alcohol.
flaked dried flaked coconut flesh.
milk not the liquid found inside the fruit (coconut water), but the diluted liquid from the second pressing of the white flesh of a mature coconut (the first pressing produces coconut cream).
shredded unsweetened thin strips of dried coconut flesh.

CORIANDER (CILANTRO)
also called pak chee or chinese parsley; bright-green-leafed herb with both pungent aroma and taste. Both the stems and roots of coriander are used in Thai cooking: wash well before chopping.

CORNFLOUR (CORNSTARCH)
available made from corn or wheat (wheaten cornflour, gluten-free, gives a lighter texture in cakes); used as a thickening agent in cooking.

COUSCOUS
a fine, dehydrated, grain-like cereal product made from semolina; it swells to three or four times its original size when liquid is added. It is eaten like rice with a tagine, as a side dish or salad ingredient.

CREAM
pouring also known as pure or fresh cream. It has no additives and contains a minimum fat content of 35%.
sour a thick, commercially-cultured sour cream with a minimum fat content of 35%.
thick (double) a dolloping cream with a minimum fat content of 45%.
thickened (heavy) a whipping cream that contains a thickener. It has a minimum fat content of 35%.

CREAM OF TARTAR
the acid ingredient in baking powder; added to confectionery mixtures to help prevent sugar from crystallising. Keeps frostings creamy and improves volume when beating egg whites.

CUMIN
also known as zeera or comino; resembling caraway in size, cumin is the dried seed of a plant related to the parsley family. Its spicy, almost curry-like flavour is essential to the traditional foods of Mexico, India, North Africa and the Middle East. Available dried as seeds or ground.

CUSTARD POWDER instant mixture used to make pouring custard; similar to North American instant pudding mixes.

DATES fruit of the date palm tree, eaten fresh or dried, on their own or in prepared dishes. About 4cm to 6cm in length, oval and plump, thin-skinned, with a honey-sweet flavour and sticky texture.

DUKKAH an Egyptian specialty spice mixture made up of roasted nuts, seeds and an array of aromatic spices.

EGGPLANT also known as aubergine. Ranging in size from tiny to very large and in colour from pale green to deep purple. Can also be purchased char-grilled, packed in oil, in jars.

EGGS we use large chicken eggs weighing an average of 60g (2 ounces). If a recipe calls for raw or barely cooked eggs, exercise caution if there is a salmonella problem in your area, particularly in food eaten by children and pregnant women.

FENNEL also called finocchio or anise; a crunchy green vegetable slightly resembling celery that's eaten raw in salads; fried as an accompaniment; or used as an ingredient in soups and sauces.

FISH SAUCE called naam pla (Thailand) and nuoc naam (Vietnam); the two are almost identical. Made from pulverised salted fermented fish (often anchovies); has a pungent smell and strong taste. Available in varying degrees of intensity, use according to your taste.

FLOUR
baker's also called gluten-enriched, strong or bread-mix flour. Produced from a variety of wheat that has a high gluten (protein) content and is best suited for pizza and bread making: the expansion caused by the yeast and the stretchiness imposed by kneading require a flour that is "strong" enough to handle these stresses. Available from major supermarkets or health-food stores.
plain (all-purpose) unbleached wheat flour, is the best for baking: the gluten content ensures a strong dough, for a light result.
rice very fine, almost powdery, gluten-free flour; made from ground white rice. Used in baking, as a thickener, and in some Asian noodles and desserts. Another variety, made from glutinous sweet rice, is used for chinese dumplings and rice paper.
self-raising all-purpose plain or wholemeal flour with baking powder and salt added; make at home in the proportion of 1 cup flour to 2 teaspoons baking powder.
wholemeal also known as wholewheat flour; milled with the wheat germ so is higher in fibre and more nutritional than plain flour.

FRUIT MINCE also known as mincemeat; mixture of dried fruits such as raisins, sultanas and candied peel, nuts, spices, apple, brandy or rum. Fruit mince is used as a filling for cakes, puddings and fruit mince pies.

GALANGAL a rhizome with a hot ginger-citrusy flavour; used similarly to ginger and garlic. Use fresh ginger if unavailable.

GARAM MASALA a blend of spices that includes cardamom, cinnamon, coriander, cloves, fennel and cumin. Black pepper and chilli can be added for heat.

GELATINE a thickening agent; we use dried (powdered) gelatine; it's also available in sheets known as leaf gelatine. Three teaspoons of dried gelatine (8g or one sachet) is about the same as four leaves.

GHEE (CLARIFIED BUTTER) with the milk solids removed, this fat has a high smoking point so can be heated to a high temperature without burning. Used as a cooking medium in most Indian recipes.

GINGER
fresh also called green or root ginger; the thick gnarled root of a tropical plant.
glacé fresh ginger root preserved in sugar syrup; crystallised ginger can be substituted if rinsed with warm water and dried before use.
ground also called powdered ginger; used as a flavouring in baking but cannot be substituted for fresh ginger.

GLACÉ FRUIT fruit such as pineapple, apricots, peaches and pears that are cooked in a heavy sugar syrup then dried.

GOLDEN SYRUP a by-product of refined sugarcane; pure maple syrup or honey can be substituted. Treacle is more viscous, and has a stronger flavour and aroma than golden syrup.

GREASING/OILING PANS use butter or margarine (for sweet baking), oil or cooking-oil spray (for savoury baking) to grease baking pans; overgreasing pans can cause food to overbrown. Use absorbent paper or a pastry brush to spread the oil or butter over the pan. Try covering your hand with a small plastic bag then swiping it into the butter or margarine.

HARISSA a North African paste made from dried red chillies, garlic, olive oil and caraway seeds; can be used as a rub for meat, an ingredient in sauces and dressings, or eaten as a condiment. It is available from Middle Eastern food shops and some supermarkets.

HAZELNUTS also known as filberts; plump, grape-sized, rich, sweet nut having a brown skin that is removed by rubbing heated nuts together vigorously in a tea-towel.

HOISIN SAUCE a thick, sweet and spicy Chinese barbecue sauce made from salted fermented soybeans, onions and garlic; used as a marinade or baste, or to accent stir-fries and barbecued or roasted foods. From Asian food shops and supermarkets.

HONEY the variety sold in a squeezable container is not suitable for the recipes in this book.

KAFFIR LIME LEAVES also known as bai magrood, sold fresh, dried or frozen; looks like two glossy dark green leaves joined end to end, forming a rounded hourglass shape. A strip of fresh lime peel may be substituted for each kaffir lime leaf.

KECAP MANIS a dark, thick sweet soy sauce used in most South-East Asian cuisines. Depending on the manufacturer, its sweetness is derived from the addition of molasses or palm sugar when brewed.

KITCHEN STRING made of a natural product such as cotton or hemp so that it neither affects the flavour of the food it's tied around nor melts when heated.

LEMON GRASS also known as takrai, serai or serah. A tall, clumping, lemon-smelling and tasting, sharp-edged aromatic tropical grass; the white lower part of the stem is used, finely chopped, in many South-East Asian dishes. Can be found fresh, dried, powdered and frozen, in supermarkets, greengrocers and Asian food shops.

LENTILS (red, brown, yellow) dried pulses often identified by and named after their colour. Eaten by cultures all over the world, most famously perhaps in the dhals of India, lentils have high food value.

LINSEEDS the seed from the flax plant. Mostly used to produce linseed oil, the grain is also used in bread.

MACADAMIAS native to Australia; fairly large, slightly soft, buttery rich nut. Should always be stored in the fridge to prevent their high oil content turning them rancid.

MAPLE SYRUP also called pure maple syrup; distilled from the sap of sugar maple trees found only in Canada and the USA. Maple-flavoured syrup or pancake syrup is not an adequate substitute for the real thing.

MIXED SPICE a classic spice mixture generally containing caraway, allspice, coriander, cumin, nutmeg and ginger, although cinnamon and other spices can be added. It is used with fruit and in cakes.

MUSHROOMS
dried porcini also known as cèpes; the richest-flavoured mushrooms. Expensive, but because they're so strongly flavoured, only a small amount is required.
shiitake when fresh are also known as chinese black, forest or golden oak mushrooms. Are large and meaty and, although cultivated, have the earthiness and taste of wild mushrooms.
swiss brown also known as roman or cremini. Light to dark brown mushrooms with full-bodied flavour; suited for use in casseroles or being stuffed and baked.

MUSTARD
dijon pale brown, distinctively flavoured, fairly mild-tasting french mustard.
wholegrain also called seeded. A French-style, coarse-grain mustard made from crushed mustard seeds and Dijon-style french mustard.

NUTMEG a strong and pungent spice ground from the dried nut of an evergreen tree native to Indonesia. Usually found ground but the flavour is more intense from a whole nut, available from spice shops, so it's best to grate your own.

OIL
olive made from ripened olives. Extra virgin and virgin are the first and second press, respectively, of the olives and are therefore considered the best; "light" refers to taste not fat levels.
peanut pressed from ground peanuts; most commonly used oil in Asian cooking because of its high smoke point (capacity to handle high heat without burning).
sesame roasted, crushed, white sesame seeds; a flavouring rather than a cooking medium.
vegetable oils sourced from plant rather than animal fats.

ONIONS
green (scallions) also called, incorrectly, shallot; an immature onion picked before the bulb has formed, has a long, bright-green stalk.
red also known as spanish, red spanish or bermuda onion; a sweet-flavoured, large, purple-red onion.
shallots also called french or golden shallots or eschalots; small and brown-skinned.
spring an onion with a small white bulb and long, narrow green-leafed tops.

ORANGE BLOSSOM WATER also known as orange flower water; concentrated flavouring made from orange blossoms.

PEPITAS (PUMPKIN SEEDS) the pale green kernels of dried pumpkin seeds; they can be bought plain or salted.

PINE NUTS also called pignoli; not a nut but a small, cream-coloured kernel from pine cones. Toast before use to bring out the flavour.

POACHING a cooking term to describe gentle simmering of food in liquid (generally water or stock); spices or herbs can be added to impart their flavour.

POLENTA also known as cornmeal; a flour-like cereal made of dried corn (maize).

PRESERVED LEMON RIND a North African specialty; lemons are quartered and preserved in salt and lemon juice or water. To use, remove and discard pulp. Squeeze juice from rind, then rinse well and slice thinly. Sold in delicatessens and major supermarkets.

QUINCE yellow-skinned fruit with hard texture and astringent, tart taste; eaten cooked or as a preserve. Long, slow cooking makes the flesh a deep rose pink.

RAISINS dried sweet grapes (traditionally muscatel grapes).

RHUBARB a plant with long, green-red stalks; becomes sweet and edible when cooked.

RICE
arborio small, round grain rice well-suited to absorb a large amount of liquid; the high level of starch makes it especially suitable for risottos for its classic creaminess.
basmati a white, fragrant long-grained rice; the grains fluff up when cooked. Wash several times before cooking.
calasparra a Spanish short-grained rice that absorbs three times its own volume of liquid, while keeping its shape; used for paella.
jasmine is a long-grain white rice recognised around the world as having a perfumed aromatic quality; moist in texture, it clings together after cooking. Sometimes substituted for basmati rice.

ROASTING/TOASTING nuts and dried coconut can be roasted in the oven to release their aromatic essential oils. Spread them evenly onto an oven tray then place in a moderate oven about 5 minutes. Desiccated coconut, pine nuts and sesame seeds roast more evenly if stirred over low heat in a heavy-based frying pan; their natural oils will help turn them golden brown.

ROCKET (ARUGULA) also called rugula and rucola; peppery green leaf eaten raw in salads or used in cooking. Baby rocket leaves are smaller and less peppery.

ROLLED OATS flattened oat grain rolled into flakes and traditionally used for porridge. Instant oats are also available, but use traditional oats for baking.

ROSEWATER extract made from crushed rose petals, called gulab in India; used for its aromatic quality, in sweetmeats and desserts.

SAFFRON the stigma of a member of the crocus family, available ground or in strands; imparts a yellow-orange colour to food once infused. The quality can vary greatly; the best is the most expensive spice in the world.

SAMBAL OELEK also known as ulek or olek; an Indonesian salty paste made from ground chillies and vinegar.

SEAFOOD
blue-eye trevalla also known as deep sea trevalla or trevally and blue-eye cod; thick, moist white-fleshed fish.
ocean trout a farmed fish with pink, soft flesh. It is from the same family as the atlantic salmon; one can be substituted for the other.
prawns (shrimp) varieties include, school, king, royal red, Sydney harbour, tiger. Can be bought uncooked (green) or cooked, with or without shells.

SEGMENTING a cooking term to describe cutting citrus fruits in such a way that pieces contain no pith, seed or membrane. The peeled fruit is cut towards the centre inside each membrane, forming skinless wedges.

SEMOLINA coarsely ground flour milled from durum wheat; the flour used in making gnocchi, pasta and couscous.

SHRIMP PASTE also called kapi, trasi and blanchan; a strong-scented, very firm preserved paste made of salted dried shrimp. Used sparingly as a pungent flavouring in many South-East Asian soups, sauces and rice dishes. It should be chopped or sliced thinly then wrapped in foil and roasted before use.

SILVER BEET (SWISS CHARD) also called, incorrectly, spinach; has fleshy stalks and large leaves and can be prepared as for spinach.

SPINACH also called english spinach and incorrectly, silver beet. Baby spinach leaves are best eaten raw in salads; the larger leaves should be added last to dishes and cooked until barely wilted.

SPONGE FINGERS also called savoiardi, savoy biscuits or lady's fingers; Italian-style crisp fingers made from sponge cake mixture.

STAR ANISE dried star-shaped pod with an astringent aniseed flavour; used to flavour stocks and marinades. Available whole and ground.

SUGAR
brown a very soft, finely granulated sugar that retains molasses for its colour and flavour.
caster (superfine) finely granulated table sugar.
dark brown a moist, dark brown sugar with a rich, distinctive full flavour from molasses syrup.
demerara small-grained golden-coloured crystal sugar.
icing (confectioners') also known as powdered sugar; pulverised granulated sugar crushed together with a small amount of cornflour (cornstarch).
palm also called nam tan pip, jaggery, jawa or gula melaka; made from the sap of the sugar palm tree. Light brown to black in colour and usually sold in rock-hard cakes; use brown sugar if unavailable.
white (granulated) coarse, granulated table sugar, also known as crystal sugar.

SULTANAS also called golden raisins; dried seedless white grapes.

TREACLE thick, dark syrup not unlike molasses; a by-product of sugar refining.

TURMERIC also called kamin; is a rhizome related to galangal and ginger. Must be grated or pounded to release its acrid aroma and pungent flavour. Known for the golden colour it imparts, fresh turmeric can be substituted for the more commonly found dried powder. Be aware that fresh turmeric stains your hands and plastic utensils such as chopping boards and spatulas.

VANILLA
bean dried, long, thin pod from a tropical golden orchid; the minuscule black seeds inside the bean impart a luscious flavour in baking and desserts. Place a whole bean in a jar of sugar to make vanilla sugar; a bean can be used three or four times.
extract obtained from vanilla beans infused in water; a non-alcoholic version of essence.
paste made from vanilla beans and contains real seeds. Is highly concentrated – 1 teaspoon replaces a whole vanilla bean. Found in most supermarkets in the baking section.

VINEGAR
balsamic originally from Modena, Italy. Made from the juice of Trebbiano grapes; it is a deep rich brown colour with a sweet and sour flavour.
cider made from fermented apples.
malt made from fermented malt and beech shavings.
rice a colourless vinegar made from fermented rice and flavoured with sugar and salt. Sherry can be substituted.

WOMBOK (NAPA CABBAGE) also called chinese or peking cabbage; elongated in shape with pale green, crinkly leaves, this is the most common cabbage in South-East Asia. Can be shredded or chopped and eaten raw or braised, steamed or stir-fried

YEAST (dried and fresh), a raising agent used in dough making. Granular (7g sachets) and fresh compressed (20g blocks) yeast can almost always be substituted for the other when yeast is called for.

YOGHURT we use plain full-cream yoghurt in our recipes.
Greek-style plain yoghurt strained in a cloth (traditionally muslin) to remove the whey and to give it a creamy consistency.

ZUCCHINI also called courgette; small, pale- or dark-green or yellow vegetable of the squash family. Its edible flowers can be stuffed.

CONVERSION CHART

MEASURES

One Australian metric measuring cup holds approximately 250ml; one Australian metric tablespoon holds 20ml; one Australian metric teaspoon holds 5ml.

The difference between one country's measuring cups and another's is within a two- or three-teaspoon variance, and will not affect your cooking results. North America, New Zealand and the United Kingdom use a 15ml tablespoon.

All cup and spoon measurements are level. The most accurate way of measuring dry ingredients is to weigh them. When measuring liquids, use a clear glass or plastic jug with the metric markings.

The imperial measurements used in these recipes are approximate only. Measurements for cake pans are approximate only. Using same-shaped cake pans of a similar size should not affect the outcome of your baking. We measure the inside top of the cake pan to determine sizes.

We use large eggs with an average weight of 60g (2 ounces).

OVEN TEMPERATURES

The oven temperatures in this book are for conventional ovens; if you have a fan-forced oven, decrease the temperature by 10-20 degrees.

	°C (CELSIUS)	°F (FAHRENHEIT)
Very slow	120	250
Slow	150	300
Moderately slow	160	325
Moderate	180	350
Moderately hot	200	400
Hot	220	425
Very hot	240	475

DRY MEASURES

METRIC	IMPERIAL
15g	½oz
30g	1oz
60g	2oz
90g	3oz
125g	4oz (¼lb)
155g	5oz
185g	6oz
220g	7oz
250g	8oz (½lb)
280g	9oz
315g	10oz
345g	11oz
375g	12oz (¾lb)
410g	13oz
440g	14oz
470g	15oz
500g	16oz (1lb)
750g	24oz (1½lb)
1kg	32oz (2lb)

LIQUID MEASURES

METRIC	IMPERIAL
30ml	1 fluid oz
60ml	2 fluid oz
100ml	3 fluid oz
125ml	4 fluid oz
150ml	5 fluid oz
190ml	6 fluid oz
250ml	8 fluid oz
300ml	10 fluid oz
500ml	16 fluid oz
600ml	20 fluid oz
1000ml (1 litre)	1¾ pints

LENGTH MEASURES

METRIC	IMPERIAL
3mm	⅛in
6mm	¼in
1cm	½in
2cm	¾in
2.5cm	1in
5cm	2in
6cm	2½in
8cm	3in
10cm	4in
13cm	5in
15cm	6in
18cm	7in
20cm	8in
22cm	9in
25cm	10in
28cm	11in
30cm	12in (1ft)

INDEX

A
alioli 69
almonds 340
   almond berry sugar cakes 262
   almond stuffing, roasted 186
   lemon butter almond slice 316
   rich chocolate almond slice 324
american cheese scones 334
apple crostata 126
apricot upside-down cakes 265
avocado
   avocado, bacon and cabbage salad 30
   chicken burger with avocado
     and bacon 80
   mexican pork cutlets with
     avocado salsa 89

B
bacon slices 340
   avocado, bacon and cabbage salad 30
   chicken burger with avocado
     and bacon 80
   prosciutto and pea pasta gratin 57
   tagliatelle with creamy mushroom
     and bacon sauce 50
bakes
   broccoli, pancetta and blue cheese
     gratin 199
   eggplant and pesto baked pasta 47
   middle eastern meatloaf 196
   potato 195
   rösti cottage pie 203
   self-saucing meatloaf 204
baking paper 340
baking powder 340
banana caramel layer cake 288
banana caramel scrolls 338
basil 340
beans 340
   whipped white beans 103
beef
   beef and crunchy wombok salad 41
   beef and mushroom family pie 112
   penang beef curry 140

(*beef* continued)
   roast beef rump with red wine gravy 181
   rösti cottage pie 203
   self-saucing meatloaf 204
   spaghetti and meatballs 58
   traditional beef casserole 171
beetroot 340
berry trifle, ultimate 218
bicarbonate of soda 340
biscuits
   caramel ginger crunchies 305
   chocolate chunk and raspberry
     cookies 315
   chocolate french macaroons 312
   macadamia anzac 305
   passionfruit melting moments 311
   peanut butter cookies 308
   slice-and-bake butter 320
   vanilla shortbread 302
blood orange 340 *see also* orange
   marmalade glaze 192
   sorbet and ice-cream slice 248
bread
   flatbreads with roasted peppers
     and zucchini 332
   olive and rosemary quick bread 331
   quinoa and seed cheese damper 331
   sourdough rye 328
   vegetable pan bagna 84
brioche 340
broccoli, pancetta and blue cheese gratin
   199
brownies, over-the-top chocolate and
   macadamia 319
buckwheat 340
buk choy 340
burger, chicken, with avocado and bacon 80
butter 340
butter biscuits, slice-and-bake 320
buttermilk 340

C
caesar salad, chicken 34
cakes/cupcakes
   almond berry sugar 262

(*cakes/cupcakes* continued)
   apricot upside-down 265
   banana caramel layer 288
   chocolate and raspberry 283
   chocolate sour cream 275
   citrus butter 272
   coffee walnut loaf 259
   featherlight sponge 256
   hazelnut plum and sour cherry 265
   lemon meringue cupcakes 279
   lemon polenta cake with
     lemon compote 247
   little chocolate hazelnut 287
   little white chocolate lamingtons 276
   mississippi mud 260
   moist coconut cake with coconut
     ice frosting 297
   passionfruit meringue 280
   poppyseed cupcakes with
     orange frosting 284
   raspberry and passionfruit
     mile-high layer 294
   raspberry yoghurt loaf 268
   rich chocolate cupcakes 271
   rich chocolate roulade 298
   rich fruit 291
   six layer chocolate 268
candied citrus 272
cannelloni straight-up 61
capers 340
capsicum 340
   barbecued salmon with capsicum
     and olive salsa 100
   potato, olive and capsicum frittata 200
   sausage spiral with grilled capsicum
     and whipped white beans 103
caramel ginger crunchies 305
caramel sauce 244
caramel top 'n' fill 340
cardamom 340
casseroles
   chilli con carne with corn
     dumplings 163
   coq au vin 160
   fast fish tagine 168
   lamb shanks with risoni and tomato 156

(*casseroles* continued)
   lemon-scented lamb casserole with winter vegetables 159
   mustard chicken 167
   osso buco 172
   portuguese seafood stew 164
   traditional beef 171
cauliflower and green pea curry 153
celeriac 340
   fish pie with potato and celeriac mash 116
char siu sauce 340
   char siu pork fried rice 73
cheese 340–1
   baked ricotta with olives 92
   broccoli, pancetta and blue cheese gratin 199
   croûtes 16
   free-form spinach, herb and ricotta pies 124
   goat's cheese and leek tart 120
   quinoa and seed cheese damper 331
   sauce 61
   tomato and goat's cheese tart with rice and seed crust 119
   zucchini and fetta fritters 108
cheesecake, new york-style 226
chicken 341
   chicken and mushroom party pies 124
   chicken and risoni soup with herbed meatballs 19
   chicken burger with avocado and bacon 80
   chicken caesar salad 34
   chicken, lemon grass and rice soup 10
   chicken sticks with harissa mayonnaise 89
   classic roast chicken and gravy 178
   coq au vin 160
   grilled portuguese chicken and rice 96
   korma 156
   lemon chicken drumsticks with citrus chilli salt 83
   mustard chicken casserole 167
   slow-cooker butter chicken 150
   spicy chicken salad 38

chilli 341
   chilli con carne with corn dumplings 163
chocolate 341
   baked pears with chocolate sauce 211
   choc-chip hot cross buns 336–7
   chocolate and raspberry cake 283
   chocolate caramel slice 308
   chocolate chunk and raspberry cookies 315
   chocolate french macaroons 312
   chocolate hazelnut torte 243
   chocolate love pots 222
   chocolate parfait with orange salad 208
   chocolate sour cream cake 275
   classic chocolate self-saucing pudding 240
   dark chocolate ganache 312
   divine chocolate and raspberry tarts 136
   ganache 271, 283, 287
   icing 268
   little chocolate hazelnut cakes 287
   little white chocolate lamingtons 276
   mississippi mud cake 260
   over-the-top chocolate and macadamia brownies 319
   rich chocolate almond slice 324
   rich chocolate and coconut tart 129
   rich chocolate cupcakes 271
   rich chocolate roulade 298
   six layer chocolate cake 268
christmas pudding, pressure-cooker, with ice-cream sauce 251
ciabatta 341
cinnamon 341
   pecan and cinnamon butter biscuits 320
citrus butter cake 272
classic pavlova baked on a plate 230
cocoa powder 341
coconut 341
   coconut ice frosting 297
   moist coconut cake with coconut ice frosting 297
   rich chocolate and coconut tart 129
coffee icing 259
coffee walnut loaf 259

compote, roasted peach and nectarine 211
cookies *see* biscuits
coq au vin 160
coriander 341
   couscous 168
corn dumplings 163
cornflour 341
cottage pie, rösti 203
couscous 341
   coriander 168
   salad 30
cream 341
cream cheese frosting 268
cream of tartar 341
creamy coconut pork curry 142
creamy pumpkin risotto 74
crème caramel 217
crostata, apple 126
crumble, spiced plum and apple 225
cumin 341
cupcakes *see* cakes/cupcakes
curry
   cauliflower and green pea 153
   chicken korma 156
   creamy coconut pork 142
   lamb keema 149
   nepalese pork mince curry 153
   penang beef 140
   slow-cooker butter chicken 150
   spicy dhal 142
   thai green prawn curry 146
curry paste 140
custard 239
custard powder 342

D

dates 342
   sticky date pudding 244
desserts *see also* puddings
   baked pears with chocolate sauce 211
   blood orange sorbet and ice-cream slice 248
   chocolate hazelnut torte 243
   chocolate love pots 222
   chocolate parfait with orange salad 208

(*desserts* continued)
   classic pavlova baked on a plate 230
   crème caramel 217
   frozen mango macadamia crunch 236
   lemon polenta cake with
     lemon compote 247
   lime sorbet and ice-cream slice 248
   new york-style cheesecake 226
   panettone custard pudding with
     macerated fruit 235
   quince and rhubarb cobbler 221
   roasted peach and nectarine
     compote 211
   slow-poached quince with
     fillo fingers 229
   spiced plum and apple crumble 225
   tropical fruit with rosewater syrup 214
   ultimate berry trifle 218
dhal, spicy 142
dressing 33, 38, 41
   garlic mustard vinaigrette 30
   lemon and mustard 120
   red wine vinegar 37
dukkah 342

E

eggplant 342
   eggplant and pesto baked pasta 47
eggs 342

F

farfalle with zucchini lemon
   garlic sauce 50
featherlight sponge 256
fennel 342
   tomato and fennel sauce 95
fillo fingers 229
fish pie with potato and celeriac mash 116
fish sauce 342
flatbreads with roasted peppers and
   zucchini 332
flour 342
free-form spinach, herb and ricotta pies 124

french onion soup 20
frittata, potato, olive and capsicum 200
fritters, zucchini and fetta 108
frosting
   coconut ice 297
   cream cheese 268
   meringue 294
   orange 284
frozen mango macadamia crunch 236
fruit cake, rich 291
fruit mince 342
   mince pies 135

G

galangal 342
ganache
   chocolate 271, 283, 287
   dark chocolate 312
   sour cream 275
garam masala 342
garlic mustard vinaigrette 30
gelatine 342
ghee 342
ginger 342
   caramel ginger crunchies 305
glacé fruit 342
glacé icing 272
goat's cheese and leek tart 120
golden syrup 342
greasing/oiling pans 342
greek lentil, spinach and dill soup 24
greek salad 194
green pea soup with mint pistou 14
gremolata 172

H

ham, blood orange marmalade glazed 192
harissa 342
   mayonnaise 89
hazelnuts 342
   hazelnut plum and sour cherry cake 265
   little chocolate hazelnut cakes 287
herbed ricotta 37

hoisin sauce 342
honey 342
hot cross buns, choc-chip 336–7
hot marmalade scones 334

I

ice-cream sauce 252
icing 256
   chocolate 268
   coffee 259
   glacé 272
   white chocolate 276

K

kaffir lime leaves 342
kecap manis 342
keema, lamb 149
kitchen string 342

L

lamb
   biryani 66
   butterflied lamb with lemon
     and herbs 107
   keema 149
   lamb and rosemary pies 115
   lemon and garlic lamb rack with
     roasted zucchini 181
   lemon-scented lamb casserole
     with winter vegetables 159
   marinated lamb skewers 104
   middle eastern meatloaf 196
   roast leg of lamb with mustard
     and herbs 184
   shanks with risoni and tomato 156
   slow-roasted lamb shoulder 184
lamingtons, little white chocolate 276
lasagne 44
lemon
   butter 316
   compote 247
   curd 279

(*lemon* continued)
   lemon and garlic lamb rack with
      roasted zucchini 181
   lemon and mustard dressing 120
   lemon and pistachio butter
      biscuits 320
   lemon butter almond slice 316
   lemon chicken drumsticks with
      citrus chilli salt 83
   lemon delicious pudding 214
   lemon meringue cupcakes 279
   lemon polenta cake with
      lemon compote 247
   lemon-scented lamb casserole
      with winter vegetables 159
   marinade 107
lemon grass 343
   chicken, lemon grass and rice soup 10
lentils 343
   greek lentil, spinach and dill soup 24
lime sorbet and ice-cream slice 248
linseeds 343

M

M&M's butter biscuits 320
macadamias 343
   frozen mango macadamia crunch 236
   macadamia anzac biscuits 305
   macadamia fillo tarts with
      caramelised pineapple 136
   over-the-top chocolate and
      macadamia brownies 319
macaroons, chocolate french 312
macerated fruit 235
mandarin jam 239
mandarin jam puddings 239
mango macadamia crunch, frozen 236
maple syrup 343
marmalade scones, hot 334
mascarpone mixture 218
mayonnaise 27
   harissa 89
meatloaf, middle eastern 196
meatloaf, self-saucing 204
mediterranean fish soup 23

meringue 279
   frosting 294
mexican pork cutlets with avocado salsa 89
middle eastern meatloaf 196
mince pies 135
mint pistou 14
mississippi mud cake 260
mixed spice 343
mushrooms 343
   beef and mushroom family pie 112
   chicken and mushroom party pies 124
   mushroom and spinach tarts
      with tomato salad 123
   really good mushroom risotto 77
mustard 343
   garlic mustard vinaigrette 30
   lemon and mustard dressing 120
   mustard chicken casserole 167
   roast leg of lamb with mustard
      and herbs 184

N

nam jim 188
nasi goreng 70
nepalese pork mince curry 153
new york-style cheesecake 226
nutmeg 343

O

oil 343
olive and rosemary quick bread 331
onions 343
   french onion soup 20
   spiced 196
orange *see also* blood orange
   frosting 284
   orange and poppy seed butter
      biscuits 320
   salad 208
orange blossom water 343
osso buco 172
over-the-top chocolate and macadamia
   brownies 319

P

panettone custard pudding with
   macerated fruit 235
passionfruit
   butter cream 311
   cream 280, 294
   melting moments 311
   meringue cake 280
   raspberry and passionfruit mile-high
      layer cake 294
pasta
   cannelloni straight-up 61
   dough 64
   eggplant and pesto baked pasta 47
   farfalle with zucchini lemon
      garlic sauce 50
   lasagne 44
   prosciutto and pea pasta gratin 57
   pumpkin ravioli with sage butter 62
   salad with tomato and crisp prosciutto 27
   shells with italian sausages 54
   spaghetti and meatballs 58
   spicy prawn linguine 47
   spinach and ricotta gnocchi
      with sage butter 53
   tagliatelle with creamy mushroom
      and bacon sauce 50
pastry 135
   rich shortcrust 115
pavlova, classic, baked on a plate 230
peach and nectarine tart 129
peanut butter cookies 308
pear tarte tatin 132
pears, baked, with chocolate sauce 211
peas
   green pea soup with mint pistou 14
pecan and cinnamon butter biscuits 320
pepitas 343
pie/s
   beef and mushroom family 112
   chicken and mushroom party 124
   fish pie with potato and celeriac mash
      116
   free-form spinach, herb and ricotta 124
   lamb and rosemary 115
   mince 135

pine nuts 343
pistou, mint 14
plums
    hazelnut plum and sour cherry cake 265
    quick and easy plum tart 132
    spiced plum and apple crumble 225
poaching 343
polenta 343
    lemon polenta cake with lemon compote 247
poppy seed cupcakes with orange frosting 284
pork
    char siu pork fried rice 73
    creamy coconut pork curry 142
    lasagne 44
    mexican pork cutlets with avocado salsa 89
    nasi goreng 70
    nepalese pork mince curry 153
    ribs with sticky barbecue sauce 92
    roast pork loin with nam jim 188
    sausage spiral with grilled capsicum and whipped white beans 103
    spaghetti and meatballs 58
portuguese seafood stew 164
potatoes
    bake 195
    fish pie with potato and celeriac mash 116
    perfect potato salad 27
    potato, olive and capsicum frittata 200
prawn souvlakia with tomato and fennel sauce 95
preserved lemon rind 343
pressure-cooker christmas pudding with ice-cream sauce 251
prosciutto and pea pasta gratin 57
puddings *see also* desserts
    classic chocolate self-saucing 240
    lemon delicious 214
    mandarin jam 239
    pressure-cooker christmas pudding with ice-cream sauce 251
pumpkin
    creamy pumpkin risotto 74

(*pumpkin* continued)
    pumpkin ravioli with sage butter 62
    roast pumpkin soup with cheese croûtes 16

Q
quince 343
    quince and rhubarb cobbler 221
    slow-poached, with fillo fingers 229
quinoa and seed cheese damper 331

R
raisins 343
raspberries
    chocolate and raspberry cake 283
    chocolate chunk and raspberry cookies 315
    divine chocolate and raspberry tarts 136
    raspberry and passionfruit mile-high layer cake 294
    raspberry yoghurt loaf cake 268
red wine vinegar dressing 37
rhubarb 343
    quince and rhubarb cobbler 221
ribollita 13
rice 96, 343
    char siu pork fried rice 73
    chicken, lemon grass and rice soup 10
    creamy pumpkin risotto 74
    grilled portuguese chicken and 96
    lamb biryani 66
    nasi goreng 70
    really good mushroom risotto 77
    risotto milanese 174
    seafood paella with alioli 69
    tomato and goat's cheese tart with rice and seed crust 119
ricotta, baked, with olives 92
risotto milanese 174
risotto, really good mushroom 77
roasting/toasting 343
roasts
    blood orange marmalade glazed ham 192
    classic roast chicken and gravy 178

(*roasts* continued)
    lemon and garlic lamb rack with roasted zucchini 181
    roast beef rump with red wine gravy 181
    roast leg of lamb with mustard and herbs 184
    roast turkey with roasted almond stuffing 186
    slow-roasted lamb shoulder 184
rocket 344
rolled oats 344
rosewater 344
    tropical fruit with rosewater syrup 214
rösti cottage pie 203

S
saffron 344
salads
    avocado, bacon and cabbage 30
    beef and crunchy wombok 41
    char-grilled prawn and corn 33
    chicken caesar 34
    couscous 30
    greek 104
    orange 208
    pasta salad with tomato and crisp prosciutto 27
    perfect potato 27
    roast vegetable salad with herbed ricotta 37
    spicy chicken 38
    tomato 123
salmon, barbecued, with capsicum and olive salsa 100
sambal oelek 344
sauces
    caramel 244
    cheese 61
    ice-cream 252
    tomato and fennel sauce 95
sausage spiral with grilled capsicum and whipped white beans 103
scones
    american cheese 334
    hot marmalade 334

scrolls, banana caramel 338
seafood 344
    barbecued salmon with capsicum and olive salsa 100
    char-grilled prawn and corn salad 33
    fast fish tagine 168
    fish pie with potato and celeriac mash 116
    mediterranean fish soup 23
    nasi goreng 70
    paella with alioli 69
    portuguese seafood stew 164
    prawn souvlakia with tomato and fennel sauce 95
    spicy prawn linguine 47
    thai green prawn curry 146
segmenting 344
self-saucing meatloaf 204
semolina 344
shortbread, vanilla 302
shrimp paste 344
silver beet 344
six layer chocolate cake 268
slices
    chocolate caramel 308
    lemon butter almond slice 316
    over-the-top chocolate and macadamia brownies 319
    rich chocolate almond slice 324
    strawberry custard 323
slow-poached quince with fillo fingers 229
soups
    chicken and risoni soup with herbed meatballs 19
    chicken, lemon grass and rice 10
    french onion 20
    greek lentil, spinach and dill 24
    green pea soup with mint pistou 14
    mediterranean fish 23
    ribollita 13
    roast pumpkin soup with cheese croûtes 16
sour cream ganache 275
sourdough rye bread 328
sourdough starter 328
soured cream 235

spaghetti and meatballs 58
spiced onions 196
spiced plum and apple crumble 225
spicy dhal 142
spicy prawn linguine 47
spinach 344
    free-form spinach, herb and ricotta pies 124
    greek lentil, spinach and dill soup 24
    mushroom and spinach tarts with tomato salad 123
    spinach and ricotta gnocchi with sage butter 53
sponge, featherlight 256
sponge fingers 344
star anise 344
stew, portuguese seafood 164
sticky date pudding 244
strawberry custard slice 323
sugar 344
sultanas 344

T

tagine, fast fish 168
tagliatelle with creamy mushroom and bacon sauce 50
tart/s
    apple crostata 126
    divine chocolate and raspberry 136
    goat's cheese and leek tart 120
    macadamia fillo tarts with caramelised pineapple 136
    mushroom and spinach tarts with tomato salad 123
    peach and nectarine 129
    pear tarte tatin 132
    quick and easy plum tart 132
    rich chocolate and coconut 129
    tomato and goat's cheese tart with rice and seed crust 119
thai green prawn curry 146
tomato and fennel sauce 95
tomato and goat's cheese tart with rice and seed crust 119
tomato salad 123

torte, chocolate hazelnut 243
treacle 344
tropical fruit with rosewater syrup 214
turkey
    roast with roasted almond stuffing 186
turmeric 344

V

vanilla 344
    shortbread 302
veal
    lasagne 44
    osso buco 172
vegetable pan bagna 84
vinaigrette, garlic mustard 30
vinegar 344
    red wine vinegar dressing 37

W

whipped white beans 103
white chocolate icing 276
wombok 344
    beef and crunchy wombok salad 41

Y

yeast 344
yoghurt 344
    raspberry yoghurt loaf cake 268

Z

zucchini 344
    farfalle with zucchini lemon garlic sauce 50
    flatbreads with roasted peppers and zucchini 332
    lemon and garlic lamb rack with roasted zucchini 181
    zucchini and fetta fritters 108

Published in 2013 by Bauer Media Books, Sydney
Bauer Media Books are published by Bauer Media Limited

BAUER MEDIA BOOKS
Publishing director Gerry Reynolds
Publisher Sally Wright
Editorial & food director Pamela Clark
Director of sales, marketing & rights Brian Cearnes
Creative director & designer Hieu Chi Nguyen
Senior editor Stephanie Kistner
Food concept director Sophia Young
Marketing manager Bridget Cody
Operations manager David Scotto

Published by Bauer Media Books, a division of Bauer Media Limited, 54 Park St, Sydney; GPO Box 4088, Sydney, NSW 2001.
phone (02) 9282 8618; fax (02) 9126 3702
www.awwcookbooks.com.au

Printed in China with 1010 Printing Asia Limited.

Australia Distributed by Network Services,
phone +61 2 9282 8777; fax +61 2 9264 3278;
networkweb@networkservicescompany.com.au
New Zealand Distributed by Southern Publishers Group
phone +64 9 360 0692; fax +64 9 360 0695;
hub@spg.co.nz
South Africa Distributed by PSD Promotions,
phone +27 11 392 6065/6/7; fax +27 11 392 6079/80;
orders@psdprom.co.za

The best-ever collection / food director Pamela Clark.
ISBN: 978-1-74245-334-7 (hbk.)
Notes: Includes index.
Subjects: Cooking.
Other Authors/Contributors: Clark, Pamela.
Also Titled: Australian Women's Weekly.
Dewey Number: 641.5
© Bauer Media Limited 2013
ABN 18 053 273 546

This publication is copyright. No part of it may be reproduced or transmitted in any form without the written permission of the publishers.

Cover photographer John Paul Urizar
Cover food stylist Kristine Duran Thiessen
Cover photochef Dominic Smith

Photographer John Paul Urizar
Food stylist Kristine Duran Thiessen
Photochef Dominic Smith

To order books phone 136 116 (within Australia) or **order online** at www.awwcookbooks.com.au
Send recipe enquiries to:
recipeenquiries@bauer-media.com.au